D0583326

Bad Brake

BAD
BRAKE

FORD TRUCKS—
DEADLY WHEN PARKED

Robert Zausner

CAMINO BOOKS, INC.
Philadelphia

Manufactured in the United States of America

1 2 3 4 5   14 13 12

Library of Congress Cataloging-in-Publication Data

Zausner, Robert, 1953–
Bad brake : Ford trucks—deadly when parked / Robert Zausner.
    p. cm.
ISBN 978-1-933822-39-6 (alk. paper)
 1. White, Jimmie—Trials, litigation, etc. 2. Ford Motor Company—Trials, litigation,
etc. 3. Trials (Products liability)—United States. 4. Products liability—Motor
vehicles—United States. 5. Motor vehicles—Brakes—Design and construction—
Standards—United States. I. Title.
KF229.W48Z38 2011
346.7303'8—dc22   2011016490

Cover design: Jerilyn Bockorick
Interior design: P. M. Gordon Associates, Inc.

This book is available at a special discount on bulk purchases for promotional,
business, and educational use.

Publisher
Camino Books, Inc.
P.O. Box 59026
Philadelphia, PA 19102

www.caminobooks.com

For Moe

Contents

Part III *Blumer v. Ford*

The following story is true. It is based on official documents, trial transcripts, personal observations, and interviews with those who were involved.

Introduction

I HAD BEEN A JOURNALIST my whole career, the last fourteen years at *The Philadelphia Inquirer*, where I developed a healthy disregard for lawyers, considering them largely underhanded schemers looking to cash in on the mistakes, or alleged mistakes, of others. A number of jokes came immediately to mind, such as, "How do you know when a lawyer's lying? His lips are moving." So when I got a call from a fellow reporter asking if I might be interested in writing a book for two lawyers in the city, I cringed at the very thought. "Are you kidding me? I'm not writing a book for a couple of —ing lawyers," I told him.

Several weeks later, annoyed at a certain editor, I asked for the lawyers' names and contacts. What could it hurt to see what they wanted? I walked over to their offices in Center City, where we chatted for more than an hour. And I discovered something that surprised and amazed me. The lawyers weren't complete jerks.

When I asked what they wanted written, their response was also a shocker. "Whatever you want," they said. "You've got free rein." Their main interest was to expose people to more than the general view of lawyers, to what they—Tom Kline and Shanin Specter—actually did for a living. "My father tells me, 'You do a lousy job of telling people what you do and why it is important,'" Specter said, quoting Senator Arlen Specter. Too often, he said, all the public sees is one side of the story, some lawyer's tacky TV ads or a news report of the occasional "runaway verdict."

I responded that I wasn't interested in doing a PR job for the legal profession or for their firm. Neither were they, they assured. They'd open their files and let me rummage around, make my own determinations, and write my own book. "Go explore. See what we do," said Kline. "Judge for yourself."

I decided to leave the *Inquirer* for one year (a hiatus that would become permanent). I got a desk at Kline & Specter, P.C., and began to delve into many lawsuits the firm had filed. The files were graphic, each named for various clients who had something in common. All were badly broken people, victims of medical errors, defective products, faulty premises, civil rights violations. Most had been horribly injured. Many had died. And they and their families, often paralyzed by grief, had had nowhere to turn for help, their tribulations of no concern to the government and their circumstances generally not splashy enough for the news media. Their only remaining recourse was to hire a lawyer to take up their cause. Sure, the lawyers would be paid for their efforts, and paid well. But that consideration wasn't the whole picture, at least not for the lawyers I was about to get to know well.

I had been at Kline & Specter for less than a week when Shanin Specter approached me and asked me to arrive at the office at 7:00 a.m. the next day. "And please wear a tie," he commanded in a gruff tone—a tone I would become accustomed to and was not offended by. (Specter, I would also learn, would rarely edit what I wrote about him, only correcting an occasional factual error or—stickler that he is—grammatical mistake.) That day we were headed to Bethesda, Maryland, to the headquarters of the U.S. Consumer Product Safety Commission. Kline accompanied us as well. Specter had recently settled a case for a client whose son had been severely injured by a defective BB gun, and now Specter was on a mission to persuade the Consumer Product Safety Commission to get 7.5 million of the guns recalled. That long day, one of many this cause would consume, included a series of meetings, some unpleasant. Weeks later the commission would vote to force a recall of the faulty product that had hurt not only Specter's client but also children all across the country. More votes and more work would take a lot of time, none of which earned Specter a dime. (I wrote about the BB gun case in my first book, titled *Two Boys*.)

Over time I watched, from a front row seat, as Specter and Kline and their army of colleagues and assistants investigated a variety of cases and causes, then planned and strategized. They welcomed challenges. They had their pick of cases, but frequently took those that other law firms had rejected, and some that they knew had little chance of a big payday. I was in court when Kline battled the nation's largest landlord on behalf of the grieving son of an eighty-seven-year-old woman who had died of heat exhaustion when the air conditioning in her apartment building was shut down for renovation work on the property. Helen Shapiro was found dead in her bathroom. Kline, angered by the death and the landlord's refusal to offer more than a $10,000 settlement, took the case, realizing that, even if he won, most juries awarded little for someone with no earnings capacity and little life expectancy. Yet he won a verdict and got an astounding $1 million for Shapiro's estate.

I learned to appreciate what these two trial lawyers do for a living, to recognize both the necessity for their work and even a certain valor in an occupation that American society too often holds in contempt.

The central case of this book, *White v. Ford*, pulls Specter, unsuspecting at first, into the legal battle of his career. It begins when he volunteers to help a small Nevada firm by providing it with information, free of charge or conditions, and it evolves into an odyssey spanning many years. It is preceded and followed by similar cases, with similarly vulnerable victims.

DERICK BOBB. Walter White. Joe Blumer.

One was a baby, another a little boy, the third a grown man. They would never know each other. Their paths would never cross. But the courses of their lives and those of their families would be forever altered by a similar occurrence, a violent episode that at first seemed like nothing more than an unfortunate accident, a matter of being in the wrong place at the wrong time.

Yet the fate that befell these three individuals was no accident. They were all victims of a mechanical contraption weighing just a few pounds and made up of several seemingly simple metal parts and gears. The device was manufactured for the Ford Motor Co. and installed in its F-Series trucks, which, for more than three decades, were the best-selling motor vehicle in the world. The device was a parking brake that, it would turn out, was defective.

Ford knew the brake was a problem. But it denied and delayed, both in fixing the brakes and in telling the public. For two decades (and counting), anyone downhill from an F-Series pickup was at risk of being hurt or killed by a runaway truck. Only luck and circumstances separated them from what happened to Derick Bobb, Walter White, and Joe Blumer.

Ford knew. But proving it, and making Ford face the consequences, would be another thing altogether.

PART I

The Battle Begins

CHAPTER 1

The Bobbs

Tammy Bobb was having a bad time. Just twenty-three, she had three kids to care for—Scott, seven, Andrew, two and a half, and baby Derick, eleven months. And she had just separated from her husband, Dave. Not that the kids noticed—Dave drove a big rig and was on the road most of the time anyway. The young family lived in a trailer park in South Central Pennsylvania, in the town of Newville. Today, more than most days, Tammy wanted, needed, to get away, to escape that cramped trailer park, if only for a few hours. It was a Sunday and Scott was at a friend's house, so she decided to load the two younger boys into her pickup truck and head for the mountains, to the family's cabin in the woods. Tammy owned the wood frame house with her mother and two brothers. It rested in a secluded, pretty spot adjacent to a state park about twenty minutes away. It would be nice to go there for a while and just relax. Besides, her pickup had a small load of wood and cinderblocks she had to drop off at the cabin.

When she arrived, her Ford F-150 climbing the last mile up a deserted gravel road, Tammy parked next to the cabin and hopped out. It was hot for September, but this spot was covered constantly in cool shade from the huge pine trees that rose up the hillside and the thick mountain laurel that covered the rocky terrain. A cold stream flowed in front of the cabin, where the family got water to drink and to boil to make macaroni and cheese for the kids. The cabin, built in a remote spot just off the Appalachian Trail in 1956, had no running water, no bathroom, no shower. Tammy had shampooed her hair more than once in the stream's crystalline currents.

The cabin wasn't much, its screened-in porch packed with old, faded furniture and a cranky generator to pump electricity into the cluttered kitchen. The place had a musty smell. But it was theirs. They had put a sign up on the cabin: "Camp Lil' Bit."

Tammy backed the truck into the driveway so she could unload the wood into one of the bins used to store firewood. She stepped down on the parking brake, shifted into first gear, and removed the key. She didn't check the manual stick shift, which Tammy, like many drivers, left in first gear as a safety precaution, the transmission as well as the brake holding the vehicle. Tammy didn't realize it, but she had shifted the truck into fourth gear, not first. It didn't really matter, though. She had set the parking brake.

She took baby Derick out in his car seat and placed it on the concrete slab that made the cabin's foundation, a sort of ground-level porch. She took Andy out and put him in the back of the truck to help her with the wood. He handed the small cut pieces of an old birch tree to his mother, stopping from time to time to peel off its white papery bark. A few of the larger pieces he rolled down to Tammy along the truck bed. It wasn't long before Derick, an energetic tyke with blond hair and a wide smile, became restless, annoyed at being strapped into his seat. He started to squirm, then holler. He wanted out.

"All right, all right. Just hold on a minute," Tammy said. She unclipped his straps and let him crawl about on the porch. Derick didn't walk yet, but he could crawl as fast as a lizard.

"Andrew, stay there and help Mommy with the wood."

Tammy and Andrew went back to their chore, Andrew giving Tammy the pieces of wood and Tammy placing them on the woodpile. Tammy had turned toward the pile when Andrew yelled out to her.

"Mom! Mom! The truck! It's moving!"

The pickup had started to roll forward, slowly, an inch at a time, down the slightly sloped driveway. Tammy's first reaction was to glance quickly back at the cabin. At the porch. *Derick! Where was Derick?*

She dropped the pieces of wood and clutched at the open tailgate. *Dumb*, she thought, *I can't hold back a truck.* Tammy ran around to the side of the vehicle. Too late. She saw that Derick had crawled to a spot on the ground next to the pickup. The rear tire approached his right arm, starting to roll over the tiny limb. She dove to the ground knees first, grabbed his arm, and tried furiously to pull it out. She yanked at his arm but it wouldn't budge. The tire held Derick's arm and it was moving toward his neck and head. Tammy pulled harder, moving him toward her and away from the tire, but only slightly, maybe an inch or two. His neck was in the clear but now the tire was rolling straight for his head. In the next few seconds the unimaginable happened. The tire rolled up and over his head. Tammy was helpless to stop it. Terrified, she could only watch and wait—Was it three seconds or three hours?—for the tire to complete its rotation, lifting the truck as it moved over her little boy's skull.

To her surprise, when the tire moved clear of Derick, he rose on his own to his hands and knees. He started to cry. A good sign? Maybe he was all right. Tammy took two big steps toward the open driver's side door to try to stop the truck, to lunge for the brake pedal, but the truck came to a halt on its own. She went to press down on the emergency brake, but it was already down. How could that be?

She looked quickly back at Derick and what she saw horrified her. His head was covered with blood, his blond hair matted with a deep red that ran down his neck and onto his orange T-shirt. She rushed over and grabbed him, spreading the fingers of one hand behind his head and neck for support and the other on his chest to turn him over. That was when he stopped breathing. Derick was out cold, his eyes rolled back into his head, his lips turning a grayish blue. Tammy held his little wrist with her thumb. No pulse.

Tammy knew CPR. She'd learned it at the local firehouse, where Dave worked as a volunteer. She lifted Derick carefully and placed him on his back. She put her mouth over her baby's and tried to force a puff of air into his chest. But she had a bad seal and the air was leaking out. She wanted to move his chin up but was afraid that his neck might be broken. She puffed again, but again it didn't work. She suddenly realized her mistake.

"He's an infant, stupid!" She yelled at herself out loud. Infants are too small to be administered regular CPR. You instead have to place your mouth over both the baby's mouth and nose. Tammy did that now and felt the subtle vibration of air moving into Derick's lungs. She pressed his chest, his heart, three or four times. Finally Derick let out a deep breath, like a long, soft sigh. She had brought him back. She had saved his life. Tammy put Andrew in the truck and lifted Derick onto the seat beside her. She rubbed his chest as he lay on his back. She started the engine, released the parking brake, and headed down the mountain, driving almost 60 m.p.h. in second gear down the twisting road, the truck bouncing violently, its rear tires sliding around the turns and spitting gravel out into the woods. Tammy knew that the nearest house with a phone was more than a mile away. When she reached it she slammed to a stop, jumped out of the truck, and began pounding on the front door.

"Help! I need help!" she shouted. An elderly man swung the door open. "Hurry! My baby is hurt! Call 911!"

Dave Bobb was at the Newville Firehouse when the call came over the radio for an ambulance. He didn't recognize the address since it belonged to someone he didn't know. Then he got a phone call. "Jesus," he yelped, "that call was for my boy, for Derick!" A friend drove Dave to the house where Tammy had gone to call the ambulance, and then Dave drove to Chambersburg Hospital, speeding along the local roadways. He arrived after the ambulance and learned that Derick had been flown by helicopter to Hershey Medical Center. Dave got to Hershey a short time afterward. Tammy reached the hospital later, her eyes streaming tears with every mile she drove, not knowing how her baby was. Would he be all right? Derick had actually stood up right after the accident, so maybe he'd be fine. Maybe the little guy would brush it off. Kids were resilient, right? Or was he dead? Was Derick gone forever? Tammy could feel the sense of dread welling up in her, mounting as she slammed the Ford into a parking spot near the emergency room doors and ran inside. Her mind and heart raced. She couldn't imagine feeling more terrible.

Until the recriminations began.

"She probably wasn't paying attention," said one of Tammy's older brothers, or so she heard days after the incident. Before anyone knew Derick's condition, before they even knew what had happened, Tammy was being blamed. Truth be told, Tammy wasn't sure herself what had happened or how.

And it only got worse. Later a woman whom Tammy considered a friend would call the government, the county Children and Youth Services office, suggesting that perhaps Derick's injury wasn't an accident at all. She reported to the authorities that the child had been scalded on his right arm just the week before, and asked, "Don't you think something funny is going on?" Derick had been burned while taking a bath with Andy, Tammy had explained to friends who saw the injury. She had just stepped out of the bathroom for a couple of seconds to put in a load of laundry when one of the boys accidentally pulled on a toy bucket that had been hanging on the cold water spigot, turning it off. Tammy had made a mistake. She wasn't a perfect mother.

Then her own husband questioned what had happened at the cabin. "Dave saw me and said, 'What the hell did you do?'" she recounted. "I said, 'Nothing.' I knew I didn't do anything wrong. I just kept saying it and saying it. 'I didn't do anything wrong!' He didn't really believe me."

While Tammy dealt with the guilt and accusing glances, the medical team worked to save her son. When one of the doctors came out to the waiting room, Dave approached him. "How is Derick? And don't sugar-coat it. Don't give me a line of bullshit." And the doctor didn't. He told Tammy and Dave that Derick might die. His condition was uncertain.

Several hours passed and the prognosis improved. Derick would survive, the doctors said, but after that the news was not good. He had endured a traumatic injury to his brain. The doctors' terminology was itself mind-bending—"acute hydrocephalus, subdural hemorrhage, subarachnoid hemorrhage, and massive central edema." In short, his skull had been crushed and he had sustained severe bleeding in his brain. The doctors told Tammy and Dave that Derick would likely remain in a permanent vegetative state.

Days went by, then weeks. Derick had his first birthday in the hospital on October 10. Tammy and Dave stayed most nights at a Ronald McDonald House nearby while their baby underwent treatment. Derick was released on December 3, 1993, eleven weeks after the tragedy at the cabin. He would continue to recover but his progress would be slow and unsure. As was his prognosis. He had brain damage—that was clear. But exactly how much damage remained in doubt. Derick might recover to a good extent, the doctors now thought, though he would always have difficulties. He probably would be blind.

CHAPTER 2

The Brakes

THE STRANGE OCCURRENCES STARTED in 1992. Ford pickup trucks were moving on their own, rolling off when drivers' seats were empty. The vehicles were running into fences, houses, other cars. First a few, then a few dozen. Then more and more.

- Mr. Bremser reported that he engaged the parking brake, leaving the engine running and the transmission in neutral, and got out of the vehicle. He heard a "pop" and the vehicle began rolling down his driveway, striking a fence.
- Mrs. Snyder reported that she was removing a boat from its trailer when she heard a "snap." The vehicle allegedly then began to roll into the lake and struck the boat.
- The vehicle was reported to be parked on an incline with the transmission in neutral and the parking brake applied. Approximately five minutes later, the vehicle allegedly rolled and struck another parked vehicle.

Reports of "rollaways" were being received by the Ford Motor Co., which then passed them along to the National Highway Traffic Safety Administration (NHTSA), as required by law. The reports concerned a particular Ford vehicle, the company's top-selling F-Series trucks, the F-150, F-250, and F-350 pickup trucks. Some of the trucks seemed to have a will of their own, not unlike the title character in the 1983 Stephen King movie *Christine*, a red and white 1958 Plymouth Fury with a murderous mind. There was just one difference. King's story was fiction. These stories were true.

At first the incidents didn't appear so serious. A fender scraped here, a bumper damaged there. And Ford seemed to dismiss the reports that the vehicles' parking brakes were somehow disengaging, terming the incidents "reported" and "alleged." But then some of the incidents began to get serious.

- Reportedly, Mr. Lynn's daughter parked the vehicle in the driveway with the engine running and the parking brake applied. The parking brake allegedly failed to hold the vehicle, which rolled and struck Mr. Lynn's house, damaging the vehicle.
- The vehicle was reported to be parked on an incline with the transmission in neutral and the parking brake applied. A "popping" noise was allegedly heard, the vehicle began to roll, and subsequently the vehicle overturned before coming to a stop.
- The driver allegedly had applied the parking brake and exited the vehicle to shut the garage door. The vehicle rolled toward the driver and struck him.

Some of the incident reports were more than a tad understated, at least by the time NHTSA got them. For instance Mr. Lynn's car had not struck his house, causing unspecified, presumably minor damage. Years after the mishap Lynn still remembered his truck rolling away as if it had just happened.

"I got out of the truck and went to open the garage," he recalled. "Then I heard a 'pop.' Just for one second I turned around and looked at the truck. Nothing. Then, I look again and I see it's moving. It rolls backwards about the length of itself. Now I had this concrete pad in front of the garage that was fairly level, and it rolls off the pad and now it's really moving . . . My daughter, Sally, who was thirty-two at the time, she starts running for the passenger side and I holler, 'Stay back! Sally, stay back!' I had the driver's door open but I couldn't run fast enough to get around it and into the truck. It was going too fast."

That was probably a good thing. Within seconds Lynn's truck rolled off his driveway and down a 27-foot embankment, its tail end striking with such force that the truck bed was shoved two to three inches into the cab, buckling its frame. Damages totaled $7,000.

"You know what, if I would've tried to get back in that truck I would have gotten hurt," said Lynn. "We were really lucky no one got hurt on that truck that day."

After he climbed back into the truck the parking brake (also called an emergency brake) popped again. "After the repairs were done, I was real careful with it," said Lynn, "and one day it just popped off again."

Without being touched. Spontaneously.

Lynn brought the truck back to his local Ford dealer to complain. "That good-for-nothin' Ford dealer said there was nothing wrong with that brake. He said, 'You just didn't put the brake on.' I said, 'Bullshit!'"

Lynn, fifty-seven and the owner of his own zinc alloy company, wasn't used to getting any guff and he wasn't going to take any from a car dealer. He made the dealer look again. The dealer sat in the truck and pushed the parking brake down to the floor. It held. Then he released it and depressed the pedal again. And again. It held each time.

"How can we fix it if we don't see anything wrong with it?" he asked Lynn. But Lynn wouldn't be dismissed. He knew he wasn't nuts, hadn't imagined it all. He was also stubborn, continuing the argument and insisting something was wrong with the brake. As the two men argued they were interrupted by a sharp and distinct sound. *Pop!* "The sucker popped off right while he was standing there," said Lynn, chuckling at the memory. The dealer immediately gave Lynn a loaner and kept his truck. He installed a whole new parking brake free of charge. He also vowed to dash off a complaint directly to Ford.

Lynn never heard back from the dealer or Ford Motor Co. He was never reimbursed for the damage to his vehicle, most of which his insurance covered. He never received a letter from Ford. He never even knew whether the incident with his truck had been reported to Ford or placed in its records.

Ford had investigated a number of the incidents. It initially forwarded nineteen complaints to NHTSA. The agency was also receiving independent consumer complaints about the moving vehicles. In those cases Ford did look into, either by sending its own representative or having a dealer inspect the truck, it found pretty much the same thing. Nothing.

- A dealer's inspection could not find anything wrong with the vehicle.
- Neither a Ford representative nor an insurance adjuster could find a problem with the parking brake when inspected.
- No problem with the parking brake was found when inspected by the dealer's service manager.
- The alleged failure could not be reproduced.

Still, a couple of the reports must have been troubling to Ford. In one, "the dealer verified that the parking brake would not hold the vehicle." In another, "the parking brake pedal was in the applied position when seen by the dealership's service manager after the incident"—in other words, the car had rolled, even with the parking brake pedal depressed.

But these reports were a mere handful out of hundreds of thousands of trucks sold. Maybe some of the drivers depressed the brakes improperly or not at all. After all, most of the brakes looked fine when they were inspected after the reported incidents. Maybe the drivers just *thought* they had applied the parking brake. It wouldn't be the first time a driver made a mistake he didn't want to admit afterward. In fact, in one of the cases Ford investigated it turned out that the owner had damaged the brake system when he tried to set it by repeatedly stepping on the release lever instead of the brake pedal. Human error or human stupidity could always be possible.

Some people might blame the truck to cover up their own mistakes. They might be too embarrassed to admit they had done something wrong. In some cases such an admission meant more than mere embarrassment. It meant paying for accident repairs or higher insurance premiums. It meant liability. Easier to blame something or somebody else. And who better than a big, faceless corporation with deep pockets? On the other hand, how many people had their vehicle roll away, blamed themselves, and never reported it to Ford or NHTSA?

TWO DAYS AFTER DERICK was hurt, an incident occurred that restored Dave Bobb's faith in his wife. That day Dave drove the F-150 that had run over his son to the Hershey Medical Center, where Derick was still being treated for severe injuries. Dave parked the pickup in the hospital lot and stepped down on the parking brake. But as he depressed the pedal he heard a clicking sound, and then the brake did something it hadn't done before. It pushed right through to the floor, without locking. An alarm went off in Dave's head. He immediately knew what had happened at the cabin. He knew Tammy wasn't crazy, wasn't concocting an excuse for the mishap. Something was wrong with the parking brake.

Of course, the Bobbs didn't know anything about Ford's history of problems with the parking brake on its F-Series truck, one of the most popular vehicles in automotive history. This type of truck, introduced in 1948 with the F-1, was by the 1980s America's best-selling vehicle of any kind, a title it continued to hold for decades. In some recent years the trucks accounted for more than half of Ford's total profits.

The Bobbs also did not know much about lawsuits or lawyers. Until now they hadn't really thought of anything except Derick. But a nurse at Hershey who witnessed their ordeal and heard the strange story of the moving pickup truck suggested that they consult an attorney. She gave them a name and arranged for an appointment. Tammy and Dave, awash in emotions ranging from bewilderment to anger, decided that they would at least like to hear what he had to say. The first lawyer who reviewed their case referred the Bobbs to another lawyer from a bigger firm located in Philadelphia. Not many lawyers, especially those with smaller rural or suburban firms, were able to take on a major American corporation. Such a battle took time and resources, often several years and hundreds of thousands of dollars. It required perseverance and toughness.

CHAPTER 3

Derick's Due

Shanin Specter, the attorney the Bobbs hired, didn't look so tough. Just thirty-six, tall and willowy, he spoke softly and deliberately. He had a gentle manner compared with that of his boss at The Beasley Firm, the legendary James Beasley, the loquacious, irascible attorney who'd won Philadelphia's first $1 million injury verdict and many more to follow. Specter was civil to clients and opponents alike. But his outer calm belied a determination to see clients get justice and to see their tormenters be held liable, punished if possible. He knew the nightmare the Bobb family must be enduring. Specter had a small child of his own, a daughter. Silvi Specter was three months old when Specter filed suit in the case.

Derick would not fully recover from his injuries, a fact that would become starkly evident in the two years following the tragedy. He did not become blind. He could see, though poorly. He was incapable of speaking, able to communicate only through a basic form of sign language. He could not use his right arm, a consequence of the brain injury, and he had weakness in his right leg, causing him to have an odd gait. He would often lose his balance, falling down as many as fifteen to twenty times a day. He couldn't do things that other kids his age took for granted, like beginning to dress themselves. Tammy had tried to potty train him, but it was no use. Other problems also began to surface. Derick had fits of frustration and an abnormally bad temper. Tammy's little towheaded angel now had moments of meanness.

The Bobbs didn't know if they had a legal case against Ford. Neither did Specter. One didn't just sue Ford. The company had burgeoned since its founding in 1903, becoming an industrial colossus with a net worth exceeding $30 billion. Ford employed a ready battalion of full-time staff lawyers and could bring in paid outside counsel as reinforcements when necessary. And it was often necessary; Ford in fact spent more money for outside counsel than on its own in-house legal department. Ford naturally didn't disclose how much it budgeted for legal expenses, but it was obvious the sum reached into the millions—many, many millions. Ford hired the best and didn't mind paying the best's bills. Lawsuits aroused little fear at Ford. For the company that had manufactured the "exploding" Pinto and equipped its vehicles with ill-fated Firestone tires, lawsuits were routine.

The accident that injured Derick Bobb could have been a mistake, an unlucky error. And even if it wasn't, how could Specter prove it was Ford's fault? How many times since Henry Ford had popularized the motorcar, selling 15 million of the affordable Model T by 1927, had a wife (or husband for that matter) backed into a garbage can or scraped the side of the garage? How many stupid mistakes did people make?

When Specter heard Tammy's story he was sympathetic yet dubious. It sounded wacky. He knew about human nature and human error. He also knew that the case, if he took it, would be a laborious one. He checked all the available sources and couldn't come up with a single legal case against Ford for a faulty parking brake. If he filed suit he would be treading on new, uncertain ground.

Specter placed his first call in the case to a man in Pittsburgh named Joe Davidson. He'd used Davidson in auto cases before. Davidson went formally by J. E. Davidson, Consultant in Forensic Automotive Mechanics. He was not a bow-tied professor, but a mechanic with dirt under his nails and experience under his belt, a no-nonsense guy who'd worked around cars all his life. Specter would ask him to check out the parking brake assembly from the Bobbs' truck. But once he reached Davidson on the phone, Specter's doubts were assuaged. Sure, Davidson told him, he'd take a look at the Bobbs' parking brake, but there was probably no need to. He was certain the brake had a problem. "I've seen a bunch of these before," he said.

In fact Davidson had considered the problem so serious and potentially widespread that he had written a letter to NHTSA's Office of Defects Investigation. Davidson began his July 9, 1993, letter the way he did everything, direct and to the point.

> Dear Sir or Madam: I believe that all light-duty Ford trucks MY92 and probably MY93 are subject to failure of the parking brake equalizer with ensuing rollaway as described in this enclosed report.

What followed was a six-page report based on a case of a rollaway truck at Cool Spring Stone Supply in Uniontown, Pennsylvania. In that incident, the truck's driver had parked the vehicle in neutral on a slight incline with the engine running and the parking brake on. "As the left door of the cab swung shut, he heard the rear brakes creak as if releasing, and the vehicle rolled backwards down the grade," Davidson noted in his report. He included a number of detailed exhibits, including diagrams and ten photographs and photomicrographs. As he told NHTSA, "I do not represent myself to be a metallurgist, but I have some experience in fracture mode recognition." He ended his report the way he had started it, with a simple single paragraph.

> OPINION. It is my opinion, to a reasonable degree of technical certainty, that the spontaneous release of the parking brake of the subject vehicle on 03 May 93 and the ensuing rollaway and resulting damage was caused by inherent defect(s) in the parking brake equalizer as manufactured.

The Bobbs' story was starting to sound a lot less wacky.

Next Specter filed a request for information from NHTSA under the Freedom of Information Act, seeking information regarding problems with Ford's brakes. It took time to get an answer from the feds, but eventually it came. NHTSA reported having received twenty-eight "Vehicle Owner Reports (Complaint Letters)." One of the first documents Specter noticed was an anonymous letter and report from Pittsburgh about a problem with Ford's brakes. Although the name of the sender had been blocked out, Specter knew immediately who had sent it. The letter was a copy of the one he'd received from Joe Davidson.

After he sued on the Bobbs' behalf, Specter filed motions for discovery, seeking memos and documents from both Ford and the manufacturer and supplier of the brake system, Orscheln Company, Inc. He traveled to Moberly, Missouri, where Orscheln was headquartered, searching through files and eventually turning up a number of important documents that he hadn't received in the vast pile of papers Ford had sent him. Maybe the car maker had lost them or tossed them. No matter—they would help his case.

One of the first things Specter noticed was a 1984 article authored by two Ford employees, Manuel Barbosa and Harry L. Worosz, about a new parking brake system Ford had developed for its Aerostar, back then the company's new compact van. The article provided some insight into what the company had touted as "the industry's first self-adjusting parking brake system." It also provided something for Specter—a motive. The same motive he had seen in other product liability cases, the same motive that so often led companies to cut costs and quality. The profit motive.

While the Ford article boasted about "improved reliability" of the new parking brake, it also noted that the new brake had significantly reduced costs to the company, which at the time was battling for market share with smaller and less expensive foreign autos. This motive was evident from the beginning of the article:

INTRODUCTION

The Aerostar Self-Adjusting Parking Brake system was conceived, designed and developed to reduce assembly labor costs and to improve reliability and vehicle maintenance. With the significant labor cost discrepancy which exists between the domestic and Japanese automotive manufacturers, vehicle component system designs that can be assembled and adjusted in less time reduce the Japanese advantage. Furthermore, systems that do not require periodic readjustment provide further savings to the domestic manufacturer in warranty charges and the consumers in maintenance costs.

The new brakes were cheaper to install at the factory and cheaper to maintain afterward. They used a ratchet-and-pawl system that made the new parking brake "maintenance-free." Simply put, the new system used a locking mechanism in which a pawl would lock into a spot on the ratchet's series of metal "teeth" to hold the brake, much like gears meshed together. The driver would press his foot down on the brake pedal, which would stop and lock when a cable leading to the rear brakes became taut. In older parking brakes these cables would occasionally loosen over time and have to be adjusted to get the proper tension. With the new system, if the cable stretched or loosened the pawl would simply catch in the next gap between the teeth further along the locking mechanism. Tension was automatic and continuous. No manual adjustments were necessary. Ever.

Ford liked this for a simple reason. Many of the adjustments in other vehicles were made while they were still under warranty—at Ford's cost. This was no longer the case with the Aerostar parking brake system, which later went into other Ford models, including the Ranger, Bronco, and F-Series trucks.

Among the NHTSA documents were the nineteen "alleged" incidents of rollaways that customers had reported to Ford. Specter noticed that most of the drivers recounted that the parking brake had released itself. Many had recalled hearing a "Pop!" just before their trucks started to roll away.

The documents Specter retrieved seemed to portray (and betray) a clear series of events at Orscheln and Ford—first questions about the parking brakes, then concerns among company executives, then a search for a way to fix the brakes, then a delay in doing so, and finally a reluctance to recall the vehicles. Specter found the plot line familiar.

He found other reports in the files, many of them technical, with diagrams and charted studies that he barely understood. But one of them gave him a jolt. This document seemed too good to be true, like a vein of gold shining in a wall of brown dirt. It was a document that convinced Specter not only that he had a case against Ford but also that he had a chance, a good chance, to go after the car company for punitive damages.

What caught his eye was a February 22, 1993, draft of a "white paper" prepared by Ford employee Tim Rakowicz, a product design engineer for the F-Series brake and rear axle system. When problems arose with the parking brake, Rakowicz had been put in charge of finding out what was going on. Rakowicz was young, a kid really, just twenty-six years old at the time, which told Specter something about what priority Ford gave its parking brake problem. Not high.

It also may have explained why Rakowicz would write such a white paper, a document only a young and naive Ford employee would be bold enough to create.

The title of the paper alone was damning: "F-Series Parking Brake Control Self-Releasing Field Campaign and Owner Notification Paper." Translation: The parking brake self-releases and the problem is serious enough that the trucks should be recalled. Specter rapidly turned the pages of Rakowicz's report.

In his white paper, Rakowicz had begun in a manner that Specter found delectably succinct, starting with a numbered notation "1. PROBLEM DESCRIPTION" contained in a box and followed by this statement: "On certain 1992/1993 model year (MY) F-Series vehicles, the parking brake control will intermittently self-release after pedal apply."

This was nothing less than an admission by a Ford employee—albeit not an upper-level executive but the person assigned to investigate the F-Series brake problems—that the parking brakes, to use his own terminology, "self-released." Specter allowed himself a thin smile. *Pop!* he thought, *goes the weasel.*

In the ensuing months, Team Specter went into action. Specter's own experts provided confirmation for what he had found in the corporate and government documents, documents that seemed to lay the blame for Derick Bobb's accident squarely on Ford. J. E. Davidson said the brake was defective. So did Campbell Laird, Specter's expert metallurgist at the University of Pennsylvania, and all those memos and documents from Ford, fully 19 feet tall when stacked page to page. It all added up to a strong case against Ford.

The documents proved, Specter felt, that Ford and Orscheln knew early on, well before the incident involving Derick Bobb, that the new variety of parking brake—initially designed and developed by Ford and then handed over to Orscheln for latter-stage design and testing—was defective. They proved that Ford was cavalier in dealing with the problem, at first telling personnel at Orscheln, according to one document, "not to worry about it," and then trying to lay the blame on Orscheln. They proved that in tests the companies were able to replicate the brake failure known as "spontaneous disengagement." They proved that it took far too long to come up with a fix and that when one was found—a plastic wedge that cost as little as 16¢—Ford was reluctant to issue a recall or even a warning, at first using the wedge only for customers who came into its dealerships complaining that their brakes had failed. The car company eventually issued a recall for all 884,400 affected trucks only when forced to do so by the government.

As part of the preparations for trial, Specter's actuarials provided an estimate of the damages due the Bobbs. The lawsuit put Derick Bobb's medical bills at $121,468.68 and his future medical and personal care at between $5.5 million and $19.8 million. His lost earnings capacity ranged from $1.2 million to $1.9 million. There was no amount calculated for pain and suffering, just one word: "enormous."

The Bobbs, Specter felt, would also make good witnesses. Tammy felt certain about what had happened on the day of the accident. She remembered pressing down the parking brake. She remembered—and could recount with gripping detail—the accident and the rescue of her son, bringing him back to life with her own breath and seeing him loaded aboard a Life Flight helicopter bound for Hershey Medical Center. She had been a good and caring mother to her three boys. Her husband was a hard-working man, a blue-collar company truck driver who put food on the table and paid the mortgage, who had been at the volunteer firehouse ready to save someone else's life when his own son had his brush with death.

In a lawsuit filed on April 4, 1994, Specter charged that Orscheln was aware its brakes had a problem with "skip-out" as early as August 1990 and that both Orscheln and Ford knew of the brake problems in production vehicles as early as April 1992. There was documentation that Ford had complained to Orscheln and demanded a fix, yet Ford had done nothing on its own to deal with the problem. The suit cited numerous cases of skip-out, or spontaneous disengagement, of Ford truck parking brakes, including three vehicles owned by Ford managers. In one case, a manager's truck had rolled into a lake. The suit also noted that a relatively inexpensive fix had been available but that Ford delayed using it. Memos also mentioned a possible recall before the accident involving Derick Bobb, but one was not issued until November 1994, at the insistence of NHTSA and months after Specter had filed suit in the Bobb case. The suit accused Ford of breaking its well-advertised promises to the public.

> Ford made certain expressed warranties to the Bobbs, including that the subject vehicle was built "Ford tough," that "Quality comes first," that Ford "strive(s) for excellence . . . in . . . safety," and that at Ford "integrity is never compromised." Ford breached these expressed warranties.

For its part Orscheln denied that its product was defective or that the company had in any way been negligent. Ford and Orscheln filed a cross-claim against Tammy Bobb, saying the accident was her fault. "The accident in question was caused by the actions of the plaintiffs themselves which amounted to negligence . . . and a misuse of the product," Orscheln stated in legal briefs. The cross-claim further declared, "Mrs. Bobb's negligence was a direct and sole cause of the minor plaintiff's injuries."

In a pretrial memorandum filed with the court outlining its defense, Ford also questioned Tammy Bobb's description of the accident. Ford planned to put on the witness stand a doctor who would testify that Derick suffered a "pinching injury, that the tire caught the back of Derick's head and that the tire did not run over Derick's head . . . that there is an apparent inconsistency between the child's injuries and the description of the accident as related by Mrs. Bobb." Ford had its own experts who would reconstruct what had occurred. Its experts also would testify about the brake design and offer their opinions "as to whether or not the parking brake control lever was properly engaged at the time of the accident or was engaged at all." They undoubtedly disputed Tammy Bobb's story.

Much of the Ford memorandum dealt with expert testimony from doctors and nurses who would testify that, despite severe injuries, Derick had recovered fairly well, that he wasn't so badly off. He had experienced "astounding improvement" in his vision; his eyes tended to drift at near vision, but the Ford expert would pronounce this "clinically insignificant." Of course, Derick's eyes might cross in the future, requiring surgery, but for now they seemed all right. His other skills also weren't so awful, the Ford-hired doctors planned to say. During an examination Derick exhibited language functions similar to that of a child twelve to fourteen months old and adaptive skills of a child fifteen to eighteen months old. Ford mentioned this as something to cheer about. The memorandum didn't mention that at the time of the examination, conducted on September 19, 1994, Derick was three weeks short of his second birthday.

The Ford experts also called the child's gait "mildly unstable," and said he suffered only "infrequent falls," not nearly as many as his mother had claimed. It blamed his other physical problems on other factors. For instance, the fact that Derick's right side did not function as well as his left could be attributed to the fact that "Derick's mother is sinistral"—left-handed, even though his parents said he had favored his right hand before the accident.

Ford went so far as to blame the child's learning difficulties on his parents, noting in the memo that "Derick has an eight-year-old male sibling who has difficulty in learning; he is a half-sibling." Sure, dumb mother, dumb sons. If there was any doubt as to Ford's meaning, the company cleared up the possible confusion when it mentioned the expected testimony of Irene Mendelsohn, a rehabilitation counselor:

> There is significant uncertainty when predicting the child's education and employment process. Thus the parents' education and employment history must be evaluated as we can assume that the child will reach that level. Here, the parents both have high school degrees. On the above bases, there is no reason to assume Derick will achieve an associate degree much less a bachelor degree.

Despite that assertion, Ford seemed to want it both ways, to say also that Derick wasn't so badly off that he couldn't do better—or perhaps Ford simply didn't notice the obvious contradiction. Directly after that expert's opinion that Derick would turn out no better than his high school–educated parents, another expert was listed who would say under oath that Derick might indeed excel. "It is possible the child will go to college," economist Joseph Mooney, Ph.D., was prepared to say.

Nevertheless Mendelsohn was of the opinion that Derick, as an adult, would likely wind up in a job that had him sitting behind a desk doing menial tasks or perhaps out and about doing light physical labor. Processing checks. Sweeping up. Ford put a rosy glow on such a scenario. "There is nothing to say that he cannot do sedentary, light to medium work . . . Ninety percent of job titles are within the sedentary, light to medium levels which indicate a wide variety of job titles from which to choose."

Was this an occupational future any Ford executive wanted for his or her child?

BY THE TIME he was ready for trial Specter was confident he could convince a jury that Ford had acted badly. His case would prove it. Trial was set for September 6, 1995, before U.S. District Judge Malcolm Muir, a short, older man with white hair and a country way about him. Muir wore plain clothes, sometimes khakis (and sometimes with yellow socks), under his black robes and ate peanut butter sandwiches for lunch. He was pleasant and unpretentious in private, but he was tough and had a reputation for disdaining the rich and mighty. He had sent more than one white-collar criminal to prison for a longer stretch than even the prosecutors had recommended. He had a nickname, though no one uttered it in his presence. Muir was known as the "Hanging Judge." He wasn't likely to be sympathetic to Ford.

While a Central Pennsylvania jury was not as likely to give a large monetary award as a panel of Philadelphians, Specter knew that these rural folks, many of them drivers of pickups themselves, had a low tolerance for irresponsibility, whether on the part of a neighbor or a big company. Specter liked his chances in court.

The case would never get there. Several months before the scheduled trial Specter got a call from a lawyer for Ford whose last name was, co-incidentally, that of another Ford product. Joe Pinto was a heavy hitter with a major Philadelphia law firm. He'd been around for decades and had represented Ford for most of his career. When Ford had a big case to defend in Pennsylvania or New Jersey, they called Pinto. He was a white-haired gentleman with soft features and a softer manner. Pinto had a reputation for being a nice guy but he knew how to play hardball.

He didn't lose cases, not big ones. He either got plaintiffs to take a settlement or he defeated them in a courtroom. He was interested in settling the case filed by the Bobbs. In a fashion not typical for many lawyers, Pinto laid his cards on the table and announced he was ready to fold his hand.

"Shanin, I want to be up front with you," Pinto said. "I know you probably have a good case."

"The best," said Specter.

"I've been at this a long time. I've never lost a big one and I don't want to start now. You know, I'm probably going to retire in a few years and I don't want to go out that way. Let's get this thing settled."

"Well, I'm willing to listen."

"Good."

"But, you know, Joe, Ford's not going to get off cheap."

"I know it." Pinto allowed himself a small smile. "I know it."

"All right. Get back to me with an offer."

It took some time but the suit was settled. And Ford did not get off cheap. The amount paid to the Bobbs, with the bulk of the money placed in a trust for Derick, was generous. It would be enough for the family to buy a house and new vehicles and provide for Derick and, truth be known, the rest of the family, for life. The amount was large, but as part of the settlement the Bobbs and Specter had to agree not to disclose it.

Specter didn't love the idea of settling or keeping his mouth shut about it. He wanted to shout the news out loud, wanted to call the news media. He wanted people across the country, people who might have had an accident involving a rollaway Ford pickup, to know about Ford's writing such a big check. But he also wanted to do—was required to do— what was right for his clients, and getting several million dollars for the Bobbs and a boy who would need care for the rest of his life was the right thing. Specter took some solace in notifying NHTSA about the settlement. Still, he had an empty feeling inside. He sensed that this fight with Ford wasn't over.

The settlement was not announced across the nation, and not a single item appeared in a newspaper or on a TV station about the settlement reached between the Bobbs and Ford. Ford's secret was safe. For now. And people were still driving Ford pickup trucks without knowledge of the defective parking brakes, still parking them on slopes, still bringing them home. Specter felt an uneasiness. He possessed what he called "guilty knowledge." He knew that something bad was bound to happen to someone else.

Indeed, in his deposition with Rakowicz, Specter had asked the Ford engineer why Ford's letter to NHTSA saying it would recall 884,400 vehicles didn't mention anything about spontaneous disengagement of the brakes. The recall notice Ford planned to send stated only that "during rapid pedal application of the parking brake, the pedal may go to the floor with little or no effort." That made the problem seem like a mere inconvenience.

"If you don't tell people that the vehicle's parking brake may spontaneously disengage and the truck may roll down a hill and hit something or hurt somebody, then you're not going to give them the information that a lot of people may need to know to cause them to come in and get this thing fixed. Isn't that true?" Specter had asked.

"I don't know," Rakowicz had responded. "They'll be informed of a recall."

Specter had been nonplussed. He had found it hard to believe Ford would have such a callous attitude toward its customers, toward human beings in general. Shouldn't people know they were possibly in danger? He had pressed the issue with Rakowicz.

Q: Don't you think the following is going to happen? Ready for this? You're going to recall these one million vehicles. A lot of folks aren't going to bring them in because they're not going to think it's a big deal that the parking brake can go to the floor during application. But they would have, a lot of folks would have brought the vehicle in if they had been told that there was spontaneous disengagement. Maybe there'll be ten thousand, fifty thousand, a hundred thousand, maybe even more people who won't bring in their vehicle because you didn't tell them about the spontaneous disengagements. Then somebody is going to have the kind of thing happen to them that Mr. and Mrs. Bobb had happen to them . . . where their brake disengaged and their vehicle rolled forward. And they didn't bring their vehicle in because they weren't told in strong enough terms about what the problem was. Now, have you considered the possibility I laid out for you?

A: I myself, I don't recall ever doing it.

Q: Well, I just mentioned it to you right now. You've listened to it. Do you think it's an unreasonable suggestion as to what may in fact happen?

A: I don't think it's unreasonable, no.

Even Rakowicz had had to admit the possibility. Yet Ford's recall would not include a notice about spontaneous disengagement, would not warn people of the potential safety hazard they faced.

Specter's questioning was not mere hyperbole. It was prescient. He had known, had felt in his gut, that someone else would get hurt. Someday, somewhere, someone was going to get killed. He had known it was only a matter of time. What he hadn't known when he deposed Rakowicz and asked him these questions on September 22, 1994, was that that moment was only seventeen days away.

CHAPTER 4

The Whites

JIMMIE DARRELL WHITE and Virginia Hooks were about as opposite as could be. He was a son of the desert, a New Mexican native with sharp angular features and bright blue eyes set in sun-baked leathery skin, his hands coarse from rugged outdoor work. She was from Iceland, as fair as Jimmie was dark, as soft as he was hard, with glasses covering bashful eyes. Jimmie, handsome despite a long-gone front tooth, was cocky, brash, and confident, even though he stood only a smidgen over 5-foot-5, 2 inches shorter than Ginny. He wore skintight jeans and a turquoise belt buckle as big as a fist. His thick head of dark hair was brushed back Pompadour-style, his sideburns long and thick. Ginny, whose stepfather was a U.S. Air Force officer who had moved the family from Iceland to New Mexico, was quiet and reserved, her voice a muted crackle, her clothing plain and in hues of brown and white, beige and cream. Her light brown hair hung straight down nearly to her waist.

But Jimmie and Ginny had one thing in common, the Iron Skillet Petro, an establishment near the main road in Grants, New Mexico, where you could fill up with gas or order a plate of fried eggs with home fries and chili peppers. Ginny was a cashier in the restaurant and Jimmie had his first cup of coffee there every morning before heading off to the gold mines, where he worked as a mechanic on everything from pickup trucks to three-story rigs.

Jimmie would look at Ginny while she worked. Sometimes she would look back; sometimes she wouldn't. The two never spoke, though, until an inanimate object, her car, brought them together. It had broken down and a co-worker suggested she have Jimmie take a look under the hood. After he fixed her car, Jimmie asked Ginny out. Their dates didn't always go well; Jimmie once took Ginny snowmobiling and she ended up being sick for days. But a romance bloomed and they married. They later moved to Spring Creek, Nevada, an extension of Elko, a mountain town of 34,000 in northeastern Nevada that was closer to Salt Lake City and Boise than to Reno and a dream world away from the glitter of Las Vegas.

Both had been married before. Jimmie's two daughters were grown and living in Montana. Ginny's daughter, Ragna, was a teenager and lived with her mother and stepfather. Jimmie and Ginny wanted another child, a child they could raise together.

Ginny had a very difficult, high-risk pregnancy and was confined to bed rest for the final trimester. But on October 22, 1990, she gave birth to Jon Walter Douglas Wayne White, named for his grandfathers, a step-grandfather, and a childhood friend of Jimmie's who had passed away. Unsure why, they started calling him Walter and it stuck. That and Buddy Boy, a nickname Jimmie was fond of for his new son.

Walter turned out to be a little lemon drop, a sweet, blond lad who never brought his parents a moment's grief. He never complained and rarely cried, even as an infant. "He would catch a fly on the window and go to the door and let it fly away. He literally couldn't even hurt a fly," his mother said. He was also very smart. Walter talked perfectly at two, in full sentences, with no "baby talk." Asked his name, he'd shoot back the answer: "Jon Walter Douglas Wayne White." By the time he was three, Walter could recite his ABCs and have lengthy conversations with store clerks, who often asked Ginny why he wasn't in school. "Because he's only three," she'd say.

The Whites doted on their young son. Jimmie, who was sometimes away on a drilling job for two or three days at a time, would come home and play with Buddy Boy for hours on end. The Whites lived in a trailer at 318 North Trescartes Avenue, a neighborhood where the homes stood fairly far apart amid bare earth and patches of scrub grass. With few trees, the community resembled a moonscape, the aluminum-sided homes plopped randomly on hilly ground that looked up to several mountain peaks. Jimmie had managed to grow a trim green lawn behind the "double-wide," an oversize trailer painted tan with green trim. On the grass he erected a swing set for Buddy Boy.

Ginny watched her son constantly. She didn't work outside the home after Walter was born, even though the extra money would have been nice. She wanted to be with Walter all day. Friends and her few neighbors warned her about being overprotective. "My mother would even tell me, 'You have to let him go. You have to let him have some freedom.' I watched him like a hawk, until that day . . ."

That day was October 9, 1994. About 4:00 p.m., Jimmie had driven his truck, an F-350, one of the bigger Ford pickups, into Elko to pick up a pellet stove he planned to install in the trailer. The truck belonged to his employer, Stewart Brothers Drilling Company, but Jimmie was allowed to use it to travel to and from job sites and during his personal time. He and Ginny's younger brother, a high school kid named Johnson Hooks, who lived with them, had unloaded the stove from the truck. First Jimmie went into the backyard to mix concrete for the slab on which the stove would rest. Little Walter, who would be four years old in a few weeks, helped him mix the cement powder with sand and water. Then he played in the backyard on his swings and with his toy trucks. Ginny had urged him to come in to take a bath. Walter had pleaded with her.

"Can't I play a little more?"

"Well, all right, a little while longer. Then it's in for your bath."

"Okay, Momma."

Walter came through the house and went out through the front door, walking along the dirt driveway that formed a semicircle in front of the house. Usually, he wasn't allowed out front, but the house was far from the road and cars hardly ever came by this deserted end of the community. Besides, Ginny checked on him from time to time through the bedroom window. The last time she looked, Walter was sitting on his tricycle, ringing its bell and singing to himself.

At one point Walter started to come back in. "The front door opened, his little hand came in, and I remember seeing his hand as he started to come in, and all of a sudden he shut the door and went back out," recalled his father. That image of Walter's small fingers wrapped around the edge of the door would stay with him.

Jimmie and Ginny were standing in the living room discussing how to position the new stove when they heard a noise from outside, a "metallic" noise, as Jimmie would describe it later. He thought one of the service boxes on his truck had slammed shut. He thought he might have left the passenger side door open on one of his trips to the truck, once to get his tape measure, later to get a small piece of flex pipe he needed to install the stove. Jimmie stood up and walked to the front door to look at his truck. *What had made that noise?* As he got to the door Jimmie noticed something odd. His truck was gone.

The phone rang. "Your truck," a neighbor told Ginny, "it's rolled down across the road."

A police report filed later that day by Sergeant John Aubrey Fosmo of the Elko County Sheriff's Department measured the distance the truck had rolled at 182 feet. The report described what had happened:

> Jimmie White's work truck had rolled across the street and was in their neighbor's yard. Both parents ran to the door, observed the

work truck was missing, then saw it across N. Trescartes in their neighbor's yard. They immediately ran to the truck, looking for their son Walter. After arriving at the truck they observed the passenger door open. However, their son wasn't in the truck.

Seeing the cab empty, Jimmie turned back toward his house. Suddenly he saw Walter lying on the dirt road, immobile. He ran to his son, spotting a dark puddle near his body. The blood looked almost black against the hard yellowish dirt. Ginny reached her boy about the same time. Both parents dropped to their knees over Walter.

"Get the car!" Jimmie shouted to his wife.

"Oh God! Walter."

"Get the car!"

"He's not breathing. Jimmie, he's not breathing!"

"Go and get the car! Hurry!"

Jimmie lifted Walter in his arms as Ginny ran back up the driveway. She jumped into their car and drove it the few yards to her husband. Jimmie had her get in the back seat, and he handed Ginny Walter's limp body. Jimmie drove as fast as he could, the Ford Topaz kicking up clouds of dirt. Ginny gave Walter CPR, holding his head back and trying to push puffs of air into his lungs.

Seconds after the Whites arrived at Elko General Hospital, the nurses grabbed Walter and carried him into the emergency room. Jimmie stayed behind, filling out forms. Ginny took a seat in the waiting room, unable to speak or move. She seemed to be in shock. A nurse came to her with some pills, something to calm her nerves. Ginny swallowed the pills without looking at them. Jimmie busied himself by calling anyone he could think of. First, he dialed his brother-in-law, Ronnie, to tell him what had happened. Then he called Johnson Hooks to tell him to move the truck out of the neighbor's yard.

"The next thing I remember," Jimmie would recall years later, "was Dr. Oswalt coming up to me and telling me my son was dead."

CHAPTER 5

The Letter

NOBODY KNEW WHAT had happened.

Walter had gotten into the truck. That much seemed obvious. And the truck had begun to roll down the driveway, which was fairly steep. As it moved, the truck had gained speed. After inspecting the vehicle, Sergeant Fosmo developed a theory as to what happened next, and he wrote it in his report filed the day after the accident.

> I believe while the vehicle was moving that the victim, Walter White, was trying to exit the moving vehicle. There were several small palm prints on the dash of the vehicle, some near the passenger door.
>
> As the vehicle passed through the slight ditch, I believe the victim finally managed to get the driver's door open. With the door opening and the jolt of [the truck] striking the ditch, I believe the driver's door was thrown open and the victim was thrown from the seat into the open door, where he was knocked slightly backward, rolling under the left side of the vehicle.

Fosmo's report went on to say that no one would be charged criminally since it was an accident. "However," he added about the parked truck, "it should have had the wheels chocked and emergency (brake) applied."

Jimmie White knew that the emergency brake *had* been applied. He was sure of it. How? Because he always put on the brake when he parked. Always. Jimmie was a creature of habit. He followed routines almost to the point of obsession. "My patterns are very set," he would say. One of them was how he handled his vehicles. He always parked them in first gear and with the parking brake on. Always.

His pals would even tease him about it. "Looks like Jimmie moved my pickup," one co-worker would tell another, because he had found the truck in first gear and with the parking brake depressed. That was the way Jimmie parked his vehicles. Always.

Jimmie could only scratch his head as to what had happened, why his truck had rolled down the driveway. Ginny never blamed him; she knew her husband too well. But the police, for some reason, came out several days after the accident and fingerprinted him. Jimmie also never blamed his wife for not having her eye on Walter the moment the accident happened. He knew she was a doting mother—that even the most watchful parent can look away for a few seconds. Neither parent ever blamed the other.

All Jimmie could figure was that Walter had gotten into his truck and, whether by accident or not, moved the stick shift from first gear into neutral. It took very little force to nudge the shift out of gear when the parking brake was set. Then Walter must have climbed over to the driver's side and released the parking brake. That part of it didn't really make sense to Jimmie. Why would Walter do such a thing? Was he playing, pretending he was driving? And even if he had tried, Walter seemed too small to release the parking brake. It took some force to pull up the hand release and someone so small would have had difficulty even reaching it. It didn't make sense but that was what must have happened. Jimmie had no other guesses.

He even told the police his speculation that Walter must have released the brake. "At the time, that was the only thing I could come up with," he would say later, years later. "I didn't believe it, but that was the only explanation I had at the time."

UNTIL MUCH LATER, almost six months later. They were long months, with Ginny trapped in the solitude of their home, a home without Walter, alone during the long day, when her daughter, Ragna, was at school. Ginny had days when she felt listless, entirely without energy. Most of the time she couldn't remember her day at all. Jimmie could scarcely concentrate on his job. Buddy Boy was always on his mind. A clinical psychologist found that the Whites had been "profoundly traumatized" by the loss of their son, that they suffered classic symptoms of post-traumatic stress disorder—nightmares, sleep deprivation, flashbacks, waves of uncontrollable emotion, and feelings of estrangement from others.

The bereavement group they'd joined hadn't worked out well. At first it helped to be with other people who had suffered losses, but then it just became a constant reminder, not that they needed one. Jimmie and Ginny thought of Walter constantly. "Whenever you least expected it . . ." Jimmie would say, then let the sentence trail off, looking down and shaking his head. "We would just go to the supermarket and see a little blond boy who looked like our son and we would have to leave."

Jimmie's sorrow turned to anger one day the following March. He was at work, finishing up, when his boss at Stewart Brothers Drilling came over to his truck, the same F-350 that had run over Walter. He handed Jimmie an envelope. Inside was a letter from the Ford Motor Co. notifying the recipient that the parking brakes on certain Ford trucks had a problem. The brakes sometimes skipped through when drivers tried to apply them. The notice didn't mention spontaneous disengagement or rollaways. It didn't have to, not for Jimmie. He stood there, feeling frozen in place as he read the words. He read them again and again. First anger, then "an empty feeling, just an empty feeling" swept over him. He'd had a revelation. "It was like a jigsaw puzzle, where everything just all of a sudden came into place," he recalled. He hurried home to Ginny, spouting like a fountain the moment he saw her. "You're not going to believe this. I know exactly what happened that day."

The next morning, Jimmie White called a lawyer. He had seen Grant Gerber's picture on a billboard along Route 27, the highway that connected downtown Elko to Spring Creek. Gerber was a referral attorney for Durney & Brennan, Ltd., of Reno. The firm was limited, all right, to Peter Durney and Tom Brennan, two middle-aged attorneys who had attended law school together and, after trying their hands at several different jobs and with different partners, decided to form their own firm in 1978. They had set up shop in a Victorian-style house built in 1906, which was extremely old by Reno standards. The house, which still had its original push-button on-off light switches, sat directly across the street from the federal building downtown. Both lawyers had good reputations in Reno and had won or settled cases for fairly large amounts of money. They had handled plenty of injury cases and knew their way around the local and federal courthouses in Reno.

The Whites' case landed on Durney's worn wooden desk. His office at the top of a creaky staircase held a jam-packed bookcase surrounded by wood paneling and muted green wallpaper. Durney was not a Fancy Dan. He had serious blue eyes that sloped downward and were topped by bushy gold-brown eyebrows. His thick reddish moustache seemed rusted in place. Durney was a trim version of the Marlboro Man, though the effect was hampered a bit by the reading glasses he wore at the office.

Durney took an immediate interest in the Whites' case. He started his research by checking to see if there had been any lawsuits against Ford for similar accidents. He found one. The case was *Bobb v. Ford*. He saw that Ford had settled for an undisclosed amount and that the plaintiffs' lawyer was Shanin Specter. Durney picked up the phone. He wanted to know if he could look at Specter's file against Ford. Specter told him about his firm's open-file policy, that any lawyer working on a plaintiff's case could look through and read or photocopy anything he or she wanted. No fees requested. No strings attached.

Durney hopped a flight to Philadelphia a few days later. He spent almost two full days reviewing the files, which were contained in several boxes stuffed with documents—photos, medical reports, Ford memos, transcripts of depositions. It was too much to take in or take with him. But Durney could see right away that there was plenty of solid information. The Rakowicz white paper, or the "recall memo," as it came to be known, was a blockbuster. Specter had been thorough. Durney was impressed, as he was when he met Specter, who was gracious and had an easy manner. Durney sensed that Specter also had a "presence" about him.

"Can I have photocopies made?" Durney asked.

"Of course. I'll have someone do them for you."

"That's okay, I can just . . ."

"I said we'll take care of it for you."

"You sure?"

"No problem."

Several days later, photocopies of the documents Durney had requested arrived at his office. If laid in a pile, the papers stood almost as tall as Durney. He searched the parcel for a bill. There wasn't any.

Specter had developed quite a file. It was almost a shame his case hadn't gone to trial with this ammunition, Durney thought. But now at least the bullets wouldn't go to waste.

A profitable confluence of factors had occurred in Specter's search for the truth of the case against Ford. As in so many other cases, one defendant had tried to put the blame on the other, which always worked to a plaintiff's advantage. While Ford and Orscheln didn't exactly accuse each other—Orscheln, after all, didn't want to lose a major customer— neither had been reluctant to turn over documents that made the other appear to be at fault. In some memos Ford criticized Orscheln for not acting quickly enough to find the problem with the brakes or, later on, a solution. When Orscheln did come up with a fix, Ford wanted Orscheln to pay to make the changes to trucks that were recalled.

This negotiating had produced a flurry of papers distributed to executives and engineers at both companies. If one had a document, the other was also likely to have it in a file somewhere—and would be required to turn it over under the rules of discovery. Neither company wanted to be caught not complying.

Durney didn't have to dig too much deeper, deciding eventually to use much of the same information—even some of the same experts—that Specter had lined up for the Bobb case. It was thus that the Whites' case in Elko, Nevada, was largely made by a lawyer in Philadelphia.

Durney did add a few nice pieces to the puzzle that made the case even stronger, especially one he picked up in Moberly, Missouri. His trip to the community of 12,000 people, in which Orscheln was the biggest employer, also served, though inadvertently on Durney's part, to send a message to Don Orscheln, patriarch of the family-run company and the town's biggest wheel.

At Orscheln, Durney discovered several interoffice memos that he had not found in Ford's files and that had not been turned over to NHTSA. The memos discussed not the brakes themselves but the devices Orscheln used to test them. These "test stands" mechanically applied and released the brakes hundreds and thousands of times to determine their durability. But the testing had revealed a problem. Sometimes the brake pedal popped right back up after it was applied; this came to be called "skip-out on apply." Sometimes the pedal popped up a little while after the brake had been set, which was simply called "skip-out," or, as the plaintiffs preferred to call it, "spontaneous disengagement." When either condition occurred, the stands shut down automatically, messing up the testing. Durney saw this as further proof that skip-out occurred.

In an interoffice Orscheln memo, one employee, Bill Tyson, summarized questions that Ford's Tim Rakowicz had asked the brake supplier about its testing procedure: "Do we document when skip-out occurs? . . . What actions did Orscheln take when skip-out occurs? . . . What have we seen in the past? . . . Basically, if we observed skip-out prior to current concerns—why didn't we report it?" Now Durney had documentation of a skip-out problem and of Ford's knowledge of the problem.

Tyson answered Rakowicz that the test stands approved by Ford were not designed to record instances of skip-out. The testers were not looking for skip-out, so they didn't write down when it happened. Yet they knew that it happened because it halted their testing.

Tyson was no longer with Orscheln, but Durney tracked him down in Nebraska and conducted a deposition. Yes, said Tyson, he had written the memos and was aware of the skip-out problem. The deposition could be used later at trial, even if Durney could not convince Tyson to travel to

Reno for a trial. (Durney knew that he probably would never get Tyson to testify in a trial. Since working with the Ford brakes Tyson had acquired a new item on his resume that would diminish his value as a witness—a criminal conviction. If it came to that, Ford indicated it would seek to introduce Tyson's criminal record at trial. Tyson told Durney that he had pleaded guilty to molesting his own daughter but that he was innocent and had entered the plea to spare his family the ordeal of a trial.)

Durney had some spare time while in Moberly. One afternoon he drove to a private golf club, where he not only was granted playing privileges for the day but also was lent clubs by the club pro. Durney was paired with four other players.

"What's your handicap?" one of them asked.

Durney was a pretty good golfer, with an 11 handicap. The others in his fivesome all claimed single-digit handicaps. And this was their course, their home turf. They gave Durney four strokes as a handicap and he agreed to a friendly wager. As the game progressed, Durney could see that the other guys weren't quite as good as they had boasted. Their past scores were low because they "bumped" the ball, moving it before each shot to avoid impediments, ruts, or uneven ground. If a ball was behind a tree or rock, according to their rules, the player could move it into the clear. It made the game easier and the scores lower. This wasn't how Durney played back in Nevada but it was how he played now.

Along the way the men got to talking. At the fourth hole Durney discovered that Don Orscheln was a member of the same club. At hole five he found out that his playing partners knew Don Orscheln. At holes six and seven he learned that Don Orscheln owned a large chunk of Moberly. At the ninth hole, one member of the fivesome confided in Durney. "Don Orscheln's an asshole," he said.

That was when Durney told them why he was in Moberly. He told them about the White case and how he planned to take Don Orscheln (and Ford) down a notch or two. At least one of his fellow players, Durney knew, would report back to Don. That was okay. Durney wanted Don Orscheln to know he was coming for him.

Durney shot an 80, eight over par, the lowest score among the five golfers. "I used their course. I used their clubs. I won their money," he would laugh later on. "And I was sure they went back to Don Orscheln and told him I was a hustler."

Durney inserted the latest information, the memos about the tests stands, into his puzzle. It showed that Ford and Orscheln knew about the brake problem and failed to warn the public or to fix it, at least in time to save the life of Walter White. The puzzle seemed complete. Most of the pieces had come from Specter but Durney added a few that would be very helpful. First Specter and then Durney summarized these complicated documents and listed them, along with their own analysis, in chronological order, from No. 1 to No. 165. They showed the breadth of the evidence in simple form and together completed a vivid mosaic of what Ford and Orscheln had done and how wrong it was.

No. 1—1984—Two Ford engineers announce the "industry's first self-adjusting parking brake system." The system lowers assembly and warranty costs.

No. 9—September 15, 1989—An Orscheln Design Potential Failure Mode and Effects Analysis recognizes "tip-on-tip tooth contact to adjuster pawl." The potential effect is described as "brake failure with resultant possible vehicle rollaway."

No. 18—March 4, 1990—Letter from Orscheln executive to Ford notes: 'The subject pawl skip-out issue has caused a great deal of concern within Orscheln Company."

No. 40—July 2, 1991—Memo from an Orscheln executive states: "If skip-out is occurring, it certainly will eventually happen with a Ford executive and/or the general public." [A later report notes several skip-outs at Ford's Arizona Proving Grounds, but a handwritten note says it's "not a showstopper."]

No. 52—November 18, 1992—Ford begins receiving notices about vehicle rollaways. One report cites parking brake "self-releasing."

No. 63—December 19, 1992—Memo details a visit by Ford engineer Tim Rakowicz and Orscheln engineers to a dealership in Canfield, Ohio, where there were reports of failed parking brakes, including one in which a truck rolled away and hit a car.

No. 72—A February 1993 Orscheln report states: 'There is no doubt in anyone's mind that the magnitude of this issue may be significant. It may very well result in a recall."

No. 88—February 22, 1993—After witnessing tests at Orscheln duplicate spontaneous parking brake release, Rakowicz issues a critical document—the first draft of his white paper titled "F-Series Parking Brake Control Self-Releasing Field Campaign and Owner

Notification Paper." The title alone concedes the brakes are self-releasing and implies owners should be notified.

No. 104—March 19, 1993—Meeting minutes cite rollaways in the Pittsburgh area, including one in which a driver was pinned against his garage and suffered serious injuries. It notes that the truck rolled away even though its parking brake remained in the applied position.

No. 136—August 7, 1993—Ford memo notes that the parking brake failed on a Ford field engineer's truck. "It dumped his boat and truck in a lake."

(September 12, 1993—Eleven-month-old Derick Bobb, of Newville, Pennsylvania, is seriously injured in an incident involving rollaway of an F-150 truck.)

No. 155—August 23, 1994—Draft of a Ford recall paper now mentions problems with 150 vehicles, 70 involving customer reports of "unexpected movement." Some complain of "spontaneous and unexpected release" of parking brakes.

(October 9, 1994—Three-year-old Walter White of Elko, Nevada, is killed in a rollaway accident.)

CHAPTER 6

A Tiger Tamer

DESPITE THE WEALTH of information and exhibits Durney had turned up in his case against Ford, he found himself outmanned and outmatched early on. It had taken time and money to develop his case. There had been trips to Philadelphia and Moberly, countless hours and costs to depose witnesses. He also needed to hire experts, top-notch experts to go up against the engineers and experts Ford would no doubt throw at him. Experts didn't come cheaply. Ford had an unlimited supply of money. Durney didn't.

Neither did the Whites. Ginny had gone back to work, taking a job as a cashier at Walmart, but she had missed days of work to meet with Durney and give depositions in Reno, a six-hour drive from Elko. Ginny and Jimmie had shelled out money for hotels and meals. They took a second mortgage on their trailer to make ends meet.

Ford had an army of legal talent, some of it in-house lawyers and some hired guns from powerhouse outside law firms. Pete Durney was a tough hombre, a first lieutenant who'd taken a bullet in his shoulder in Vietnam. But he was only one man in a two-man firm. In the months before the trial was scheduled to start, on July 13, 1998, Durney was bombarded with twenty-seven pretrial motions filed by Ford and Orscheln, whose cases had been merged.

Durney knew that the judge assigned to the case, U.S. District Judge David Hagen, would grant no delays. Discovery had been a laborious process, and it had been almost three years since the suit had been filed. Pretrial motions had to be answered fast, and one mistake could lead to a key witness or piece of evidence being excluded from the trial.

With the trial date looming, Durney realized he had a tiger by the tail. He needed help. Ford's many motions were a tactic, Durney knew, designed to delay, intimidate, and overwhelm him—and perhaps force him into a too-little and too-early settlement. Durney wasn't intimidated but he was overwhelmed.

He did get some help for free, thanks to a strategic error by Ford. The car company had filed a cross-claim against the Whites, another bullying tactic—what could it hope to win from the couple who lived in a trailer in remote Elko, Nevada? It could scare them, but the Whites didn't scare easily. Jimmie was too red-hot mad at the company he felt had murdered his son.

What the cross-claim did do, however, was involve another attorney, one appointed by Jimmie's employer's auto insurance carrier, which could be forced to pay off if the Whites lost the cross-claim. Now an insurance company was footing the bill for a second lawyer and the carrier, on Pete Durney's advice, picked a sharp-minded, fast-talking attorney named Don Nomura to represent the Whites. Nomura's firm was larger than Durney's and, although his role was limited, Nomura and his firm's resources would help. As things turned out, Nomura would eventually prove an especially painful foe for Ford.

Even so, Durney still needed help to deal with the onslaught of motions and maneuvers the giant company would throw at his two-man firm. He needed someone whose firm had some muscle and who could get up to speed very quickly on such a complex case. There were piles of documents to read, tons of facts to memorize. Durney didn't need a national search to come up with a name. Shanin Specter already knew the case inside out. In suing Ford for the Bobbs he'd actually developed the bulk of the Whites' case.

Durney called Specter and asked him to sign on. Specter would have to fly out West and be away from home and his practice for several weeks. He checked with his partner, Tom Kline, though he knew it wasn't necessary. Kline would welcome another fight against Ford.

"Go!" said Kline, knowing that his partner still had a bad taste in his mouth from the Bobb settlement. It had been a good settlement, but still . . .

"You sure?"

"We'll get by. Go get a verdict against them this time."

Kline & Specter, which at the time included nine lawyers and a sizable support staff, would help answer all those Ford motions. Specter would also help foot the hefty bill to hire experts.

By this time in his career Specter had won a fair number of cases. He and Kline, who had occupied the office next to Specter's at The Beasley Firm for more than a decade, had left to start their own firm three years earlier. They had already built quite a reputation despite the admonition from their former boss, James Beasley, that they would never do as well out on their own.

Specter would himself gain a Beasley-like status as a take-no-prisoners practitioner. And he would take on a persona much like that of the feared yet respected Beasley. Specter was all about business when he stepped off the elevator at the firm's offices, which in future years would grow to occupy nine floors of the building, with some thirty attorneys, a half dozen of whom were also doctors. On non-trial days lawyers and assistants moved in and out of Specter's office like ships through a busy seaport. He made quick decisions on even the weightiest of matters. Specter was sometimes curt but always civil, even to opponents in a courtroom. He was rarely ruffled. His shoes were shined, his tie knotted and tight to his throat, even at the end of the workday. In the office he prohibited the wearing of jeans. He didn't own a pair himself.

Specter wasn't big on small talk. He didn't care about the weather (unless it threatened to rain out his beloved Phillies). Once, asked in a questionnaire to describe his personality, Specter jotted in the large blank space afforded him only one word: "Direct." And he expected the same efficient use of words from his employees, some of whom trembled in his presence. One time, during a meeting Specter headed, a woman staffer grew so nervous that when it came her turn to speak she found herself unable to utter a single syllable. She managed a motion excusing herself and hurried out of the conference room.

Specter expected people, especially those who worked for him, to listen when he spoke, without interruption, even when he paused to think for a moment. On more than one occasion he had been heard urging an associate not to finish his sentences for him. But he also listened when others spoke and he solicited opinions, often, and from many people—fellow attorneys, assistants, clerks. During trials he'd ask his co-counsels, some of them young and far less experienced, what they thought about every facet of the proceedings, even his opening and closing speeches. Sometimes he accepted their suggestions; sometimes he did not. He also asked clients for their opinions, including them in strategy sessions following a day in court. And as resolute and as decisive as he was, Specter also was not above changing his mind. He was smart enough to know that he didn't know everything and to admit without hesitation or compunction when someone else was right—and he was wrong—and alter course.

Specter's meticulous and demanding nature made him both tough and gratifying to work for. Attorneys assigned to work on a trial with him, like soldiers assigned to General Patton, had to be well prepared, ready to snap to attention or to provide an intelligent and studied answer at a moment's notice. If Specter wasn't always gentle in stating his demands, well, too bad.

And if Specter was brusque it was because he hated wasting what he considered life's most precious commodity: time. He cherished every hour of every day. His own personal and family time was important to him. Like his famous father, U.S. Senator Arlen Specter, he played squash whenever possible, several days a week at a minimum. He had his secretary schedule court times and opponents, even when he was on trial out of town. In later years Specter would win a gold medal as part of the 45-and-over U.S. squash team at Israel's Maccabi Games. It was on the squash courts at the University of Pennsylvania that he had met Tracey Pearl, herself a varsity squash player. One day, Specter asked her to play, then asked her to have dinner with him. Then he asked her to marry him.

By the time the case of Walter White went to trial, Specter had three children. Silvi was now four and a half years old, six months older than Walter White, who died thirteen days shy of his fourth birthday. Perri was two and a half, and Lilli was not quite a year old. Specter could imagine how the Whites felt at losing their only child. Besides his skills as an attorney, Jimmie and Ginny White would also have Specter's empathy.

DURNEY HAD NEVER seen Specter in a courtroom but he had been struck by the younger lawyer's ability to store and compartmentalize facts. He had read the Bobb depositions in which Specter relentlessly and mercilessly grilled witnesses. He knew Specter had attended the University of Pennsylvania Law School and had studied law for a year at Cambridge University, where he had debated and won. Durney felt that Specter had a "presence" that would impress a jury. So he told Specter he wanted him to sit "first chair," to lead the case. To open. To question witnesses. To close. *White v. Ford* would essentially become Specter's baby.

"You want to come out and try this case?" he asked Specter.

Specter hesitated for a second, surprised by Durney's selflessness. Lawyers rarely gave up such a starring role. But Durney wanted the best for his clients, he said, and he felt Specter would deliver it.

"Sure," Specter said, "I'd love to come to Nevada."

"Well," said Durney, now feeling more upbeat about his case than ever, "the first thing you're going to have to do if you're going to come out here is to learn how to pronounce it properly."

"What?"

"It's not Nev-ah-da," said Durney. The proper pronunciation, he lectured, was with the second syllable enunciated with an "a," as in "cat." "It's Nev-a-da."

For his part, Specter wanted something from Durney. "Let's not tell these other lawyers right off who's going to try the case," he said. Durney complied. But when Ford learned Durney had hired Specter, they assigned their lead role to someone who had dealt with Specter before. Joe Pinto would be heading to Reno too. What Ford might not have known was the conversation Specter had had with Pinto before settling the Bobb case, the conversation in which Pinto had conceded that the facts of the case didn't stack up well for Ford.

There was a second, more personal, reason Specter hesitated before agreeing to make the trip to Reno for what was expected to be a three-week trial. He had another commitment scheduled for right before the trial, a commitment on which rested, as Specter put it, "domestic tranquility." Specter and his wife, Tracey, had planned—paid the airfare, booked the hotel rooms, made arrangements for the kids to be cared for—a nine-day trip to Holland and Belgium. Their last day abroad was scheduled to be Sunday, July 12. The trial was set to start at 9:00 a.m. on Monday, July 13.

There was no way Specter was going to miss doing the trial. There was no way Specter was going to tell his wife they weren't going to Europe. One thing helped him do both. The rotation of the Earth. Like something out of a Superman episode—the one where he flies so quickly around Earth he goes back in time—Specter was able to keep his date in Reno by traveling westward over nine time zones. He and his wife departed Antwerp at daybreak, then drove to Amsterdam, where they caught a Sunday noon flight that arrived in Philadelphia at 3:00 p.m. Specter rushed home, packed his bags anew, took a shower, and then rushed back to Philadelphia International Airport just in time to catch a flight to Minneapolis, then a connecting flight to Reno. The whole trip, Amsterdam to Reno, had taken 20 hours, actually, 24 hours, counting driving time to and from the airports.

Specter had been true to his word while in Europe, not working on the case during the vacation. Instead, he had his secretary send the key documents he needed to review the case via Federal Express to his last stop, Antwerp. The packet of papers was nearly two feet thick. As soon as he and Tracey had taken their seats on the plane crossing the Atlantic, Specter tore open the parcel. "As far as I'm concerned," he told his wife, "the vacation is over." While other passengers slept, Specter spread his papers over a table tray in the business class compartment. Over the next eight hours he focused, unwavering, on the essential facts of *White v. Ford*. Moments before his flight touched down in Philadelphia, he was done.

When Specter arrived in downtown Reno at 11:00 p.m. Pacific Time, the air was warm, even for July. Reno, a town of 180,000 that billed itself as "The Biggest Little City in the World," was more than 400 miles north of its younger and far more glamorous sister city of Las Vegas. Reno struck Specter as an odd place and oddly familiar. It looked like some of Pennsylvania's smaller cities, like Harrisburg, except with casinos instead of a state capitol building. And while the streets of Harrisburg bustled during the day and were empty at night, Reno was exactly the opposite. The Western city glistened at night with its makeup on, the bright casino lights forming a dazzling smile from a distance. In the daytime, its plain face appeared haggard and hungover. Its sidewalks were nearly vacant.

Few people flew to Reno to party. It wasn't Vegas. It drew a few conventions, but most of its visitors came by car, many from across the nearest border, with California. Plenty of locals also hung out, nursing beers in the sports betting parlors or playing the nickel slots. The casino at Harrah's, where Specter would reside for the next three weeks, was populated during the day by old ladies and out-of-work men who had long hair and wore baseball caps. "Glamour" was not Reno's middle name.

More than a few people ogled Specter as he walked through the casino to the elevator that took him to his sparse accommodations, a corner room with a king-size bed, a desk, a folding table he had ordered, and little else. The looks he got weren't his imagination or ego. People actually turned and looked, and for a reason. Specter was an oddity at Harrah's. He was a man dressed in a suit and tie.

Moments before the trial commenced the next day, Durney found it hard to suppress a twinge of excitement. And relief. Not only because the show was finally about to begin after years of work, but also because he knew at that moment, as Specter entered the courtroom, that he had done the right thing in handing the Philadelphia lawyer the reins to his case. He knew Specter had just made a long trip and hadn't slept much. But he appeared bright-eyed and confident. If he was tired, he didn't show it. If he felt awkward in this new setting, in a courtroom that was foreign turf for him, he didn't show that either. He seemed in command.

"Good morning, Your Honor," he said to Judge Hagen just after 9:00 on that Monday morning. "Shanin Specter for the plaintiffs."

CHAPTER 7

"Ford Tough"

COURTROOM NO. 6 WAS a quiet, modern space on the eighth floor of Reno's federal courthouse. Rich-looking teak covered the walls, the spectator benches, the railings, the jury box, the judge's dais. The chairs were a comfortable black leather, the carpeting a deep blue with gold dots. Light was supplied economically by five large Tiffany half-globes suspended in a row from the 25-foot ceiling. The room's dark feel made it seem cooler than it really was.

It also seemed solemn, quite unlike the judge who occupied it. Judge Hagen was a sprightly older man who walked with a bounce and had led an intrepid youth and middle age, having raced sailboats along courses that took him as far as Australia. Hagen was anything but stern-faced or stuffy. He smiled easily. (And the wood in his courtroom was veneer, not solid, he made sure to tell visitors lest they think that taxpayer money had been spent too lavishly. The judge even kept a sawed-off sample on his desk as proof.) Hagen was known as fair and smart, not pompous or stuck in his ways, and not afraid to correct himself if need be.

The lawyers and the judge were able to dispense with last-minute motions on the first day since many of the major disputes had been settled weeks earlier. Hagen had denied Ford's motions to exclude the testimony of the plaintiffs' expert witnesses. Ford had claimed, relying on a 1993 Supreme Court decision, that the experts' testimony was not within the realm of accepted science. But Hagen disagreed. The experts were in.

He also allowed evidence from the Bobb case, evidence from all prior incidents of skip-outs or rollaways, and evidence of parking brake malfunction on Ford trucks other than the F-Series and the Bronco. Ford had sought to bar it all. Hagen also ruled as admissible the deposition testimony of Tim Rakowicz if Ford would not agree to voluntarily produce him as a witness at trial. Specter preferred to have the Ford engineer and author of the now-infamous "white paper" appear live before the jury. But under federal rules, the witness, in Michigan, could not be compelled to appear because he was more than 100 miles away. Yet a decision to keep Rakowicz from appearing at trial presented pitfalls for Ford, particularly the plaintiffs' ability to pick and choose what they wanted to present to the jury from his prior deposition testimony—and without Rakowicz getting the chance to explain or expand on his original answers. Faced with this prospect—and the inevitable critical comments by Specter about Rakowicz being a no-show—Ford decided to put him on a plane to Reno.

One significant ruling by Hagen went Ford's way. While deciding that NHTSA documents regarding Ford trucks could be used as evidence, the judge ruled that the plaintiffs could not use the company's recall notice for 884,400 trucks as evidence against Ford. Under the federal rules of evidence, a company's "subsequent remedial measure" could not be used as evidence against it. The logic was simple—it wasn't right to punish a company for eventually doing the right thing. To do so would be to discourage recalls of unsafe products. So any mention of Ford's recall was out.

Specter mentioned Ford's recall early in his opening statement to the jury.

> And in '94 the federal government concluded, "Oh, yeah, there's spontaneous disengagements. You ought to get cracking, Ford." And you will learn that they let it be known that they were going to make these vehicles be recalled. So along about July or August of '94 Ford decided, you will learn, to recall the vehicles. There was only one problem with that. They didn't do it.

"Objection!" hollered Orscheln's lawyer, Max Steinheimer. Joe Pinto jumped to his feet and requested to see the judge at sidebar.

"There was an exclusionary order with regard to the recall. It was not to be mentioned or any aspect of it . . . I don't think it can be cured and I'd move for a mistrial," said Steinheimer.

Pinto also demanded a mistrial. "This is in direct contrast of your order," he told Hagen.

On the contrary, insisted Specter, calmly and politely asserting that he had not violated the judge's order. He had not mentioned Ford's "subsequent remedial measure"—key word "subsequent"—as prohibited by Hagen. He hadn't mentioned the actual recall notice, but instead the government's (NHTSA's) August 1994 threat and Ford's *decision*—not the notice—to recall the trucks. That was several months *before* the October 9 accident that killed Walter White. It was not "subsequent" to the incident. In fact, Specter added, Ford did not begin issuing recall notices until November, and Jimmie White didn't get his until the following March.

Pinto argued that Specter was playing word games. "But the [government] letter telling Ford they were going to have to recall is the same thing as the recall," he said, turning to Specter with a scowl. "You were supposed to avoid the mention of the recall."

Hagen denied a mistrial but warned Specter not to make any further mentions of the recall.

Specter didn't want to press his luck, didn't want to irritate the judge—whom he hadn't met until a day earlier, which was unusual for such a major case—but he felt the issue was important enough to continue the argument a bit further. He also thought he could convince Hagen. The judge's rulings on other motions seemed so on the mark to him that he felt Hagen simply must have gotten this one wrong or that he had it right but hadn't expressed his opinion well. Either way, he felt Hagen's mind was open enough that he could change it. He would give it a try.

Specter insisted one more time that he was not mentioning Ford's actual recall but the company's discussion of it *before* Walter White's accident, including Rakowicz's white paper recommending a recall. "Are you saying that his recommendation of recall is not part of the case?" he asked the judge.

Hagen hesitated a second. This was a crucial decision, a defining moment in the matter.

"Well, no," Hagen said. Then he added, "If Ford's own persons are internally recommending recall, that's a different thing. . . . What Ford did internally, this is an admission on the part of Ford. . . . If my order is capable of being interpreted [as] taking away from the plaintiff an admission by the defendant, then right now I revise the order in that respect."

Hagen reversed his earlier decision and ruled that Specter could continue to refer to Ford's letter about a recall, though he could not use the actual recall notice as evidence unless Ford invoked it first, which, Specter knew, Ford would now do. Not to introduce the recall notice at this stage—with the fact now out that Ford had discussed and considered a recall—could lead the jury to believe that Ford never followed up with an actual recall, that it never tried to remedy the problem. Ford couldn't afford to do that and would in fact mention the recall later in the trial. Suddenly the recall was back in as evidence.

Specter continued his opening statement. He showed the jury diagrams of how the brakes worked and why they had failed, though he vowed to keep the technical details to a minimum. In truth, Specter never fully understood himself how the contraption worked, except that the teeth of the ratchet and pawl (which looked like parts of two gears) sometimes didn't lock up right and slipped, releasing the brake. He figured that anything he couldn't understand after 10 minutes was something he'd never be able to explain to the jury.

He gave a brief description of the brake system, starting with the Ford Aerostar, and explained how problems began to develop soon after the self-adjusting brake was installed in Ford vehicles. He talked about later vehicle rollaways, how Ford's project engineer, Tim Rakowicz—"He is going to be here tomorrow morning to talk to you"—had documented reports of such incidents, which included vehicles used by three of Ford's own executives. "And he [Rakowicz] felt sufficiently strongly about it that he made a recommendation to Ford that they do what? That they recall all of these vehicles that had these brakes in there."

Specter told the jury that Ford had rejected that recommendation. Later, it decided on a short-term fix—the plastic wedge. The wedges were on dealers' shelves in early 1994, long before Walter White's death, but Ford did not issue a notice to owners. It merely made the part available to customers who brought their vehicles to the shop with complaints about the parking brakes. Later that year, in August, two months before Walter White died—and years after NHTSA had begun receiving reports about bad brakes on its consumer hotline—the federal government finally asked Ford to recall the vehicles. Ford promised to do so in a timely fashion, but did not. The recall did not begin until November and did not reach Nevada until March 1995.

Specter also told the jury about the Whites, who, while Ford debated the problem and delayed a recall, were raising a toddler, the only child from their marriage, never suspecting that something was wrong with Jimmie's F-350. Not until their "rendezvous with tragedy." But don't decide the case for the Whites because you feel sorry for them, Specter told the jury.

> I'm sure you feel sympathy for the Whites. We all do. The Whites are not here for your sympathy. They don't want your decision to be affected by considerations like sympathy. That would be improper. The court has already told you that. The court will tell you that again in his charge to you.
>
> The Whites are here for responsibility.
> The Whites are here for accountability.

They're here for you to make an accounting and a fixing of responsibility for what happened.

Pinto, near the outset of a brief opening speech sought to displace some of the blame. "A company like Ford, and it's similar to General Motors and Chrysler, for a fact don't make most of the components in their vehicles, but they outsource the components and have them manufactured by other companies and then basically these large companies are assemblers of their vehicles."

Pinto acknowledged that the brakes did indeed develop a problem, but he asserted that it was not one that affected safety. The problem, as he described it, was one of skip-through on apply—the parking brake pedal pushed through to the floor when being applied, thus not engaging the brake. This was not a danger, he explained, because a driver would instantly know that the brake had not engaged. "And all that had to be done to correct that problem was to reset the parking brake." Simple, if it didn't work the first time, just push it down again until it did.

There was no "spontaneous disengagement" of the brakes after they were set, he said. At least not any that Ford could replicate.

What about Rakowicz's concerns about rollaways? "In the beginning," said Pinto, "Timothy Rakowicz believed that these rollaways must be a problem. He investigated them and, after all of the efforts, the conclusion was that there was not a problem with spontaneous disengagement."

He told the jury that young Walter had been playing "out there in the front yard by himself, unsupervised." And he said, "There are questions, serious questions, about . . . whether or not the parking brake was properly engaged by Mr. White."

Steinheimer, Orscheln's lawyer, talked far longer in his opening statement than Specter and Pinto combined, taking the jury on a rambling, technical journey in which he fumbled with diagrams and brake parts and the court's visual projector. He introduced a laundry list of dizzying technical terms:

> The two cables then come forward connecting to an equalizer, which is the other green piece, and then a single cable runs to a forward mounting bracket, which is up here at the front, near underneath the parking brake assembly. And from the forward mounting bracket another cable runs to the parking brake lever or assembly and enters the bottom of the assembly. Now, the auto-adjust feature, the self-adjust feature, can compensate for conduit elements.

Conduit elements are those portions of the cable that have a heavy outside protection and that bend around the frame member.

So the force is perpendicular to the contact. It's perpendicular to the face of the load-bearing surface. Now the next thing one needs to look at is where the pivot point is. And the pivot point is the center of the whole pawl. And what happens, the perpendicular force generates torque. In other words, torque is the circular force.

Steinheimer went on like that for a while until finally he must have realized he was losing his audience. "So I've mentioned briefly," he began to say at one point, then realized the folly of such a statement, "maybe not as briefly as I intended. . . ." He conceded later, "Now, I think I've probably bored you enough with brake stuff." At one point, the judge interrupted Orscheln's lawyer and called for a 20-minute break, when he told Steinheimer, "You appear to be getting your second wind."

Specter couldn't follow Steinheimer's speech and he figured the jury couldn't either.

Like Pinto, Steinheimer denied there was such a thing as spontaneous disengagement of the parking brakes. He acknowledged a problem with applying the parking brake but called that simply "an annoyance . . . and inconvenience." There had been no proven instances of spontaneous disengagement, he said. He also acknowledged that there had been cases in which trucks rolled away on their owners, but said, "There are many causes for rollaway in vehicles. For example, driver error. People on occasion believe they applied a parking brake when they didn't. That's one example." Another, he said, was when someone overloaded a truck with too much weight for the brake to bear. Another was worn brakes or "broken parts." Rollaways were a part of life. "Vehicle manufacturers have always received reports of vehicles rolling away. It's something that comes with the automobile," he said, trying to make light of a serious situation. "If it's a wheeled object, it could roll away. You put a lawn mower on a steep hill, it's going to roll away."

Like Pinto, Steinheimer pointed a finger at his co-defendant, noting Ford's role in developing the brake system. "Orscheln," he told the jury, "developed this parking brake assembly to the engineering specifications and requirements that were put together by Ford with input from Orscheln."

Normally that would have ended the opening speeches, with the defendants going last, both after Specter. Two against one. But the countersuit against the Whites meant that Don Nomura got the final word before the witnesses took the stand. Nomura got to remind the jury of what Specter had said, to tell them the case wasn't just about pawls and ratchets and torque.

> The fact of the matter is that on October 9, 1994, late Sunday afternoon, a little boy's life was lost because of a Ford and Orscheln part that failed in the brake, resulting in his death.

He told the jury that Ford claimed there was no defect in the brake system, "but then they took the relatively extraordinary step of suing Mr. and Mrs. White." Nomura railed against Ford not so much for a faulty brake but for not warning the public sooner about the possible danger. As he would toward the end of the case, Nomura left the jury with a powerful image to illustrate the actions of his clients and those of Ford. "If there's a vicious dog in the neighborhood next door . . . you have a greater concern of having your child outside if you know about that versus not knowing about it."

> Who had knowledge of the risk to the people who use these vehicles?
>
> Who had knowledge of prior incidents and discussed them and identified them in their studies?
>
> Who kept the knowledge to themselves, did not share it with the public, did not share it with the Whites?
>
> Who failed to warn the public of this knowledge?
>
> That's where this case runs.
>
> That's where this case gets decided.

CHAPTER 8

The Engineer

Specter simplified the case. He had only a few major witnesses, and only a few to appear in person. He planned to read portions of the testimony of Tammy Bobb, whose young son had also been run over by a rollaway Ford truck. There would be testimony, live and through depositions, from Ford and Orscheln employees to back up his long list of evidence and exhibits. There would be testimony from several experts and members of the White family. Specter felt his case would be concise yet compelling.

One strategy Specter employed was to call a defendant's witness as his own. He wouldn't wait to cross-examine a company's employee after the employee had taken the stand for the defense and told its version of things. He would call the employee first. Specter also liked to use a defense witness to help introduce key evidence and exhibits into the record. *Is it true that this document says such and such?* It was like forcing the enemy to help load the plaintiffs' pistol. In the White case, he would enlist Tim Rakowicz, whose testimony would consume most of two days, or half of the plaintiffs' entire case.

Rakowicz was the key to Specter's case. He was the young Ford project engineer who had dealt more closely than anyone with the parking brake problem, having been put in charge of investigating the dilemma of rollaways more than six years earlier, back in 1992. He had gone to Atlanta and Ohio to inspect vehicles. He had been present for tests. He had been Ford's chief liaison with Orscheln in trying to pinpoint the problem and then fix it. No one knew more about the parking brake in the Ford F-Series trucks than Tim Rakowicz. If Specter could use Rakowicz to support his case, he would be far down the road to getting a verdict against Ford.

Specter began his questioning of Rakowicz, now thirty-two years old, by using something else of Ford's as if it were his own. This tactic was the equivalent of thievery, though legal thievery. Ford had advised the plaintiffs' team that it had a model of the parking brake it intended to use to prove its case. Specter immediately asked to see it. Ford produced the model and Specter was wowed by it. The model stood about five feet tall and was made of multicolored translucent plastic so that jurors would be able to see the inner workings of the brake system. It was quite an apparatus, made to scale yet much larger and prettier than the real thing. Pete Durney was taken aback for a second when he first saw the huge mechanical device. It must have cost $30,000 or $40,000 to make, he figured. Ford really did spare no expense in defending itself against lawsuits.

Specter asked Ford to produce the model for trial so the plaintiffs could use it for their case as well. Ford said no. So the matter went before Judge Hagen, who ruled that the automaker had to produce the model as an exhibit for the plaintiffs.

"Your Honor," interrupted W. Chris Wicker, one of Ford's three attorneys at the trial. "I think you meant to say 'defendant.'"

"No, I meant to say 'plaintiffs.' I thought it should have a plaintiffs' exhibit number because it's a plaintiffs' exhibit."

"I think," chimed in Pinto, "just before this that we agreed that it was a defense exhibit."

Specter didn't care either way. He just wanted to use the model. "Judge, I didn't pay for it. I don't want to get a bill," he said, making light of it all.

"All right then, it's a defense exhibit," Hagen surrendered.

But by being allowed to use it first, having Rakowicz employ the model to identify various parts and positions, Specter had essentially staked claim to it. At Ford's considerable expense. If the judge thought it to be a plaintiffs' exhibit, so would the jury. And if Ford had planned to use the model to impress the jury, that opportunity had been lost, though Specter did inform the panel that the expensive contraption belonged to Ford. Later in the trial, when Ford put on its defense, there was no longer a need to use the model, and Ford didn't. Specter had an explanation for that, though it was hardly hifalutin legal terminology. After he had used the model as his own, he explained, "It had cooties."

SPECTER USED RAKOWICZ, an earnest-looking young man who wore wire-rim glasses and a trim black beard, just as he had used the plastic model. He had the engineer, who gave slow, careful answers, acknowledge that he was "one of the major players in the investigation" of the parking brake problems and also that the brake was originally introduced to, in Specter's words, "save some dough for Ford." Rakowicz described the "tip-on-tip" condition of the brake gears that prevented the pawl and ratchet from meshing properly. He also confirmed memos among corporate engineers and executives, including one between two Orscheln employees that showed that both companies knew early on of the problem with spontaneous disengagement, or brake "skip-out." The memo read: "After my conversation with Seepaul Lyman at Ford on July 1st, '91, I feel we need to establish a plan on what we need to do to prevent adjuster pawl skip-out from occurring. . . . It certainly will eventually happen with a Ford executive and/or the general public." Seepaul Lyman was Rakowicz's predecessor as Ford's project engineer.

Specter had Rakowicz detail his visits to inspect reports of bad brakes in Georgia, Ohio, and Canada. He asked the engineer about a confidential supplement to one report stating that "two things happened that Tim did not want included with Ford's copy of the report," including one incidence of skip-out in an F-150. Such an omission had the smell of a cover-up. Rakowicz said under oath that he didn't remember making any such statement about leaving information out of reports.

"Well," Specter followed up, "that would be a wrong thing to do if it was done, correct?"

"You're asking me to go back six years and go through my thinking. I don't recall."

"If there was a vehicle that had adjuster pawl skip-out in the plant, shouldn't Ford know about that? And shouldn't the documents that go to Ford include that?"

"They should," Rakowicz acknowledged, adding, "The more data we have, the better. That's just general. Everybody can understand that. So we would want to know about everything. But to have me comment on this and recall that, I just don't remember that."

Specter concluded the line of questioning by noting that a copy of the confidential supplement had been found in Orscheln's files, but not in Ford's.

> Q: Do you know that this document does not exist in Ford's files?
> . . . Do you know that we obtained this from Orscheln?
> A: I don't know how you obtained it.

With Rakowicz on the witness stand, Specter entered his barrage of evidence into the record—documents, reports, memos, even voice messages retained by Ford and Orscheln. (He used blow-ups his firm routinely referred to as "BMFs." And they really were big mothers.) Included was the information that brake problems were found in 4 percent of the vehicles spot-tested at one Ford plant. Another report detailed an incident in which a "loud bang" was emitted from a Georgia Power Company truck whose parking brake, which had been set for 10 minutes, suddenly let loose, causing the truck to roll into a transformer.

Rakowicz tried to fight Specter on a number of points. One dealt with memos on the testing of the brake, a test in which engineers from Ford and Orscheln were able to duplicate spontaneous disengagement, or skip-out. Rakowicz had relied on the test back when he was investigating the problem. Now, years later and after he had been promoted to another position at Ford, Rakowicz questioned the validity of the test in which a metal pin was used to start off the pawl and ratchet in a tip-on-tip condition.

> Q: Didn't you say in four documents, Ford and Orscheln documents, that you thought it was a valid test?
> A: I was so driven to find out what was going on that I was hoping to latch on to anything that might help describe it, and so I don't know what I said, but in reviewing the test and in further discussions, we were, we determined as a team collectively, and I think everybody agreed, that we were prohibiting the pedal from operating as it was intended, and we considered it not a valid test.
> Q: Are you denying that you said in four documents that you thought it was a valid test?
> A: I may have initially.

To Specter, this sounded like revisionist history. Rakowicz first said the test duplicated spontaneous disengagement but later, when other Ford employees were involved, he deemed the test not valid. This sounded suspiciously like peer pressure, or boss pressure. Specter pressed the point.

> Q: And then you wrote: "The condition has been duplicated during parking brake hill hold testing on February 19, 1993, at the supplier facility using a part removed from a problem vehicle." Is that what you wrote?
> A: Yes.
> Q: And you were referring to the pin test.
> A: Yes.

> Q: You didn't say in this document that you didn't believe in that test, did you?
>
> A: It does not say that.

Then Specter produced a voice mail message Rakowicz had left for an Orscheln executive in which he said he believed "the way the tests we ran on the hill with the pin representing a tip-on-tip or an actual roll-to-roll condition I think is good and I think it is an accurate way." Rakowicz said he didn't recall the message, but that he did remember that his opinion "wasn't shared by the rest of the team, including our experts." Rakowicz said he later came to agree with those other experts. The proof, he said, was in his depositions in the Bobb and White cases. Specter followed up.

> Q: Well, I recognize that when your employer was sued that you gave the same statement in deposition. I'm asking about stuff before the lawyers got involved. I'm asking about when you were preparing documents at Ford in connection with your engineering duties as a Ford Motor Co. employee. Is there a document that you authored or that refers to you as believing that that tip-on-tip pin testing was invalid?
>
> A: Not to my recollection.

Specter pulled out another memo written in Rakowicz's own handwriting in which he mentioned as a likely cause of the rollaways "disengagement after apply."

> Q: So . . . your view at this time was that one of the most likely causes of this concern was disengagement after apply. . . . Correct?
>
> A: Yes.

Later Specter quoted from another memo in which it was stated, "Light Truck Engineering [at Ford] feels that Orscheln's original design was deficient."

> Q: Is that what it says?
>
> A: Yes.
>
> Q: Were you part of Light Truck Engineering?
>
> A: Yes.
>
> Q: Did you share that belief?

A: The belief was that skip-out shouldn't occur.

Q: As this is phrased, did you share the belief that Orscheln's original design was deficient?

A: Yes.

And later still:

Q: Do you have a recollection that Ford was considering changing suppliers?

A: I have a recollection that we threatened, yes.

The most crucial piece of evidence was the draft of a white paper Rakowicz had written on February 22, 1993. The document had become well known to both sides. It flatly mentioned that the brakes would "self-release" and suggested a recall, though it didn't use that exact word. But the intent was clear, especially to those at Ford and Orscheln who had gotten wind that Rakowicz was writing the document.

"Tim did tell Bill about a white paper he is writing for a recall committee," was the way one memo put it, referring to Orscheln's Bill Tyson. If the executives at Ford saw nothing else of importance in that memo, they noticed that single sentence and those two words—"recall committee." Those words raised red flags at Ford. Later, the sentence was underlined, with a handwritten note in the margin by Ken Gutowski, Rakowicz's boss. The notation read: "Purge all copies with this comment—not true."

What was not true, at least not technically, was that Rakowicz was writing the white paper for a company recall committee. The paper was instead intended for Ford's Critical Product Problem Review Group (CPPRG), which could then discuss a recall. The difference was pretty much one of semantics, a formality. Rakowicz's sentiment seemed crystal clear: He was concerned about the F-Series parking brake, very concerned. In his mind he had been writing a paper for a possible recall.

Q: Do you deny that you told the folks at Orscheln in December of '92 that you were working on a white paper for a recall committee? Do you deny you said that?

A: I may have said it.

Yet Rakowicz now insisted that he had been wrong, that Gutowski had been right in demanding that the mention of a recall committee be purged. "I wrote something that was not true," Rakowicz said, adding later in his testimony, "It's not a recall committee. That is the answer; it is not a recall committee. Ken knew that; I did not."

He also tried to backpedal on his belief, back when Ford and Orscheln were seeking the cause of the rollaways, that spontaneous disengagement was to blame. Specter read to Rakowicz from his own report that "the parking brake control will intermittently self-release after pedal apply." Again, Rakowicz grudgingly acknowledged the truth.

> Q: That's what you said?
> A: That's what's written on the paper, yes.
> Q: And you wrote it?
> A: Yes. At that time, yes.
> Q: And was it true when you wrote it?
> A: No, it's not.
> Q: Wasn't true when you wrote it?
> A: It was at the time. It was an explanation of a theory that we had.
> Q: Does this say this is an explanation of a theory?
> A: It doesn't say that directly, but that's what it was.
> Q: Well, let me help you, Mr. Rakowicz. . . . I'm going to give you the entire document and I want you to tell the jury if anywhere in that document you say this is a theory.

Rakowicz pored over the document. Several minutes passed.

> Q: Are you ready to answer my question?
> A: Yes.
> Q: What's the answer to my question?
> A: It does not say that.

If Gutowski's "purge" note had the stink of a cover-up, a similar odor emanated from a memo written by an Orscheln executive in response to a voice message he had received from Rakowicz. It seemed to say that Ford didn't want to have any mention of disengagements or skip-outs but wanted all references to use the term "skip-through." In such cases, drivers were not in harm's way, the note suggested, because they could immediately tell there was a problem and simply reapply the brake. Such a minor malfunction didn't result in rollaways. The memo indicated that Ford wanted everyone to use the same terminology, sanitized terminology that ignored the safety problems with the parking brake.

Rakowicz's actual white paper, when it was admitted at the trial, was five pages in black and white that in a criminal case might have been termed a confession. Rakowicz hadn't minced words, not even in the title: "F-Series Parking Brake Control Self-Releasing Field Campaign and Owner Notification Paper."

His report began by stating a problem that Pinto and Steinheimer had contended in their opening speeches did not exist: "*On certain 1992/93 model year (MY) F-Series vehicles, the parking brake control will intermittently self-release after pedal apply.*" This was not skip-through on apply. It was self-release *after* pedal apply, after a driver thought the truck was safely parked.

The white paper went on to describe the "root cause" of the self-release problem as a "tip-on-tip condition" that occurred when the teeth of the gearlike ratchet and pawl did not interlock, but instead came to rest "tip on tip." When this happened, a driver could believe the vehicle's parking brake was engaged. Then when the driver climbed out of the truck, any jarring or movement—the slamming of a door, someone unloading materials from the truck bed—could be enough to make the metal gears slip apart and disengage the brake. As Rakowicz put it in his white paper:

> If a parking brake lever assembly with this condition were to exist on a customer's vehicle, they would experience the following effects:
>
> a. The parking brake pedal apply will feel normal.
>
> b. The customer will leave the vehicle and in an arbitrary amount of time, the parking brake control will self-release. A popping noise will be heard if the customer is within hearing distance. The parking brake pedal will remain in approximately the same position that it was applied to.
>
> c. If the vehicle is on an incline, the vehicle will potentially roll down the incline.

In addition, under a notation "INVESTIGATION AND VERIFICATION," Rakowicz cited reports by Ford, warranty analysis, and visits to three dealers to examine the reported problem. These visits did not dispel the notion of faulty parking brakes; rather they verified the problem. As Rakowicz noted:

> The condition has been duplicated during parking brake hill hold testing on February 19, 1993, at the supplier [Orscheln] facility using a part removed from a problem vehicle.

Ford would later deny that engineers had been able to recreate the self-release "phenomenon," a word Rakowicz used. The company would claim that the self-release had happened under test conditions that were artificially produced, using the metal pin. Though conducted by Ford and Orscheln employees, Ford would insist that the test didn't count.

Rakowicz's paper also cited the number of vehicles affected: all 1992 and 1993 F-Series trucks. Under the heading "Estimated % Units Defective"—yes, he'd used the word "defective"—Rakowicz wrote: "All production."

He had listed several possible immediate solutions, including returning to the old parking brake system used in 1991 and prior years and staying with the new system but eliminating the self-adjusting feature. But he left no doubt that he felt a change was essential. In his notation, "PREVENTATIVE ACTION," he recommended: "Develop design change to completely eliminate the possibility of this condition occurring."

The most damaging part of the report for Ford was what Rakowicz recommended for the current parking brake. The statement was clear and unequivocal: "All service stock of 1992–1993 parking brake controls must be purged."

Whatever language Ford wanted to use was all right with Specter but he knew what "purge" meant. It was tantamount to a recall. To any layman it meant getting rid of the parking brakes on all those 1992 and 1993 trucks, a number that Ford, in another document, put at 884,400. Rakowicz, without using the word, had suggested a recall.

In yet another part of his white paper Rakowicz noted what actions Ford had taken up to that point to fix the problem. The entry read: "None at this time."

There were later drafts of the white paper, drafts presumably written after higher-ups at Ford had seen the original. These later drafts read differently. Very differently. For instance, no longer did "No. 1, PROBLEM DESCRIPTION" simply state that the brake "will intermittently self-release after pedal apply." Now it referred to what Ford wanted to make the focus of attention: "skip-through on apply." The new PROBLEM DESCRIPTION section made it sound as though there wasn't even really a problem:

> During pedal application, the adjustment pawl may not totally engage with the ratchet, and the pawl may skip over one or more teeth on the ratchet. If this occurs, the parking brake system will not achieve full or near-full tension, potentially resulting in park-

ing brake ineffectiveness. (Generally, if the brake release is used and the pedal reapplied, the parking brake will operate as intended.)

But Ford had known more. It was aware of rollaways. It knew about accidents and about people getting hurt, yet the latest white paper minimized the problem. It suggested that if the brake did not totally engage, the driver should simply set it again. No big deal.

RAKOWICZ'S SECOND DAY on the witness stand began with Joe Pinto complaining to the judge about a television show that had aired the night before. The CBS show, *Public Eye with Bryant Gumbel*, had been about problems with gas tanks in some older model Ford Mustangs. Featured was a woman whose two young sons had burned to death in one of the cars, and she was on the air accusing Ford of murder.

Pinto wanted the judge to question the jury to see if any of them had watched the show and whether they would hold this information against Ford in this case.

> PINTO: I didn't see the TV show last night, but I understand from other people who did that there was an exposé about Ford Motor Co.
> HAGEN: It's about time.
> PINTO (to the court reporter): Did you get that? Would the record reflect he said it in jest?
> SPECTER: And all counsel are laughing, including Ford counsel.

When Pinto continued to protest, Specter mentioned that he had been watching TV too.

> SPECTER: Your Honor, I also saw something last night about the Ford Motor Co. on television. I saw a commercial talking about how Ford is committed to a better environment. And it made me wonder about whether Ford had spiked the Reno media market with additional positive advertising in light of the trial.
> HAGEN: Is this the conspiracy theory?
> SPECTER: I'm not a conspiracy theorist, Your Honor, but it seems that there is both good and bad out there with Ford.
> HAGEN: Mr. Pinto, what do you propose?
> PINTO: Well, my initial reaction, of course, was to come in and ask for a mistrial. But after giving it some sobering thought, I think

> at the very least we have to have some type of a modest voir dire
> of the jury to see if anybody on this jury may have been adversely
> affected.
>
> HAGEN: Do you want to suggest questions to me or do you want me
> to wing it?
>
> PINTO: Well, when you say do I want you to "wing it," you scare me
> a little bit.

The judge asked if any of the jurors had watched a TV show "having
to do with automobiles." None of them had. No harm, no foul.

Specter got back to Rakowicz and his February 22, 1993, white paper.

In his testimony now Rakowicz backed off his previously stated concerns over the parking brakes. Specter would try to seal off his retreat.
Having had him testify before in his deposition for the Bobb case, Specter was aware of what Rakowicz might say. He also knew he could
use the deposition if the young engineer tried to stray from his original story.

For instance, Rakowicz was saying now that he did not believe the
brakes self-released, that spontaneous disengagement did not occur.
What had changed over the years?

> Q: You feel it [spontaneous disengagement] does not happen?
> A: I don't think it does, no.
> Q: Would it be fair to say that you don't know?
> A: I think with the testing we've done and the inability to substan-
> tiate and prove it, I would say it does not happen.
> Q: Back in 1994 I asked you at page 64 [of the deposition] about this.
> And I said, "Your answer to the question is: 'I don't know if it
> ever occurred.'" What was your answer?
> A: I said "yes."

Specter wanted to establish two more things before he let Rakowicz
off the witness stand. One was Ford's failure to warn drivers about the
problem with the truck parking brakes. The other was the fact that even
when Ford finally did recall the trucks it did not acknowledge a safety
hazard. Specter pointed to Ford's notice to NHTSA that it would recall
the vehicles in question. He read it aloud:

> This is to inform you that the Ford Motor Co. has decided in
> response to the urging of the Office of Defects Investigation to

recall for modification of the parking brake control assembly those vehicles . . . that are equipped with manual transmissions. Although Ford does not believe that the condition to be rectified by this modification involves an unreasonable risk to motor safety, we will . . . notify owners.

The condition to be addressed involves certain 1992 through 1994 model year Ford F-Series trucks, F-150, 250, 350, Bronco MVPs and certain '93 and '94 model year Ranger trucks and Explorer MVPs with manual transmissions. . . . The condition may occur occasionally when the parking brake control lines up in a tip-on-tip relationship.

If this occurs, the pawl may skip over more teeth than the ratchet during park brake application, which could prevent the system from achieving full tension.

When this occurs the parking brake goes to the floor with little or no effort during application. This could result in parking brake ineffectiveness if the parking brake is not released and reapplied. If the vehicle is not left in gear, the vehicle could roll freely if the parking brake application is not effective.

Ford, even in its recall, was still refusing to own up to the real problem.

SPECTER: And what was really happening here was that Ford was putting the label of this problem as being skip-through for the government and eventually for others, and not putting the label on as being rollaway, spontaneous disengagement. But that was the true condition that was being addressed by this proposed recall. That was what was really going on, right?

RAKOWICZ: I don't agree with that, no.

Q: Ford didn't want to tell people that vehicles were rolling away, correct?

A: The alleged vehicle rollaways that we had, we did not know what was happening with them. So I think it's inappropriate to tell somebody we [did] know what was happening.

Q: Ford never told people that vehicles were rolling away, correct? They never told the general public the vehicles were rolling away, correct, prior to October 9, 1994, prior to this boy being killed?

A: Not to my knowledge. I know that NHTSA was aware of it.

Q: Right. But NHTSA is not the general public, correct?

A: Correct.

Q: Did you, Mr. Rakowicz, in July 1994, consider that people, did you consider whether people should be told about the spontaneous disengagement issue at that time?

A: I don't remember. Again, I know that we were aware of it and we were investigating it.

Q: Taking a look at your deposition from September 22, 1994, at page 151 . . . you were in my office, correct?

A: I was in your law offices, correct.

Q: And this was three weeks before Walter White lost his life, correct? . . . And I said to you, "Do you think that Ford Motor Co. ought to tell consumers . . . that they ought to bring in their vehicles, the vehicles being recalled, because, number one, the parking brake might spontaneously disengage and the vehicle might roll, as well as the reason . . . you said they were going to use when they notified consumers, which is that the pedal might go to the floor during application?" What was your answer?

A: I said, "I don't know."

Q: And I said, "Have you thought about that question?" And what did you say?

A: "Yes."

Q: And I said, "Have you discussed it with your colleagues?" What was your answer?

A: "Yes."

Q: So between July and Septmber 22, 1994, before this boy was killed in October, you talked to your colleagues about telling folks in this proposed recall letter not only about skip-through on apply but [also] about spontaneous disengagement, right?

A: At the time, we were concerned about the alleged vehicle rolls, yes.

Q: Instead of doing what was considered by you and your colleagues, which was to tell people about those spontaneous disengagements and vehicles rolling away and skip-through on apply, what you actually decided to do was to tell them only about skip-through on apply, what Ford decided to do only was to tell them about skip-through on apply and not spontaneous disengagement? . . . The discussion that you had with your colleagues did not result in Ford telling people about rollaways?

A: Right.

In fact Ford knew that the *real* problem, the one with potentially severe safety consequences, was not skip-through on apply at all. It was spontaneous disengagement, which resulted in trucks rolling away. And people getting hurt.

Specter had proof of this. It was right there, right in front of everyone's eyes. The proof was in the company's actions. The proof was that when it finally did recall vehicles to fix the brakes, Ford recalled only those vehicles with manual transmissions. Why only those vehicles? Because the others, those with automatic transmissions, could not roll away even if the parking brakes did suddenly disengage. That was because the automatic transmission would hold the vehicle in place if the brake failed. Unlike trucks with manual transmissions, which drivers could park in neutral, trucks with automatic transmissions had to be put in "park" in order for a driver to remove the key and walk away. The trucks with automatic transmissions had a built-in safety backup. The trucks with manual transmissions did not. A faulty parking brake was a danger in a truck with a manual transmission, but not in a truck with an automatic transmission.

By recalling only trucks with manual transmissions, Ford was virtually admitting that the problem was not skip-through on apply, a mere inconvenience, but a safety hazard—and that 884,400 potentially dangerous trucks were on the road.

Specter's questioning about this put Rakowicz on the defensive. Specter hoped it would be a turning point in the trial. He noticed the defense lawyers sit up in their soft leather chairs when he started down this path. He didn't pull his punches.

> SPECTER: Now, let's talk about what this is really, really about. What this is really about is that there wasn't a recommendation to recall the vehicles that had an automatic transmission because when you put the vehicle in park, if for some reason the brake disengages, the vehicle is still going to hold. Correct?
>
> RAKOWICZ: First of all, I want to make it clear that in my position I don't recommend a recall nor do I make decisions about recalls. I, what I can comment on is that an automatic transmission, you know, there are standards for the ability of the transmission to hold the vehicle. And so if an automatic transmission is in park, it's going to stay where it's going to stay.
>
> Q: Right. But if you don't recall the vehicles that have automatic transmissions people are still going to experience skip-through on apply in automatic transmission vehicles. Right?

A: We already went over that point.

Q: Am I right?

A: If the pedal assembly . . . Sure.

Q: So what Ford was doing here is Ford was putting a phony label on the reason why there was going to be a recall, and that phony label was, "We're doing it because of skip-through." But the truth was, "We're doing it because of spontaneous disengagement." And the reason we know it's a phony label is that this fix wouldn't fix skip-through in vehicles that had automatic transmissions. Right?

  This fix wouldn't fix vehicles that had automatic transmissions because there would still be skip-throughs on those vehicles?

A: We already talked about [how] skip-through could occur on automatic transmissions, so yes. If you had the fix on automatic transmissions, you wouldn't get skip-throughs.

Q: But this wasn't going to fix it for automatic transmissions. This was saying, "We'll leave the vehicles with automatic transmissions out there and, impliedly, people will still experience skip-through"?

A: In an automatic transmission they could still experience skip-through.

Q: But what this fix would do, what it would accomplish is that for people who had manual transmissions, those people, if there was a recall and the wedge were put in, those people couldn't experience either skip-through or spontaneous disengagement if this recall went through?

A: We discussed this before. The wedge would eliminate that.

Q: And you folks at Ford knew that there's all kinds of times that people that have manual transmission vehicles will leave their vehicle in neutral with the parking brake on? You live in Michigan, right?

A: Yes.

Q: You get up in the morning; it's a cold morning. You get up and put the vehicle in neutral and start the vehicle and you've got the brake on. You go back inside and have a cup of coffee while the vehicle heats up, and occasionally you might leave the vehicle in neutral.

A: I don't know. I don't have a manual transmission.

Q: If you did, and the parking brake were to disengage spontaneously . . .

A: Given several assumptions, such as the grade [incline], such as the weight of the vehicle, et cetera, yeah. I mean if it's in neutral, by definition, and the parking brake is either not applied or for some reason comes up, then yeah, it won't hold. Sure.

Q: It's a cold morning in Michigan, but you have an automatic transmission and you go out to start the car up. You leave the vehicle in park. You go back in the house, have a cup of coffee, the brake disengages spontaneously, the vehicle's not going to roll because the vehicle is in park?

A: Yeah, the transmission will hold it. Sure.

That night, Specter met Joe Pinto and another Ford lawyer, Ray LeBon, for dinner. The trio slid into a green leather booth at an Italian restaurant in the Silver Legacy Hotel, where the Ford team was staying for the duration of the trial. They ordered beer and red wine before the food arrived. It was hardly extraordinary for opposing counsel, even bitter courtroom rivals, to get together quite amicably after hours and share casual, even candid conversation. These three lawyers had sat down before to discuss the case and a possible settlement but they had made little headway. Maybe it was time to try again.

Specter felt momentum had swung in his favor. He had noticed LeBon scurry out of the courtroom during his cross-examination of Rakowicz, which in itself was unusual. Lawyers didn't generally walk out during key testimony. It came near day's end, as Specter elicited what he felt was such an important admission from the engineer—that Ford knew only its trucks with manual transmissions were a problem because those with automatic transmissions would hold the vehicle in park if the parking brakes failed. And that the company had reason to believe they might fail.

"I couldn't help but see you walking out of court. Where were you going?" Specter now was examining LeBon.

"To call Ford."

"What did you tell them?"

"I told them I was hanging black crepe in the courtroom."

This was LeBon's way of saying he had told the folks in Dearborn that the case was not going well up to this point. Specter knew that LeBon and Pinto wanted to settle. Even Judge Hagen on the next day of trial would pull the attorneys aside and say, "I never interject myself into the settlement of issues of cases I'm trying, even when they're being tried to a jury, but . . . I'm really surprised that this case is being tried. This strikes me as a case that the parties should be hammering out a settlement on. That will be the end of my remark on that."

Both Pinto and LeBon had acknowledged to Specter that they were bothered by Ford's conduct, the delay in issuing the recall, and the wording of the recall. They felt they could win on the question of whether the brake was defective, that the plaintiffs faced a difficult task proving such a proposition to the jury. Yet they also knew that it was months after Walter White was killed that his despondent father received notice in the mail that something was wrong with the brakes.

Specter knew something else that had little to do with the case and a great deal to do with the business of law. At this point in a lawsuit there was much less incentive, financial incentive, for a defense attorney to keep going. Plaintiffs' lawyers lived for the thrill and payday of a verdict. They only got paid if they won, either a verdict or a settlement, and they got nothing if they lost, even having to swallow expenses, which generally ran into six figures for major cases. On the other hand, defense lawyers were paid by the hour, and most of those hours came in developing the case for trial, for research and depositions and pretrial motions. Once a trial commenced, the meter on billable hours was just about up. Defense lawyers didn't make more money if they won or lost a verdict, though winning was clearly better. A losing verdict could mean losing a client, which was big business in a case like this, with an important corporate client at stake. Such a loss was a gamble, one not worth taking unless the odds were greatly in the defense's favor. Settling the case, while not a courtroom victory, was a safe escape route. It allowed a client to cut its potential losses (not to mention avoid bad publicity) and the defense lawyers to claim at least a partial win.

Pinto and LeBon indicated to Specter that they wanted to settle. LeBon had said that the case wasn't going well for Ford and that he could envision the car company losing a verdict, if it came to one. But was LeBon being unusually candid or was he playing possum? Either way Specter knew that Ford would not surrender easily. While he had scored points with the jury, Ford still had its own defense to put on. The defense team was also aware, as was Specter, that the plaintiffs' case was largely circumstantial. There was no hard proof that the brake had spontaneously disengaged, there were no living eyewitness to the event, and there was no way of knowing positively that Walter White hadn't released the parking brake on his own. Although they hadn't loved Ford's actions in issuing the recall, they felt that they and the company's hired technical experts could convince the jury that the parking brake was not defective, or at least create enough doubt in the jury's mind about whether it was. And no defect, they felt, meant no plaintiffs' verdict.

Plus, Ford's executives were evidently proving a hard sell on a settlement. Specter knew that they had been told by their original attorney in the case that the company could and would win. And there was some evidence that was true.

"We did do two trials using mock juries," LeBon had told Specter months earlier.

"And?"

"We won both times."

Specter knew that such mock trials were useful, much as focus groups were to soft drink makers or cell phone manufacturers. They often produced verdicts that accurately predicted the real outcome. But they also could be wrong, failing to anticipate the strategy and skill of an opponent. Specter smiled at LeBon.

"Who played the role of plaintiffs' counsel in those mock trials?" he asked.

LeBon responded with a dismissive wave. He didn't mention a name.

"Well," Specter continued, his smile broadening, "you didn't call me to do it."

CHAPTER 9

The Experts

Rakowicz's testimony had gone well for the plaintiffs, but it wasn't enough. Specter knew that Ford would present experts to rebut the notion that it had a dangerous product out on the road. So he got his own expert. Not just an expert, an expert's expert. Campbell Laird, a materials scientist and metallurgist, had everything you could dream of in an expert witness. He had the look—white hair and an intelligent face. He had the sound—a confident voice that still held more than a trace of his native Ardrishaig, Scotland, even though he had lived in the States for more than thirty years. He had the resume, a professor of material science and engineering since 1968 at the University of Pennsylvania, the Ivy League university whose law school Specter had attended. Laird's particular expertise was determining "how things break" and how accidents happen.

He had spent eight years earning his undergraduate and doctoral degrees at the University of Cambridge. He had also taught at a few other impressive institutions—the University of Vienna, the Sorbonne University in Paris, and the Governmental Laboratory for Research Materials and Standards in Helsinki. Laird, in his late fifties, had been published nearly 300 times and had won fourteen awards, including Cambridge's Darwin Prize for his doctoral thesis.

Laird had also spent some time in the corporate world, learning firsthand about products and companies like Ford. Well, not *like* Ford, but Ford specifically. Laird had taken a leave of absence from Penn to spend five years at Ford's scientific laboratory in Dearborn, where he did research into the fundamental properties of materials.

Laird was smart and knowledgeable and fast on his feet. He was a likeable chap, and he came across that way.

By the time the *White v. Ford* trial started Laird was an old hand at giving his expert opinion for legal cases. Specter did not hide the fact. He wanted the jury to know that Laird had testified before. And he had

Laird note that he had testified for both plaintiffs and defendants—"very close to 50/50"—and in some cases on behalf of major corporations. He was not a professional plaintiff's expert. He could be objective.

Q: Do you have experience in evaluating the same type of brake that is the subject of this lawsuit previous to this case?

A: Yes, sir. I have been involved in the failure analysis of a brake very similar to the one of interest here.

Q: And who was the owner of that brake?

A: The owner was a person called Bobb.

For this case Laird examined not only the parking brake from Jimmie White's truck but also the documents, reports, and memos circulated among the engineers and managers at Ford and Orscheln.

He subjected the brake to a battery of tests, including visual inspections under a variety of magnifications. He noticed a "bit of damage" and smoothening of the metal where the pawl and ratchet had come together tip-on-tip. At 1,000× magnification, he had detected a slight crack in the metal and a "granular structure" where bits of metal had broken off. Another tooth had a chip in it. "So that again is supportive evidence of repeated tip-on-tip impacts between the pawl and its partner ratchet teeth," he testified.

Laird noted one tooth that was very badly damaged, enough so the damage could be seen with the naked eye, and several others that had suffered significant damage. One showed wear that produced a "curvy effect." Any of these weaknesses could result in the teeth getting stuck in a tip-on-tip position, the precursor to a spontaneous disengagement.

At one point in his testimony Laird stepped down from the witness stand to point out damage in a series of electron microscope photographs he had taken. He talked for some time, finishing his explanation of the pictures with a stark conclusion.

All this evidence then indicates that there were multiple episodes, including the very significant episode of tip-on-tip damage and skip-out that occurred on the date of the accident involving Walter White.

Laird concluded as well that the brake system had a design defect. The self-adjusting feature meant that the ratchet would move up along the teeth of the pawl as the brake cable slackened with use. This movement over time to a higher and higher tooth was intended to keep consistent tension in the brake cable. But this same movement, Laird testified, meant that as the ratchet moved up along the teeth, "at some stage inevitably" the teeth of the ratchet would strike the teeth of the pawl. This would create damage. And that damage would promote the tip-on-tip sticking of the two metal parts. When one or more tips then disengaged, it could happen suddenly and forcefully and cause the entire series of teeth to skip-out, releasing the brake.

Laird went on to cite reports and studies showing that Orscheln was well aware of the design defect, including a company failure analysis that noted, as Laird termed it, the "inherent weakness" of a pawl-and-ratchet system. He also cited the development of a dual-pawl system in which two sets of teeth were used in a slightly "offset" fashion so that if one stuck tip-on-tip, the other would be properly engaged and hold the brake. (Ford ended up switching to such a system in later models.) Laird said this would be inexpensive, noting such a design change would cost an estimated 87¢ per brake.

But design changes were not made for many years and only after a number of accidents. The Aerostar was the first to experience problems but, noted Laird, that vehicle had been equipped with an automatic transmission, which essentially provided a backup brake system. Specter told Laird that problems with later vehicles, including the F-Series, were at first largely ignored because skip-out didn't happen very often.

> Q: Now, would a reasonably prudent manufacturer close [out] a skip-out issue due to a low occurrence?
> A: Speaking as an engineer, if a problem involves a safety problem and where the potential for serious consequences is high, rare occurrences are insufficient. There are manufacturers who have, who adopt a different policy; they don't want their reputation to be tarnished by anything. When they encounter a problem, they do something about it and they fix it.

He was not talking about Ford.

Laird spoke about the wedge, the temporary fix Orscheln had devised, how it could be easily installed and that it cost pennies per piece when mass-produced. But Ford delayed a recall and widespread use of the inexpensive plastic part, at least in time to save Walter White. It could have been worse, of course. Some F-350 trucks, like the one that had killed Walter, had also been retrofitted in various parts of the country for use as school buses.

Laird was convinced about his conclusion and he was convincing as well. Toward the end of Laird's direct testimony, Specter asked him for a summation. Specter telegraphed the question for the jury, then lobbed the softball across the plate. Laird crushed it.

Q: Dr. Laird, let me ask the question this way, if I may. Have you formed an opinion based on a reasonable degree of engineering certainty as to how this accident occurred?

A: Yes, sir.

Q: What is that opinion?

A: My opinion is the vehicle was in gear, in first gear, the brake was applied, young Walter got into the cab, somehow released the gear from the first position to neutral. As a result of that the truck was released and rolled down the hill, in which event we know he was thrown out and killed. Subsequent to the accident, the brake was found in a down position.

Orscheln's Steinheimer jumped up to object. It wasn't an agreed-on fact that the brake had been found in the down position. No one knew for sure how it was found right after the accident because the truck had been moved back to the Whites' driveway before the police arrived. Judge Hagen sustained the objection, which turned out to be a good thing for Team Specter. Laird got a do-over.

LAIRD: Should I begin the answer again?

SPECTER: Please.

A: Based on the documentary evidence as provided by depositions, based on my analysis of the brake and the tip-on-tip impact and the history of the user, based on the additional facts of the accident, it's my opinion that the brake was applied and it spontaneously released, that the gear had to be changed from first to neutral with the brake applied in order for that to happen.

Laird explained that Walter, not yet four years old, would not have been strong enough to pull the stick shift out of first gear if the parking brake had not been applied. If the parking brake had been off, the transmission would have been holding the full weight of the truck, among the largest in the F-Series.

Laird's scientific studies also confirmed the likelihood of a tip-on-tip condition leading to spontaneous release of the parking brake. The analysis, proclaimed Laird, "demonstrates that without equivocation and supports the opinion."

Also, Laird said, it would have been difficult for little Walter to have reached the parking brake release because it was located at the far left of the cab. He noted that the police officer who investigated the accident did not find the boy's handprints on the driver's side of the cab, which had been covered with dust. His prints were all over the right, or passenger, side of the cab.

The defense's cross-examination of Laird seemed ill prepared. Pinto, for instance, probably was instantly sorry the moment he asked Laird about secondary causes of the accident, suggesting that perhaps there was a cause other than the brake self-releasing. "I don't know about that," Laird began. While Laird was a metallurgist and not on the witness stand as an expert on accident scenes, Pinto's question gave him an opening to state his opinion about it. Laird sounded like a Scottish Columbo, rambling yet convincing, as if he were on the brink of a discovery about how Walter could have released the parking brake, but then . . .

> No, it couldn't have happened that way. In fact, he couldn't have released that brake!
>
> Let's consider other aspects of the evidence. Let's consider, for example, the dust and the handprints. There are no handprints reported by Sergeant Fosmo on the driver's side. If Walter had released the brake, he couldn't get at it on the floor of the truck because the, if he was approaching from the passenger side because the four-wheel drive lever was in the way and the phone was in the way, and the best way he could have gotten at it, if he knew it was there and had seen it, would be . . . The steering wheel was also in the way.
>
> There's not much more than the thickness of a man's thigh between that and the seat. The best way he could have gotten at it would be to lie along the seat, put one hand on the dashboard, and reach down with the other to pull it. There are no such marks of hand marks. I think that's important evidence.

Laird's information had come from Sergeant Fosmo, whose testimony Durney had taken during a relatively brief deposition. Fosmo did not appear in court but his prior testimony had been read into the record. He was a veteran officer who had taken advanced police training courses in accident reconstruction and who had investigated, by his account, some sixty to seventy accidents.

Fosmo had said two things that Specter especially wanted on the record.

One was that he did not think Walter White could have released the parking brake. "To crawl over and release the emergency brake, then to pull it out of gear, I just did not think that a three-year-old would be able or that he could do that, but it was very unlikely."

The other was that Fosmo had found the truck "very dusty" and that handprints were easily visible in the cab. Yet he had found none on the driver's side. "I took photos of everything that was pertinent to any handprints, and there were none that were visible to me on the driver's side," he had testified.

And there would have been if Walter White had moved to that side to release the parking brake. As Professor Laird put it:

> Because he would have to support himself with one hand on the dashboard in order to reach down and react his pull on the lever, otherwise he would fall onto the floor. So he would have to do that.
>
> PINTO: Would I fall on the floor if I reached down to pull the lever on the release mechanism? I wouldn't, would I?
>
> A: But you're not 35 inches tall.
>
> Q: Of course I'm not. Is that how tall the boy was?
>
> A: Sorry, that was his weight in pounds. I believe he was 42 inches tall.

Steinheimer didn't fare much better with Laird. He tried to get technical with the professor. A mistake. "I probably asked the wrong question," he said to Laird at one point. "I'll withdraw the question."

When the defense lawyer did get in a question, Laird's answers only seemed to showcase his expertise. For example, when asked about "load-carrying range," Laird dazzled the jury and seemed to confuse Steinheimer.

> LAIRD: Well, it depends on the area of the mark because the, in order for that to be satisfied we would require that the load that's applied through the brake divided by the area of the impact has to be equal to or less than the yield stress and shear, which in this material is about 170,000 pounds per square inch.
>
> STEINHEIMER: You've obviously lost me in the math.

When Steinheimer stated that it took a long time to develop alternative designs, offering an excuse for why it took Orscheln and Ford so long to fix the parking brake, Laird had another ready riposte.

Q: And normally that development takes several years?
A: That's under our old, unacceptable ways of doing business, it did. And we've learned from the Japanese that we better get our act together and speed it up.

The defense attorneys kept trying to trip up Laird. They cross-examined him once, then after Specter posed a few more questions, cross-examined him again. Hagen finally began to tire of it. "This better be the last round," he said at one point. The lawyers finally ran out of questions—long before Laird ran out of answers.

TWO IMPORTANT THINGS happened late on this, the fifth day of the trial.

After the lunch break Pinto had to see the judge at sidebar. The defendants wished to drop their cross-claim against Jimmie and Ginny White. Ford no doubt now realized that the suit against the deceased boy's parents had been a mistake. Not only did it make Ford seem cruel and callous, but it also added a lawyer, in the person of Don Nomura, to the plaintiffs' side. However, dropping the suit against the Whites would not be so simple.

PINTO: We would like to dismiss the claim against Mr. and Mrs. White. But I have a problem with how we communicate to the jury and would make a suggestion that we just tell the jury that that claim has been resolved, Mr. Nomura's presence is no longer necessary.
JUDGE HAGEN: I appreciate your desire to get Mr. Nomura out of the courtroom, but I was wondering what he has to say about this request.
NOMURA: Your Honor, I don't think telling them it's resolved is an appropriate resolution. I think that there can be a motion made in the presence of the jury. We will not object to the motion and the court can dismiss the action against them.
HAGEN: Is that acceptable to Ford?
PINTO: I don't see why it's necessary to do it in the presence of the jury.

NOMURA: Joe, it was a claim that was made and identified for these jurors as something to be litigated in this suit and for me to simply wander off and that claim to be disappeared without saying there's some resolution . . . what is that?

Pinto wanted the cross-claim to simply go away. Nomura, though the dismissal would give him a legal victory, had now become invested in the trial. He wanted the jury to know that Ford had conceded the point, that it was Ford's decision to drop the suit against the parents of Walter White. Hagen showed little sympathy for Ford.

"Well, it seems to me that by asserting this claim Ford may have climbed onto the back of a tiger and . . . the only means of dismounting is for the cross-claimant and the party claimed against to come to an agreement as to what I tell the jury," said the judge. If they couldn't agree, Hagen said he was disposed to tell the jury, at a minimum, that Ford had dropped the claim.

"Okay," Pinto agreed after discussing it with Nomura. The judge would say that Ford had dropped the claim. Pinto must have realized this was the best deal he could get. The jury would hear of Ford's surrender on a minor battleground, but at least Pinto would be rid of Nomura. If he stayed on the case to its conclusion, Nomura would be permitted to make a closing speech in addition to Specter's. Nomura could be a real pain in the neck. Pinto wanted him off the case.

Pinto admitted this to Specter when the two men, stuck out in the desert city far from their Philadelphia offices, had dinner together on Friday nights. There was not enough time to go home for the weekend but not enough trial work to keep them busy on Saturdays. Specter would say later in court that he liked Pinto, and he'd mean it.

On this Friday night as the two shared a bottle of red wine at LaStrada, a restaurant in the El Dorado Casino that had a twinkling ceiling and the saturated smell of garlic, Pinto called Nomura a "Japanese Zero." The reference was to the Japanese fighter pilots of World War II. Specter took the remark not as a racial slur but as a compliment; the Zeros, despite being the enemy, were ferocious fighters. Specter figured he also probably meant it in a not-so-flattering manner since the exact term Pinto used was "a fucking Japanese Zero."

Pinto wanted Nomura grounded, but like the Zeros, Nomura (a native Californian who had attended UCLA) had a surprise for his foe when the issue of his removal from the case arose in court.

HAGEN: [to the jury] You've seen Mr. Nomura in the room and heard his participation and his explanation for his participation, namely that there was a claim brought by Ford against the plaintiffs. That claim has now been dropped by Ford and so that claim is no longer in the case and you're not to consider it or even speculate about it. Mr. Nomura will be taking his leave, I guess.

NOMURA: Your Honor, actually, I will not be taking my leave. I told counsel I will stay until the conclusion of the case. I'm associated with Mr. Durney and Mr. Specter and the plaintiffs.

HAGEN: Okay.

Pinto threw his pen down against his yellow legal pad. So did one of the other Ford lawyers. Ford and Orscheln would not get to play two-on-one against Specter after all. Nomura had agreed to stay and help. The case was too exciting, too important, for him to simply walk away. He had only asked Specter for one thing.

"So he's going to stay in the case?" Pinto asked Specter later on.

"Yep."

"So what's he get out of this deal?"

"A final argument."

"That's bullshit," said Pinto.

"For punitive damages."

"Well then he won't get a final argument. There won't be any punitive stage."

"We'll see, Joe."

"It won't get that far."

"We'll see."

CHAPTER 10

The Family

JOHNSON HALLDOR GUNNAR HOOKS, as he gave his name during his initial deposition, was the brother of Ginny White, a younger brother who had moved in with the Whites after his and Ginny's parents died. He had lived with the Whites, who were his legal guardians, for two years.

Portions of Hooks' depositions were read into evidence at trial, with Judge Hagen's directions to the jury that such testimony was to carry the same weight and importance as that given live and in person. Hooks would not appear at the trial. He now lived more than 100 miles from the federal court district in Nevada and could not, under the court's rules, be compelled to make the trip. Specter didn't insist that Hooks return to Nevada for the trial. There was nothing to be gained by it, at least not for the Whites. Specter wasn't going to give the Ford and Orscheln lawyers an opportunity to try to embarrass Hooks, to try to depict him as somehow less responsible than the experts in dark suits who filled the courtroom. Specter let Hooks stay in Albuquerque and let his depositions do the talking for him. The depositions, he felt, spoke eloquently enough.

Hooks' words brought to mind the Mel Brooks character Fabiola, a rock and roll star (played by Brooks) featured on the flip side of the 1960 hit comedy record *The 2000 Year Old Man*. When Fabiola is asked how old he is, he answers that he's about twenty . . . or thirty. Why doesn't he know exactly? "Man," he tells the interviewer [Carl Reiner], "I'm busy layin' out sound."

When the accident happened that killed his nephew, Johnson Hooks was in his bedroom, oblivious to the commotion going on outside. He hadn't heard a thing. Why not? "My music was on," he testified at one of two depositions. Hooks wasn't dumb. He was simply afflicted with a condition that tended to dull the senses. He was a teenager.

In person, Hooks was an imposing character, an Icelandic giant. He stood 6-foot-6 and weighed about 300 pounds, with a paunch around his middle. But he was, like his sister, quiet and gentle by nature. Quizzed by the Ford and Orscheln lawyers at his depositions, Hooks, who was eighteen and a senior at Elko High School at the time of the accident, didn't remember what day of the week it had been when his brother-in-law's truck rolled down the driveway, killing three-year-old Walter.

> Q: The police report indicates the accident was on a Sunday. Does that sound correct?
> A: I don't know what day it was. I don't pay attention to what day it is unless I'm in school.
> Q: Do you remember if you went to school that day?
> A: No, I didn't.
> Q: It was probably a Saturday or a Sunday?
> A: Well, it could have been during the holiday too.

After the accident, after Walter had been hospitalized, after Hooks had talked to Jimmie at the hospital and had driven the truck off a neighbor's property and back onto the Whites' driveway, Hooks repaired once more to his room, with a neighborhood friend, Steve.

> Q: Did you and he discuss the accident anymore?
> A: No.
> Q: What did you talk about?
> A: We played a video game.

No, Johnson Halldor Gunnar Hooks did not seem like the ideal witness. But there was one thing that Hooks was certain about, one thing that he swore to in his depositions. Like a typical teenager, Hooks didn't necessarily know what day of the week it was, but he clearly remembered a minor detail that most adults might have long forgotten. That detail was a linchpin in the Whites' case, but it would take Hooks a while to get to it in his testimony about that horrible day.

First, he remembered being alerted to the accident by Ragna.

> I came out of my room and my niece was crying and I asked what was wrong.
> And she goes, "Walter got hurt."
> And I said, "What happened?"
> And she goes, "The truck rolled down the hill."
> And I go, "What?"
> And she goes, "The truck rolled down the hill."
> And I said, "Which one?" And she said "Jimmie's."

And I go, "The white one?"

And she said "yes." And so I looked out the window and the truck was down in the neighbor's driveway.

Hooks then walked out of the house and down to the truck. He saw a black splotch on the road near the truck.

I didn't know at the time it was blood but I saw that.

He walked back to the house to talk to his niece some more. Hooks called the hospital to find out about Walter, but was told the hospital could not release any information because he was not next of kin. Being an uncle didn't count. Finally Jimmie called the house.

And I go, "Is Walter going to be all right?"

And he said, "The hospital doesn't know for sure."

And I think I asked him again and he said, "Johnson, just don't worry about that right now. If the truck is in the way of the neighbor, I need you to move it out of their way."

Hooks hung up and searched for the keys. He found them on the dining room table, picked them up, and walked back outside and down the road to the truck. He bent down and removed a few rocks that looked to be in the way of the tires. Hooks had a driver's license and had driven trucks before, but not this one. He shifted into reverse, but the Ford wouldn't budge. He hopped out of the truck and, with the help of a neighbor, switched the tire hubs to the four-wheel-drive position. Then the truck was able to pull itself out from the ditch in which it had crashed, resting against several trees.

Q: When you first got in the truck and sat in the driver's seat for the first time . . .

A: Uh-huh.

Q: Did you look to see where the gearshift was?

A: Yes.

Q: Where was it?

A: No, I guess I didn't really pay attention to where the gearshift was.

Q: Do you know which gear the gearshift was in when you first got in the truck?

A: No.

Q: Do you know whether the parking brake was on when you first got in the truck?

A: No.

Q: You don't know?

A: I didn't, I didn't look.

Q: Did you ever touch the parking brake itself or the release mechanism at the time you were trying to get the truck away from the trees?

A: No.

Good news for the defendants, it would seem. Hooks did not recall—hadn't noticed, really—whether the brake pedal had been in the depressed position. But he did notice and recall something that happened a few minutes later.

Q: What did you do when you parked the vehicle?

A: Pardon?

Q: Tell me how you parked it.

A: I stuck it in or left it in first. I turned off the key. And I pushed on the emergency brake. It went down a little ways and I got out of the truck.

Q: Before that day had you ever touched that emergency brake before?

A: No.

Q: Did you notice anything that you thought was unusual when you put the brake on?

A: When I got it up there?

Q: Yes.

A: It went, it only went down like an inch.

Q: Did you press pretty hard on it?

A: Yes.

That the huge lad was unable to press the brake down more than an inch could only mean one thing. It had already been applied. Jimmie White had seen to that.

This important fact about the brake being set was not one that Hooks remembered expressly—as if he were *trying* to remember an important fact about the brake—but one that he remembered in a roundabout way because the brake only went down an inch. He didn't analyze what that meant. But it could have meant only one thing. The truck had rolled away, even with the parking brake pedal applied. Meaning that little Walter had not released it and Jimmie had not forgotten to apply the brake. The brake had failed.

THE SIXTH DAY of trial, the fourth day of testimony. It was time to show the jury just how much damage Ford had done, the price Walter White's family had paid.

After entering deposition testimony from a few more witnesses, including Ford and Orscheln employees, Durney called to the stand Dr. Diana Eberstine, a clinical psychologist from California who had reviewed the Whites' case and spent more than two days with them at their home in Elko.

> DURNEY: What did you learn?
> EBERSTINE: I learned that they're very family-oriented people. They're quiet people who primarily socialize with a few friends and family. They were devoted parents. They were very religious people.
>
> I found that they had been profoundly traumatized by probably one of the most gruesome child deaths I've ever heard recounted, and I unfortunately have heard a number of them.

Eberstine's evaluation found that the Whites were suffering from post-traumatic stress disorder, including intrusive thoughts, nightmares, and flashbacks. Ginny in particular had "vivid, horrible flashbacks of the trip to the hospital when she was trying to give CPR to her child in her arms." After a time she had fewer nightmares but they were replaced by something that, in a way, was worse—good dreams. "You have this lovely memory of the person that you've lost," Eberstine explained, "then you have to wake up to reality and they're gone."

Ginny also had severe panic attacks, irrepressible and sudden feelings that someone in her family was unsafe, that something had happened to one of them. She would occasionally run out of the house, jump in her car, and go searching for Ragna, fearing that some tragedy had befallen her daughter. This occurred despite Ginny's agoraphobia, a fear of going outside her house, which afflicted her in the months after Walter's death. Eventually she would venture outside to a store, but with fear in her heart and a picture of Walter in her purse. Ginny also had difficulty eating. She suffered what Eberstine termed "classic symptoms of survivor guilt, shown by her reluctance to take medications and statements such as, 'I deserve to suffer.'" Ginny often had a glassy "ten-foot stare," as Eberstine called it.

Jimmie would sometimes get so upset at memories of his son's death, said Eberstine, "that he would just go mentally blank, which again is something commonly seen in very, very traumatized people. At times at work he would pick up a tool that he had used with Walter and he would become overwrought with grief."

Durney, seeking to preempt forthcoming defense testimony, told Eberstine that another doctor, someone from her own profession, would tell the jury that within five years the Whites would no longer suffer a clinical emotional impact. This would all fade away.

> DURNEY: Do you agree with that?
> EBERSTINE: No.
> Q: Why not?
> A: Well, I think they will still have, there will still be an emotional impact on them for the rest of their lives for what they've gone through. . . . Just because somebody doesn't have symptoms that will qualify them for a diagnosis doesn't mean that on Easter or Halloween you don't feel sad or grief.
>
> The fact that your child is not there to share it, or when Ragna graduates from college Walter won't be there, the grandchildren that they had hoped to have, all the other things that are associated with their future world that would have been part of their world with Walter, is gone."

THE NEXT WITNESS was Diane Robinson, Jimmie's sister. She had come to his house after he and Ginny returned home from the hospital. She described walking into the house, seeing a crowd of people, family and friends, Sergeant Fosmo.

Ginny was off in a corner, crying.

> And then I went across the room and I sat with her and she called to me and she was saying, "My baby. My baby is gone." And we prayed. Together we prayed out loud that he didn't feel any pain. . . . We didn't talk. She cried. And then my brother took her and put her to bed and laid her down, and he sat next to her in the chair and she just cried the whole time. She kept crying, "my baby, my baby," all night long.

Jimmie had looked more in control. He was a tough man, short but muscular, hardened from years of rugged outdoor labor. He talked to the men from the sheriff's department for a while and seemed to be doing all right. But he wasn't. Diane recalled what happened to Jimmie next, her words recreating the scene so vividly that the jury could easily picture it. And would not soon forget it.

> My brother was in the kitchen and they all walked outside and it was dark, it was night, and they all walked outside. And a few minutes later the front door opened and they came in and they were carrying my brother. There were four men carrying Jimmie and they took him over and put him in a chair and he just poured out of it just like he was water, right out of that chair like he had no bones.

Robinson said her brother and sister-in-law had left most of Walter's possessions—his bed, his toys, his posters—just where they had been, unmoved, untouched. Before she stepped down from the witness stand, Robinson left the jury with one more image about Walter and his parents.

> When he died, his little shoes were by the front door. And they stayed there for over a year.

Jimmie White would finally get his day in court.

Nearly four years had passed since the accident but Jimmie, now thirty-seven, still had rage in his heart. He hated Ford. If he saw a Ford ad on TV, he'd change the channel. Or turn the TV off. His new truck, a Dodge, displayed a decal on the back window depicting a little boy peeing—on the Ford logo. Jimmie hated Ford. Ford had killed his son.

But he kept his cool on the witness stand. It was important that he do so. At first with Durney handling the questioning, Jimmie sounded more like an expert witness than a plaintiff. After receiving Ford's recall notice, Jimmie, who had trained early in his career as a Ford mechanic, had done some experiments of his own. And after some protest by the defense, the judge permitted him to testify about his findings.

Jimmie's tests didn't involve electron microscopes or some of the other fancy equipment Campbell Laird had used. Jimmie had simply taken a piece of wire and hooked it to the knob of the stick shift of his F-350. Then he attached the wire to a fish scale that measured up to 50 pounds.

The purpose of his test was to see how much force it would take to pull his truck out of first gear if the parking brake was off, if the transmission was holding the truck in place on an incline, in the same spot where it had been parked in his driveway on October 9, 1994. Could Buddy Boy have pulled the truck out of gear with the brake on?

On his first attempt, Jimmie pulled at the shift with 30 pounds of force. It wouldn't budge. He pulled a second time until the scale reached 35 pounds. Again it would not pull into neutral. He didn't try it again with greater force for fear of harming the transmission. It was still the company's truck, after all.

Jimmie had never intended his experiment to be evidence in a legal case. He just wanted to satisfy his own curiosity. No way could Walter have pulled the truck out of first gear if the parking brake wasn't holding the truck. He just wasn't strong enough. Not that it mattered. Jimmie knew he had set the parking brake. He always did. And with the brake set he was able to pull the shift out of gear with the fish scale barely registering any force at all.

> Q: Did you have a custom and practice with regard to parking brake application?
> A: I set it all the time and I always set it the same. There was no special application as far as stepping on it or anything.
> Q: Have you always made it a habit to set the parking brake?
> A: Always.
> Q: Ever any variation in that habit in your life?
> A: The only time I wouldn't set parking brakes is if I was getting ready to pull the rear drums for inspection, because you can't pull the rear drums with the parking brake set. But other than that, yes, they were always set.

Jimmie recounted the worst day of his life for the jury, about seeing the truck in the neighbor's yard, of finding Walter unconscious near a pool of his own blood, about the ride to the hospital.

> And the next thing I remember was Dr. Oswalt coming up to me and telling me my son was dead.

Jimmie talked about the years since the accident. He said that he and Ginny had discussed having another child but that the doctors had told them that was unadvisable. Ginny had had a difficult pregnancy with Walter. The couple attended a bereaved parents' group for a time, but it hadn't helped. Seeing a psychiatrist in Elko had helped some.

Q: Dr. Eberstine told us that she visited your home in the summer of last year, the summer of '97. Has the pain diminished at all since you visited with Dr. Eberstine?

A: The pain of the loss? No.

Jimmie had been a conscientious mechanic. He'd worked on his own trucks and maintained them carefully. He made sure they were inspected on time and that they passed. The thing that bothered him most, he told the jury, was that he had never known the parking brake might have a problem. Not until it was too late. Had he known a fix had been available, that Orscheln had developed the wedge, he would have run down to Gallagher Ford, the nearest dealership, to correct the problem. Why hadn't Ford warned him?

Q: What would you have done to protect your family had either Ford or Orscheln notified you that they had been experiencing problems with the parking brakes that had been installed in their 1992, 1993, even 1994 model year F-Series trucks and that . . . they had been hearing reports that some of them across America were rolling away?

A: I can guarantee you I would have taken that vehicle in and had it fixed if I had known there had been a fix for it. If there hadn't been a fix available, I can guarantee you that truck would have been parked so it would never roll.

Q: In fact, at some point after the accident you learned that there was a fix, a wedge?

A: Yes, sir.

Q: How long did it take you to take the truck to Gallagher Ford once you learned about the wedge?

A: I was told about the recall, or the notice, that morning and I had that truck in before it opened that day.

Q: How long did it take them to put the wedge into your vehicle from the point in time when you drove it into that dealership until the point of time that you drove it out?

A: It was approximately half an hour.

Pinto tried to establish a few points during his cross-examination. One was that the Whites, though loving parents, had not been watching Walter when he climbed into the pickup truck on the day of the accident. Jimmie had been watching him. So had Ginny. But, Jimmie had to admit, not when Walter went into the front yard and climbed into the truck.

He also acknowledged that he had told Sergeant Fosmo that he thought Walter had released the parking brake. But that was before he had seen the recall notice, when "that was the only conclusion I could come up with at the time."

Pinto apparently wanted to throw some doubt on the testimony of Johnson Hooks about the parking brake being set. Hooks had driven the truck all the way back to the Whites' driveway and when he stepped on the parking brake, it depressed only about an inch. Pinto couldn't get Hooks to Reno; he knew that. So in questioning Jimmie he seemed to suggest, without actually saying so, that perhaps Jimmie and Johnson had made up the notion about the parking brake's position. But Jimmie said that the two hadn't talked that much about it, let alone concocted a story. Pinto seemed surprised to learn that Jimmie hadn't even been prepped about Hooks' testimony before taking the stand. He certainly didn't seem to expect Jimmie's answers.

> Q: Have you read his testimony, the testimony that he [Hooks] gave at his deposition about what happened and what he did the night of the accident?
> A: No, sir, I have not.
> Q: Has the lawyer read it to you?
> A: No, sir, he has not.
> PINTO: Okay.

Durney stood to question Jimmie White once again. He asked that Plaintiff's Exhibit 164 be admitted into evidence. This was Ford's recall letter. While Ford, after a previous ruling by Hagen, was now willing to talk about the recall notice, it didn't want the actual document brought before the jury. One reason was that the notice characterized the problem with the brakes as a "defect." And not just a defect, but one that was "safety-related." Ford's own letter sounded like a confession. But Pinto argued before the judge that it would be unfair to let the jury see the notice because the actual wording was not Ford's, it was NHTSA's. It was government-mandated wording.

PINTO: You had previously ruled the recall was out unless the defendants chose to introduce it. Secondly, the defendants have not chosen to introduce the recall letter.

HAGEN: The recall letter has been discussed upside-down in this case for the last week.

PINTO: I agree with that, but the recall letter itself is prejudicial.

HAGEN: Show me the prejudicial part, please.

PINTO: This right here. It's required by the National Highway Transportation [Safety] Administration that that be the wording that is used and it sounds like an admission by the Ford Motor Co. . . . The real point of my objection is that it says a "safety-related defect."

SPECTER: Well, that's right and, Mr. Pinto, I believe that if Ford doesn't believe that it's a safety-related defect, they can come to court and say so.

PINTO: The fact that the recall is before the jury, I think that the words "safety-related" are prejudicial. We have maintained throughout this case that the problem with this vehicle was not safety-related.

Pinto argued the government made the company use those damning words. Specter argued that Ford "can't have it both ways"—play the role of the good guy that acted responsibly in issuing the recall letter yet deny what it said in the letter was correct. Hagen allowed the introduction of the recall notice as evidence.

GINNY WHITE DIDN'T want to be in court. Painfully shy and soft-spoken, she was barely audible at times. She still had that "glassy stare" the psychiatrist had talked about. But Ginny managed to make it through her brief testimony.

She talked a little about Walter. She talked about Ragna, who was now eighteen and attending Menlo College in California. She talked about the day of the accident, how she had told Walter to stay in the backyard, how he had strayed to the front to ride his tricycle, how she had watched him through the window—except for a few fateful minutes.

She talked about the moment she realized the awful, terrible truth. And about trying to ignore it.

GINNY: And I got in the car and started it and saw my husband bringing my son up the driveway and he told me to get in the backseat, and I did, and he handed me Walter and he took off to the hospital.

DURNEY: At that point in time did you think Walter was alive?

A: No.

Q: Notwithstanding that belief, did you administer CPR?

A: Yes, I did.

Q: All the way to the hospital?

A: Yes, I did.

Joe Pinto had Ray LeBon cross-examine Ginny, wishing to forgo this grim task himself. LeBon was brief, seeking to make the point with the jury that the Whites, despite their usual vigilance, had on this occasion allowed their son to play outside unsupervised.

Q: Ma'am, was Walter generally allowed to play in the front yard without supervision?

A: It wasn't without supervision. I usually watched out the windows.

Q: Ma'am, what were you doing at the time that this happened?

A: My husband and I were discussing plans for the pellet stove.

Q: Was the TV set on?

A: Yes, it was.

Q: Were you watching TV?

A: No, sir.

So then why was the TV on? LeBon didn't ask the question, but the thought hung in the air. Some of the jurors might have wondered. LeBon had perhaps sown some doubt. If some jurors were looking to let Ford off the hook, maybe this provided an excuse to do so. Big corporations, after all, couldn't be responsible if parents let their tots climb into trucks and play with the stick shift.

Specter doubted these suggestions were enough to turn the trial. He felt good about the case he had presented, its documented facts, irrefutable evidence, and honest, plain-talking victims in Jimmie and Ginny White. Ford and Orscheln were about to produce several witnesses, their own experts and some other company engineers and executives, but none who had been as involved with the parking brake as Specter's witnesses or the Ford witness he had transformed into his own, Tim Rakowicz.

Specter was content with what he saw in the faces of the six neatly dressed jurors who had listened attentively to Ginny White tell about the loss of her child.

"The Whites rest," he told the court.

CHAPTER 11

The Case for the Defense

SPECTER HAD KEPT his cast of characters to a minimum. He knew that juries appreciated the restraint and that fewer witnesses minimized the risk of a problem. Now Ford and Orscheln would parade their witnesses to the stand. Orscheln had a handful of experts and company employees lined up to testify. Ford would use seasoned experts—expert "testifiers," Specter called them—while keeping its own engineers and executives back home, safe from scrutiny and, worse, the possibility of making a mistake on cross-examination. Ford's witnesses were experts not just on technical matters but also on defending products. They were accustomed to appearing before juries and jousting with plaintiffs' lawyers. They made few mistakes, if any.

Some jurors would likely be impressed by this band of professionals. Specter relished the challenge they presented. If he couldn't jab holes in the defense witnesses' testimony, he would try to at least tarnish it, to scratch off some of the luster. "Reasonable doubt" wasn't enough to defend a civil case. The jury would instead decide the outcome on which case it felt was stronger—the plaintiffs' or the defendants'. Specter felt his witnesses had tipped the scale heavily in his clients' favor. The defendants would try to tip it back.

Gutowski and Blewett

The first testimony for Ford came in the reading of the deposition taken from Kenneth Gutowski, Rakowicz's supervisor at Ford. This testimony established the parameters of the defendants' case.

Skip-through on apply did occur, said Gutowski, but "the team did not consider it a safety concern because the operator would notice a difference during the apply." He remembered Rakowicz's concerns and recalled talking about them with the young engineer. Gutowski acknowledged having written the notation "Purge all copies with this comment—not true" about Rakowicz's white paper for a recall committee.

"That is my writing, yes," he said and then explained that his purge note was not some nefarious action, but simply routine. "Always a supervisor reviews words for clarification, and this was not correct. It was not a white paper for a review recall committee . . . It was grossly in error. It wasn't at the recall stage . . . Therefore, by purging it and reissuing it correctly, not to purge it to hide it, but reissue it with the correct word was the intent." Routine—nothing insidious about it.

Gutowski shoved part of the brake problem, or at least its solution, onto Orscheln. "We let Orscheln do the testing," he said. Ford had relied on Orscheln to find the problem and the solution. He denied any existence of spontaneous disengagement. The so-called pin test that had replicated that problem didn't count, said Gutowski, "because they tricked the whole system into aligning in the tooth-on-tooth condition that would not occur in the real world."

STEPHEN BLEWETT, a consulting engineer with twenty-six years of experience and a master of science degree from the University of Southern California, had conducted an accident reconstruction three years after the incident in Elko. He didn't so much offer a theory of how the accident had occurred as he presented a litany of measurements relating to force—how much to open the truck door latches, how much to pull the shift out of first gear with the parking brake not set, how much to remove the truck from gear on a level surface, on a slope, etc., etc. It was his job, here in the courtroom, to set the stage for witnesses later on.

But the answers he gave even to his own attorney seemed iffy, especially for an expert. For instance, if the truck had been parked on a slope in first gear and the parking brake was not engaged—one of the defense theories of the accident—how much force would it take for someone to pull the stick shift from first gear into neutral? Well, said Blewett, more than 15 pounds. On cross-examination, Specter asked again how much more force it would take. Blewett said he didn't know because the scales he used in his testing only went up to 15 pounds. The fish scales used by Jimmie White, who never laid claim to being an "expert," went to 50 pounds. Jimmie had gotten up to 35 pounds of pressure before stopping for fear he'd damage the transmission.

> SPECTER: You could have used another scale to do this also. Right?
> BLEWETT: Sure.
> Q: You could have used a fish scale?

A: That's correct. And then the question is what the accuracy of that scale is.

Q: You know that Jimmie used a fish scale to test pretty much the same thing?

A: I wasn't aware of that.

What was the degree of the slope on which Blewett had parked the truck for his experiment? "I did not measure it," he responded.

Did he know the precise spot the truck was in when it started to roll? "No, I don't."

Did he use the police photos to position the truck in the same spot for his tests? "No, I did not."

In doing his tests and taking his own pictures, Blewett had photographed the truck on a flat surface. In fact, he had taken sixty-one photos in all. But for his second test, this one with the truck parked on a grade, there was no photo. Why not? "I apparently overlooked that," he testified.

Had he overlooked it on purpose?

SPECTER: Now, as an experienced accident reconstructionist, have you ever heard about the, oh, expression—"know what not to photograph"?

BLEWETT: No, I have not.

Q: How about the concept "know what not to photograph"?

A: I would say yes.

Q: Tell the jury what that concept is.

A: Well, there are things that if you take pictures of that are clearly not substantiated by the evidence, they're not necessary to take, and that someone will look at that photograph they're taking and try to make something out of it.

Q: I see. That's one way of putting it. Would a different way of putting it be that if you photograph something which is not terribly helpful, that photograph can then be used against the client for whom you've taken the photograph?

A: Sure.

Q: Now, was there anything else that you didn't photograph except for the position of the vehicle when you did your measurements of it?

A: I took my pictures of the area and the vehicle. As to other pictures I should have taken, there's probably some I should have taken.

Specter asked if anyone else was at the scene when Blewett went to the Whites' house to take his photos and reconstruct the accident. Yes, there had been, said Blewett. Among those at the scene was Eugene Wait, Ford's original lawyer in charge of the case before Pinto was called in to take over.

Blewett further acknowledged that he had not tried to position the truck in the same spot as in the actual accident. The site had been altered, he said. The grading of the driveway had been changed and the Whites had built a porch where the truck once had been parked. Well then, Specter wanted to know, why didn't Blewett test the truck on a slope that had the same angle as the ground the truck had been parked on at the time of the accident? Blewett reminded him that the area had been altered. He could no longer place the truck on the exact spot at the same angle.

But Specter insisted it could be done, that there was a way that Blewett—or anyone with an understanding of basic geometry—could calculate the degree of the slope on which the truck had been parked. You didn't have to actually place the vehicle on the exact spot. After all, Blewett had the police officer's photographs of the truck and where it had been parked before the accident.

Q: Now, as an experienced accident reconstructionist, sir, you can take that photograph and you can make a pretty close estimation as to what that slope is, can't you?

A: From the photograph?

Q: Yes.

A: No.

Blewett wasn't getting it. He would any second now.

Q: Well, let me suggest to you that what you do is you look at the house and the house tends to be level, correct?

It was common sense. Houses were built level. If you had the house on a level line and the truck in the same photo at an angle, you could just take a protractor . . .

A: I can probably make some approximations, yes.

Q: Did you do that?

A: No, I did not.

Wayne Soucie

Anyone could see that Orscheln's Wayne Soucie was a nice guy, a "regular guy." He grew up in a small town, "took my first gas engine apart in second grade," attended the University of Missouri, and later worked as an engineer. He held nine U.S. patents. The company's manager of design development when the self-adjusting brake was invented at Orscheln, Soucie, a thin, fair-haired, middle-aged man, had never testified in court on behalf of his company's products. He had never been on a witness stand. He didn't sound like the other expert witnesses. He sounded like what he was, a regular guy telling what he knew.

> SPECTER: They pay your way out here and your way back?
> SOUCIE: I hope somebody will.

Specter knew the jury would like Wayne Soucie.

He talked about Orscheln's efforts to find the cause of the brake problem, including coming up with more than twenty-five prototype fixes. While defending Orscheln, he did not let Ford off the hook. During the search for a cause and a solution, his company had met weekly with folks from Ford and later on had spoken with them in daily telephone conferences. Ford knew what was going on every step of the way.

Orscheln was never able to make the brakes spontaneously disengage, said Soucie. He tried to explain how some of the vehicles had rolled during the "pin test" that Orscheln had conducted. Once was when a truck was on a 20 percent grade and it began to roll—but the brake never disengaged; the load was simply beyond the point at which the brake would hold the vehicle. A second time the truck rolled when technicians started to push on the pedal to increase the pedal load; in that case, said Soucie, the pedal pushed through on apply. A third time the brake disengaged after Orscheln had a man, a large man of 200 pounds, kick the pedal repeatedly. On the twentieth kick or so the brake disengaged. But, said Soucie, a subsequent inspection of the disassembled brake showed a structural failure—that the test had exceeded the strength of the metal pawl.

From anyone else, this might have seemed like old-fashioned excuse-making. But coming from Soucie, the explanations sounded plausible.

His final conclusion: "We took extreme actions with regard to force, energy, sustained time, and we were never able to recreate or cause a spontaneous disengagement."

Orscheln's attorney, Max Steinheimer, asked Soucie about the photographs Sergeant Fosmo of the Elko County Sheriff's Department had taken at the scene the night of the accident, after the truck was moved and parked back in front of the Whites' house. The photo was critical. It seemed to show the brake pedal in the up position, not depressed, as Johnson Hooks had testified.

Specter jumped up with an objection to using the photo to interject an opinion that the brake had not been applied. The plaintiffs had not been informed about such testimony, and their experts had already been sent home. It wasn't fair, he protested at sidebar, out of the jury's hearing. Judge Hagen agreed. Rules were rules. Testimony about the photo would not be permitted.

Steinheimer argued that Orscheln didn't inform the plaintiffs about the photo and what it purported to show before the trial because the defense didn't realize it then. Now it did and now the defense should be allowed to present the evidence, especially considering its potential impact.

Hagen wasn't biting. "If the lightbulb went on in your head, Mr. Steinheimer, and you got that idea about comparing these two photographs, then you should have told plaintiffs' counsel because this is really an additional opinion you're getting from your witness, isn't it?"

When testimony resumed, Soucie acknowledged under cross-examination that Orscheln designed the wedge that fixed the brake problem in 1993, long before the fatal accident.

Specter also presented handwritten notes on the results of Orscheln's pin tests. The notes seemed to conflict slightly yet importantly with what Soucie had told the court. Specter read one part aloud: "Additional application to pedal that the vehicle was creeping and the lever popped and would not hold the vehicle on slope after twenty seconds."

Q: Is that what it says?
A: That's what it says.

The brake had "popped." The report did not say it had skipped through when being applied. Still, the witness insisted, that's what had happened, no matter what the notes said. Soucie didn't know who wrote those notes. He further testified that he did not agree with Tim Rakowicz's conclusion that there had been spontaneous disengagement. And Soucie disagreed with another employee's opinion in a written report that "all ratchet-and-pawl mechanisms are prone to this type of failure mode periodically." The January 4, 1993, analysis report had been changed to remove that language, Specter noted. Soucie explained that the opinion about the brake system was wrong and the author was told to rewrite his report, yet the original document had not been discarded. Although Soucie disagreed with the comments, the author of the report was not ordered to eliminate them, as Rakowicz had been ordered by Gutowski to "purge" his comments about a recall committee.

> SPECTER: You wouldn't want to purge anything, correct?
> SOUCIE: No.
> Q: That's not the policy of the Orscheln Company, right?
> A: No, it's not.
> Q: You folks don't use that kind of language at Orscheln, right?
> A: No.

But, as the jury knew, Ford had.

Stuart Brown

Stuart Brown had earned his Ph.D. in mechanical engineering from the Massachusetts Institute of Technology and was currently the director of the Boston office of Failure Analysis Associates, a firm with 500 employees. Brown studied why things failed. He was Orscheln's answer to Campbell Laird. He had done work for many companies, among them Motorola, Intel, Gillette, and Johnson & Johnson.

Brown had been asked by the defense to examine Orscheln's ratchet-and-pawl brake assembly system. As part of his examination, he had collected literature, done research, traveled to Missouri to inspect brake assemblies, performed an analysis based on engineering drawings, reviewed high-speed videos of the brake system in operation, examined "exemplar parking brake assemblies," and inspected an F-350 truck similar to Jimmie White's.

His conclusion: "Once the parking brake is applied, fully applied, and the driver walks away from . . . the truck, the vehicle will stay—excuse me, to be more precise, the ratchet and pawl will stay engaged and will not spontaneously disengage."

Brown followed with a lengthy explanation of how he had reached this conclusion. He examined the design and found it "appropriate." The materials that had been used were also adequate, with the metal properly "case hardened." He used diagrams to help the jury "step through the different contact geometrics" of the ratchet-and-pawl system. He testified that the metal-toothed mechanism has a "bias towards engagement," not toward skipping out.

Specter had several questions about Brown and about his analysis. First, how much was he getting paid for his efforts on behalf of Orscheln? Brown said he couldn't say exactly, but that it was roughly $40,000, "and it may be a little bit more than that." That was far more than the $28,000 an average worker in Reno's Washoe County earned in a year.

Specter also wanted to know whether it was true that 70 percent of Brown's failure analyses was conducted for defendants in legal matters, for companies that called and said, "We've been sued. We have a problem with a product. Would you look at the product? Would you help us defend the product? Would you come into court and testify?"

Replied Brown, "I can't give you a number, but I can say it's more than half." Specter suspected it was a great deal more than half. His own expert, Campbell Laird, had told the jury that in the past he had testified about half the time for plaintiffs and half for defendants, a fact that made him appear objective. Specter doubted this was the case for Brown. He pressed the issue.

How many times, he asked, had Brown testified *against* a company. The answer did not necessitate complex calculations. The number was zero.

Q: Have you ever come into court and testified that a product was defective?

A: No, sir.

Brown assured Specter on cross-examination that the designs he had studied were of brake systems that were in pristine condition, without any wear or damage. But Specter wanted to know why. Why use a perfect brake rather than one like the parking brake in Jimmie White's truck, in which some of the teeth of the mechanism were chipped or broken?

Q: You could have taken this brake, you've got all this ability, this background, you went to MIT, right? You could have taken this brake and you could have done a set of drawings which reflected this brake's condition with this brake's deformations, chipping, and broken teeth. Correct?

A: No. I, we're talking about scale of effort here.

Q: Well, sir, has there been any effort spared in this case?

A: No, I'm saying that when you get down to that level of detail, we're talking, you know, potentially many years of effort.

Q: Did you actually see the brake that was involved in this case?

A: No.

Specter noted that Brown had traveled to Orscheln's facility in Missouri. He mentioned that Ford had returned to Orscheln some fifty parking brakes that customers had alleged to have failed.

Q: Now, did you look at those fifty brakes?

A: No sir, I did not.

Q: Or any of them?

A: No, sir.

Two Michelles

The judge began the second day of defense testimony by barring the depositions of Michelle Bailey and Michelle Thornall, who had testified for the defendants that they found "comparative negligence" on the part of Walter White's parents—basically, that Jimmie and Ginny had caused their son's death. Hagen found their deposition testimony unfairly prejudicial and potentially confusing for the jury. Not to mention ridiculous.

"If letting a little kid play outside in a rural neighborhood, outside the immediate presence of his parents . . . every parent who has ever raised a little kid in rural America has been negligent day in and day out," said Hagen. The judge himself was an Arkansas native who was sent to live with relatives in Wisconsin for a while when his father faced tough economic times.

"I would have a terrible time finding that a rural parent created an unreasonable risk of harm to his or her child by allowing the child to play out of doors without someone with that child every moment of the day," he said. "It would have driven my uncle and aunt crazy if they would have had that obligation with me on the farm, I'll tell you."

James Varin

James Varin was your prototypical Ford witness, a former Ford employee who knew the operation, yet a witness who could not be held responsible if he made a mistake because he no longer worked there. Varin had been "principal reliability engineer" for the company's light truck division. He left Ford after ten years, retiring in 1981. Now he was a consultant in the field of automotive engineering. "Almost all" of what he did, Varin acknowledged when questioned by Specter, involved "activities related to litigation, and almost all of that was related to product liability litigation." Even during his decade at Ford, Varin had spent, he estimated, about two-thirds of his time defending the company in legal cases.

> SPECTER: And how many cases have you been involved in since then for Ford?
>
> VARIN: Maybe 100 to 200. I really don't know.
>
> Q: Have you ever testified in any of those cases that a Ford product was defective?
>
> A: No. I've made that finding, but I've never been given, never been asked to give that testimony.
>
> Q: Because when you tell them [Ford] that, they don't want you to bring it into court?
>
> A: No. It's because when they realize that, I think they resolve the case without it going to court.

In other words, Varin was telling the jury, when Ford found in the past that it had a defective product it paid off the plaintiff. What Varin left unsaid was: *Unlike in this case, because there was no defect.*

It was a clever response and one that Specter couldn't let go uncontested. He got Varin to say that he had only done consulting work on two occasions for a plaintiff and that he had never, not once, testified against Ford. Specter's next question drew an objection and the judge ruled that Varin did not have to answer. That was all right with Specter.

> Q: Do you know what happens to experts who testify against Ford in relation to the question of whether Ford will hire them again?

Varin went on to explain the "functional evaluation" he had performed on the brake system in Jimmie White's truck and that he found its "apply and release characteristics" were "acceptable to my standards." He agreed that one tooth in the brake system had been damaged but that that was "not in any way related to anything that could have caused the accident to happen."

He noted that the pedal on the parking brake showed deterioration that came from "very hard, very forced applications . . . more vigorous than is typically observed." That also could have caused the damage observed on the brake's pawl tooth. "The appearance of this pedal," said Varin, "shows that the person who operated this parking brake operated it with a lot of force and . . . probably very rapidly, and that kind of operation was probably what led to the kind of damage that is shown in this tooth number eight." He compared the pedal to that in the truck of Tammy Bobb, which he'd also examined. The Bobb brake, Varin said, showed a "very gradual wearing down on the ridges of the pad." The wear on Jimmie White's pedal was much more severe.

Though the company used the slogan "Built Ford Tough," Varin was implying that Jimmie White had been too tough. But he wouldn't say that directly, Specter found out on cross-examination.

> Q: You wouldn't say this is vehicle abuse, is that correct?
> A: No.
> Q: You wouldn't say this is misuse, correct?
> A: No, I wouldn't.
> Q: You don't claim that this happened because Mr. White over here misused the vehicle, do you?

Varin agreed that he had not.

Specter, who was as familiar with the Bobb case as anyone in the courtroom, also pointed to differences between the Bobbs and the Whites and their trucks. For one thing, Jimmie used his truck for work and the Bobbs didn't. Jimmie's truck had also logged nearly three times the miles, 60,000 compared with just 23,000.

> Q: And Mrs. Bobb, she wasn't in the mining industry, was she? She was a housewife, correct?
> A: Yes.
> Q: And Mr. Bobb wasn't in the mining industry either, was he?
> A: No.
> Q: They lived in central Pennsylvania, right?
> A: Yes.
> Q: Not a place where you have the grit and gravel and residue of a mining operation that you do in Elko, Nevada. Right?
> A: Well, there are lots of mines in Pennsylvania. I don't know to what extent they frequented them, but there are a lot of mines in Pennsylvania.
> Q: But they weren't miners. Right?

A: Not that I know of.

Q: They weren't mechanics and didn't supervise a mining operation, right?

A: No.

Varin concluded that there had been no skip-out of the brake, no spontaneous disengagement. Testing could not replicate such a thing, except
for the "pin test," which Varin dismissed as producing not spontaneous
disengagement but "forced disengagement." His conclusion of what had
happened:

> I think most likely the last operator of the vehicle neglected, forgot
> to apply the parking brake and left the vehicle perhaps in gear with-
> out the parking brake applied. Another almost as likely possibility
> is that young Walter White disengaged the parking brake while he
> was inside the vehicle, disengaged by pulling the release handle.

Specter wanted to show that Varin was hardly an objective observer.
He had investigated more than 100 cases of rollaways, or cases of "unattended vehicle movement," as Varin put it. His conclusions had never
varied.

Q: Every time you've done an investigation, which is more than
100, you came to the opinion within a reasonable degree of engineering certainty that the reason for the rollaway was the
fault of the driver. Correct?

A: Yes.

Varin had testified at length about a variety of other causes for rollaways. There were leaking rear axle seals, overloaded vehicles, vehicles
towing boats, worn rear brake linings. Sometimes, he went on, several
of these things happened in combination. So what, Specter wanted to
know, did any of this have to do with Jimmie's truck?

Q: Leaking rear axle, that could cause it. That didn't happen here.
Right?

A: I don't have any reason to believe it did.

Q: The brake doesn't hold. That didn't happen here?

A: I don't believe that was the cause of the rollaway.

Q: It wasn't towing a boat, was it?

A: No.

Q: Excessive worn rear brake linings? That didn't happen here either, right?

A: I don't have any basis for believing it did.

Q: Well, you don't think any of these things happened at all, so I guess they didn't happen in combination. Right?

A: I don't have any reason for believing that they did. No.

Jeffrey Germane

The second week of the trial ended in a heated argument between the lawyers over Ford's final witness, professor and accident reconstructionist Jeffrey Germane. The argument arose from the same photo that had come up earlier, the one taken by Sergeant Fosmo of the interior of Jimmie's truck on the night of the accident. The one that seemed to show the brake in the upright released position. The one the judge had ruled earlier that Orscheln could not use to try to show that the brake had not been applied. Now Ford wanted a crack at using the photo.

Specter voiced his objection, saying it was too late to bring in a new expert opinion. He had not been given notice of such testimony. "If they had photographic evidence from that night which demonstrates the position of the pedal . . . then they need to tell us that," he told Hagen. "If they have . . . a man that was going to come in and say he'd give an opinion on that, we need notice of that so we can have the vehicle examined by our experts for exactly the same purpose. This is grossly unfair."

Pinto argued that the position of the brake was not an opinion at all. It was a fact. Facts could always be introduced. It was never too late. "You can look at the . . ." he began to say.

But the judge interrupted. "No, it's not a fact. It's an opinion." He had already ruled on this issue earlier, he said, and his ruling stood.

Though Specter won the critical ruling, he wasn't satisfied. Not hardly. He'd been around this block before.

> SPECTER: Your Honor, I would ask, because this is an exquisitely sensitive aspect of this case, I would ask that Mr. Pinto speak to Dr. Germane before the doctor takes the witness stand so that it's absolutely clear that he's not to get into this either on direct or cross-examination.
>
> PINTO: How can I ask him not to get into something on cross-examination if you ask a question that requires the answer?

SPECTER: I am not going to ask a question about the photograph and what it shows. Okay? I'm not going to ask that question.

I just want to be clear that I know Dr. Germane. He's a very experienced witness, testifying in court all over the place. I don't mean anything negative by that, but I want to be sure he understands that, number one, you're not going to elicit the opinion and, number two, I'm not going to seek it either. Because I don't want this guy blurting out in answer to a question that I ask that this is what the photograph shows.

Pinto persisted in arguing the point. "In my estimation, it is a very important fact," he told the judge. "In the interests of justice, to block a fact like this out of the case is against the interests of justice. . . . This parking brake is clearly in the up position in Sergeant Fosmo's photograph. If it's in the up position, all of your testimony by Johnson Hooks falls apart."

The argument was intense, and the sidebar about it the longest of the trial. Finally, Hagen had had enough. "Mr. Germane is an expert witness who will not testify that the parking brake was in any particular position," he said.

Step back. Move on with the trial.

Germane testified that he was an expert in accident reconstruction. He'd earned his doctorate at Brigham Young University, where he remained a professor. He operated Germane Engineering, which was basically Jeffrey Germane. Much of his work came from testifying in court for car companies and their attorneys.

Germane said he believed Walter White had fallen out of the driver's side of the truck, where the parking brake release was located. He said his conclusion was based on a number of things, including the fact that Walter was struck by the left-side tires. His testimony differed from prior opinion that Walter had fallen from the passenger side. Germane also believed the truck's doors had been left open. This was based on the height of the door latch—about 6 inches over Walter's head—and because it would have taken about 13 pounds of pressure to push in the button on the door latch.

But Germane's main finding offered the jury a direct contradiction from what it had heard from the plaintiffs:

I believe that there's no physical evidence, based on the evidence that I reviewed, that substantiates spontaneous release of this emergency brake.

Germane went on to offer a variety of scenarios of how the accident might have happened. Whether by accident or not, Walter White at some point somehow "pulls the parking brake and the truck rolls." It could have happened as he climbed into the truck or later on. According to one scenario espoused by Germane, "The boy enters the vehicle, he disengages first gear, and he releases the parking brake and the truck rolls."

Specter realized his cross-examination could be volatile. He didn't expect it would burst into flames. He was about a minute into his questioning when he asked why Germane had not considered reports of rollaways when he did his accident reconstruction.

> Q: Wouldn't that be an important thing for an accident reconstructionist to consider when he's trying to figure out how an accident happened, to know whether there had been reports of a product malfunction?
> A: In this particular accident there was physical evidence that the brake pedal was not down.

Hagen's eyes flashed and he jumped in immediately.

> HAGEN: The answer of the witness is stricken. The jury will disregard it.

But the cat was out of the bag. *Physical evidence that the brake pedal was not down? What evidence?* The jury might wonder. Germane, of course, was referring to the very thing he was not supposed to mention, the Fosmo photos. Specter asked for a sidebar with the judge.

"That is a disgrace. I can't believe it. I can't believe it!" Specter told Judge Hagen, insisting this mention by Germane of "evidence"—disallowed evidence—was clearly breaking the rules. "He gave an entirely unresponsive answer. He is absolutely cheating of the worst sort."

"Your Honor," Pinto broke in after a minute, "I apologize."

But it wasn't really an apology, just the way Pinto started his explanation.

"The reason he answered the question the way he did was because he believes sincerely, and he did incidentally use the photographs when he created his opinion. I told him we are not to refer to the photographs and the position of the parking lever as it's shown on any photographs in responding to any questions. Now, unfortunately, I told him the photographs and I didn't think to take it one step further and [tell him] not to mention the position of the parking brake. And I think that's what he's trying to say, why . . ."

"No," broke in the judge. "I know exactly what he's trying to state."

Specter demanded that the judge strike Germane's entire testimony. "It's absolutely the worst thing I've ever seen practicing law," he said.

"You're young yet," interjected Pinto. "I've seen a lot worse."

Specter, who was forty, didn't laugh. Neither did the judge.

Pinto belittled the incident, saying no harm had been done. The jury had been instructed to strike the statement. The jury probably didn't even know what Germane was talking about. It would be "extreme," he said, to strike all of his testimony.

"I'll tell you what would be extreme," responded Specter, "a default judgment." He was referring to the most extreme of rulings from the bench, suggesting that Hagen unilaterally decide the case against Ford, taking the verdict out of the jury's hands and leaving it only to decide the amount of damages.

Hagen didn't know what to do. He felt that that Germane had intentionally flouted his ruling. Germane, he said, "decided he was going to be cute, as many experts attempt, and wait for what he thought was a good opening to get the answer in. That's exactly what he did."

"Now the question I'm agonizing over is whether the bell can be unrung by my simple admonition to the jury to disregard his answer." Hagen decided to strike Germane's answer and move on. "Let's finish up with this guy," Hagen said, a tone of disgust in his voice.

But Specter wasn't having it. "Your Honor, I don't want to continue with my cross-examination of this witness at all. I mean, my problem with this guy is the guy is absolutely no good."

"Wait a minute," Pinto started.

"You wait a minute," said Specter, hot now. "He is a cheater. That is what he is and that's what he is doing."

Specter and Pinto went back and forth for a time. Finally, Specter said, "The difficulty we have here, Your Honor, is we're on the verge of Ford Motor Co. being whacked for an enormous amount of money and they will do anything they can. I'm not talking about Mr. Pinto over here. But just so we're clear about this, Mr. Germane is a fourteen-year consultant to the Ford Motor Co. . . . They want to do anything they can, including getting this case mistried right here and right now. And that's what's going on here. If I go back out there and ask him another question for which that's not a responsive answer, he may say it again."

"Your Honor," protested Pinto, "there is absolutely no evidence that it was intentional."

"Yes, there is, and let me tell you what it is," Hagen shot back, giving Pinto a sharp look. "I've watched this witness during his direct examination. I've seen his willingness to get in whatever he can with respect to a question even if it isn't in response to the question. I've seen him attempt to make an argument when there was no question pending. . . . And so I know this kind of witness, Mr. Pinto. I've tried a few cases, and I believe that he did what he did intentionally. I think he thought he was being cute."

There was a deadlock in the courtroom. Specter wouldn't go on with his questioning of Germane. Pinto didn't have another witness. Germane was his last. Perhaps Orscheln could recall one of its witnesses, Stephen Blewett, to explain some things, Specter suggested. That was fine with the judge. But now Orscheln's Steinheimer was up in arms.

"We decided to time our witnesses and our evidence so that we ended with something that we thought was going to be strong and part of our case and we're done. And opening it up with a reconstructionist after that fiasco might be worse than not putting him on at all. . . . I do not want to do that. I don't think I should be made to do that since this was not my problem and I didn't create it and I didn't generate it."

Hagen still didn't know what to do, and he didn't mind admitting it. "This is really troubling," he said, wrinkling his forehead. "I can't let this go and I don't want to be too draconian in my ruling. I've just got to think about this. This just screws up everything."

"I'm sorry, Your Honor," Germane said at one point.

"He made a mistake," said Pinto.

"I don't believe it," said Specter. "I don't believe it."

Hagen would be saved from his dilemma, at least for the moment. It was almost 4:00 p.m. on Friday. He could take the weekend to think about it. He would render a decision first thing Monday morning.

NOT ALL THE PARTIES in the case would wait that long.

Pete Durney walked back across Stewart Street to the Victorian-style house that held the offices of Durney & Brennan. He would catch up on things for a few hours before heading home. He'd been there barely an hour when he looked outside and spotted Steinheimer standing in the parking lot. Steinheimer, for some reason, was looking once more at Jimmie White's red and white Ford F-350, the truck that had run over Walter

White. It was being kept at Durney's nearby offices for the duration of the trial.

"Hello, Max," Durney said as he walked down the steps of his office and into the lot.

"Hi."

"Takin' a last look?"

"Yeah," Steinheimer said, a melancholy smile creasing his face.

"What do you think of the case?"

"Well, I'm thinking maybe we should try to reach a settlement."

"Well, I'm sure we'll probably take the policy limit," said Durney, fully aware that Orscheln was covered by its insurance carrier for a maximum of $3 million.

"You know a lot of that has already been spent."

"How much is left?"

"About one-point-eight."

That was $1.8 million. Orscheln had already spent $1.2 million on the case for expenses—travel, discovery, hiring experts. And legal fees. The lawyers had been putting in overtime on the case and billing for it. Durney figured that Orscheln was worried about the verdict, more than Ford was. Not only could a jury award more than $1.8 million and force the smaller company to dip into its own pocket, it could also award severe punitive damages, maybe enough to jeopardize the company itself. Durney figured that Orscheln didn't want to find out.

"I don't think $1.8 million's going to do it," he said. "You're going to have to do better."

By Monday morning Orscheln did do better. It came up with $250,000 more of its own money, bringing the total offer to $2,050,000. It wasn't a lot, but it would eliminate the all-or-nothing financial risk of the case, providing a sort of insurance policy against a losing verdict. It would cover Durney's and Specter's expenses. It would also ensure that the Whites, win or lose against Ford, would suffer no monetary loss. They had missed work and spent their own money to participate in the proceedings. They had taken a second mortgage on their house to help pay their bills. A settlement with Orscheln meant at least they would not walk away broke.

It was a deal. Orscheln could go back to Moberly.

WHEN THE TRIAL resumed, Hagen had reached his decision on Jeffrey Germane. He found the defendant in the case, now only Ford, to have failed to conform to the federal rules of civil procedure by giving excluded testimony "in answer to a question that could not possibly have been interpreted to call for such an answer."

But the judge refused to strike Germane's entire testimony. He could continue to testify but not argue "explicitly or implicitly" that the Elko Sheriff's investigation showed the parking brake to be in the released position. What's more, Hagen warned, if Germane strayed from the prohibition one more time, if he mentioned "evidence" that the brake pedal had not been depressed, Hagen would not only strike such statements but also take things further, a giant step further. Hagen would tell the jury "that no such evidence exists." Ford didn't want that. And just to make doubly sure it wouldn't happen again, the judge also struck the Fosmo photograph from the record.

Specter resumed his quizzing of Germane. He didn't have much left and he didn't want to offer Germane another opportunity to stray. So he kept it short and tried to keep Germane's responses controlled and focused. He asked why Germane had not included spontaneous disengagement when considering various scenarios for the accident.

Q: When an accident reconstructionist does their job, they're supposed to reconstruct the accident. Right?

A: That's the objective. Correct.

Q: And an accident can occur for many different reasons. Right?

A: That's correct.

Q: You have cited some of the reasons the accident may have occurred. Right?

A: Correct, what I think is most probable.

Q: Excuse me, that question called for a yes or no answer. Is that correct?

A: Sometimes I can't answer yes or no.

Q: Sometimes you may not be able to, sir, but that question called for a yes or no answer. Correct?

A: Okay.

Q: You did not evaluate the question of whether there was a product defect. Right?

A: Correct.

Q: And therefore you did not evaluate the question as to whether a product defect caused the accident. Correct?

A: I'm not sure I can answer that yes or no.

Q: Did you examine the parking brakes themselves?

A: No.

Alfred Darold

Alfred Darold, a thirty-five-year Ford employee, had been chairman of the company's Critical Product Problem Review Group, or CPPRG. He testified that his group, for which Rakowicz had written his white paper, was not—repeat, *not*—a recall committee nor did it have authority to issue a recall. But he acknowledged the group could refer matters to a recall committee. It seemed like a case of semantics. The CPPRG was the first major step to a recall.

Darold also testified that no spontaneous disengagement had taken place, merely skip-through on apply, no safety issue, only "an annoyance" to drivers. The recall, he said, came only because NHTSA had expressed concern and was threatening to request that Ford recall the trucks.

Darold was not supposed to have been Ford's last witness. But Germane's testimony had not gone exactly as planned. He had not turned out to be quite the star witness the defense had hoped. Now Pinto wanted to close the trial with Darold giving Ford's explanation of why those recall notices were sent out so late. Ford had told NHTSA in August 1994 that it would send recall notices and the first letters did not go out until November. Jimmie White didn't get the recall notice until March 1995, five months after his son's death. Pinto felt a need to diminish the impact of that testimony. He wanted Darold to talk about the "bureaucratic" delays that had made it take that long. There was nothing insidious about it, just the normal time involved in notifying such a large customer base.

"There are 890,000 letters that have to be sent out, 890,000 wedges that have to be provided to the field to dealerships . . . across the country to be able to implement the recall," Darold said. Ford's policy was not to issue a recall until its dealerships had at least 50 percent of the parts needed for a repair. "Needless to say, you can't manufacture a million or a half million of anything overnight. So that takes time." Writing and sending letters also took time. Ford had contracted an outside firm to research vehicle registrations to get the addresses of people who owned the trucks. Another firm was hired to get the letters and stuff them into envelopes. It all "takes time," said Darold.

Specter understood that things didn't happen overnight. But what if Ford had begun the process earlier? He noted the date of Tim Rakowicz's white paper and recommendation for a recall.

> Q: If the decision to make the recall had been made on February 22, 1993, how long would it take to effectuate a recall?

Darold didn't give an answer. He refused to. But Specter's point had been made. Had the company acted sooner, the recall notice, even if it had taken five months, could have reached Elko, Nevada, well before October 9, 1994, the date that Walter White died. Ford had delayed. Ford did not want to admit to a safety problem with its brakes, still wouldn't admit it. Had Ford had its way, it might *never* have issued a recall. Specter had evidence of this. He would use this witness to play his last ace. Darold, who had gotten off the witness stand to point at charts for Pinto, remained standing for questioning now by Specter. He looked awkward and exposed.

Q: You only did it [recall] because NHTSA made you do it, right?

A: We did it because NHTSA was interested in having it done, yes, and we accommodated NHTSA.

Q: Right. And if there had been no NHTSA you wouldn't have done it, right?

A: Based on our understanding of the facts of the brake and the design, the spontaneous disengagement does not occur and the only . . .

Q: Excuse me, Mr. Darold. Excuse me, Your Honor. I think the question called for a yes or no answer. The question again, Mr. Darold, was if there were no NHTSA you wouldn't have done it. Right?

A: If there were no NHTSA . . . we probably would not have done the recall.

Q: And the proof . . . that you wouldn't have done the recall is that you never recalled the vehicles for the people of Mexico, right?

A: I'm not aware that there are vehicles in Mexico to be recalled.

Q: You don't sell these trucks in Mexico?

A: I know trucks were sold in the United States and in Canada. I know trucks were sold in other areas. I am not aware that trucks were sold in Mexico.

Q: Are you aware of the document we went over with Mr. Rakowicz in this case where it said . . . that the vehicle population in Mexico was not included? Are you aware of that document?

A: I don't remember that.

Q: You recalled the vehicles in the United States because of NHTSA and you recalled the vehicles in Canada because of Transport Canada, but you didn't recall the vehicles in Mexico because they don't have the equivalent of NHTSA or Transport Canada in Mexico. Right?

A: I don't know that that's true or not.

But it seemed obvious that it was. There had to be *some* Ford trucks in Mexico and other countries. In fact, Ford started making the F-Series around the time the North American Free Trade Agreement took effect, and its overall sales to Mexico soared from fewer than 2,000 in 1992 to more than 30,000 in 1993. And most people knew, probably better in Nevada than in other parts of the country, that plenty of used vehicles from the Unites States ended up south of the border. Plenty of 1992 and 1993 F-Series trucks were being driven around—or being parked on slopes—all over Mexico right now.

Specter didn't tell the jury all this. He didn't have to. It was just common sense that some trucks wound up in Mexico, where Ford had handled the brake problem not with a recall but with silence.

It was also common sense, jurors had to know, that Ford could have warned almost a million owners sooner than the several months it took to produce a letter, find the addresses, and get the letters in the mail. Specter posed the question to Darold, who by now had become hostile, saying he didn't understand questions and trying to avoid giving direct answers. And though Specter prided himself on always being polite, his patience had worn paper-thin.

Q: And you wouldn't have to use the method of sending out a letter if you didn't want to, right? You could use other methods to supplement that as well if you wanted to, right?

A: I don't understand what you mean.

Q: Well, have you ever heard of something called television?

A: Sure.

Q: You could make a ten-second or a thirty-second television advertisement and purchase time and make a broadcast for the people of, just for example, Elko, Nevada . . . "Bring in your Ford vehicles." Right?

A: There are certain regulations that are imposed on [our industry] by NHTSA and NHTSA requires that we do what we did.

Q: NHTSA requires that you send a letter but NHTSA does not require that you limit your method of communication to mail only. Right?

A: That's true.

Q: Right. You could use television, correct?
A: I suppose that's possible.
Q: You could use radio, right?
A: I suppose that's possible.
Q: You could take out an ad in the newspaper, right?
A: Yes, that would be possible.

Ford could have done more. Lots more. The company had delayed not only the recall but also compliance with earlier government requests for information about the parking brake problem. NHTSA had sought documents by an October 29, 1993, deadline, then gave Ford an extension to December 22. It didn't receive the data until the following February.

Q: So the whole date, the reason the recall . . . was backed up all the way to August [was] in part because NHTSA wasn't able to make a demand on you to recall before then because you hadn't gotten information to them, right?
A: That's possible.
SPECTER: Nothing further.

Pinto didn't want the trial to end that way. Not with Specter forcing a damaging admission from Ford's last witness. Pinto would have the last word, but he didn't exactly sprint across the finish line.

PINTO: Do you know who the suppliers of the wedges were?
DAROLD: I don't recall.
PINTO: Okay. If you don't recall, we can't ask you to tell us. Thank you.

Hagen looked up, seeming surprised. Was that it?
"Please call your next witness," he said to Pinto.
"We have no more witnesses, Your Honor."

CHAPTER 12

Closings

CLOSING ARGUMENTS WERE IMPORTANT. Specter's speech could determine the difference between a victory that would send a potent signal to corporate America and a defeat that meant a three-year-old boy had died in vain.

He had to do two things. One was to convince the six jurors that the bulk of the blame for the accident rested on Ford's shoulders. He also had to convince them that Ford had acted "with oppression or malice," the threshold for punitive damages.

Such damages, Specter was well aware, were the weapons for holding companies accountable, the only tool to help ensure good corporate citizenship. The car companies in particular had been successful over the years in blocking legislation to hold corporate executives criminally liable when products they knew to be defective resulted in injuries or death. New bills kept getting introduced—including one by Senator Arlen Specter in 2000, which never came to a vote—and they kept failing. In fact, Shanin Specter knew of only one case from years ago in which a prosecutor forced a criminal case against a company for a personal injury or death. The company was Ford.

An Indiana prosecutor got a grand jury to return criminal indictments of reckless homicide against the carmaker's deadly Pintos. Ford had announced in June 1978 that it would recall 1.5 million Pintos with faulty fuel systems but didn't actually start sending the notices to car owners until two months later—and twelve days after an accident resulted in a fire that incinerated three teenage girls inside a Pinto. At trial, Ford won acquittal, a verdict aided by a judge's ruling that the prosecutor could not introduce a memo circulated among Ford executives that suggested the company would rather take its chances with lawsuits than spend $11 per car to fix the Pinto's faulty gas tanks.

The Whites' case, Specter felt, was similar, but the cost of the plastic wedge needed to fix the F-Series parking brake would have been 16¢, not $11. A hell of a low price to place on human life. He knew there was only one way to make Ford pay for its decision. And pay it should. The company hadn't merely screwed up; it had played dumb, then lied. It had acted with bad intent. Specter had to convince the jury of that. He set the stage early in his closing speech.

> You are going to have the opportunity to hold the Ford Motor Co. accountable for their conduct. That is an awesome and vitally important responsibility.

Specter was not brief in his closing. He began where the problem began, with the Aerostar, which Ford in one document had referred to as a "headache." Ford knew of the problem very early on, Specter said, "So wouldn't a reasonable person make sure that the problem was solved?"

Yet it wasn't. That was clear in the ensuing years, when reports of rollaways started to stream into Ford. "Vehicles," Specter told the jury, "just don't roll away."

> Again, Ford did nothing even after its engineer in charge of the product, young Tim Rakowicz, wrote a white paper mentioning "spontaneous disengagement," after the phenomenon was demonstrated using the "pin test," after Rakowicz recommended a recall.
>
> Now, why doesn't Ford want to recall the product? I think the answers are perfectly obvious, but let's discuss them if we could. The first thing they don't want to do is they don't want to pay for the cost of recalling the product because that's an expensive proposition.
>
> Number two, they don't want to delete the self-adjust feature of the parking brake because if you do that, then when the vehicle is under warranty and you bring it back in you actually have to go to the trouble of having the fellow in the dealership check that brake mechanism and do it himself because it won't self-adjust, and that's going to cost whatever that's going to cost because once you delete the self-adjust function now it's something else that's got to be done as far as warranty.
>
> Number three, why else? We don't want to tell people in this country our vehicles roll away. Now, why don't we want to tell people our vehicles roll away? Now here again the answers are perfectly obvious, but let's just highlight them for a moment. The first thing is that it's mighty embarrassing to tell people that our vehicles roll away.

What an ethical and reasonable and responsible seller and man-ufacturer would do . . . when you make a mistake and have a prob-lem, you act. And you own up. And you say your vehicles are rolling away. We're recalling the product. And maybe somebody says, "Look at Ford. Their vehicles roll away." But maybe lives are saved because the company did the responsible thing and brought the vehicles back.

Instead, Ford ignored, delayed, covered up. It denied that the prob-lem existed, claiming it could not recreate spontaneous disengagement in tests, even though it had done so using a metal pin to simulate actual conditions. Still, argued Specter, a test wasn't necessary to realize there was a problem.

Now, do we have to be able to create snow to know that it happens? Of course not. Do we have to be able to duplicate spontaneous dis-engagement to know that it happens? No. Isn't it enough that vehi-cles are rolling away and rolling away?

The fact that Ford did not recall trucks with automatic transmissions was proof that Ford knew of the dangers, knew the brakes could release and that trucks left in neutral or fourth gear could roll away. But Ford lied, Specter told the jury. Even when it finally issued a recall, the com-pany pretended the problem was skip-through on apply, not self-release of the brake. And in doing so, Ford sought to purge records, to sani-tize opinions. It held meetings, namely among members of its product review group, in which no minutes were kept. Specter compared these actions to another, sinister group that held tightly to a vow of silence. He did not mention the Mafia by name, but the parallel was clear.

Now the Whites do not accuse the Ford Motor Co. of engaging in organized criminal activity. However, can you think of any other business activity that would not keep records of something as im-portant as what occurs in the Critical Product Problem Review Group? Any entity that would not keep records of something as important as that within their own environment aside from an organized criminal activity? That's the only entity that wouldn't keep careful records . . . because those records would provide the truth, and we can't let a jury know the truth, so we're not going to keep records.

Ford had come into court with experts and excuses. It was asking the jury to believe not the written documents but what it had said in court now, years later. Specter, borrowing a line from Winston Churchill, said Ford surrounded the truth with "lies, lies, lies. A bodyguard of lies." He painted a picture of Ford's offices that he felt the jury would remember.

> Those dark rooms with no windows and no records, but only se-
> crets, secrets, keeping the truth from the American public, those
> secrets preserved by the bodyguard of lies . . .

Ford knew not only about the problem but also about a relatively inexpensive solution. It knew about the plastic wedge Orscheln had developed. It knew that vehicles that had rolled away no longer did so after the wedge was installed. Yet it still put off a recall.

> And remember Mr. Rakowicz told you, "Yes, we were considering
> telling people about spontaneous disengagement in about July and
> September of 1994." He had his deposition taken [in the Bobb case]
> the month before Walter White was killed. And he said, "We've
> been thinking about it for the last two months." If they had only
> done it. If they had only done it, we wouldn't be here. Walter White
> would be getting ready to go into the second grade. He wouldn't be
> in the cemetery.
> It's sickening. They didn't do it. They didn't care. Because they
> figured they could get away with it.

It was the jury's job, Specter solemnly told the six people in the jury box, to make sure Ford didn't get away with it.

> Only you, only you stand between their conscious disregard for the
> safety of everybody in this country, including Walter White, and
> getting away with it.
> Only you.

Joe Pinto rose and approached the jury box slowly. "I have a pain in my stomach over cases like this. This is no fun," he told the jury, expressing his regrets to the Whites "for the terrible tragedy they went through, and I think for the people that I work with at Ford Motor Co., who feel the same way."

Pinto had a tough job in front of him. Did the people at Ford really feel as badly as the parents of Walter White?

Specter had minimized the effectiveness of Ford's experts, belittled them, really. None of the Ford or Orscheln witnesses seemed to pack the punch of the testimony Specter had elicited from Tim Rakowicz, which was backed up by his memos and his white paper. Pinto didn't have many cards to play. He began by appealing to the jury's sympathy, not for Ford but for himself.

> This is a tough case. I've been at this business for a long time, and as I look around I'm probably the oldest guy participating in this case.

"Second oldest," chimed in Judge Hagen, injecting a bit of humor into what Pinto had intended to be a dramatic moment.

Pinto pressed on. He thanked the jury for paying attention and working hard. "Because I'm worn out," he said. "Coming in and working 8:30 to 5:00 sounds like an ordinary day, but our job didn't end at 5:00 and I'm wondering how . . . I can hardly talk and I hope I'm able to speak loud enough through all this." He told the jury a few moments later, after dropping his notes onto the floor, "I'm getting too old for this business."

Then Pinto admitted what he had to.

> I think you heard me say early in the case this parking brake involved a problem, and I'm not going to take that back.

But he denied that spontaneous disengagement had occurred in Ford's brakes or that the product resulted in the death of Walter White. He played down the incidents of rollaways, noting that only 200 cases were reported out of 884,400 vehicles. "And there's lots of reasons why cars roll away," he said.

Pinto denied that Ford had lied or kept secrets. If Ford had "purged" documents, as Tim Rakowicz's boss had written on a memo, how did the plaintiffs obtain them? "Ford turned it over in discovery," Pinto asserted. Ford turned over documents even though some of them seemed incriminating, he said, though perhaps stressing that fact a bit too much.

> This collection of liars, people who won't keep their records because they don't want them to show up here in court. Well, I've never seen a worse collection of records in my life that have been

produced in this case that would seem to incriminate somebody because people put their thoughts down on paper. And I've heard of cases where they destroy records, but you got them, you saw them because Ford Motor Co. produced them.

Pinto barely mentioned Tim Rakowicz's testimony. Rakowicz, he said, was a "rookie" who at first thought the brakes had spontaneously disengaged. "Well, later he changed his mind," Pinto said. "People change their minds."

Pinto spent considerable time, by contrast, on the deposition testimony of Johnson Hooks. It had been a seemingly minor part of the case, though Pinto termed it "the plaintiffs' linchpin in its case."

> This whole case rests on the reliability of the testimony that was given in the deposition by Johnson Hooks. I don't know why Johnson Hooks . . . didn't come into this courtroom and testify. I mean, he's a family member. We can't subpoena him, he's out of the state, but he was actually the ward of Mrs. White until he was eighteen years old. Don't you think maybe it would have been good if we had Johnson Hooks here to evaluate him, to question him in front of you, and to hear what he had to say?

Pinto hinted that perhaps Hooks' testimony that the brake had been applied—that he was only able to press it down another inch after moving the truck from the neighbor's property—had been fabricated. Pinto didn't actually make the accusation.

He mentioned Jimmie White receiving the recall notice from Ford.

> I don't blame him for being irate when he saw that letter. And it's human nature to think, "Oh, Walter didn't do that. It was Ford's brake problem." What would you expect him to do? So he gets a hold of Johnson and he talks to Johnson, tells us what Johnson told him, remember that?

Hooks, said Pinto, had testified that he had not ridden in Jimmie's truck the day of the accident. But Jimmie testified that he had, that both of them had gone into town to pick up the pellet stove.

> Johnson Hooks didn't remember he was in the truck on the day of the accident. . . . Now he remembered a year later that he stepped

on the pedal and it only went down an inch . . . How could he possibly, I ask you, remember what he did with the truck after the traumatic event that took place when he couldn't even remember that he had gone to town that day with Jimmie White and picked up that pellet stove? How could he remember that he didn't release the parking brake?

And you know something, I've been in a lot of cases and I don't think he, I can't say he's lying or anybody is lying here. But people, people think things are true and they're sometimes assisted by other factors that occur, like an explanation that we got a recall letter, and we're trying to figure out if something is wrong with the brake and, let's remember, if you can, what happened that night. All I can say is that Johnson Hooks is not a reliable witness for a number of reasons that we see here.

Pinto blamed others for the brake problem and for Walter's death.

He blamed Orscheln. "In the first place," he told the jury, "it wasn't Ford's brake. They didn't manufacture it, but they sure tried to get it fixed." Once a problem was detected, he said, Orscheln assured Ford it had been corrected.

In the middle of 1990, Orscheln wrote to Ford, and this is during the development period for the F-Series, and Orscheln told Ford, "The issue is closed. We solved the problem."

Pinto also blamed the Whites. Jimmie, the evidence suggested, had left a door of the truck open, allowing Walter to climb in. The small child could not have opened the door himself.

And I have eight little grandchildren running around and I very rarely lock the doors of my cars, but I close them because I don't want my kids or my grandchildren getting in my cars. . . . We do know, and nobody disputes, that somehow that night Walter did get in the car, probably through an open door, and that Walter moved the gearshift lever. Now, we know that's not Ford's fault.

Pinto took care not to be callous toward Jimmie and Ginny White. He almost apologized for putting the blame on them. "This is a very emotional case," he told the jury, "but I've got to represent my client, even, even this big monster company deserves to have legal representation."

You'll remember when we started this case, you all told this trial judge here that you could be fair to this faceless, big corporation, just as you could to Jimmie White and his wife. And that's what we're going to ask you to do."

BECAUSE THE BURDEN of proof in civil cases lay with the plaintiff, Specter was permitted a final rebuttal before the jury left the courtroom to deliberate a verdict. But his remarks were limited to comments Pinto had made in his closing. It had to be purely ad lib.

He began by saying he did not call any individual, witness or attorney, a liar. Juries didn't like such personal accusations, Specter knew. They could hold it against a plaintiff.

> But you have not gotten the truth from them in this courtroom. That is the fact. And the fact is that the truth is in those documents, and they run from those documents.

Believe the documents, he was saying. Believe the records culled from the very files of Ford and Orscheln. Believe what you see in black and white. And, speaking of those documents . . . Specter then seized on Pinto's statement in his closing speech.

> Now, Mr. Pinto says he's never seen such a bunch of incriminating documents in his entire life. And I appreciate his candor. And he is right. Neither have I.

Specter also set the record straight about Ford's voluntarily turning over those documents. It was not, he told the jurors, a matter of corporate goodwill.

> And let me tell you about why they turned over the documents. If you have a document and it's discoverable in a case and you don't turn it over, it's obstruction of justice and you go to jail. Now, nobody at the Ford Motor Co. apparently is willing to go to jail over this issue. They would rather pay money. And, frankly, money is in a lot of regards very inadequate. Maybe somebody ought to go to jail. But that's not why we're here. This is a civil case. This is not a criminal case. And they didn't destroy the documents because nobody is willing to go to jail over the issue. Hooray for Ford Motor Co.!

Specter poked a hole in Pinto's assertion that only some 200 vehicles had been affected out of 884,400.

> How many people were there all across America whose vehicles rolled away who thought they must be stupid? Who never thought there was a problem with the parking brake because they trusted the Ford Motor Co., and therefore they never called Ford or NHTSA and said, "My vehicle rolled away." Probably quite a few. He doesn't count those in his 200 cases because they were never reported. They never called in. And if these people continued to have their way . . . then it's still going to be a secret because their recall letter said, "We're doing this for skip-through on apply, not for spontaneous disengagement." So therefore nobody knows it and it continues to happen.
>
> So that 200 could just as well be 2,000 or 20,000. We just can't know because they haven't given the necessary information to the American public so that people would then respond accordingly.

About Johnson Hooks not remembering he had driven to town with Jimmie White on the day of the accident, Specter had a ready reply.

> So what?
>
> Mr. Pinto told you that lawyers can always find inconsistencies, and he's a fine lawyer.
>
> PINTO: Thanks.
>
> SPECTER: You're welcome.
>
> And so he can find an inconsistency between what somebody said here, somebody said there. Is that an inconsistency on a critical issue? It seems to me that it is not. Johnson Hooks, they took two shots at him. They took two depositions. They rake him over the coals for umpteen hours; that's the best they can come up with.

About Tim Rakowicz changing his mind that spontaneous disengagement occurred in the parking brake and that tests confirmed it, Specter also had something to say.

> Mr. Pinto sticks to the claim that no one has concluded there was spontaneous disengagement. Where have we been? What about NHTSA? Didn't they conclude that? Didn't Tim Rakowicz conclude that? Mr. Pinto says he changed his mind. Where is the docu-

ment in his hand to prove that he changed his mind? I know when he changed his mind—when he got here.

Then Specter brought something up that Pinto had said at the beginning of his speech. It was something personal Pinto had shared with the jury, the pain he had felt over this case.

Some people say that you shouldn't let the jury know that you like your opponent because maybe the jury doesn't like the opposing lawyer, so why tell them that you like him? But I like Mr. Pinto. We come from the same place. He's my friend. And he's done the best he can. As have I.

This is a harder case [for Ford] than it is for Mr. and Mrs. White. But there's a reason for that. There's a reason, there's a reason. They're wrong. They deserve to lose. Not Mr. Pinto necessarily, but his client.

Mr. Pinto tells you that he's sick to his stomach. You know why Mr. Pinto is sick to his stomach? I think you do.

I ask you to return a verdict for the Whites.

CHAPTER 13

A Big Bet

Now the waiting began.

Specter and Pete Durney walked across Stewart Street to Durney's office. They knew it could be a long time before the jury returned with a verdict. The verdict sheet was long and complex. It contained fifteen separate questions with a serpentine list of instructions: "If you answered 'yes' to Question 2, answer the next question. . . . If you answered 'no' to Question 3, do not answer Question 4. . . ."

First the jury had to agree on whether the parking brake system was faulty. Question 1 read: "Was the product in question defective in design?" It was a fairly straightforward question. Specter didn't see any way the jury could answer "no." Clearly, he believed, the brakes were defective.

But things got a little trickier after that. Question 2 read: "Was this defect a proximate cause of the death of Walter White?"

The verdict sheet also asked whether the product was "defective for Ford's failure to warn." Should Ford have warned the public—and specifically Stewart Brothers Drilling, Jimmie White's employer—sooner about a problem with its brakes? And did that failure result in Walter's death?

Then the jury had to look at the role of Walter's parents. Had they been negligent? If so, did that contribute to their son's death, and how much? What percentage of the blame, if the jury found there was blame, went to Ford and how much to the Whites?

If Ford was at fault, was it liable to pay damages to the Whites? And how much?

Finally, was Ford liable for punitive damages? This was the hardest part of a case to prove. It was difficult enough to prove a company's liability, never mind to prove to a jury that it had acted "outrageously" and with malice.

Specter was used to waiting for verdicts, including those on election nights when he had worked on his father's campaigns. He was experienced enough to believe that he could speculate on a positive outcome. He was also experienced enough to know that you never knew.

Both Specter and Durney had a lot of catching up to do on other business, other cases. Specter had also not seen his family in nearly three weeks. He missed his kids and his wife. When he called home, Tracey gave her husband something he didn't expect—more legal work. Her OB/GYN had been sued for malpractice. Could Shanin help?

This was hardly Specter's bailiwick. Usually he made money *suing* doctors, not helping them out. He got on the phone and spoke to the doctor's lawyers and his insurance carrier's lawyers. Then he called the plaintiff's lawyers. Then the doctor's lawyers. After more of this back-and-forth Specter was able to broker a settlement, a payment that was agreeable to both sides. The doctor's insurance would pay. Specter had negotiated the deal. By phone. From Reno. For free. All in a day's work.

Meanwhile, day one of deliberations by the jury came and went with no verdict.

DAY TWO FOUND Specter and Durney again waiting across the street in the creaky old house owned by Durney & Brennan. Specter was busy working the phones, dealing with associates who were handling other cases. One call was not about other cases.

"Hello, Shanin," said Joe Pinto.

"Joe. How are you?"

"Good, good. Listen, I want to communicate an offer to you." Pinto said it with little confidence, in a voice that told Specter it was an offer he could and would refuse.

"Go ahead."

"Two and a half million."

"Okay. I'll communicate it to my client."

It was a lowball offer for a case that had gone so far—and so well, in Specter's estimation, for the plaintiffs. But he knew not to expect much from Ford. A few months earlier, just after Specter had taken the case, Ford and Orscheln had asked that he and Durney travel to San Francisco for a mediation session. Orscheln had offered peanuts, a few hundred thousand dollars. Ford had offered nothing. The session was no more than another strategy to show the companies were willing to hang tough while wasting Specter's and Durney's time and money.

Now, offering $2.5 million was Ford's way of trying to opt out of the case on the cheap. Specter had seen such tactics before and would see them again. Wait until a moment in which the plaintiff—usually some poor soul who needed cash to pay his bills—was biting his nails, waiting for the jury, and then make a lowball offer. Get him on the edge of his seat and dangle some money in front of his eyes. Often the plaintiff bit.

Specter hoped Jimmie would say no to Ford's offer. But Jimmie was the client, the boss. What Jimmie said would go. But Jimmie had advantages over other unfortunates. For one, he already had Orscheln's money. Also—and it was hard to consider this as an advantage—the Whites did not have an injured child to care for. Their son had no medical expenses. Buddy Boy was dead. The Whites might be tempted to take Ford's offer, Specter knew, but he hoped they wouldn't.

Specter wasn't close to guessing Jimmie's thoughts. He and Ginny wanted to tell Ford to shove its offer. But they had felt bound by another consideration. They were concerned about the effect of their decision on Pete Durney and Shanin Specter.

"We don't want to settle with Ford. We're not in it for the money," Jimmie told his lawyers. "But we know how hard you fellas have worked on this case, how much you put into it. So if you want to take the settlement, we'll abide by that decision."

Specter was not a terribly expressive or emotional man but at that moment he could have kissed Jimmie White. He wanted to grab that tough little man and wrap his arms around him. Instead he smiled.

"I didn't come all this way to settle, Jimmie," said Specter, his mind dredging up thoughts of Derick Bobb. "I came here to get a verdict."

The jury deliberated all of the second day without one, though. As Specter walked through Harrah's to his hotel room later that day, he did something he had never done in Reno. He took a seat at a blackjack table. Specter, wearing a navy suit, starched shirt, and red tie still pulled tight to his throat, stood out amid the few other players, dressed in jeans and baseball caps. He was alone at the table, just him and the dealer, an attractive young woman who began shuffling several decks for the evening's first customers. She eyed Specter with curiosity. Reno was a casual sort of place. He was not a casual-looking guy.

"What's someone like you doing playing at a $5 table?" she asked as Specter moved a red chip onto the green felt.

"Lady," he said, "I made the biggest bet of the day in Reno. I just made a $2.5 million bet."

CHAPTER 14

Deliberations

THE DELIBERATIONS IN *White v. Ford* were not entirely affable. In the private confines of the jury room, several jurors raised their voices. Some argued. A few had their feelings hurt. Having so much to discuss, so much to decide, was arduous, emotional work. The verdict sheet was complicated. And in the federal court system, the verdict had to be unanimous. Yet in the end the six jurors not only would agree on a verdict but would also say that a decision had never been in doubt, that they all had really known, had known in their guts, what the outcome would be the minute they left the courtroom.

One day of deliberations would pass. Then another.

The waiting was difficult. Soon, the jury had to render its judgment. Specter would know whether his gamble—and the years of work—would pay off or whether the jury would absolve Ford of any responsibility in the death of Walter White. Specter didn't enjoy the waiting or the feeling of being powerless, with nothing left in his arsenal or intelligence to push the jury toward what he felt was a just decision. But in a way, these hours and days provided a certain solace, a chance to exhale with the knowledge that he had done everything he could.

During one of those quiet hours, Specter sat in the empty courtroom, put his head back, closed his eyes, and let his mind drift. He thought back to his earliest days as a lawyer, back to The Beasley Firm and his small office there. He remembered his first case as a lawyer, his first time in a court. A chuckle escaped his lips. He could laugh now.

THE CASE HAD BEEN one of eighty-five that Specter had found dumped on his desk when he arrived for his first day of work on August 26, 1984, at The Beasley Firm. Specter remembered entering the austere lobby of the Girard Building on South 12th Street, a tired-looking thirteen-story edifice located a few blocks from the courtrooms of City Hall. He rode the elevator to the fifth floor and walked along a wooden parquet floor to his new office, a cramped and dim space that looked out onto an alley, the sun's rays blocked by the larger surrounding buildings and an adjacent air shaft. The office afforded sunlight only about one hour of the day when everything aligned perfectly—when there was a cloudless sky, when it was around noon, and when it was summer. Only then did Specter, who loved the sun, have a sliver of natural light steal into his spartan quarters.

He had all these cases waiting for him and he wasn't even a lawyer yet, not officially. He still needed to find out whether he had passed the bar exam and then be sworn in as a member of the bar. But Specter wasn't about to complain. Not to the legendary James E. Beasley, a freewheeling personal injury lawyer who was fond of cowboy boots and flying vintage airplanes and who had won the first million-dollar personal injury verdict in Philadelphia, with many more to follow. Like newly minted doctors doing their hospital residencies, the young lawyers who worked for Beasley were expected to toil long and hard, to handle a heavy workload, and to jump into the fray without hesitation. Standing 5-foot-9, Beasley was a powerfully built man who wore a trimmed moustache and a broad bravado. He was a no-nonsense, demanding boss who rewarded lawyers who toed the line, booted those who didn't.

One case that Specter inherited already had a trial date and nearly three boxes stuffed with medical records, depositions, and other documents. The case of Adelaide Lusky was not a great case, not even a good one. None of the other lawyers knew exactly why Beasley took the cases he did, nor did they ask. They just did the best they could to win them.

By the time Adelaide Lusky was sixty-one years old, she had been experiencing difficulty swallowing for a few years and had been treated by her family doctor. When nothing seemed to help, he sent her to a specialist who, following a series of X-rays and a GI series, decided to perform an esophagoscopy, the placing of a scope down Lusky's throat to try to determine the cause of her dysphagia. But the apparatus tore a microscopic hole in Lusky's esophagus. What ensued were two operations to try to fix the damage. As a result, Lusky suffered what she said was awful pain over the course of several weeks. "I was in such agony—the pain was excruciating—I felt like dying," Lusky said in deposition testimony. She had bouts where she vomited and coughed up blood. She also had a scar running from behind her ear to near her collarbone and a loss of sensation near her chin. But the bottom line was that she had emerged from her ordeal without any major permanent disability. She had healed and by and large was now fine except for the scar. She also claimed her problem with swallowing had, after an initial improvement, returned.

(And also that, as her son Ronald testified, "She can't yell the way she could before.")

Otherwise, Lusky was basically okay. In fact, in a statement of facts the defense presented one of her doctors reported that following the operations, on January 6, 1981, "she was healed and she and her husband were taking a trip to Florida."

So even if Specter could convince a jury that the specialist, Louis T. Broad, M.D., had been negligent—and the defense could argue that such an injury was part of the presumed risk of the original procedure, the esophagoscopy—it was going to be difficult to convince its members that a hefty award was warranted. No one should have been scarred or forced to experience unnecessary pain, but could Specter seriously make a convincing argument for substantial damages?

Some six weeks after arriving at Beasley, Specter was informed that he had passed his exam and he was sworn in as a member of the Pennsylvania Bar the same day. The next month the Lusky case was set for trial. An attempt to settle the case failed. Specter had asked for $100,000 and Dr. Broad's attorney countered with something lower—zero. So a jury was picked and a trial commenced.

Specter's argument on Lusky's behalf was straightforward. He told the jury that such a perforation of the esophagus was not, contrary to the defense claim, routine or expected. He also contended that she had not been properly advised of certain aspects and risks of the esophagoscopy, even though she had signed consent forms. And that her damages, though perhaps not debilitating, included "scarring, sensory impairment on one side of the face, [and] deepening of the voice."

The first closing speech of Specter's legal career comprised seven pages of handwritten notes on a yellow legal pad. It left nothing to chance, not even his reminder to recognize the judge and jury:

> Please the Court
> Thank the jury

Specter, in a theme he would repeat many times during his career, asked the jury to use "common sense" to decide the case. On the issue of causation, he said, there was no dispute. Dr. Broad perforated his client's esophagus, which caused an abscess. And, he said, Lusky received poor quality care "from day one," starting when she entered Thomas Jefferson Hospital for the procedure with her X-rays under her arm, and nothing else. "How hard would it have been for Dr. Broad to pick up the phone and order her records?" asked Specter. "What was the hurry?"

The method of insertion of the scope, colloquially termed the "blind method," was also not a preferred method for a patient such as Lusky, who had a problem with swallowing. Finally, Specter argued, the patient was not adequately informed of the risks of the procedure, including the possibility of an abscess or change of voice. Sure, he said, Lusky had been shown a form but, "There's a big difference between having a form shoved in front of you and being told that when they do stick a tube down your throat, he might perforate your esophagus."

For damages, Specter asked the jury to consider, in addition to medical costs, past and present pain and suffering. And also future pain and suffering, including the fact that this experience had caused Lusky to fear a further procedure that might correct her still-existing problem with swallowing. He also asked for compensation for disfigurement, namely, the scar on Lusky's neck and her deepened voice. He concluded:

> Ladies and gentlemen, this is the Luskys' day in court. This is their one chance to be compensated for what has happened to them. We are confident that after you have reviewed the evidence and the testimony in light of your common sense you will find for the Luskys and return a substantial verdict on their behalf.

The defense followed with its argument that Dr. Broad had done nothing wrong. A perforated esophagus was part of the risk of the procedure. Sometimes it happened. Doctors, no matter how careful, were not infallible. They were not God and could not be held to impossible standards. And Lusky knew this. The proof was that she had signed a consent form that detailed the risks. Besides this, Lusky was essentially fine now. Yes, she had a scar on her neck and perhaps her voice was slightly different, but she was hardly an invalid. A doctor had reported that despite her continued complaints even her dysphagia had been cured.

After the defense attorney's closing speech there was silence in the Philadelphia Common Pleas courtroom of Judge Louis G. Hill. After a few seconds the judge cast a quizzical look at Specter.

"Mr. Specter?"

"Yes, Your Honor?"

"Your rebuttal?"

Specter hadn't prepared a rebuttal. And for good reason. He didn't know he was allowed one. He'd been a lawyer, a real lawyer, for only a matter of weeks. He was green and now slightly red-faced. This was his first trial, his first closing argument. And his first chance at a rebuttal, the important last word either side would have in the case.

Specter, flummoxed, collected himself and stood briefly. "Your Honor," he managed, "I think everything's been said that should be said."

That was it. The five-day trial was over except for the judge's charge to the jury. And the verdict, which the jury reached after only two hours of deliberations.

> QUESTION 1: Was Defendant Louis T. Broad negligent?
> JURY: No.
> QUESTION 2: Did Defendant Louis T. Broad fail to obtain from Mrs. Lusky an informed consent?
> JURY: No.

Specter had recorded his first verdict and his official won-loss record in a court of law stood at 0–1.

But he wouldn't accept the defeat, not easily. Specter filed a motion for a new trial. Several aspects of the judge's charge to the jury had bothered him. But he focused largely on one, the judge's instruction on how the jury should decide whether Lusky had been properly informed of the procedure's risks. Judge Hill had said that to find Dr. Broad negligent, the jury needed to determine that he had failed to pass on information about the risks of the procedure in such a way that had the patient known of those risks, she would have decided against having the procedure. Basically, with this instruction, even if the doctor had failed to inform his patient, it was all right as long as the risks were not so bad as to make her back out.

Evidence suggested that the jury took this instruction to heart. During its deliberations it had asked the judge to repeat that portion of his charge. Specter was nonplussed by it all. He noted in his motion that the closing instruction as to informed consent was stipulated in Pennsylvania law. It was there in black and white, detailing the proper charge for the jury. And the judge had exceeded the bounds of the law.

Judge Hill, it turned out, recognized his own error. He called Specter and admitted it to the young lawyer. But rather than rule on the issue, he suggested Specter go directly to the defense lawyer and negotiate a settlement. Which was just what Specter did. He told opposing counsel that he expected to win his motion for a new trial, that the judge had said as much to him and suggested the two sides talk it out. The doctor's lawyer considered and got back to Specter with an offer of $5,000 to settle the case.

IT WASN'T MUCH. But it was, evidently, more than Specter might expect to win in another trial. And was that really what he wanted? He had already lost the case before a jury once. He informed his client of the offer and also told the Luskys that if they accepted, they would get nothing since it would not even cover the $6,000 in expenses incurred by The Beasley Firm. (It never occurred to Specter to somehow split the settlement and cover only part of the firm's costs.) To say the Luskys were unhappy was an understatement. They instructed their attorney not to accept the settlement and to drop the case. Drop it, and forget the $5000. If they weren't going to get paid, neither were Beasley and his newest attorney.

Specter laughed lightly to himself. How things had changed since that first case. For one thing, his new office at Kline & Specter was on the nineteenth and top floor of a Center City building, complete with skylight and plenty of sunshine. More importantly, Specter had become at ease and confident in a courtroom, even thousands of miles from his home. He even took pains not to seem too polished, generally wearing similar blue suits with red ties to court each day and mindful to leave his cuff links back at the hotel. He didn't want to seem flashy.

And now much more was at stake. Not that Adelaide Lusky's discomfort wasn't important, but this latest case involved the life of a little boy and his parents' lifelong grief. It also involved the potential safety of 884,400 other drivers across the country.

CHAPTER 15

The Verdict

BY 3:15 P.M. ON THE third day of deliberations, the jury announced to the judge that it had finally reached decisions on all fifteen questions. It had a verdict. It was one that would surprise both sides.

> We, the jury in the above-entitled action, find as follows on particular questions of fact:
> QUESTION 1: Was the product in question defective in design?
> ANSWER: Yes.

Specter and Durney exhaled. It was a good start but it was only the start. Of course the product was defective. They assumed they would win the jury over on that question. Now the hard part, finding that the product and Ford's actions caused the death of Walter White and that Ford was liable.

> QUESTION 2: Was this defect a proximate cause of the death of Walter White?
> ANSWER: No.

We've won, thought Pinto. *We've won!*
We've lost, thought Durney, disbelief falling over him like a shroud. *Oh God, we've lost. We worked so hard, had such a good case. How could we have lost?*
Specter, too, felt the sting of defeat, a rare feeling for him. He said nothing, except to himself. *All this, and we've lost.*
Durney, despite his deep tan, looked pallid, almost sickly. Specter remained expressionless, or at least he tried to. The Whites had lost. Still there was the rest of the verdict to be read.

> QUESTION 3: Was the product in question defective for defendant Ford's failure to warn?
> ANSWER: Yes.

Okay. That was good for the plaintiffs. But it was only half of the answer.

> QUESTION 4: Was the defect for failure to warn a proximate cause of the death of Walter White?
> ANSWER: Yes.

Pinto looked stunned. The blood returned to Durney's face. The jury had found a second defect of sorts, something besides the problem with Ford's brakes, something worse—Ford's failure to warn the public, the Whites in particular, about a dangerous defect. And while the jury found that the brake system, though defective, had not been responsible for the death of Walter White, it now determined that Ford's failure to issue a warning had been. In short, it wasn't Ford's actions that had killed the child. It was Ford's silence.

This was a complete turnaround. Defeat had turned to sudden victory. But it still wasn't over. Not nearly.

> QUESTION 5: Was defendant Ford negligent with respect to the product in question?
> ANSWER: Yes.
> QUESTION 6: Was Ford's negligence a proximate cause of the death of Walter White?
> ANSWER: Yes.

Not critical to the Whites' case, but good. They already had one finding that Ford was responsible. This was affirmation.

Specter knew what came next. It could mean another turnaround, could obliterate their victory. Now the jurors would say whether the Whites were also to blame for the accident, for Walter's death. Ford had claimed that the child had not been supervised, that Jimmie had left the truck doors open, that Ginny was looking somewhere else when her son walked out the front door and climbed into that truck.

> QUESTION 7: Were plaintiffs Jimmie and Ginny White contributorily negligent with respect to the accident?
> ANSWER: Yes.
> QUESTION 8: Was Jimmie and Ginny White's contributory negligence a proximate cause of the death of Walter White?
> ANSWER: Yes.

A pained expression came over Ginny's face. She'd been wounded, gored. Jimmie felt a swirl of emotions, none of them good.

This finding by the jury was bad but not entirely unexpected. It was natural the jury would find the Whites partly to blame. But how much? Who was more to blame for the death of Walter White, the Whites or Ford? The jury was about to proclaim a "percentage of negligence" (Question 9). Specter looked intently at the jury forewoman, Luanne Oroszi, as the court clerk announced the decision.

> Jimmie and Ginny White's negligence: 40 percent.
> Defendant's negligence: 60 percent.

In a way, it didn't matter as much as it seemed. Even if the jury had found the Whites more than 50 percent negligent, Ford still would not have won the case because it was about more than just negligence. Ford's failure to warn had sunk the company.

Finding the Whites 40 percent negligent also would not reduce any damages award. Under Nevada law, a punitive award for intentionally—and that was the key word, "intentionally"—improper conduct could not be reduced because of negligence by another party that was unintentional. Just because someone else made a mistake didn't mean Ford's punishment should be lessened.

The jury pressed on.

> QUESTION 10: Is Ford liable to plaintiffs Jimmie and Ginny White for negligent infliction of emotional distress?
> ANSWER: Yes.
> QUESTION 11: Is Ford liable to plaintiffs Jimmie and Ginny White for intentional misrepresentation?
> ANSWER: Yes.

This simply meant that Ford had to pay the Whites.

The next three questions were about money. The jury awarded reimbursement for Walter's funeral and medical expenses, $5,434.57.

For the past suffering of Jimmie White the jurors awarded $350,000. They also had not evidently been convinced by the testimony of Ford's witness, the psychologist who had said that this suffering would abate, all but ending after five years. The jury awarded an additional $800,000 for Jimmie White's future suffering. It awarded the same amounts to Ginny White, for a total of $2.3 million.

It was not a huge award. Not for such a lengthy, emotional trial. Not for a case that took years to develop. The award was in fact less than the settlement Ford had offered just a day earlier. The Whites could have had $2.5 million for the asking.

But the jury wasn't finished.

> QUESTION 15: Do you find by clear and convincing evidence that Ford acted with oppression or malice in the conduct upon which you base your finding of liability for the death of Walter White?

This was the big one. This was the question of punitive damages, generally a far larger award. Should Ford not only have to compensate the Whites for their loss but also be punished? This was always a tougher sell for a jury. Did it believe that Ford acted in an outrageous manner, with malice? Did it believe that Ford lied, concealed the truth? Did it believe that Ford placed the almighty dollar over the well-being of its customers, over the value of the life of a three-year-old boy from Elko, Nevada?

> ANSWER: Yes.

CHAPTER 16

Pennies, Dimes, and Dollars

Now FORD WOULD BE PUNISHED. The only remaining question was how harshly.

Maybe not too harshly, Specter thought. The jury had not been generous with compensatory damages, awarding $2.3 million. It didn't seem likely the jurors would deal a severe blow to Ford in this, the final stage of the trial. It was Specter's job to convince them to do so.

There was one more stage of speeches to go. Specter would start, followed by Pinto, then a plaintiffs' rebuttal. The courtroom was not packed. There was no major media coverage, no throng of reporters or spectators. In fact, fewer people were in court than during the rest of the trial. The expert witnesses had returned to their offices and universities. There were empty chairs where Orscheln's lawyers and employees had sat. Ford's witnesses, its experts and its engineers, were long gone. Not a single Ford executive was on hand to accept the company's punishment. That would be left to the soldiers, its lawyers.

It had all come down to this. Now, almost four years since Walter White had been killed.

THE PROCEEDINGS GOT UNDERWAY at 8:30 a.m. First Pinto had some matters to discuss with Judge Hagen. He asked that Specter be barred in his speech on punitive damages from mentioning Ford's net worth or financial condition as a consideration for the jury.

"Denied," ruled Hagen. He would permit Specter not only to refer to Ford's wealth but also to introduce a balance sheet showing total Ford stockholders' equity as of December 31, 1997. The amount was fantastic: $30,734,000,000. "And just once again," Specter would tell the jury in a moment, "the figure is three, oh, seven, three, four, zero, zero, zero, comma, zero, zero, zero."

Second, Pinto asked the judge to place some limit on the amount of punitive damages. He asked him to consider a Nevada statute that set a ceiling at three times the compensatory damages or, in this case, roughly $6.9 million.

Denied again. Hagen would not limit the jury.

For his part Specter objected to the judge informing the jury that any punitive damages would go to Jimmie and Ginny White. "The purpose of punitive damages," Specter told Hagen, "is not to compensate the Whites. It is to punish the Ford Motor Co. And the implication in the phraseology that the court has written there, or the inference that may be drawn, I should say, is that this is something which is being done for them, and it's not being done for them."

Hagen agreed. His instruction to the jury was short and simple.

> In arriving at any award of punitive damages, you are to consider the following: One, the reprehensibility of the conduct of the defendant. Two, the amount of punitive damages which will have a deterrent effect on the defendant in light of defendant's financial condition.

Specter started his speech sounding like a mathematics tutor. Ten percent of Ford's worth was $3 billion, he told the jury. One percent was $307 million. Even one-tenth of 1 percent was $30.7 million. But forget all of that, he said. "These numbers defy my understanding. Thirty billion dollars is not something I understand, not something that I think most people understand." He talked about how Ford had committed the most reprehensible act possible—"the taking of a human life and loss of a human life, especially the life of a child."

How could that be measured in dollars? Specter wanted to leave the jury with something striking, something that would portray the amount of money Ford possessed—and how much it could afford to pay—in a graphic, memorable manner.

> Let's forget about $30 billion. Let's just put that aside and let's forget about Ford and let's talk about this in terms of just a person, a human being. After all, Ford is entitled to be treated—you know they're a corporation—just like a human being. And let's say that some person did what you have found that Ford did here. And that person, they're not worth $30 billion. In fact, all they have in the world is what's in their pocket, and what's in their pocket is not $30 billion. It's $30. Same first two numbers. Forget about all these zeroes. Thirty dollars. That's all there is. That's all they have.

Specter reached into his right pants pocket and pulled out three $10 bills. He laid them out on the veneer wooden railing that separated him from the six jurors.

> Now, if you take 10 percent from that person for what he has done, 10 percent, that's $3.

He reached into the right-hand pocket of his suit coat and withdrew three single dollar bills. He placed them on the railing next to the three tens.

> Now if I've got thirty bucks in my pocket and we take away $3, that hurts. That hurts. That's 10 percent. But if you say 1 percent [to] somebody who is worth $30, what's that? That's 30¢ . . . How much does that hurt if I've got thirty bucks in my pocket, you take away three dimes?

Next to the singles he placed three dimes.

> If you take away one-tenth of 1 percent from somebody who is worth $30, do you know what that is? Three cents. Right?

As he placed three pennies next to the dimes, Specter made a motion as if flicking lint off his shoulder. That was how Ford would regard having to pay one-tenth of 1 percent. Like a minor irritation, an annoyance. Like a piece of lint. The three pennies on the railing next to the dimes and the singles and the $10 bills didn't look like much at all.

And that, Specter said, would not do.

> There are 884,000 people in this country who have these vehicles who got a letter that [Ford] didn't tell them the truth as to why these vehicles were being recalled. You know all of that.
>
> They must know and you must speak loud enough so that they know that they can get their vehicles back in and get this 16¢ wedge and put it in their car to save the lives of their children and themselves and anybody who is downhill of a parked vehicle that has had this problem, and there are 884,000* of them across this country.

---

*The lawyers frequently rounded 884,400 down to 884,000 in court.

Will Ford do it themselves just based upon what you've told them in your verdict? I don't think so. There's no evidence that Ford would ever do anything unless they're forced to, forced to by the federal government, forced to by you ladies and gentlemen.

Your verdict for punitive damages must be loud enough so it is on the front page of every newspaper tomorrow morning, so every person in this country knows, if they have that vehicle, they can take it into the shop and get it fixed. Nothing short of that is going to get the job done.

Finally, on the issue of damages and punishment, these people at Ford who make these decisions, these decisions that people who you have found exhibited conscious disregard, conscious disregard, these people must know, they must feel it.

They have to have a message sent to them in an unmistakable way. They've got to feel it in their gut like Mr. Pinto told you he felt it in his gut when he gave his closing address to you.

Remember when Diane Robinson said that when they brought Jimmie White back home and they put him in his chair the night his son was killed, that he slipped out of his chair and crumpled on the floor like water? Remember that?

If you want to be heard, if you want Ford to listen, if you want them to change, if you want people to be safe, your message must be loud enough and strong enough and clear enough so that Alex Trotman, the president of that company, and everybody else who has anything to say about this subject pours out of their chairs like water and crumples to the floor.

Thank you.

Pinto rose and approached the jury. He was a short man with white hair. He looked older than when the trial had started three weeks ago. He started speaking slowly and softly.

It's very difficult for me to come to you now after having lost the case and speak about anything, but now I've got to come here and balance out some of the things that Mr. Specter has told you.

Bear in mind that you have already awarded compensatory damages to the Whites for their grief. . . . I think Mr. Specter is emphasizing the message you have to give to Ford, and I can tell you that Ford has already gotten the message. . . .

The judge interrupted to ask Pinto to speak up. "It's hard to speak loud after what's happened to us, but I'll try," he replied, then added for the jury, "In any event, you've gotten the message across that we should be punished."

Pinto pleaded for mercy. He told the jury that the $30 billion Specter mentioned "isn't the money that Ford has in its pocket," that it was Ford's net worth and was invested in buildings and machines and the business of making automobiles.

He asked the jury to consider that Ford did eventually recall the trucks, although he acknowledged, "I think you've already given your message about the way they've done it." Most of the vehicles had been fixed, he said, and Ford and Orscheln came up with a better design for vehicles manufactured in later years. "So a lot has been done to rectify the situation that you found requires punishment," he said.

There wasn't much more he could say in conclusion. So Pinto didn't say much more.

> Now, what can I tell you? Just be fair. That's all. There's no reason to be outrageous, talk about the amount that Mr. Specter has asked for.
>
> All I ask you to do is be reasonable and put an amount that considers the fact that you've already awarded the total damages and that you be fair.

The plaintiffs' rebuttal was something of a surprise. At least for Pinto and Ford. As Specter had promised, he would yield the final words of *White v. Ford* to Don Nomura. To say that Nomura was keyed up, "juiced," as they said in his native California, was an understatement. He had worked on what he would say for the last two weeks, then just last night he had thrown it all away and started over again. He was ready now, more than ready.

Nomura had barely spoken, starting with the jury's "opportunity to save lives," when Pinto rose to object. It was "very unfair" for Nomura to get a chance to give a second speech, he told Hagen. Chris Wicker, a second Ford attorney, complained that he'd never seen a different lawyer give a rebuttal. "I'd probably agree with you," the judge said, "but the objection comes too late." Nomura was underway and he couldn't be stopped. The "Japanese Zero" was swooping in for the finishing blow.

When he restarted, Nomura corrected something Pinto had said, that most of Ford's money was tied up in buildings and machines, that it didn't have anywhere near $30 billion in cash lying around. Actually, Nomura said, holding a corporate ledger sheet, Ford had total cash reserves, marketable securities of $20,825,000,000.

He then talked about a vision he had awoken with every morning of the trial, the vision of a father holding his dead son in his arms, of Jimmie stroking the hair of his lifeless child, then later having to endure the insult of being sued by Ford.

> I have another vision of this case, too. . . . Two months ago there was a kindergarten graduation for my five-year-old, and there were twelve kids lined up with mortarboard hats that they had made from crepe paper stuck on the top and glued onto the top of a coffee filter. They looked just like mortarboards to them. They were wearing their best clothes and they marched up and took their diplomas, and at five years old I had never seen them happier or more proud of themselves.
>
> That's a small thing in that small moment and we've all seen that. It's not unique to me. It's not unique to you and certainly not unique to the decision makers at Ford. They know about the joys that children bring. They know also that when children die it's so much different . . . it's so much different than when adults die. Adults die and they've had a full life, they have accomplishments, they have experiences, they have memories. When children die, children die only with their dreams and your dreams for them.

Ford knew that children might get hurt because of its faulty brakes, Nomura said. Ford knew "the horror that would be visited upon families across the country." But the giant carmaker based its decisions not on the value of human life but on "cost-effectiveness." It was willing to take chances with people's lives, with children's lives.

> And if perchance a horrible accident should occur, we'll [Ford] defend that case. We'll spend millions in defense. We'll hire every expert that we can find. We'll talk about parabolic curves, we'll talk about broken ratchets and pawls and say it's just superficial. We'll hire nice people like Mr. Pinto to come in, and he is a nice man, but he's not Ford. It's a grandfatherly visage that he provides in here, but he's not Ford.
>
> He stands before you and says, "I'm sorry. We get the message. Ford's sorry, too." But look over at the table. Three attorneys. They

didn't make the decisions in this case. And Ford is not even present. They don't even have the dignity to come to court and hear your verdict and understand your verdict.

No one even shows up at counsel table on the day of the verdict, the day of judgment, the day to hear what you have to say. Have they gotten the message as he said? I don't think so.

There is a boardroom in Detroit, Michigan, and they're sitting around. They won't come; they won't tell you they're going to change. But they're waiting. They're watching. They're listening. And they're wondering whether it's going to be business as usual tomorrow or whether they're going to be forced to change, and they're waiting to hear from [six] people from Washoe County who have control over that.

See, I don't want to hear tomorrow or next year about other fathers holding their children dead in their arms and stroking their hair. I don't want to hear tomorrow or next year about little shoes by the front door empty forever. I don't want to hear about lies, excuses, and promises to recall, promises that "we've gotten the message" when they haven't, promises such as that.

I'd like to hear something about the truth now.

I'm haunted by this case and I'm going to tell you we're going to be haunted so much more if you let this opportunity pass and you don't punish them so hard that they never do this again and change their ways.

I've practiced in Washoe County for twenty years and I've been before many juries, most of that for the district attorney's office representing people in the county against criminals. My work hasn't changed so much after all. In all those years I've never had to beg a jury for a result, but maybe I've never had anything as important as this happen. I'm begging you today to do the right thing. Save some lives.

Pinto objected. Nomura's statement went far beyond any rebuttal. But Pinto was too late. Nomura was done. Nomura had said his piece. The jury left the courtroom to decide Ford's punishment.

IT DIDN'T TAKE LONG. Just a few hours.

At 1:30 p.m. the lawyers were called back to court. The clerk read the decision.

We, the jury in the above-entitled action find as follows:
   What amount of damages, if any, do you find should be awarded
as punitive damages?
   ANSWER: $150,884,400.

The amount was $150 million plus $1 for each of the 884,400 Ford
trucks sold with faulty parking brakes.

CHAPTER 17

Not the End

As SPECTER HAD HOPED, plenty of newspapers carried accounts of the outcome of *White v. Ford.* It would have been hard not to. The total award, nearly $153.2 million, was the second largest product liability award in U.S. history, eclipsed only by a verdict against Chrysler a year earlier.

People had in fact noticed. Even the jurors in the case had been angry with Ford. Long after the trial one of them, Clarice LaRose, a soft-spoken, attractive middle-aged woman who worked in a bank, said that what bothered her most was that Ford had not warned drivers about spontaneous disengagement of its parking brakes. "It still bugs me. I still wouldn't buy a Ford. They said at the trial to think of Ford as a person. Well, if you're a person and you know there's something wrong, don't you have a responsibility to tell me?"

Yet Ford never did take action to inform drivers of the true nature of the problem with its brakes, never did acknowledge that spontaneous disengagement occurred. Although many of those trucks had been fixed, many had not and were still being driven around with defective parking brakes. And without their owners' knowing the potential hazard.

Specter worried that another child, another Walter White, could become a victim. He wrote to NHTSA, informing the agency of the outcome of his court case, notifying it that the problem still existed. He asked that NHTSA order Ford to conduct a second recall, this one informing owners about the true problem, about spontaneous disengagement of its parking brakes. Of course if NHTSA ordered a new recall with a new recall letter, that would be a tacit admission that the NHTSA-approved first letter had been inadequate. The agency decided against another recall and in its letter to Specter did not state a reason. So some drivers would remain uninformed about the danger that possibly awaited them. Specter could only hope that the news accounts of his case would reach them.

While he relished his victory against Ford, Specter couldn't foretell the twists and turns that lay ahead, couldn't imagine the long and arduous road he would have to travel to finally reach a conclusion in the case of *White v. Ford*. The war was far from over.

FORD, AS SORRY as its lawyer had said the company was, appealed the verdict. It filed a number of post-trial motions with Hagen, including one seeking a new trial. The judge denied them all except one—a motion to reduce the punitive damages. Hagen, bound by Nevada precedent in the case, felt that the Nevada Supreme Court would not uphold the award on grounds of "proportionality." The punitive award was so much larger— about sixty-five times—the $2.3 million in compensatory damages awarded to the Whites. The most the Nevada Supreme Court had ever upheld in the past was a multiple of thirty. Hagen followed that example, reducing the punitive damages in *White v. Ford* to $69,163,037.10, less than half the jury's award. But Specter was not upset. He felt that $69 million would be enough to punish Ford.

Ford also appealed the case to the U.S. Court of Appeals for the Ninth Circuit, located in San Francisco. At the least, this move would tie up the case for some time, though Specter had no idea it would be so long.

People in Elko also read the stories of the case against Ford. Many of them assumed, as was often the case when large damages were awarded, that Jimmie and Ginny were now rich, that they'd hit the lottery.

Although the Whites would receive compensatory damages from the case, they wouldn't get a cent from the lion's share of the verdict, the punitive damages, for years. If ever. The legal wrangling wasn't over, not nearly.

Jimmie and Ginny had taken leaves from their jobs while the trial was going on. After it was over, Ginny returned to her position as a cashier at Walmart, only to find that her locker had been cleaned out. Her boss had assumed she would quit after winning her legal case and had given her job to someone else. Jimmie returned to work and was on the job a full week as a mechanic at Stewart Brothers Drilling before he discovered that his medical benefits had been terminated. And so was he. His bosses figured he was rich and didn't need employment.

Without jobs, Jimmie and Ginny decided not to look for new ones, not right away. They took a year off from working. They needed time to heal their wounds. They traveled, visiting relatives in other states. Maybe they would help console them. They had their money from the settlement with Orscheln, but it wasn't as much as it had sounded at first. And the Whites had run up substantial debts during the trial and the months preceding it. No money had come in and plenty had gone out.

The money from Orscheln was used to pay bills. The Whites bought their trailer outright. They paid Ragna's college tuition. They sold their two Fords and bought new autos; Jimmie's new pickup was a Dodge. The Whites not only visited relatives but also helped them out with loans, car and mortgage payments. Before long the money from Orscheln was mostly gone. In a way Jimmie was glad. "You feel funny spending it because you know where it come from," he said.

THE YEARS PASSED. Ginny took a new job, working a cash register at Sierra Jewelry and Loan, a pawnshop in downtown Elko. Jimmie started working for another drilling company, making $15 an hour, good pay in Elko. Jimmie didn't mind working again. It kept his mind off things, most of the time.

"I still have days where I get up and I feel really depressed. I go to work and I don't feel like doing anything. . . . It happens to me when I least expect it," he said one day, seated at his kitchen table, a spot from which he could survey most of his house. From the looks of things, a visitor not familiar with the tragedy that occurred there so long ago might have thought the Whites' son was still alive. Walter's pictures were everywhere, on bookshelves, in frames on the walls, on the refrigerator. The blow-up of Walter used for the trial was framed and displayed on the wall in a small room Jimmie used as an office. Jimmie had insisted on having the photo back, unable to stand the thought of his son's likeness lying in the darkness of a basement storage room somewhere. Walter's videotapes—*Pinocchio, Casper the Friendly Ghost, Tarzan, Lion King*—remained on the shelf below the TV set in the living room. His toy trucks and race cars were in a nearby box. His tricycle sat out back in a shed. Walter's tiny, steel-frame bed rested against a wall in the Whites' master bedroom, covered with his favorite stuffed animals. Ginny looked over at the bed with hurt blue eyes, telling a visitor, "I just can't put it away."

The house was quiet now, lonely. Even Guppy, Walter's dog, had died.

Ginny derived solace from God. She attended services every Sunday at the Church of Christ, though she rarely visited the cemetery. "I can't fathom the thought of him being down there," she whispered through quivering lips.

Jimmie felt just the opposite. Also a devout Christian, he had not been to services since the accident. "I'm too angry to go," he said. "I still have a hard time figuring out how He could let this happen to us." Yet he felt drawn to Walter's grave site. When Ginny went to church on Sundays, Jimmie visited the cemetery. "I don't know how I could make it through the week if I didn't go to the cemetery," he said.

One day Jimmie drove his Dodge truck along the dirt roads of his neighborhood and onto the two-lane asphalt highway, then through the streets of downtown Elko. The license plate on his truck read "Buddy B." Jimmie pulled into the Elko Cemetery adjacent to Elko High School, a school Walter would have attended had he lived. The echoing sound of a basketball could be heard bouncing somewhere in the distance. Jimmie walked slowly, almost mechanically across the neatly manicured lawn. He stood above Walter's grave on the chilly May afternoon, snow still blanketing the mountains that loomed over Elko. Jimmie stood there without a coat, wearing jeans and a black denim shirt, silent as he shivered slightly against a brisk wind. He peered down at the polished marble stone, its etched figure of a Care Bear, the flags of the United States and Iceland, and read once again the painful words: "White—Jon Walter Douglas Wayne. Oct. 22, 1990–Oct. 9, 1994. We Love You Buddy Boy."

LEFT: *Derick Bobb at six months*
(COURTESY OF THE BOBBS)

RIGHT: *Diagram of parking brake*
(FORD TRIAL EXHIBIT)

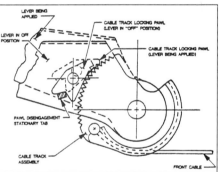

BELOW: *The Bobbs' Ford F-150 parked outside their mountain cabin, Camp Lil' Bit* (COURTESY OF THE BOBBS)

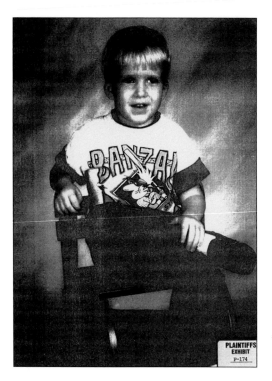

Jon Walter Douglas Wayne White
(TRIAL EXHIBIT, COURTESY OF
THE WHITES)

Jimmie White's truck parked outside the family trailer
(ELKO COUNTY SHERIFF'S DEPARTMENT)

ABOVE: *Shanin Specter (left), Don Nomura, and Pete Durney examine evidence in a weekend meeting during the first* White v. Ford *trial* (AUTHOR'S PHOTO)

RIGHT: *Portrait of U.S. District Judge David Hagen outside the judge's courtroom* (AUTHOR'S PHOTO)

BELOW: *Ford engineer Tim Rakowicz* (PHOTO FROM VIDEOTAPED DEPOSITION)

Jimmie and Ginny White leaving the federal courthouse during the second White v. Ford *trial* (AUTHOR'S PHOTO)

Specter awaiting the verdict in the second trial, with bet slips on the table in front of him (AUTHOR'S PHOTO)

Plaintiffs' lawyers entering the former offices of Pete Durney during a break in the second trial (AUTHOR'S PHOTO)

PART II

Round 2

CHAPTER 18

The Waiting Game

Jimmie White waited a while after the verdict and the filing of an appeal before he started checking on his PC for decisions by the Ninth Circuit Court of Appeals. He would sit in his back room, the portrait of Walter peering down at him, and click his way to the court's pages on the Internet to see if there was any news on *White v. Ford*. Every day he checked, day after day. Months lapsed into a year, then two years. Still nothing.

His mind kept taking him back to the day of the verdict, when he listened as the judge excused the jurors and watched them file out of the room. And moments after, when both sides had walked out into the granite hallway. Joe Pinto had approached Jimmie and made an astounding admission. "My heart just wasn't in it," Pinto said, looking sheepishly into Jimmie's tear-filled eyes. "I have grandkids." He had done the best job he could for Ford and indeed had felt that the company had won the case, that the jurors had made a mistake, voting on emotion rather than the cold facts. But Pinto had never relished the case. It had been hard for him to come to court each morning and look at Jimmie and Ginny sitting in the first row.

Pinto would retire to Florida not long after the trial. Several years later, reminiscing about the case and his career, he would proudly tell a visitor, "I have eight grandchildren now." His wife, Lillian, quickly corrected him. "Nine. He loves children and it did break his heart," she said. During the trial Pinto had shared the facts of the case with his wife, every excruciating detail.

Pinto nodded. "It was very difficult for me to try a case like that, with a child killed in that way," said the lawyer, looking frail now, a sliver of the vibrant battler he had once been. Cancer had invaded his colon, his lungs, his brain, and he was dying. Lillian helped him walk slowly to the couple's backyard pool set in a private patio ringed with alternating red and white geraniums and overlooking a golf course.

But Pinto's memories of the trial remained vivid and his opinion of the case unwavering. He felt that an appeal was justified. He did not feel that Ford should have lost. "It does not make any sense," he said of the verdict. How could Ford have been found liable—and punished with a $153 million verdict—if the brake defect had not caused Walter White's death? How could the jury find that the defect was not what caused Walter White's death yet punish the company so severely for not *warning* about the defect? It wasn't logical. "Failure to warn about what?" he exclaimed, his face reddening as he struggled to rise from an outdoor chair.

Pinto continued to defend Ford to anyone who would listen. But when asked if Ford had done nothing wrong at all in regard to the death of Walter White—sending the recall notices late and even then not revealing the true extent of the brake problem—he avoided a direct answer. Instead he smiled. "What I said was my client did not produce a product that caused this injury."

What the appellate court would decide was anybody's guess. Jimmie was anxious about its ruling, but all he could do, all anyone could do, was wait. Two years became three, three became four. . . .

CHAPTER 19

The Sad Case of "John Smith"

IN THE INTERVENING YEARS Specter would have a number of major cases, many of them involving badly hurt children or young adults. One that stood out, that Specter still felt deeply inside himself even years later, was the case of David Caruso, a young man who entered a hospital with a treatable malady but had a tube placed improperly in his throat. The tube had slipped, cutting off his airway and his oxygen. Alarms rang out on the hospital floor, but no one responded for six minutes, six minutes in which Caruso suffered severe brain damage, leaving him in a near-vegetative state. At trial Specter did something unusual, something he hadn't done before or since. He gave his closing speech in the first person, speaking as if Caruso were speaking for himself, telling the jury about his family and his fiancé, his once-held future plans, dreams and aspirations lost. Some members of the jury cried. Then they handed down what at the time was a record verdict in a Pennsylvania medical malpractice case—$49.6 million.

IN ANOTHER CASE Specter represented five-year-old Destine Weightman, who sank to the bottom of her apartment complex swimming pool while two lifeguards were not doing their jobs. At trial Specter showed a photograph of the lifeguards lying on their backs, one with her eyes closed and the other listening to a Walkman. Destine was left unable to see or speak or respond to any external stimuli—except pain. But what irked Specter as much as anything was that after the tragic incident the "heartless apartment complex management," as the *Philadelphia Daily News* put it, tried to evict the family from their Upper Darby, Pennsylvania, apartment. A jury in that case handed down a $24 million verdict. But perhaps no case bothered Specter more than that of yet another injured youth. The case was terribly sad, as was the legal outcome, in Specter's view, even though it was a seven-figure settlement. Specter was visibly shaken as he walked back to his office from the federal courthouse the day the case ended. For someone so even-keeled, almost stoic, Specter seemed a jumble of emotions—anger, pain, frustration. He seemed ready to scream or cry. The case, like that of Walter White, involved a car company—although because of the confidential settlement both the company and Specter's client would remain anonymous.

The lawsuit involved a horrific head-on car crash and a fourteen-year-old boy who had been badly injured, left paralyzed from the waist down for life. The seat of the car in which the boy—call him John Smith—had been a passenger had been equipped only with a lap belt, a device that was found time and again to be dangerous and was replaced in later models with the safer three-point lap-shoulder belts. The lap belt had directed the entire force of the violent collision to the boy's midsection, doing irreparable damage. By the time the case went to trial in December 2001, John Smith was twenty years old, an adult, though one barely capable of living alone. Yet he was very much alone. The accident six years earlier had claimed the life of his mother. His father, a truck driver, was never around to help him. John had no job. With an IQ of seventy-two, John, living on government benefits, had few prospects.

The trial began in federal court and the plaintiff's side was, in Specter's estimation, doing well. After the closing speeches concluded and the jury started to deliberate, Specter advised John of the company's offer of $1 million. When Specter told John of the offer, his eyes went wide. *One million dollars!* He jumped at the money like a starving dog at a steak. "Yes," he told Specter, "take the offer."

Specter raised an eyebrow. It wasn't enough, he told John. Not after all these years. Not after all his suffering. He would never have the use of his legs, never be rid of the pain he endured. He would need medical care for the rest of his life. From an attorney's perspective, the case had taken years to put together and bring to trial; boxes of documents—evidence of the automaker's knowledge that the belts were unsafe—lined a wall of the courtroom. The car, a small 1984 model sedan, had been saved all this time and rested during trial in the bowels of the federal building, where the jury had viewed the twisted wreckage just days earlier, seemingly impressed by the fact that passengers who were not wearing the lap belts had emerged unscathed, while John was crippled for life.

During the trial Specter made hay of the fact that the car company offered the superior three-point belts only as an option when it had other, less important items—such as cigarette lighters—as standard equipment. Cloistered in a small, antiseptic room adjacent to the court, Specter and two associates told their client all this. "Hang on, John. Wait for the jury's verdict. It's a matter of hours now. You've waited all this time, all these years. Just hang on." (Even if they somehow lost, Specter decided that he would take care of his client financially, that he'd take the money from his firm's bank account if it came to that. He'd even discussed it with his partner and close friend, and Tom Kline had agreed.)

John, tears in his eyes, confusion in his mind, reluctantly agreed to reject the million-dollar offer. But when the jury deliberations went into a second day—and the car company upped its offer to $1.5 million—the temptation became too much for him. It was a lot of money. He'd be rich, at least compared with how he was living now. After a night at home, lying awake, thinking about all that money—and the horrible thought of the jury possibly deciding the case in the car company's favor—John came back to court and ordered his attorney to take the settlement offer. With his sorrowful eyes downcast and refusing to meet Specter's, he insisted that this was his final decision.

"Take the settlement. I can't take the chance if we lose," he said.

"John, listen to me. We're not going to lose," Specter implored.

"But what if we do?"

"We're not going to."

"I can't take that chance. I can't."

"John, please, you've taken my advice up to this point and we've done all right."

"I want to take the money."

"Just hold tight for a few more hours."

"Take the money. That's my decision."

Specter, exasperated, acceded to his client's wishes. Before he did, though, he went to the manufacturer's lead lawyer in the case and told him the offer was rejected. The amount was not enough. The defendant's lawyer immediately made a phone call and then increased the offer again, this time to $2 million, a sign to Specter that even the company knew its initial offer had been low. Specter took the increased amount.

After the jury was dismissed its members indicated they had been leaning toward a substantial award against General Motors, much more than John got. If he had only waited those few more hours. Specter left the courtroom and walked the fifteen blocks back to his firm. A few minutes after he arrived at his desk, Kline stepped into his office. He had heard the news.

"How are you?" Kline asked.

"I'm crushed," replied Specter.

He knew that most cases, about 90 percent, settled before a jury reached a verdict. Hell, most of them settled before a jury was picked, before the first piece of evidence was submitted. Sometimes it was the best and most reasonable course. Just not this time, not this case. Months later John was broke. After the settlement check came through, he had also refused Specter's advice to place his money in a trust that would keep it safe, earn interest, and pay him a monthly allowance. John had met a young woman and married her. Not long afterward, his new wife left him and took most of the money out of the couple's bank account, according to John's uncle, with whom John had gone to live out West.

At 6:15 a.m. on February 5, 2003, a year and two days after John received his settlement check, his uncle walked into John's bedroom to wake him for the day. He found John lying in an awkward position, his face down in a trash can next to his bed as though perhaps he had been trying to vomit into the cylinder. The uncle lifted his nephew and saw that his face was black and blue, a collection of blood having settled in his youthful, cheerless features. John was dead. The cause was officially ruled an accidental overdose of painkillers. His uncle felt that it was also a case of a broken will, that John, his body and his hope shattered, had simply given up on life.

IF THE CASE had any effect on Specter, it served only to harden him. It had made a committed man even more resolute. Despite receiving a check from the automaker, he considered the case a failure. The large corporation had acted wrongly—had been a "bad actor"—yet had not been forced to atone for its sins, escaping a guilty verdict and the glare of public scrutiny. To the car company, Specter knew, the settlement was a pittance.

Ford, if he had anything to do with it, would not get off so lightly when it came to a little boy named Walter White.

CHAPTER 20

Do-Over

FOUR AND A HALF YEARS after the verdict in Reno, the Ninth Circuit issued its opinion in the case. It was a split decision, 2–1.

The appellate panel threw out the $69 million award, saying it was based on erroneous jury instruction, and sent the case back to Hagen for another jury to set an amount for punitive damages. This was a blow to the plaintiffs, but hardly a victory for Ford. The Ninth Circuit held that Ford had acted with "implied malice," which covered not only conduct intended to injure a person but also "despicable conduct which is engaged in with a conscious disregard of the rights or safety of others." Still, the court also wrote that the jury's punitive award went beyond the "territorial limitation" by considering the impact of Ford's acts on people other than Nevadans.

Other states had different laws regarding liability. And punishment. For instance, Judge Andrew J. Kleinfeld, who wrote the majority opinion, estimated that in his home state of Alaska damages in such a case would have been limited to roughly $7 million, with half going to the state treasury. "By imposing ten times what Alaska would allow, with all the money going to the Whites and their attorneys, rather than [giving] half of it to the state government, Nevada has created very different incentives from Alaska for manufacturers, distributors, and plaintiffs' attorneys."

Specter found this particular mention of the plaintiff lawyers' fees insulting. (And wasn't Kleinfeld aware that punitive damages were subject to taxation, meaning that some 40 percent would, after all, go to the government?) He also felt Kleinfeld's logic was tortured. The jury hadn't trespassed across any territorial boundaries. It had acted in a simple and straightforward manner, setting an award it felt would punish a company as big as Ford for reprehensible national conduct. (Those 884,400 trucks were everywhere, not just in Nevada.) Besides, what folks did or didn't do in Alaska had nothing to do with it.

Specter was, of course, disappointed to lose the $69 million award. But, truth be known, all this latest decision meant was that he would have to go back to court to try the amount of punitive damages again before a jury. The jury's verdict for Ford's liability and for punitive damages would stand. The question was only a matter of how much.

MORE MONTHS WENT BY. Specter and the Reno lawyers had several conference calls with Ford's attorneys and Judge Hagen about a second trial to have a jury decide the amount of punitive damages. The discussions were very cordial, at least on the surface. Ford was willing to drag things out, to use every recourse available. And Specter wouldn't blink. If Ford wanted to dawdle, it was okay with him. A second jury would see things the Whites' way and award hefty punitive damages and the appellate courts would ultimately have to approve some sizable award. If Ford wanted to drag things out he was prepared to wait. That's what he told Ford. And he meant it. In December 2003 Specter got a call from John Osgood, an attorney who said he managed the Product Litigation Group for Ford. He said that Ford wanted to work toward settling the case. He wanted to know Specter's thoughts.

"Nothing's changed," Specter said. "We've said it all before. Ford needs to make a serious eight-figure offer in order to get the ball rolling on settlement."

Osgood then launched into a discussion of two recent appellate court rulings that he said seemed to limit punitive damages to roughly nine times the compensatory damages—at the very most. But Specter shot back that those same court decisions allowed for exceptions to any limits, and that the egregious nature of Ford's act—its intentional failure to warn people about a dangerous truck that killed an innocent three-year-old boy—could certainly qualify as such an exception. The two hashed the debate over for some time, talking about the language in the prior cases. Then Osgood made an offer.

"We're willing to offer three times the compensatory damages."

"Rejected."

"That's about $7 million." The amount was the same as Judge Kleinfeld on the appellate court had noted would have been allowed under the laws of his home state, Alaska. Specter didn't wait even a full second before responding.

"Rejected," Specter repeated crisply. He didn't elaborate. Osgood seemed taken aback.

"Don't you want to take the offer back to the lawyers in Reno, Pete Durney, Don Nomura?"

"No need."

"How about your clients? The Whites?"

"Of course I'll take it to them, but I am authorized to reject any offers of this nature."

There was a pause. Osgood was waiting for more from Specter. All he got was silence. Finally, Ford's representative spoke up.

"Well, don't you have a counter?"

"No."

"You have to."

"No, I don't have to."

"There must be some number."

"Look, as soon as Ford makes an eight-figure offer, we'll be glad to make a counter. That's been our position and it's still our position."

Specter wanted the bidding to start at $10 million. Unless Ford was willing to enter that ballpark, Specter wouldn't play ball.

Osgood replied that he would be sending a letter about Ford's offer through Durney's office to be forwarded to Kline & Specter. He wanted Durney to see the money on the table with his own eyes.

Specter relayed his conversation with Osgood in a one-page memo to Durney and Nomura. It ended with a brief sentence that conveyed his adamance on the issue: "Let's stay the course."

CHAPTER 21

Making the Rules

Yᴇᴛ ᴀɴᴏᴛʜᴇʀ ʏᴇᴀʀ would pass before both sides would respond to the appellate court's ruling and the case would be returned to Judge Hagen for retrial. The judge chose January 2004 for the trial, then delayed it until March. It was coming up on a decade since Walter's death. He would have been thirteen by this time, an eighth grader. Since the trial, Specter had had a fourth daughter, Hatti, who was already three years old.

Ford, seeking a different outcome, filed nineteen pretrial motions aimed at limiting the plaintiffs' lawyers. Specter filed three.

Ford wanted to exclude evidence of the company's financial status. It didn't want a repeat of Specter mentioning the company's $30 billion net worth, citing appellate cases that it said barred mention of the company's worth as irrelevant and unduly prejudicial. Hagen noted that Ford's lawyers had used "selective quotation of certain passages" from these precedents. For instance, he said Ford had omitted one important phrase from a U.S. Supreme Court case relating to a defendant's wealth: "That does not make its use unlawful or inappropriate." Key words—DOES NOT.

Ford also used Nevada Supreme Court rulings to press its point, but Hagen noted, "Once again, Ford has quoted the authorities selectively." A sentence from the same opinion directly contradicted it: "The wealth of a defendant is directly relevant to the size of an award, which is meant to deter the defendant from repeating his misconduct as well as punish him for past behavior."

Ford also asked Hagen to preclude Specter from again pulling out his dollars, dimes, and pennies to demonstrate Ford's relative wealth and a suitable punishment. Ford's lawyers argued that such a demonstration could produce an excessive verdict. However, Hagen ruled that Specter could, if he wanted to, use the same comparison, that it was a "simple illustrative exercise . . . [and] is relevant and helpful to the jury's determination of the proper amount" of punitive damages.

Ford asked that Hagen bar any discussion of the company's recall notice, which did not mention spontaneous disengagement of its parking brake or the "skip-through" problem. Ford's argument was that the re-call notice was mailed after the incident and therefore had no bearing on Walter's death. Specter argued that the notice was indeed fraudulent, that Ford knew the brakes would disengage and intentionally had not mentioned that fact. Hagen agreed, finding that the evidence could support a jury finding that Ford's recall notice was "something less than completely forthright." And even though the notice was mailed after Walter's death, the company's "continuing failure to warn other customers about precisely the same defect arguably 'replicates . . . prior transgressions' of the sort that injured the Whites."

Ford further asked that the plaintiffs be prohibited from appealing to the jury's emotions, such as asking them, as was the case in the first trial, to keep a "vision" in their minds of Jimmie holding his dead son in his arms, or Don Nomura's describing his own son's kindergarten graduation (which Jimmie would never experience for Walter). Hagen cautioned the lawyers to stay away from "golden rule" statements asking jurors to put themselves in the place of Jimmie or Ginny White. The courts generally consider such statements prejudicial and as appealing to the passion of jurors. But the judge gave the plaintiffs' lawyers latitude, ruling that mentioning the Whites' pain and suffering was valid "in evaluating reprehensibility" of Ford's actions in deciding punitive damages. He said, "The Whites did lose a child, and did suffer, and Ford did continue to put other people at risk by failing to warn of the defect."

The judge did grant Ford's motion seeking to exclude another type of commentary, remarks referring to Ford as a "faceless" corporation, a corporation based far from Nevada. Hagen specifically mentioned Don Nomura's reference in the first trial to a "board room in Detroit." He also cautioned Nomura against again bringing up his past career as a prosecutor and his comment at the first trial that his job "hasn't changed so much after all." Yet Hagen said he had no problem with the Whites' lawyers asking the jury to "send a message" to Ford through a large punitive verdict. "Indeed," said Hagen in turning down Ford's motion, "as the Whites point out, the whole point of a punitive damages award, which is grounded in retribution and deterrence rather than compensation, is to 'send a message' regarding the wrongfulness of a defendant's conduct."

Hagen also denied Ford's request to prevent a range of evidence from coming before the jury, including evidence of people injured by the defective Ford truck in other states, including the testimony of Tammy Bobb, the Pennsylvania mother whose son, Derick, was injured in a roll-away mishap. Hagen found that even though the jury's mission was to hand down punishment for the harm caused to Walter White and potentially to other residents of Nevada only, mention of those other cases from other states was allowable "when it demonstrates the deliberateness and culpability of the defendant's action" in Nevada.

The rulings by Hagen were critical in setting the stage for a second jury verdict on punitive damages. The judge had refused to allow Ford to muzzle the plaintiffs. He had dampened any hopes Ford may have harbored in having a second jury hear only part of the story about its defective trucks and the death of a little boy.

Hagen's rulings were as close to pitching a shutout as Specter could have hoped. Now there were a few other things Specter hoped the judge would see his way. First he asked that Ford not be allowed to mention that the first jury had found that the defect in Ford's truck had *not* caused Walter's death. (Its failure to warn was found to be the cause.) Yet Specter wanted to be able to mention the defect itself. Hagen's ruling: Granted.

Specter also wanted there to be no mention of the first jury's $2.3 million award for compensatory damages. Ford argued that the amount should be mentioned and the second jury instructed of the appellate court's "reasonable relationship requirement" between punitive and compensatory damages. Hagen disagreed, citing the U.S. Supreme Court's reluctance to "impose a bright line ratio which a punitive damages award cannot exceed." In the event of an excessive jury award, it would be up to him and if necessary the appellate courts to decide. "All the second jury needs to know," he ruled, "is that the Whites already have been fully compensated for their losses, including the emotional distress caused by the death of their son."

Before the second trial would commence, Hagen had also asked both sides to present him with proposals on how he should instruct the jury. They did. And he rejected both, instead fashioning his own one-page statement in which he would outline the history of the case, how "the brake failed to hold" in Jimmie's truck, how Walter White climbed or fell from the Ford F-350, how "the rear dual wheels of the truck rolled over his chest." Hagen would tell the jurors that Ford had already been found liable in the boy's death. He would tell them they were there to decide only the amount of punitive damages. He would also say, "Ford knew the parking brake was prone to failure prior to this accident but continued to sell it without recalling it and without warning customers of the danger."

CHAPTER 22

Return to Reno

JIMMIE AND GINNY WHITE packed their car with enough clothes to last them a week. Jimmie pulled his vehicle down the sloped driveway that led from their trailer and out onto the highway toward Reno, 230 miles away. The Whites were glad to be leaving Elko. The town seemed to have become smaller since they had won their case against Ford. Folks had become distant, even resentful.

"They thought we were rich," said Jimmie.

It was a common malady among the victors in lawsuits. People thought they'd become instant millionaires. A millionaire was a particularly big deal in Elko, where there weren't many of them. Maybe none. Jimmie felt that everyone, even people he considered friends, looked at him differently after the verdict, after that $150.9 million punitive damages award, even though he'd never seen a cent of it. The whole town knew who Jimmie White was now.

Even when he went into the bank with his paycheck on Fridays, the tellers addressed him as "Mr. White."

"I'd known this one teller for years. I said to her, 'Don't you ever call me Mr. White again.'"

But for a lot of the fine folks of Elko, Jimmie no longer existed. He had become Mr. White, the guy who "won" all that money from Ford.

IT WOULD TAKE almost five hours to reach Reno, and Ginny could feel their emotions grow stronger with every mile. They hadn't been to Reno since the trial. They dreaded going back, dreaded dredging up all those awful memories, memories of October 9, 1994, memories that always bubbled just below the surface, ready to spring up at them without notice. Yet they wanted to face Ford once again, to exact the final and momentous revenge the appeals court had denied them. The trip to Reno was like the walk to the schoolyard to fight the class bully. They felt fear and apprehension, yet the adrenalin was pumping. And Jimmie, his leg bouncing nervously as he sped along the interstate, could scarcely wait. Sure, he was scared. But his anger was stronger than his fear.

Jimmie had changed a lot in the nearly six years since the first trial. Ginny looked the same but her husband did not. The once wiry little guy who used to wear tight jeans and longish hair now looked more like an accountant than a cowboy. He still wore the big silver and turquoise belt buckle his father had given him, but now it rode a few notches further along the belt. Jimmie had gained about 40 pounds in the last year, going from 125 to 165 pounds. He no longer had a taut appearance, though his weight gain wasn't such a bad thing, considering it started when he quit smoking a year earlier. Jimmie had his hair cut short into a slightly choppy style parted on one side. His backlit blue eyes were now obscured somewhat by wire-rim glasses. There was one more change in Jimmie that affected his appearance and even his manner. He had used some of the money from the Orscheln settlement to fix his teeth, twenty of which had been broken, chipped, or knocked out entirely from a fall on a concrete porch years ago. No longer did Jimmie have slightly yellowing teeth with gaps; he now had two gleaming white rows. That change and the extra weight made Jimmie look different. His speech had also changed, the Western twang accented now by a slightly whistling lisp.

But one thing had not changed. Jimmie and Ginny still longed for their son, for Buddy Boy. Ginny still suffered from dreams in which Walter kissed and hugged her, saying "I love you, Momma." Then he'd walk away, his image growing smaller and smaller until it disappeared. The dreams, though less frequent now, haunted her, making Ginny fearful of closing her eyes at night. She still experienced sudden pangs of sadness, usually when something reminded her of her son. On their arrival in Reno she and Jimmie had visited a local mall just to pass the time, when she spotted a woman with a little boy in a stroller. A little blond boy. A little boy who looked like Walter. Her eyes filled with tears. "Jimmie, I have to leave," she said. And so they had.

Jimmie and Ginny stayed strong and stayed together in the years after Walter died. They never blamed each other for the incident, nor had they done the only thing that was worse—blamed themselves. Other couples had, and it had cost them. Neighbors of the Whites, Steve and Anna, had lost a child in a drowning incident. Their eight-year-old son had lifted the cover off their pool and climbed in. When the heavy plastic fell over his head, he had been forced underwater. When he tried to swim to the top for air, he found that the cover had fallen back down, flush onto the water's surface. His four-year-old brother tried to help but he wasn't strong enough to lift the tarp. He ran inside for his mother but it was too late. By the time she pulled her older son from the water he was dead. The Whites consoled their friends, spending hours with them in their home and steering them to groups for grieving parents. Noted Jimmie, "They're not doing so good now." But he and Ginny were determined to persevere. They had even looked into adoption (Ginny was unable to have more children of her own). They were still in their early 40s, young enough to start again. They had tried to adopt a child from a friend of Ragna's, but a judge ruled that because of problems in the birth mother's family, the child had to go to a couple who were unknown to the birth mother. The Whites were out.

"After this is all said and done and the dust settles and we figure out where we're going," said Jimmie, mentioning Oregon and Washington. "I'd say there's a pretty good likelihood we'll try to adopt. Maybe an older child, to give one of them a break. Everyone wants babies."

Jimmie and Ginny were both weary when they arrived in Reno. Neither had been sleeping much and the closer the retrial came, the less sleep they got. It wasn't as bad as the last trial, during which Jimmie had been constantly sick to his stomach, waking in a sweat in the middle of the night to throw up or leaving during trial recesses to vomit in the nearest men's room. Jimmie was a fighter. In the courtroom he had been stoic, never allowing his head to fall or his eyes to droop. He would soldier on again now. He would do it for Walter.

Jimmie wasn't the only one who'd changed over the last six years. Pete Durney had grown a beard tinged with gray. Don Nomura still jogged six miles or so every morning, but his days of running marathons were over, his knees and his busy law practice shortening his running distance. He was still physically and mentally as tight as a steel drum, but his portrait, like Durney's, had been touched by age's paintbrush, his thick, spiky black hair now showing strokes of white.

Specter looked largely the same, a little grayer yet still lithe and energetic. Over the years he'd had a number of trials and major verdicts, the most recent a $20 million jury verdict for a college student who had suffered brain damage when inattentive nurses failed to hear alarm bells at his bed in the intensive care unit, leaving him without oxygen for too long. Specter had won that verdict (plus an usually rare verdict for punitive damages, even if only for $15,000) despite the fact that the student had been admitted to the hospital for self-inflicted injuries. He had set himself on fire in a suicide attempt.

Between the last Ford trial and this one, Specter had also endured "the worst day of my life." The Specters and five other couples, including their close friends Todd Albert, a Philadelphia orthopedic surgeon, and his wife, Lauren, had taken a trip to Morocco and on February 18, 1999, had arranged to be driven over the Atlas Mountains from Ourzazate to Marrakech in a convoy of three sport utility vehicles. When he saw the foreign-made vehicles, Specter complained, as did several others in his party. They were not equipped with rear passenger seat belts. But there wasn't much to be done at that point, so they hopped in, letting the hired local drivers negotiate the narrow, curvy roadway alongside the mountains. National Highway No. 9 did not have guard rails for the most part. As one of the SUVs behind Specter's was rounding an S-curve, an oncoming car traveling too fast caused it to veer toward the outside of the roadway. One tire went over the side of the road and then, in one terrifying instant, the vehicle toppled over the steep embankment. The SUV rolled over once, smashing out several windows. Then it rolled again, ejecting Lauren Albert from the interior. On the third roll, the large vehicle crushed her body. The SUV came to rest 100 feet below the road. Passengers, including Todd Albert, who had been in the front seat, suffered only scratches and bruises. But Lauren Albert, 41 years old, was dead.

Later Specter rode with his friend and his wife's body in the back of a pickup truck down the mountain to a morgue. That three-hour ride, mostly silent and seemingly endless, was one that would remain embedded in his memory forever.

When he returned to Philadelphia, Specter set about investigating and then filing suit against several responsible parties, chiefly the SUV manufacturer. The company had not sent finished cars to Morocco, only kits that had to be assembled on site. While the cars that drove off its assembly lines had seat belts, those sent as kits did not. The lawsuit against a European firm for an incident that had occurred in Africa was filed in Philadelphia. Part of the settlement with the automaker, whose name was to remain confidential, was an agreement that it would never again sell a vehicle of any kind—kit or otherwise—without belts for all the seats.

On a chilly day in March 2004, nearly six years after the first trial, Specter again found himself on a plane heading westward. He would land in San Francisco and rent a car—a Ford product, intentionally—for the three-hour drive through the Sierra Nevada Mountains to Reno. He was angry at Ford, angry that all these years later it had still not issued a warning, a real warning citing dangerous brakes, to the owners of certain 1991–1993 pickup trucks. He was angry that Ford still was not ready to take its punishment for the death of a three-year-old boy. Walter White had been dead for almost a decade.

Ford had been able to prolong the battle until most of the affected trucks had been retired. In the interim many people had been hurt. After notifying NHTSA of the Whites' fantastic verdict against the automaker, Ford had supplied the agency with additional data about rollaways. David Caputo, the Harvard-educated Kline & Specter associate (and later partner) who drafted and responded to pretrial motions for the second trial, had obtained and meticulously sifted through the data. What he found seemed astounding—1,149 drivers of Ford trucks had reported experiencing rollaways, with 54 suffering injuries. That was many more than the 70 customer reports of "unexpected movement" of trucks Ford had cited in a 1994 memo. And far more than Specter knew about—and the jury was told about—in the first *White v. Ford* trial.

Specter worked his BlackBerry while Caputo drove the Lincoln Aviator. The two discussed details of the case and strategy while Specter checked his e-mails, most of them having to do with the U.S. Senate election back in Pennsylvania. His father was in a fight for his fifth term in office and his political survival. Arlen Specter was battling in a Republican primary against Congressman Patrick Toomey, a conservative whose candidacy was being pushed hard by the ultraconservative Club for Growth. The well-heeled group had made Pennsylvania a key battleground, railing against the moderate Specter as being too liberal to represent the GOP. It was out to get, as the group itself had put it, Specter's "scalp." The threat was real. While Specter was ahead in the polls by 18 points in early March, with an April 27 primary, Shanin Specter was concerned. There were too many undecided voters still out there and he knew that, especially in primaries, the most ardent (and conservative) Republicans were most likely to show up to vote. His father's "favorable" rating had been eroding among "core primary voters," those considered strongly GOP or very conservative. The previous August, Specter's favorable rating among this group was 57 percent, but by early March it had slipped to the low 40s. Meanwhile, Toomey's favorable rating among core primary voters had started at 21 percent some seven months earlier, when he was a relative unknown, and had risen steadily to 49 percent by March 1 (and would continue to soar until it hit 69 percent). By early March Arlen Specter still scored better overall and with more moderate and progressive Republicans, but could they be counted on to turn out at the polls? If not, Toomey could surge ahead at the finish line. Certainly, the race was going to be close.

The younger Specter remembered vividly one election his father had lost, his bid for a third term as Philadelphia district attorney. Shanin Specter was fifteen at the time, and seeing his father defeated had broken his heart. He never wanted to see that again. He would continue to help run the campaign during the trial, reviewing and editing ad copy and scripts and giving instructions on how much to spend in which markets and in what time slots. All this from the tiny typewriter pad on his BlackBerry.

Incoming e-mail: "Toomey's running ten-second spots on cable in the Lehigh Valley."

Specter: "Good. Keep our thirty-second spots up there. And don't make the buys until the last minute you have to. We don't need them knowing what we're doing."

Specter's prediction would come true. As the primary election neared, Toomey would creep closer and closer in the polls, from 18 percentage points behind, to 12, and then within single digits.

ON MONDAY MORNING, the day before the trial was to start, a few motions still had to be filed and Specter assembled the full team in Durney's former office at 36 Stewart Street, the old wooden building he'd given up for a more modern space in the Reno suburbs. The building, across the street from the federal courthouse, was only partially in use and Durney had secured the first floor conference room. It would make a good base camp.

CHAPTER 23

Wheeler Dealer

AFTER THE MEETING Specter checked into his room at the Silver Legacy Resort Casino in downtown Reno. The Silver Legacy, built ten years earlier, was the newest hotel in Nevada's second largest city, the poor little sister to Las Vegas. The typical hotel room rate in Reno was about $50.

The city hadn't changed much in six years, at least not for the better. The downtown looked the same, maybe a little seedier. Specter walked along the main drag, Virginia Street, passing older folks and conventioneers. Bowlers were everywhere, wearing matching shirts and toting ball bags on rollers en route to a tournament at Reno's seventy-eight-lane National Bowling Stadium. Signs boasted of a coming National Tattoo Association and a gathering of female construction workers. Andrew Dice Clay was featured on billboards around town.

Specter wanted a cup of coffee but all he passed were souvenir shops, sidewalk casinos, liquor stores, pawnshops, loan stores, and wedding chapels, of which there were eleven in Reno. One advertised its "silver package"—use of the chapel for thirty minutes, a personal wedding coordinator, a keepsake photo session, an organist for thirty minutes, a small bridal bouquet, and one boutonniere—all for $399 Fridays and Saturdays, $379 Sundays through Thursdays. Another establishment in Reno—once known as the "Divorce Capital of the World" because of Nevada's liberal 1931 law requiring only a six-week residency for a couple to unhitch—advertised a complete legal divorce package for $379.

The day before, Specter and Caputo had seen two young couples climb out of an SUV at the Silver Legacy. The bride wore white and the rest of the wedding party had on blue jeans and flannel shirts. "Let's get drunk!" hooted the best man. Specter wondered how long it would be before the newlyweds took advantage of the $379 divorce special.

SPECTER DIDN'T KNOW what to expect from Malcolm Wheeler, Ford's new lawyer. Wheeler had lost just one major case in a fairly lengthy career defending big corporations, and in that case he had won a reversal on appeal. Over several decades he had resolved many Ford lawsuits. A half dozen had gone to jury verdicts and Wheeler had won them all. Wheeler had protected well the Blue Oval, Ford's well-known escutcheon.

Wheeler hadn't started out working for corporate America. In fact, he hadn't set out to become a lawyer. The son of a government auditor, Wheeler was raised in the Panama Canal Zone and headed for the Massachusetts Institute of Technology to become a physicist. The notion faded when he saw the competition. "I decided I wasn't smart enough," Wheeler recalled. Once he abandoned science, he was lost as to a career goal. So Wheeler took his B-plus average and applied to law school at Stanford. Even with his degree, he didn't practice law much. He taught full-time at Kansas University for three years before joining a law firm in California, where he handled antitrust cases but also worked pro bono defending young adults arrested on drug charges. Hippie defense work.

In 1977, while at Hughes Hubbard & Reed, Wheeler was called by Iowa University about a teaching job. He visited the school and liked what he saw. On his return to California he informed his law firm he was quitting to return to academia. "This couldn't have come at a worse time!" one of the partners told him. A big case had just come in for which Wheeler was well suited. There had been a number of explosions involving Ford's popular car, the Pinto. There was a case that might develop into a criminal procedure. "We want you to do it," they told Wheeler. It was a quandary. He wanted the Iowa job but the Ford case also fascinated him. So he did both. Iowa let him teach just one semester per year and clumped his classes together on Mondays and Tuesdays. From Wednesday through Sunday and during the eight other months of the year, he worked on cases, particularly Ford's. In August 1978 the nationally publicized trial opened in an Indiana courtroom. Ford, with Wheeler at the defense table, won acquittal.

That was a long time ago. In 1990 Wheeler decided to move with his wife and two children to Denver. He traveled so much, defending clients in so many states, that he could live almost anywhere. Denver was a central location with clean air and safe streets. Wheeler, with one paralegal in tow, moved his office. In February 1998 (three years after Klin & Specter formed in Philadelphia) he joined with a group of other lawyers to start his own firm, Wheeler Trigg & Kennedy. The firm started with nineteen lawyers and a handful of prized Fortune 100 clients, including Ford and DaimlerChrysler, later adding other corporate giants, including Whirlpool and Pfizer. Only six years after opening his own firm, Wheeler arrived in Reno to come to Ford's rescue once again. By now his firm had thirty-seven lawyers and a staff of ninety.

The White case would be a little difh. nt for Wheeler. A jury had already found Ford liable and the verdict, including punitive damages, was upheld in the appeals court. Only the amount was to be decided. It was a bad situation. But Wheeler had been known to make the best of a bad situation. In 1990 he was Ford's attorney when it ended a twelve-year-old patent infringement lawsuit filed by Robert W. Kearns, the inventor of the intermittent windshield wiper, a device he claimed the auto industry stole from him. (Wheeler was brought in six weeks after Ford had lost at trial and helped settle the case for $10.2 million, far less than the $141 million Kearns had sought. The settlement was considered a victory for Ford. By comparison, Chrysler later settled with Kearns for $30 million.)

Wheeler realized his new case would be difficult. So many things were working against him, especially the first jury's verdict and the instruction that would be given to this new jury that it ' ad to follow the first jury's decision. All except the amount of punitive damages. "It certainly makes it very interesting to walk into a courtroom and know the judge is going to tell the jury all these bad things about your client," he would say. Wheeler also knew that Specter and his crew had unearthed more bad information on Ford in the years since the first trial, including the 1,149 incidents of rollaways through 1999. Imagine if the first jury had known that.

The case had been dumped in Wheeler's lap barely eight months ago, along with seventy-two boxes of materials. He would have to bone up on the details, and fast. To make things worse, in pretrial motions, Hagen had ruled against Ford in almost every instance. But the more Wheeler examined the documents, the more he felt he could make a case that Ford had been a responsible corporate entity, not the loathsome profit-hungry colossus Specter had made it out to be. Wheeler was convinced that everyone at Ford had tried hard to discover and solve the problem with the brakes. Neither Ford nor Orscheln was ever able to prove that the brakes spontaneously disengaged, yet Ford had made design changes—it had shortened the brake release rod so it wouldn't be inadvertently kicked and free the brake, new documents showed—and installed the plastic wedge and later replaced the brakes altogether. Just to be safe. The company had issued a service bulletin to dealers and later recalled the trucks, even sending not one but four letters to each owner. "I truly believe they were trying to do the right thing," Wheeler said. "I'm going to try the case I think is the truth."

But he knew his behemoth client was the underdog. Specter had been fighting this war for years, ever since the parents of Derick Bobb had called his office. Specter had lived with the material for six years and was trying the case a second time. As Wheeler put it, "There was one person who was doing this for the second time and improving on it. And there was another person who wasn't."

WHEN WHEELER FIRST stepped into the courtroom in Reno, his appearance surprised Specter. He was fifty-nine but looked a lot younger. When he walked, he glided. He didn't look like old Joe Pinto or even Ed Gray, the gray-suited, gray-haired lawyer Specter had faced in a case against General Motors. Wheeler, a California native, did not have the cookie-cutter semi-military look of the corporate lawyer. He wore a tailor-made midnight blue suit and an air of supreme confidence. His dress shirt was so white it seemed to emit light, as if plugged into an electrical socket. Wheeler seemed to have stepped off a page in GQ. He was thin, even thinner than Specter. Wheeler's distinguishing feature was his long, straight black hair, hanging halfway over his ears and over the back of his shirt collar, in something of a Beatles-style cut, except parted to one side. His entire look and demeanor was the flipside of Joe Pinto, a shorter man with white hair and often a slightly defeated look. If Wheeler was trying to show that he was kind of a hip, modern guy and not your typical gray-clad corporate lawyer, he'd already achieved his first success in White v. Ford.

Specter, by contrast, took pains to appear understated, almost nondescript. During the two-week trial, he would wear a blue suit with a white shirt and red tie every day. Different blue suits and red ties, but the same somewhat subdued uniform every day. He wanted to be a familiar sight, someone the jury would listen to, not look at. Outside the courtroom, Wheeler and Specter were quite the opposite. Wheeler went to work most days when he wasn't on trial wearing jeans and an open shirt. Specter was a stickler, almost always in a suit, wearing cuff links and shined shoes, a tie pulled tight to his throat.

It seemed like a parade when the lawyers walked into the courtroom on the first morning of the trial. Eight men, four from each side and all in dark suits, took their places in the front of the room. For the plaintiffs there was Specter, Caputo, Durney, and Nomura. Wheeler had local counsel at the defense table with him along with two other men in suits nearby. A legal assistant as well as three other lawyers sat a few rows back in the courtroom.

"These attorneys get paid by the minute, don't they?" joked a potential juror.

Jimmie and Ginny White sat in chairs behind the plaintiffs' table, holding hands, as they would throughout most of the trial, his thumb gently stroking hers. Ginny wore the gloomy frown that seemed her permanent expression, while Jimmie sat with his jaw firmly clenched. They were exhausted but determined not to show it.

The trial began the way all trials seem to begin, with the judge calling potential jurors and most trying to avoid service. The excuses showed variety. "My father's sick," said one man. One woman suffered from neuralgia. Another had a realtors' conference. Another's sister was flying in to visit. "I can't see well enough to drive at night and I live 91 miles away," said one woman. One man had recently started a new job. Another had a job interview—in an hour. Hagen let them all go. He didn't want jurors in such an important case who didn't want to be there. And some of them did.

"Oh, please pick me," thought Connie Martin, a single woman in her thirties. Hagen had explained the basics of the case and Martin found it enthralling.

Hagen noted that "Ford knew" its parking brake was prone to failure and continued to use it. He told the potential jurors about Walter White's death, which brought tears to Ginny's eyes. He told them about the prior jury's findings, though not the amount of its awards. He told them of the appeals court's ruling.

"This is where this jury takes over," said Hagen.

Each side, the defense and the plaintiffs, could strike three potential jurors. The jurors were asked about their jobs, their families, if they had ever sued someone, if they knew any of the lawyers.

One, Catharine Armour, had worked with Pete Durney's wife about ten years ago. She was a secretary at the elementary school where Pete's wife, Martha, had taught.

"Would this prevent you from rendering a fair and impartial verdict?" Armour was asked.

"No, absolutely not," she responded. Armour, to Specter's surprise, would be kept on the jury.

Another potential juror obviously enjoyed his few minutes in the limelight.

"Despite what people say, I'm not retired," he said in response to one question. Allen Humphreys also said that, yes, he had sued someone, a bowling alley, about thirty years ago. A ball machine had returned Humphreys' ball with a chunk missing. He complained and the alley manager told him to take a hike. Humphreys did—to court. He won his claim and the bowling alley was forced to fix the ball. "They put epoxy on it and it was as good as new," he beamed. "I still use it today."

Specter liked Humphreys' make-them-do-the-right-thing attitude. He also liked that he was a mechanic and would be able to understand the trial's finer technical points. What Humphreys didn't tell the lawyers, what he wasn't asked, was that he once worked fixing cars at a Ford-Suzuki dealership. He was kept on the jury.

Specter also liked Cynthia Lavan, who had also filed a suit. Hers was a little more serious. Lavan had been part of a class action against the manufacturer of the Dalkon Shield, the defective intrauterine birth control device. Specter knew that she was an employee trainer at a large company. What he didn't know was that Lavan worked for a car company, General Motors.

The jury was set at eight, eight Nevadans who would again decide Ford's punishment. Overall Specter was happy with the jury. It seemed a little too old for him, particularly two of the jurors. Older folks, he'd found, generally gave smaller awards. But he felt good, even lucky, to have landed Armour—why hadn't Wheeler tossed Pete's wife's colleague from the jury?—Humphreys, and Lavan. He felt that all three could be convinced that Ford had done wrong. He would be right, it would turn out. About one of them.

"THIS WAS WALTER WHITE," said Specter, holding the large color portrait in front of the jury, the portrait that Jimmie White had kept at home. Specter didn't want to be melodramatic, but he did want the jury to get a glimpse of the lad, to know that Walter was a real, flesh-and-blood person. Jimmie's face flushed and he began breathing heavily when the photo was shown.

Specter briefly reiterated his case—the reports of rollaways, Ford's report of one injury when it knew there were more, the government's request for a recall, Ford's sluggish acquiescence, its delay, and the fact that it didn't really state the problem, the hazards associated with the brake problem. He showed them the ratchet and pawl, the plastic wedge used as a temporary fix.

The public was never told, even until now, that the serious problem was rollaway.

Judge Hagen called a recess for lunch. Specter was glad. He wanted the jury to have some time to think about what he had told them.

"My speech is ringing in their ears right now," he told Durney and Nomura over tuna sandwiches in Durney's old conference room across the street. "They're thinking over lunch how much to give."

Nomura suggested that Specter should have mentioned a few other things, specifically the $23 million cost of the recall and how Ford had tried to avoid it.

"No, I purposely didn't tell them that and I'll tell you why," said Specter. "I don't want the jury to award $23 million. I may have years ago. Not now."

Specter had wanted to mention two numbers, one far smaller and the other much bigger. One was the cost of the plastic wedge—16¢ apiece. The other was $11.5 billion, Ford's net worth, sharply reduced from previous years but still impressive.

The lawyers talked over lunch about the jurors and about Wheeler. What could be his strategy? What was Ford's super-sharp lawyer going to argue? Would he do something similar to what Pinto had done at the first trial, which was basically to admit that Ford was wrong and appeal to the jury for leniency or, as Pinto had put it, to "be fair?" Ford had lost that case. Its behavior had been found outrageous and a punitive verdict upheld. What else could Wheeler do?

They were about to find out.

As Wheeler walked toward the jury box it was evident that he was older than he first appeared. A few gray strands showed in his carefully coiffed black hair. But Wheeler, with his high energy, came off well. He was liquid, mellifluous in both manner and voice. He glided about the courtroom. His voice was steady, sure, and soothing.

Ford had done nothing wrong, nothing at all. In fact, he told the jury, the company had bent over backward to make sure it did everything right.

It had started by buying its brakes from Orscheln, the "premier parking brake company in the country," at a price higher than what other companies might have paid. (This comment also served to let the jury know that Ford didn't make the brakes, defraying blame from the automaker.) Sure, Ford later received some complaints about rollaways, but only a handful. "Only six reports. That didn't seem like that much," said

Wheeler, noting the hundreds of thousands of trucks that had rolled off the assembly line.

When a problem finally was suspected, said Wheeler, Ford tried its best to analyze it. When, for instance, it found that some people were kicking the parking brake's release rod, knocking the brake out—again, not Ford's fault—it changed the design and shortened the rod. "Ford investigated . . . and made changes quickly," said Wheeler.

When spontaneous disengagement was suspected, Ford again investigated and pushed Orscheln to do so as well. Tests were run and run and run. But spontaneous disengagement could not be proven. What about the tests that did demonstrate the problem? Well, said Wheeler, those tests didn't prove anything because they were conducted under a "wholly artificial situation," with workers kicking the brake system and jumping up and down on the vehicles' bumpers. Those tests didn't count.

Even so, Ford still acted. It had Orscheln create the wedge to put into the parking system to try to prevent rollaways. It didn't have to do that at all. Ford also notified dealers in a bulletin about the possible problem and the fix. It sent out news releases. Then, Wheeler told the jury, "Ford agreed to do the recall, even though testing could not prove that spontaneous disengagement occurred." The wording of the recall, he added, conformed to government safety requirements. And then Ford sent out four additional notices to vehicle owners. These were "extra steps" that Ford didn't have to take. The recall got a 79 percent response, well above the average industry rate of 70 percent, said Wheeler.

What more could Ford have done? It investigated. It tested. It made a fix even though it couldn't replicate the problem. It notified dealers. It issued a recall. It sent owners repeat notices.

What's more, Wheeler said, the Ford employees were not heartless, greedy souls bent on covering up a problem with the brake system. Just the opposite. Tim Rakowicz, the engineer assigned to find and fix the problem, had done everything possible and was never able to find evidence of spontaneous disengagement. What about his "white paper" suggesting the opposite and recommending a recall? A mistake, said Wheeler. Now that Rakowicz had seen other documents, he realized the folly of his prior testimony. And Alfred Darold, the second witness scheduled for the trial, didn't think there was a problem. Heck, he'd even bought a Ford F-Series truck for his wife and two daughters to drive around in.

No, Ford was no big, bad wolf. The company and its employees had done everything possible. They had done their best. "That's why,"

Wheeler said, moving to the jury box, "at the end, we'll ask you to say that punishment is not appropriate."

Wheeler's strategy was thus revealed. He would not, as Joe Pinto had done before him, beseech the jury to "be fair" in levying a punishment. He would instead insist—the prior jury's ruling be damned—that Ford had done nothing wrong. Wheeler was not trying to minimize the damage. He was going for absolution. He was going for broke.

"It's an all-or-nothing defense," said Specter after the trial recessed for lunch.

"They're really shooting for the moon here. They're swinging for the fences," said Nomura. "It's a pretty gutsy move."

If Wheeler could convince the jury that Ford had done nothing wrong, perhaps he could pull off a victory and get them to award the smallest of damages—zero. But there was a risk. If the jury didn't believe that Ford had done nothing wrong, this argument could seem arrogant or, worse, that Ford was trying to put one over on the jury. If Wheeler's strategy didn't work, Ford might face a huge verdict.

"It's a big-lie defense," said Specter, alternating among a notepad, a tuna hoagie, and his BlackBerry, which brought news of his father's Senate election.

"We can tell the jury," added Caputo, "that Ford lied to NHTSA, it lied to the public, and now it's lying to you."

"They're saying that Tim Rakowicz was ill prepared before and now he's back to make it right? I don't think they can sell that fish," Specter said. "They're saying that Ford's employees weren't uncaring or heartless or stupid? I'm going to argue that, in some combination, they were."

Specter polished off his sandwich and began punching messages into his BlackBerry. His calm in the face of fire soothed the other lawyers. Specter didn't think any of the jurors would buy Wheeler's strategy.

He didn't realize how wrong he was.

THE JURORS had listened intently to Wheeler, expected behavior during an opening argument. Specter had seen jurors fade away as trials went on. He'd even seen jurors dozing at past trials. (His partner, Tom Kline, had one trial in Philadelphia in which a juror kept falling asleep despite a judge's repeated admonitions. After the case was settled the judge informed the juror that he'd be coming back. As a defendant, charged with contempt.) But these jurors were interested, Specter could tell. And he had to admit that Wheeler had been good. But now the street fighting began. There would be less time to prepare speeches. The lawyers would be working on the fly, examining and cross-examining.

There would be only three witnesses at this trial. Two were from Ford: Tim Rakowicz, the young Ford engineer in charge of looking into the brake problem, and Alfred Darold, a Ford executive who had testified in scores of trials in Ford's defense, including in the first *White v. Ford* trial. Finally, Wayne Soucie, an Orscheln engineer, would take the stand for a brief testimony.

Specter had decided against putting Jimmie or Ginny on the stand. It would serve no purpose. This trial was only about the amount of punitive damages, not whether Jimmie had set his truck's brake on that fateful day. Nor would Campbell Laird, Specter's expert witness, testify about how spontaneous disengagement of the brake system could occur. Specter did not have to prove the entire case against Ford all over again.

Or so he thought. Not everyone on the defense team was convinced. Now that Ford had taken a new tack, in essence pretending the first trial had never taken place and denying—despite the previous verdict—that it had done anything wrong, maybe bringing back Laird would have been wise. Or putting Jimmie on the stand. Maybe the jury would go for Ford's argument. And how could it be convinced to give a large award if it didn't hear from Jimmie or Ginny, if it didn't feel the pain of their loss?

But Specter felt confident he could convince the jury by letting it hear from Ford's own people. He felt that Rakowicz was making things up, trying to skirt the truth, and he felt confident the jury would see through him. Juries, Specter knew, could always smell a rat. And Rakowicz, he felt, was a big one. So was Darold. Specter felt he could expose them for what they were—company men toeing the company line.

CHAPTER 24

Rakowicz Redux

IT WAS SPECTER'S JOB once again to go up against Tim Rakowicz, to try to pick apart his story. Specter didn't dislike Rakowicz. In fact, he had sympathy for him. He had no proof, of course, but after all these years and testimony—Rakowicz had first been deposed for the Bobb case so long ago—Specter had a working theory. As a bright and idealistic young engineer at Ford, Rakowicz had been placed in charge of reviewing a potential system problem. And he had diligently done just that and he had gotten it right—there was a problem, indeed, a big problem. Rakowicz had put it in writing. He had recommended a recall. Alarm bells went off at Ford and the wagons were circled, but not around Rakowicz and his findings. He got no backing by his superiors or his superiors' superiors. He was forced into a corner, made to compromise, to backtrack, to retract. By the time he was questioned in the first White trial, he denied that the brakes failed and he suffered convenient memory losses about the facts of his investigation. The innocent, candid engineer was no longer either.

At the first White trial years later, Rakowicz had been well prepared in what to say. He disputed portions of documents he had helped to develop and he still had problems recalling important details. Specter felt this could not have been a comfortable position for Rakowicz, yet he toed the company line. It would have been better, better for Rakowicz and better for Ford, Specter felt, if he had simply been more open, if Rakowicz had told the jury that, yes, back when he looked into the matter and wrote his white paper he believed that the brakes were bad and that a recall was warranted and he still thinks that, but that Ford was a large company where such important decisions and changes happened slowly, perhaps too slowly in this case. If Rakowicz had made such an admission, there was little doubt Ford would have lost the case. But the jury likely would have appreciated his openness, and perhaps it would have found Ford's behavior was not reprehensible and not deserving of punitive damages, or at least not such a huge amount. It was only Specter's theory, his gut feeling.

So as he embarked on yet another examination of Rakowicz, he did so with a mixture of emotions. He needed to attack this witness, to debunk his testimony, and yet would do so with little animus for the man—and Rakowicz was no longer a kid—on the witness stand. Part of Specter felt sorry for Tim Rakowicz.

Rakowicz's hair had become somewhat thinner on top, but otherwise he looked pretty much as he had six years earlier at the first trial. He still had a serious demeanor belying his age. He wore a gray suit, blue shirt, and maroon tie. He would wear the same uniform throughout his four days of testimony. In his slightly high, soft, almost boyish voice, Rakowicz tried to sound friendly. That demeanor didn't last very long.

Specter let it be known right from the start that his examination would be no cakewalk. He started his questioning by bringing up Rakowicz's deposition from the Bobb case, the case in which a Ford truck "ran over the head of a little boy." Rakowicz responded that he never examined the brake from that case. The brief Q-and-A seemed innocuous, but Specter simply wanted to get information from the Bobb case into this trial. He thought he might face a battle, that Wheeler would object. To his surprise the defense lawyer didn't say a word.

Specter showed that he was in charge. When Rakowicz tried to launch into long explanations, speeches that strayed far from the questions, Specter immediately reined him in. He looked at the judge and raised repeated objections.

Finally Hagen interrupted and peered down at Rakowicz. "Please concentrate on the question," he said. And again, moments later, Hagen told the witness, without the "please" this time, "Answer the question."

Rakowicz was able to answer some questions he hadn't been able to answer at the 1998 trial. He remembered details now that he hadn't remembered before. He corrected statements he had made before, some of them incriminating to Ford. "My recollection is better today because I had a chance to look at the documents," he explained, looking at the jury.

Indeed, Rakowicz seemed much better prepared. He seemed to have all the answers now, the right answers. And his delivery was more polished. He looked at Specter for his questions, then faced the jury with his answers. And he thought before speaking, pausing a second or two to look up at the ceiling or scratch his chin, then giving his answers. It was convincing but things were just starting to heat up.

DAY TWO OF RAKOWICZ'S testimony brought a litany of similar statements from the witness: "I don't know." "I don't recall." "It depends." While Rakowicz's memory was now crystal clear on some points—most notably that spontaneous disengagement of the brakes never occurred—he had major memory gaps on some subjects.

Didn't Rakowicz once say, "We have to get skip-out resolved?" Specter asked.

"I don't remember," replied the witness.

Rakowicz denied that his now-infamous "white paper" written in February 1992 was ever meant to recommend a recall. Specter reminded him of his answer at the last trial when Rakowicz was asked if he'd ever told the folks at Orscheln that a recall was the purpose of the paper. His answer then, "I may have."

Could he say now whether he uttered those words in 1992? "I can't," said Rakowicz.

Reminded that the white paper mentioned the brakes "self-releasing" and contained a statement that they "will" intermittently self-release—not that it was a mere possibility—Rakowicz said the actual occurrences were very rare, just six reports among 500,000 trucks produced in the first year. He said he hadn't known that at the first trial. So when did he learn that fact? Said Rakowicz, "Probably a few days ago." Yet there were reports of at least twenty-one rollaways by the time Rakowicz wrote his report, including reports to dealers and the government. Didn't Rakowicz know about them? "Yes," he acknowledged. A few of the jurors looked befuddled.

And couldn't there have been many more that were never reported? Couldn't there have been people whose trucks rolled away who thought they had simply forgotten to set the brake? "People might think that, sure," Rakowicz said.

Rakowicz had written in his paper that sometimes the brake "would remain in the down position." Correct? "Yes," he had to admit.

Did Ford ever do a survey asking about rollaways? "No."

One main point Rakowicz wanted to make at this trial was that his 1992 white paper had been wrong. Just plain wrong. He hadn't known, twelve years ago, things he knew now. For one, the tests that were done were invalid. If he knew then what he knew now he would never have written the report. He was sticking to the new story. There was no such thing as spontaneous disengagement.

Specter thought this was a lot of bull. It was revisionist history at best. At worst the witness had been coached and rehearsed to the point of perjury. Specter asked a question for which he thought he knew the answer but he was surprised by Rakowicz's response.

Q: Did you ever write that this report was wrong?
A: Yes.

Yes? "Where?" Specter wanted to know.

Rakowicz responded that a document written in 1994 proved that the white paper had been wrong and that he never sought a recall of the vehicles. The proof came in a document that used the word "theories" in discussing the brake problem. It seemed like a stretch, hardly "proof."

Q: Does this say the paper was "wrong"?
A: No.

Then Specter produced a Ford document dated April 1994—*after* the one that used the word "theories"—in which the possible causes of rollaways were given ratings from one to three, with three the highest. In this report, skip-out of the brakes was rated a three—a "most likely" cause. If spontaneous disengagement was only a theory, it was still a top one at that time.

Q: You didn't think it did not occur. You thought it was "most likely"?
A: No, sir.

Rakowicz pointed to another piece of evidence he said proved spontaneous disengagement did not occur, that refuted his white paper. A report written in August 1994 mentioned that skip-out had been "impossible to duplicate." Again Specter didn't consider this proof at all, coming so much later in the game and not directly stating that the phenomenon had never occurred, just that Ford had not duplicated it.

But wait a second? How could Rakowicz have done this report? He had just told Specter a day earlier that he no longer worked on the F-Series brake problem after he had been transferred to another department in June 1994. "I was moved but was asked to write this paper," explained Rakowicz. "I didn't think of it yesterday when you asked me." Specter gave the jury a wry look. Rakowicz could remember back twelve years, but not one day?

Specter used Rakowicz to introduce new evidence. Had he seen another document, one that came years later, in which Ford listed 1,149 reported cases of rollaways? Rakowicz wasn't sure. The report had also mentioned 54 injuries and 1 fatality. At mention of the fatality, Jimmie White put his arm over his wife's shoulders, his lower lip quivering. Several of the jurors looked over. Everyone in the courtroom knew what the Whites must have been thinking. *Reports of 1,149 rollaways, 54 injuries, 1 fatality. Why us? Why Walter?*

Specter asked about five rollaways reported from the Pittsburgh area and at least four injuries. Rakowicz remembered various aspects of those cases. "Six years ago you didn't remember. Your memory improved?" Specter wanted to know. "Yes," said Rakowicz. On another point he added, "At the last trial you tricked me."

But why had Ford reported only one injury to NHTSA in August 1994, when Rakowicz knew of at least four, plus the case of Derick Bobb? (Specter knew Rakowicz knew about Derick. He had deposed Rakowicz in the Bobb case.)

> Q: Ford had a lot more reports than one injury. Correct?
> A: Yes.

DAY THREE OF RAKOWICZ'S testimony brought more questions about rollaways.

The engineer had said that the rate of incidents was extremely low. Specter mentioned the Ford Ranger plant at which two of fifty trucks were found to have experienced skip-out of the parking brakes.

> Q: Two of fifty. Four percent. Is that a low occurrence?
> A: No, sir.

Specter brought up the time in Louisville in July 1993 in which a batch of trucks was found to have inoperable parking brakes. The plant gates had been locked to prevent shipment of the trucks. A report had mentioned that skip-out was a "design-inherent condition." Another report mentioned that the parking brakes were a "Top 5 warranty concern."

> Q: Was it a "Top 5 warranty concern"?
> A: I don't recall.

Rakowicz testified that a number of things caused rollaways. Many times people just didn't set the brake fully and walked away from their trucks, even as they were moving slightly, a condition called "creep."

Specter rattled off a number of individual cases involving rollaways, one of which involved a Ford engineer's truck rolling into a lake.

> Q: Do you think a Ford engineer would exit a truck while it was still moving and allow it to roll into a lake?
> A: No, sir.

Rakowicz had said the brake problem was merely a "customer inconvenience." Usually the brake popped back up immediately after a driver had tried to set it and the driver simply had to press it down a second time. No big deal. That was why safety wasn't mentioned in the service bulletin sent to dealers along with the plastic wedge designed to fix the problem.

> Q: You didn't tell them it was a safety issue, correct?
> A: Yes.
> Q: But rollaway is a safety issue. Correct?
> A: Absolutely.

Now Specter went on to a major point from the first trial. Ford had not recalled trucks with automatic transmissions, even though they had the same faulty parking brake system. There could be only one reason for this—because trucks with automatic transmissions would be shifted into "park" when left standing and, therefore, would not roll away. Automatic transmissions provided a backup of sorts to the parking brake. Recalling only the trucks with manual transmissions was proof that Ford considered the brakes a safety problem and not merely one of driver inconvenience. If the recall was merely over driver inconvenience, Ford would have recalled all the trucks. The conclusion was inescapable: Ford knew the manual transmission trucks were unsafe, yet it didn't clearly state that and would not admit it, even to this day.

Specter would wrap it up on this point. This line of questioning and Rakowicz's answers would prove to be perhaps the most critical of the entire trial.

> Q: You weren't including the automatics because the recall wasn't about skip-through on application, Mr. Rakowicz. The recall was about rollaway, correct?
> A: The recall—what we were urged to recall by the safety administration as a precautionary safeguard against rollaway.
> Q: The recall was about rollaway, correct?

A: My answer stands, yes, sir.

Q: But you described it to the world as something that was being done for skip-through on application, correct?

A: We described it as "skip-through."

Q: Can the question be answered yes or no?

A: It deserves a little bit of explanation.

Q: Can the question be answered yes or no?

A: Would you repeat it, please?

Q: You described the problem to the world as "skip-through on application" and not "rollaway," correct?

A: Yes, sir.

Q: You gave a phony reason for the recall, correct?

A: No, sir.

Q: If you were really recalling for skip-through on application, then you would have recalled the automatics, too, correct?

A: We recalled because the . . .

Q: Can you answer the question yes or no?

A: It deserves a little bit of an explanation.

Q: If you were recalling the vehicles for skip-through on application, you would have recalled the automatics as well, correct?

A: Not necessarily.

Q: Mr. Rakowicz, we'll go into this in some detail, but do you recognize as you sit here on the witness stand that your explanation to this question and the ones just preceding it have changed since you testified six years ago?

A: No, sir. I don't recall my prior testimony.

Q: You were asked about this in exquisite detail the last time you testified, correct? For at least half an hour we talked about this, correct?

A: I remember it, yes, sir.

Q: And it's memorialized in the trial transcript, correct?

A: Yes, sir.

Q: And you were here for the opening statement, correct?

A: Yes, sir.

Q: And you heard me tell the jury that there was a phony reason given for the recall, correct?

A: Yes, sir.

Q: And you've read the transcript of your trial testimony, you told me, a couple of days ago, at least twice, correct?

A: I probably read my transcript maybe as far as a month ago.

Q: So you did this [recall] because the government wanted you to. Is that correct?

A: Yes, sir.

Q: If the government hadn't told you to do it, you wouldn't have done it, would you have?

A: I don't think so, no, sir.

Q: What the government was worried about was rollaways, correct?

A: They were concerned and they asked us to do it as a precautionary measure.

Q: They were concerned about rollaways, correct?

A: Yes, sir.

Q: And that was a safety issue, correct?

A: Yes, sir.

Q: And so the recall was done for a safety issue, correct?

A: Potential, yes, sir.

Q: And in order for people to know the importance of what they're doing when they get a recall notice, they have to be told the truth about why the vehicle is being recalled, correct?

A: Yes, sir.

Q: And rollaway is a safety issue, correct?

A: Yes, sir, absolutely.

Q: And skip-through on apply is not a safety issue, correct?

A: Yes, sir.

Q: But people were never told that the vehicles were being recalled because of rollaway, correct?

A: Yes, sir.

Q: People were told the vehicles were being recalled because of skip-through on apply, correct?

A: Yes, sir.

Q: So people were told that the recall was not for a safety issue, correct?

A: No, sir.

Q: Well, the form may have said safety, but the substance of the communication, which is skip-through on apply, is not a safety issue, correct?

A: Yes, sir.

Q: Do you agree that it's more likely that somebody will bring the vehicle in more promptly if they're told the whole truth about the safety nature of the reason for the recall?

A: I don't know if I can say that.

Q: Doesn't that make sense to you?

A: I can't comment on people's behavior relative to recalls. There are a lot of people that don't heed recalls.

Rakowicz pressed the point that the recall had experienced a high compliance rate, a rate of nearly 80 percent. But Specter noted, even at 80 percent (which the plaintiffs disputed), that meant that 170,000 people still had not brought their trucks in for repair. And many of those who did may have taken months, acting perhaps only after receiving their third or fourth notice. Specter knew human nature. People, if told their trucks or cars were unsafe, would come in sooner than if told there was a convenience problem with their brakes. He felt the jurors would understand this, too.

Q: Did you see yesterday that there were, as of 1999, 1,100 complaints that Ford reported to NHTSA as of that time concerning rollaway?

A: I don't recall the number.

Q: Well, how many of those 1,100 occurred on the 170,000 vehicles that never came in because Ford didn't tell people that the vehicles were being recalled for the reason of rollaway, Mr. Rakowicz?

A: I wouldn't know.

Q: How many of the fifty-four injuries reported by Ford to NHTSA were included among the 170,000 vehicles that didn't come in?

A: I don't know.

Q: How many of those fifty-four injuries occurred while somebody . . . to somebody whose vehicle eventually came in but it took longer to come in because they didn't think that skip-through on apply was enough of a reason to bring their vehicle in?

A: I don't know.

Q: The people of this country still don't know that the vehicles were recalled for reason of rollaway, correct?

A: Yes, sir.

Q: Well, if the vehicles have a useful life of about twenty years, and if they were made between 1992 and 1994, then they're on the roadway now because they're only ten or twelve years old now, and they'll be on the roadway for another eight, ten years, correct?

A: Yes, sir.

Q: And all those people don't know that these vehicles were recalled because of rollaway, correct?

A: Yes, sir.

Q: Don't these people deserve to know that, Mr. Rakowicz, yes or no?

A: Yes, sir.

Specter didn't let it drop there. On the third day of testimony, with Rakowicz trying to be elusive and Specter trying to be patient and hold him to a line of questioning, the witness had finally made this important admission. Specter had painstakingly led Rakowicz to this point, had wrung from him an admission that Ford had not told the truth—or at least not the whole story—in its recall notice. In fact even after one jury had rendered a verdict that it was the faulty recall notice that had caused the death of Walter White, Ford still hadn't come clean, still hadn't told the public the real reason for the recall. Specter had a few more drops to squeeze from Rakowicz about the public's right to know.

Q: Are you going to tell them?

A: I think . . . I don't know how they're informed, through their letters.

Q: [But] the letters they've gotten don't say that, correct?

A: Yes, sir.

Q: Are you telling me that Ford is now going to tell people the truth about why the vehicles were recalled?

A: Well, we told the truth in our letter based on what we knew. We did, so we put in our letter what we believed to be true and NHTSA approved it.

Q: No, sir. You told me before that people deserved to know the reason for the recall, which was rollaways. Now, is Ford planning to tell people this now, ten years later?

A: I don't know, sir.

Q: Have you asked anybody that question?

A: No, sir.

Q: Do you think that's a pretty important question, Mr. Rakowicz?

A: Yes, sir.

"Wow! Wasn't that bitchin'?" Specter had been unable to believe his own ears. Now, with the judge calling the lunch recess, Specter and company were back in Durney's office, the wrapped tuna sandwiches in a pile in the middle of the conference table.

"What just happened there?" Specter asked.

"He's ready to give it up!" replied Nomura. "He just said that people deserve to know and we should have told them."

"I was floored," said Specter. He had seen Rakowicz come full circle, reverting for a moment—a crystallizing moment—to the innocent, candid young engineer whom Specter had met many years ago. Rakowicz had dropped his guard and told the truth. *Ford had not done enough to inform people of the rollaway problem with its trucks.* Rakowicz had admitted it. Finally.

There was excitement in the cramped, wood-paneled room.

"We got nothing like that in the first trial. He did, Don. He gave it up."

"I was stunned," said Nomura. "I expected Rakowicz to say something like, 'We didn't want to panic the public, or to cause public alarm because we didn't think spontaneous disengagement happened.' He'd been asked the question before. It was like it was unanticipated."

It had been quite an admission.

Wheeler followed. He would try to rehabilitate his witness. He would try to show that Specter had tied Rakowicz in knots and he was now trying to untie them.

Q: Did any Ford test show that spontaneous disengagement had occurred?

A. No.

Q: Did any Orscheln test show it?

A: No.

Q: Did any NHTSA test show it?

A: No.

Wheeler made a point of it. Even tests by the government, an independent party in all of this, failed to turn up a problem. (He didn't mention that NHTSA had itself tested only eight brakes.)

"You tried very hard to prove spontaneous disengagement?" "Yes," said Rakowicz. He had simply and earnestly been trying to find the problem. It was frustrating that the tests kept coming up negative. He had "brainstormed" with Orscheln engineers. He had done "every conceivable test." He had communicated with dealers across the country. He had traveled to various places around the country to investigate.

Rakowicz had no reason to lie, he said. It was his job to uncover problems. What would have happened, Wheeler asked, if he had failed to report finding a problem to the higher-ups at Ford? "I would have been fired," said Rakowicz.

But he had not found spontaneous disengagement. It was thus a "close call" on whether to issue a recall, Rakowicz said. Ford knew rollaways were occurring but was unable to demonstrate that it was a problem with its brakes that was causing them. And, as everyone knew, rollaways were a common occurrence in the car business. One of the most common problems was simply that people didn't press down hard enough on the brake. Nevertheless, Ford decided to recall the trucks. As Rakowicz put it, "Because NHTSA wanted it and rather than argue with them . . ."

What about his white paper in which he had mentioned that the brakes had a tendency to skip out? Rakowicz said it had been "based on my misunderstanding of the test results." It had been a mistake.

He also backed the decision by his boss, Ken Gutowski, to "purge" the notation that he had written the report for a recall committee. "Gutowski was correcting Orscheln because they were wrong about what group I was writing the paper for."

> Q: So as you sit here today, was there more you could have done faster or additional tests you could have done to try to prove spontaneous disengagement?
> A: No, sir.

THE TRIAL'S FIRST WEEK had ended. The finish line was in view.

But first, the weekend, and some downtime. Jimmie and Ginny decided to stay in Reno, taking time to rest. Jimmie had been too keyed up to sleep well, some nights closing his eyes for only an hour or two. They would relax over the weekend, or try to. They would eat some nice meals. One afternoon they took a few magazines and a bag of dirty clothes to a Reno laundromat.

Specter unwound in his own fashion. On weeknights he'd try to get in a game of squash, once with Durney arranging for him to play the pro at a Reno club. (Specter lost the match but he won one of four games.) Specter and Caputo had dinner at a nice restaurant each night, one evening at a shoreside table on nearby Lake Tahoe. On another night all the plaintiffs' lawyers went to Pete Durney's house in the country for martinis and salmon steaks. (Specter stuck with a dark beer.) But on weekends Specter wanted to get out of town, and pronto. On Friday morning, the last day of the trial's first week, he instructed Caputo to be packed, to load and gas the Lincoln Aviator and be ready to move out as soon as the trial recessed for the weekend. They drove the three and a half hours to San Francisco, one of Specter's favorite cities. Hotel rooms had been booked and dinner reservations made. There was the waterfront to visit, with its crisp, fresh breezes and a view of Alcatraz, and an art deco auction Specter wanted to attend. Maybe he'd hit Chinatown for dim sum.

The drives to Frisco and back also gave him time to help out with his father's Senate campaign. Specter feverishly worked his BlackBerry and telephone, dispensing orders on which TV ads to run and when, where to position staffers, and how much money to spend on what, as well as strategy for his father's upcoming debates against Pat Toomey. Specter would like to have been there to play the role of Toomey in a preparation debate but he was 3,000 miles away. (He had done such political debates before. He had played the role of the Democrat in preparing Tom Ridge for a debate in his first race for Pennsylvania governor in 1994. Specter, anticipating what Democrat Mark Singel might say, had done well against Ridge. Too well. Ridge ended up forgetting it was just a test run and got angry with his "opponent.")

"I have us at Postrio at 9:30 tomorrow night," Specter told Caputo, referring to Wolfgang Puck's well-known San Francisco restaurant. "I think you'll really like it." The trial seemed a complete afterthought. And it would barely cross Specter's mind, at least not until Sunday night, after he had made the trip back to Reno and hunkered down once again with Durney and Nomura to map out the remainder of the trial. His co-counsel looked very different than on trial days. Nomura showed up in running shoes and a sweat suit. Durney was wearing shorts and sandals, a blue shirt with a brown vest and a baseball cap proclaiming "UC White Mountain Research Station."

The lawyers bounced ideas around, but there wasn't really much to say. Rakowicz, they all felt, had largely surrendered his credibility. A few things were left to ask him, and to reiterate. One thing Specter wanted to ask about was Rakowicz's preparation for trial. He wanted to ask if Rakowicz had been told by Wheeler to minimize his role in the whole brake fiasco, to say he was less involved in the process than he really was, and to say less than he really knew.

"Wheeler's going to object," said Durney. "It's client-lawyer privilege."

"Then I'm going to say it's the exception to the rule, that there was a crime, the crime of fraud, that he suborned perjury," said Specter through a clenched jaw. And he meant it. He felt that Rakowicz had been lying—fudging the truth, at best—and that he'd probably been coached on how to do it.

Offered Nomura, "And if you say who told you to minimize your role and Wheeler stands up and cites client-attorney privilege, he's answered your question."

"Oh, I'm excited," said Durney.

"I'm going to do it," said Specter.

A devilish smiled crept onto Nomura's face. He liked when lawyers stepped across the line a little. "Boy," he told Specter, "you're getting to be a real cowboy."

"I don't care. I've waited six years. I'm going to do it. I don't give a fuck."

And when the trial resumed, he did it.

> SPECTER: Isn't what you were trying to do with both me and Mr. Durney back when we took your depositions was to minimize and understate your role in connection with this problem?
> RAKOWICZ: No, sir, absolutely not.
> Q: Nobody coached you to minimize or understate your role, Mr. Rakowicz?
> A: No, sir.

Wheeler did not take the bait. He did not object, leaving Specter without an opening to mention fraud or perjury or suborning perjury. Whether Wheeler simply missed the opening or decided not to object was unknown. But Wheeler had been silent for most of Specter's questioning. Ford had lost the vast majority of its pretrial motions and Wheeler evidently felt that Judge Hagen would have ruled against most of his objections. So rather than risk losing a litany of legal points in front of the jury, Wheeler apparently had decided to remain as silent as he could during Specter's interrogation.

Specter was content as well. Though he had wanted to force a confrontation with Wheeler, the jurors had nonetheless heard the allegations that Rakowicz had been "coached," with no immediate rebuttal. He pressed the issue.

Q: How many hours have you spent looking at documents and otherwise preparing for your testimony?

A: I couldn't even guess, sir.

Q: Well, you told us that you spent a couple of days each time on four separate occasions with the lawyers, correct?

A: Yes, sir.

Q: How many hours a day would you work with them?

A: Eight hours, eight to nine hours.

Q: So a total of eight days; is that correct?

A: Approximately.

Q: Times eight and a half, that would be seventy hours, correct?

A: Yes, sir.

Yet if all this preparation had made Rakowicz more certain of the facts than at the first trial, how was it, Specter wanted to know, that he had been "unfamiliar" with various reports, reports that listed rollaways and accidents involving Ford trucks? How could he not have known certain facts of the case, facts inimical to Ford's case? And how could he not have known, even at the first trial, some very simple things, things that didn't require any preparation, such as the fact that Ken Gutowski was his boss?

Q: And if I had asked you that question back in 1999 or '98 or '97, you would have known who was your supervisor, wouldn't you, Mr. Rakowicz?

A: Maybe not.

Q: You could possibly forget the name of your supervisor?

A: Yes, sir.

Specter was sure the jury was seeing through Rakowicz like plate glass. How many members of the jury who held jobs, and most held jobs, didn't know who their boss was?

And Rakowicz did not remember an earlier conversation he had had under oath with Specter about the Bobb case. Specter had asked whether it might be possible that because of the tepid language of the recall letter perhaps owners had not brought their vehicles "because they weren't told in strong enough terms about what the problem was." Rakowicz had agreed at the time that that was not an "unreasonable suggestion." That possibility was not something Rakowicz wanted to acknowledge now at this trial, but it was hard to avoid. Specter had Rakowicz's acknowledgment from the Bobb deposition in black and white. And he read it aloud.

> Q: Now, do you recollect that conversation with me?
> A: No, sir.
> Q: And that was three weeks before the White child was killed, correct?
> A: Yes, sir.

Three weeks before Walter White was killed, Rakowicz acknowledged that perhaps people didn't bring their trucks in because the recall notice did not contain strong enough wording. Maybe if he had asked Ford to put something out, an emergency notice, something . . .

But Rakowicz would not budge from his insistence that Ford did nothing wrong. Even in the one instance in which 4 percent of Ford trucks tested had brake problems—a rate the engineer had earlier acknowledged was not a low occurrence—he refused to be critical.

> Q: Four percent would be very bad?
> A: Not necessarily.
> Q: It would be very bad if this were a frequent occurrence?
> A: It depends.

Specter thought he saw a few jurors smile. Wheeler, who had worn a grin through much of the trial, wasn't grinning now.

Specter continued the grilling. He felt the jury, after five days of testimony, becoming frustrated with Rakowicz and his elusive answers, answers that seemed rehearsed, answers that had changed since 1998. Answers that, in many cases, weren't answers at all.

ONE THING TEAM SPECTER had discovered over the weekend, thanks to Caputo's unrelenting research, was that Rakowicz had been wrong about one instance of rollaway. Rakowicz had testified that one truck that had rolled away had done so because it had been overloaded. The weight of the truck plus that of a trailer and generator had exceeded the suggested load limit by 3,000 pounds. But over the weekend Caputo checked something most car owners don't bother to even glance at—the owner's manual. He determined that the gross combined vehicle weight was greater than Rakowicz had testified. In fact, the load limit had not been exceeded. The truck had not been overloaded. Couldn't Rakowicz have checked the owner's manual himself? Specter made the most of it.

> Q: So when you told the jury that it was over the weight recommended by Ford to load the vehicle by 3000 pounds, that was false, wasn't it?
>
> A: I perhaps was confused at that point.
>
> Q: Well, how many times had you gone over this before?
>
> A: I probably read each document maybe twice.
>
> Q: Well, didn't you check it in the owner's manual before telling all these things to the jury?
>
> A: No, sir, I didn't.

And how could Rakowicz deny that he wrote a white paper that recommended a recall because of the brakes releasing spontaneously? The report had been titled: "F-Series Parking Brake Control Self-Releasing Field Campaign and Owner Notification Paper."

> Q: And "self-releasing" refers to spontaneous disengagement, correct?
>
> A: Yes, sir.
>
> Q: And "field campaign" refers to recall, correct?
>
> A: Yes, sir.
>
> Q: So this document could just as easily be titled "F-Series Parking Brake Control Spontaneous Disengagement Recall and Owner Notification Paper," correct?
>
> A: No, sir. The titles were standard based on the format.
>
> Q: But the words are synonymous, correct? A "field campaign and owner notification" is a recall, correct?
>
> A: Yes, sir.

If Rakowicz felt that the pin test that revealed spontaneous disengagement was not a valid test, why hadn't he told that to the jury in the first trial? "I don't recall my prior testimony," said the witness. Rakowicz had also said at the first trial that he didn't know who had devised the pin test. Now he remembered that it was Wayne Soucie, an engineer at Orscheln. And he had testified years earlier that he did not know what the Field Campaign Review Committee (FCRC) was at Ford. "I'm not familiar with that term or that committee name," he had told the jury in 1998. Now he knew what it was and what its meeting had been.

> Q: This FCRC meeting to decide to recall these brakes, that was
> the culmination of two years of your work at Ford, correct?
> A: Yes, sir.
> Q: Right. You started to work on this problem in September 1992.
> You had collected the information. . . . You had written a paper
> in February 1993, which you presented to the CPPRG. You did
> more testing. . . . You were asked to prepare a report on the
> subject. . . . You did so, and it all culminated in a meeting on
> August 23, 1994, with the FCRC, correct?
> A: Yes, sir.
> Q: And then two years later you tell Mr. Durney over here that
> you're not familiar with the term "field campaign review com-
> mittee" or that committee name, correct?
> A: Yes, sir.

Sometimes a little thing could make a big difference in a trial. An odd
statement, a slip of the tongue. If Rakowicz had any credibility left by
late Monday afternoon, a week into the trial, his comments about a place
named Lorain, Ohio, population 68,000, may have been the clincher. A
team of Ford engineers had made the 80-mile trip from company headquarters in Dearborn to Lorain in December 1992 to check out a brake
problem on Ford Econoline vans. At the first trial in 1998, Rakowicz had
testified that he was uncertain whether he went along. Now, looking
at a document about the trip, Rakowicz's memory was better. Now he
remembered being there.

Specter found it hard to believe that Rakowicz would have made such
a trip without remembering it several years later for the first trial. When
he saw the document produced by Wheeler, a document he had never
seen before, Specter realized it would have been virtually impossible for
Rakowicz not to have remembered the trip. The new fact supplied by
the document was just how long Rakowicz had been away from home
in Lorain.

> Q: Do you recall the transcript says that you testified in the first
> trial that you don't recall that you went on that Lorain trip, sir?
> A: Yes, sir.
> Q: How long was that team there?
> A: We were there from November 21 through December 4.
> Q: Thirty days hath September, April, June, and November. So that
> would be, the twenty-first through the thirtieth would be ten

days, and four days in December. That would be fourteen days, correct?

A: Yes, sir.

Q: And where is the Lorain assembly plant?

A: It is in Lorain, Ohio.

Q: Pretty far from home?

A: No, sir.

Q: Would you be able to make a commute there every night back and forth?

A: No, sir, it was a long drive.

Q: Okay. So if you were there, you would have driven there and stayed overnight, correct?

A: Yes, sir.

Q: Okay. And it was a two-week trip, correct? That's what that document says?

A: Yes, sir.

Q: Right. And in the first trial you told us that you didn't remember being there, correct?

A: Yes, sir.

Q: Two weeks, right? Don't you think if you were in Lorain, Ohio, Mr. Rakowicz, for two weeks, you would have remembered that?

A: No, sir.

Specter allowed himself a slight laugh at the answer. It was incredible. First Rakowicz didn't remember who his boss was. Then he didn't remember staying at a hotel in Lorain, Ohio, for two weeks. Two whole weeks. That's how long this trial would last, and who among the jurors would forget spending two weeks in the jury box? No one, Specter was certain.

The whole notion of purging documents—as suggested in Gutowski's notation about Rakowicz's writing for a recall committee—stuck in Specter's craw. He knew that cover-ups existed everywhere, even in the highest government circles. Remember Watergate? If he had been able to find a notation about purging a record, he could only imagine what he had not seen, what records might have actually been purged. Was the jury wondering the same thing? Specter decided to wrap up his questioning of Rakowicz by planting the seed.

Q: You told Mr. Wheeler [that by] April 21, 1993 . . . you had decided that . . . and tell me if I've got this down correctly—

spontaneous disengagements were not occurring. Was that your view at that time?

A: On or around that time, yes, sir.

Q: Yet you listed spontaneous disengagement in your handwriting as one of the most likely potential causes of this problem, correct?

A: It was listed as potentially most likely.

Now Specter showed Rakowicz the document in which potential causes were rated by number, with one the lowest and three the "most likely." Spontaneous disengagement was rated as a three.

Q: So this must have been a misprint, right? That really should have been a one instead of a three, correct, as "unlikely," not "most likely," correct?

A: No, sir.

Q: Wasn't this an error, Mr. Rakowicz? Don't you want to tell the jury this was an error, putting a number three there?

A: No, sir.

Q: Shouldn't that document have been purged, Mr. Rakowicz?

A: No, sir.

Q: Along with the other documents that should have been purged?

A: I don't know which other ones you're referring to, sir.

Q: What else got purged, Mr. Rakowicz?

A: Nothing.

SPECTER: Nothing further.

CHAPTER 25

Zero

THE TRIAL WAS VIRTUALLY OVER at this point. For both Specter and Wheeler, Rakowicz had served as an instrument to place the basic facts before the jury. He had been on the witness stand for the better part of five days. Just two witnesses were left, and they would be fairly short work.

The first, called by Specter, was Alfred Darold, who had been employed by Ford since 1963—more than four decades—in one capacity or another. Darold was an older man, but he appeared robust, with a rigid gait and a no-nonsense look about him. He had a craggy face and very white skin, giving him a pale, almost scary look against his black suit. If he wanted to make a few extra bucks, he could have worked nights at the funeral parlor down the street.

But Darold didn't need any extra money. He earned a good living doing just what he was doing now, testifying at trials. Darold was as close to a professional witness as one could get. He made $220 an hour for his time, for preparing for trials and sitting through them as well as testifying. That was roughly $2,000 a day for his time in court alone. Federal jurors were paid $40 a day.

Darold was retired now, working as a consultant to Ford. When he worked for the company full-time, he had also spent much of his efforts defending Ford in court. He did what Ford termed "design analysis." The term was code for defending Ford products and providing lawyers with technical advice and testimony when needed. Over the last twenty-five years Darold had testified at many trials. "Probably," he figured, "in the hundreds." Probably more trials than all the lawyers in the courtroom combined.

That was curious, Specter pointed out to the jury, since over a seven-year period during which the F-Series brake problem arose Darold was also chairman of Ford's Critical Product Problem Review Group, or CPPRG, at Ford. That was the group to which Rakowicz had presented his white paper, a group that could recommend a recall. Specter pointed this out to the jury—a man who worked with company lawyers defending the company against lawsuits also was in charge of a committee that could recommend recalls.

Specter was keenly aware of Darold's trial skills. He had been Ford's anchor witness in the first trial. Specter knew he wouldn't elicit any shocking admissions from the long-time company man and defender. But he would chip away at him on a few critical points.

One was the fact that Ford had taken nearly five months to respond to NHTSA's request to issue a recall.

> Q: And Ford taking five months to answer a letter from NHTSA for an EA [engineering analysis] is bad, correct?
> A: Not necessarily.
> Q: Well, what do you think, Mr. Darold? Yes or no, is it bad in this case?
> A: It would be preferable for us to answer sooner but it's not necessarily bad that we were delayed. The magnitude of the task, discussion with NHTSA, could very well have explained it.

Yes, sooner would have been better, Specter had forced Darold to concede. And he also got Darold to acknowledge that when the owner notifications finally went out, it didn't happen all at once but in waves and over many months. Only 76,000, fewer than 10 percent, were sent in the first batch, mailed December 16, 1994. Then 182,092 more were sent in early February 1995. The bulk of the notifications were not sent until March 16–22. And some owners were not identified until later, with 5,341 sent notices in June and 11,600 more in August 1995—almost a year after Ford had notified NHTSA that it would issue the recall.

Darold, like an experienced boxer, tried to slip Specter's jabs. He couldn't feign memory lapses, as Rakowicz had. Darold had too much experience for that. He instead would make speeches, answering simple questions with lengthy explanations that strayed from the original question. Or he tried to. Specter objected repeatedly, claiming the witness was being nonresponsive. He wanted his opponent to stand still and take his lumps. He demanded yes or no answers where appropriate, cutting off the ring when Darold launched into long-winded explanations. Finally, when Darold tried launching into another speech, Specter had had enough. He put a halt to it.

> Q: Excuse me, now—now, Mr. Darold, first of all, on these questions that I'm asking you, every time I ask you a question that

can be answered yes or no, you give me an answer and then you give me a "because" which is then going to be followed by a long explanation with a bunch of excuses, correct? Yes or no.

A: No, sir.

Q: You're a very experienced person answering questions, correct?

A: Yes, sir.

Q: Right. You've testified I think you told us a couple hundred times, correct?

A: In various circumstances, I believe that's true, yes.

Q: All right. Now, to deal with some basic concepts of grammar and the English language, you know that if a question contains the word "why," then an answer would appropriately contain the word "because." Right?

A: Yes, sir.

Q: Now, have you heard me use the word "why" in any of my questions, sir?

A: No, I can't remember that you did.

Q: Okay. I'm going to try to do a good job of flagging all my "why" questions for you, okay, Mr. Darold?

A: Thank you.

Q: Thank you. Now let's get back to where we were.

Darold could only smile at Specter's approach. He knew what was going on and he didn't seem to mind terribly that Specter had figured him out so early in the game. That didn't mean he would totally abandon his strategy, forcing Specter to cut him off several more times.

Q: And you're aware, sir, are you not, that as of the time that Ford sent this letter to the government on August 30, 1994, they actually had in their files not less than eight reports of injuries being sustained by people in connection with alleged rollaways. Correct?

A: I understand that's true, I understand there were reports of others that have subsequently been found, and in fact . . .

SPECTER: Your Honor, excuse me, Your Honor. I believe the witness has answered the question.

HAGEN: Yes, the question has been answered.

Specter traveled quickly over a lot of ground. The CPPRG did not keep minutes of its meetings. Far fewer rollaway accidents were reported after the wedge fix, undeniable proof, it seemed, that the brakes had been the cause. If NHTSA had not forced Ford to recall trucks, the company wouldn't have. ("That's possible," Darold said, only to be shown that at the 1998 trial he had said "Probably.") Ford, if it had truly wanted to warn people, could have put advertisements on radio and television about the brake problem, urging drivers of its trucks to at least, "Please use chocks!"

WHEELER DID A concise and good job with Darold in his examination. He kept it short, trying to shed any picture Specter may have painted for the jury of Ford as a malevolent creature with only the bottom line as its conscience.

> Q: What role, if any, did financial considerations play in your, CPPRG's, consideration and treatment of this parking brake issue during the period from when it opened on October 26, 1992, until it was closed in 1994?
>
> A: None.
>
> Q: Why not?
>
> A: We were considering technical issues, we were considering engineering issues, we were trying to make engineering decisions about technical issues. Finance just doesn't fit in there.
>
> Q: If you, Mr. Darold, had concluded in, let's say, mid-1993 or fall of 1993, that there was a safety defect in this parking brake, would it have saved money for Ford or cost Ford more money for it to delay recommending this issuing to the recall committee for consideration?
>
> A: Delay would only cost money.
>
> Q: Why is that?
>
> A: Well, the longer that the decision is delayed, potentially the greater the population of vehicles involved. The more the vehicle—the more there are of vehicles involved, then if there is a [recall] campaign, ultimately there's more vehicles that we have to go get, there's more customers that we have to inconvenience. The sooner, the better is really the key. If we could get it done quickly, well, the quicker we could get it done, the better off we would be. We were always motivated to get it done quickly.
>
> Q: During the time that you were on CPPRG just as a member or as the chairman, can you recall any time when anybody criti-

cized you or the CPPRG for having pushed an issue up to the
recall committee for its consideration?

A: No, not at all. That's what we were expected to do.

Q: How many recalls did Ford Motor Co. initiate in calendar year
1994?

A: Twenty-five.

In fact, Wheeler was posturing, Ford was a good company that had
done everything possible to ensure safety. And Darold had that in mind
at all times. He had nothing to lose by blowing the whistle on a bad
brake system if in fact it was a bad brake system.

Q: Is there any way that you know of in which your career would
have been harmed if you had referred the parking brake issue to
the recall committee prior to August of 1994?

A: No, not that I know of.

Q: Is there any way that you knew of . . . that you could have
helped Ford Motor Co. by not referring the issue to the recall
committee if you had believed there was a defect?

A: No, not at all. If I knew that there was a defect, not referring or
not going forward would be just the opposite. That would cause
trouble.

Q: Was there any significance in what you just said, any significance to the fact that this was the F-Series trucks we're talking
about as opposed to some other vehicle?

A: Yes.

Q: What is that?

A: The F-Series vehicle was then the best-selling vehicle in the
country, or in the world, for that matter, for ten years or more.
Today it's the best-selling vehicle in the world for over twenty
years. That vehicle is important to Ford and its reputation is
Ford's reputation. So we want to do everything we can to protect the reputation of that vehicle because that reflects directly
on Ford Motor Co.

Wheeler took it a step further. He got personal with Darold, the man
who, as chairman of the CPPRG, could have pushed the recall ahead
sooner. But he hadn't. He hadn't because he had trusted Ford's trucks

and their brake systems, trusted them with his own loved ones. Not only had Darold not pushed for a recall warning customers earlier, but he also hadn't even mentioned the supposed brake problem to his own family. He had bought a Ford Explorer with the same brake system for his wife and daughters. This last statement was convincing. Darold trusted his family, its very well-being, to Ford engineering. What greater testimony could be made?

Q: Are you married, Mr. Darold?

A: Yes, I am.

Q: Were you married to your wife back in those days?

A: Yes.

Q: Did you have children?

A: Yes, we do.

Q: How old were they?

A: At that time the children were about sixteen and eighteen, that time being '94.

Q: Who drove these Explorer vehicles that had this parking brake system in your family?

A: My wife drove the Explorer more than I did, and with the children principally. And the children were learning to drive or were early drivers, and they drove the Explorer more.

Q: At any time, Mr. Darold, during the period when you had those vehicles for your family, did you tell them, "Watch out for the parking brake"?

A: No, I did not.

Q: Did you tell them anything unique about the parking brake?

A: No.

Q: Mr. Darold, if someone at Ford was responsible for the fact that the Light Truck Engineering CPPRG did not send this parking brake to Ford's recall committee before August of 1994, who would that person be?

A: That would be me. If the CPPRG was responsible, I was the chair and I bear that responsibility.

Q: Is there anything, as you're sitting here today, Mr. Darold, that you know of that you think you should have done in order to push this issue for consideration by the recall committee before August of 1994?

A: No, not at all.

WHEELER: Thank you, Mr. Darold.

Specter listened to this testimonial about Ford trucks, about how Darold and his family and other Ford employees drove Fords and trusted them with their lives. Now he had a few questions of his own.

> Q: Mr. Darold, let's start off where we ended, just about, which is this question about what kinds of vehicles you and other engineers at Ford Motor Co. drive. You fellas drive a lot of Chevys?
> A: No, sir, we do not.
> Q: How would that look if you pull up into the Ford office driving a Chevy?
> A: Well, some people do it. I choose not to. Most people choose not to.
> Q: Right. You're on the Ford team, right?
> A: Yes, sir.
> Q: Not the Chevy team, correct?
> A: That's correct.
> Q: Most of the fellows don't pull up in Chryslers, correct?
> A: That's correct.
> Q: Or Mercedes Benzes?
> A: That is also correct.
> Q: Ford people don't tend to drive anything but Ford vehicles, correct?
> A: By and large that's correct.
> Q: You fellas get a price break on those vehicles, too, don't you?
> A: We're proud of our vehicles. We enjoy driving them.
> Q: Do you have my question in mind?
> A: Yes, I do.
> Q: You fellas get a price break on those vehicles, correct?
> A: In some circumstances, yes.
> Q: That would include you, correct?
> A: Yes.

More than a few of the jurors were smiling. So was Darold, slightly. The very image of a Ford executive pulling up to the company headquarters in a Chrysler was certainly amusing. A Mercedes-Benz, even more so.

But the underlying truth wasn't amusing. That Ford never told its customers of the real danger with its vehicles' brake systems wasn't funny at all. The fact that Darold chose not to tell his own family didn't make it any better. Specter decided to close his case on this point.

Q: Last thing, Mr. Darold. Pardon me for discussing your family with you, but your lawyer raised it, so I must. Did your daughters know that there had been eight injuries reported to the Ford Motor Co. as of the time of the recall when they decided to get in the vehicles and use these vehicles?

A: No, sir, they did not.

Q: Did they know that there had been fifty-four injuries reported in these vehicles as of '99?

A: In '94, sir, that would be impossible.

Q: Did they know in 1999 that Ford Motor Co. told the federal government that there were fifty-four injuries reported to them in connection with allegations of vehicle rollaway?

A: No, they did not know that.

Q: And do they know how many injuries have been reported to Ford Motor Co. up through March 16, 2004?

A: Of course not.

SPECTER: I didn't think so. Thank you, sir.

MALCOLM WHEELER SHOWED UP for court to begin Ford's defense bruised and battered. Literally. He had what looked like a brown spot on his forehead that descended below his right eye. The spot was a bruise and some dried blood. The lawyer explained to the court that he'd been walking down the street near the courthouse the night before, reading while he walked. It was a bad idea. He walked right into a metal pole. He laughed a short laugh.

Testifying next as a witness called by Ford would be Wayne Soucie, the Orscheln engineer who had dealt with the brake problem. Soucie had testified at the first trial. His time on the stand had been brief and relatively mild.

Soucie looked a little older than at the first trial but he still had a boyish face and a soft voice. He mentioned that he had built a self-propelled tricycle in the sixth grade, had gone on to become an engineer, and now had twenty-two patents to his credit. He supervised more than forty engineers in Orscheln's Research and Development department. Wayne Soucie seemed like a nice guy.

He had been a good witness at the first trial and would be a much better one this time, for a simple reason. Orscheln had sold off its brake division and no longer relied on Ford for a major portion of its business. Soucie had no reason to appease Ford. He had no reason to lie at trial. "Does your income depend on this trial?" Wheeler asked him. No, it did not, Soucie said. "Are you being compensated for being here?" No, though Ford was picking up Soucie's expenses.

Wheeler wanted the engineer from Orscheln on the stand to corroborate some of the things Tim Rakowicz had said. And Soucie did. He stood in front of Ford's big plastic model of the brake system and used a pointer to explain how it worked. He put on reading glasses to look at documents. In a monotone voice he described the problem with the brakes. He seemed earnest.

His testimony boiled down to simple concepts. Yes, there were operator reports that the brake would push through to the floor when applied. Yes, there were reports of rollaways. But no, spontaneous disengagement did not occur.

No matter how many brakes they tested at Orscheln and no matter how many tests they conducted, they simply could not replicate the alleged spontaneous brake failure. Ford had been cooperative throughout the testing process, Soucie added. It had provided parking levers, data, results from field trips. He and Tim Rakowicz spoke often. Laboratory and field tests were conducted in which the parking levers were kicked, in which trucks were jumped up and down upon, in which vehicle loads were increased to put more pressure on the brakes, in which trucks were parked on steep inclines.

> Q: Did you ever recommend any testing to further examine, further try to find out what was going on with the rollaway issue and have your proposal rejected by Ford?
>
> A: No, no. They were cooperative with trying to get to a resolution.
>
> Q: As of today, Mr. Soucie, are you aware of any test that's been done by anybody, whether by government engineers, research engineers, university engineers, industry engineers, anybody, who has been able to show that spontaneous disengagement occurs in any of these brakes?
>
> A: I haven't heard of any test results that replicated that particular failure mode.

And what about that notorious white paper, the document the plaintiffs had hung their hat on? According to Soucie, it had been a mistake. Plain and simple, Rakowicz had screwed up. Soucie said he had talked to the Ford engineer on February 23 or February 24, 1993, a day or two after he wrote the white paper intended for the CPPRG, the committee that could recommend a recall. That was a few days after Soucie had informed Rakowicz about the results of the latest testing, including the "pin test" in which they were able to make the brake stick in a tip-on-tip position. The test results had concerned Rakowicz. But, said Soucie, that was only because Rakowicz hadn't fully understood the scope of the testing; he simply didn't get it.

> Q: What did you tell Mr. Rakowicz about the test, Mr. Soucie?
>
> A: Basically . . . my impression was that he didn't understand his initial comment or his initial review of the data where the mechanism hadn't disengaged at rest, it had disengaged when additional force was being applied to the lever.
>
> Q: When you say "when additional force was being applied to the lever," what do you mean by that?
>
> A: Well, basically, in, like, cycle one where we had done, trying to replicate what would be going on in the field or potentially in the field with load shift, people opening and closing doors, vehicle jumping, being moved up and down due to different conditions around the vehicle, nothing had happened.

Test one, nothing happened. In a second test, Soucie said, the truck did begin to move but only because the engineers had gone overboard in trying to create a rollaway. He testified that in that test "the operator actually was kicking the side of the pedal from the driver's position. The people who were doing this test basically were kicking down on the lever to see whether they could get it to disengage. The angle at which they were kicking, they were kicking down on the lever, was actually applying force to the top of the pedal which increased the load and would be just like a skip-out on apply on that particular condition." Okay, there was rollaway in these instances, but it was not because of spontaneous disengagement. Under these test conditions, it was more like skip-out on apply.

In a third test, vehicles did start to creep away. But Soucie said this test also didn't count because engineers had put just enough tension on the brake to barely hold the vehicle. The brake had disengaged but only after the operator tried to press down on it further. Again, skip-out on apply. When these same trucks had their brakes fully applied and were left alone, in a "static" state with no banging or jumping, they didn't budge, even with the gears in the tip-on-tip condition and when fully loaded and parked on a 20-degree slope.

Q: What conclusions, if any, did you, Mr. Soucie, draw from that test series, those three cycles of tests?

A: Well, basically, that the static tip-on-tip, the typical forces that a vehicle might encounter with regard to opening and closing doors, wouldn't have an effect on a tip-on-tip condition, that if additional force was applied, that you could cause a skip-out on apply condition, and that even repeated tip-on-tip conditions didn't modify the ability of the mechanism to be able to support full-system load for an extended period of time.

Q: What conclusions did you reach, Mr. Soucie, about spontaneous disengagement, if any?

A: Well, basically, with the data that we'd been able to collect, we weren't able to replicate a disengagement under load or a spontaneous disengagement, even after or even as a result of extreme cable force or extreme outside force to the mechanism, far beyond what would be expected in a particular vehicle.

Q: Did you ever change your mind about that?

A: I haven't found any data that would change my mind on that data.

Specter had sat with his head back and his eyes closed for much of Soucie's testimony. That was partly because he was trying to show the jury he didn't feel Soucie's testimony was worthwhile. He also knew something Ford did not, something that allowed him not to pay terribly close attention to this testimony. Specter planned to let Don Nomura cross-examine Wayne Soucie.

Nomura was a bit of a wild card and a wild man. The appeals court had reversed the first verdict on other grounds but also said that Nomura had gone too far in his closing speech, that it had been inflammatory. While this jury seemed to be responding to Specter, there was no telling how it would respond to a change of drivers at this point in the race. It might find Nomura refreshing. Or annoying.

Nomura's style was vastly different from that of Specter or Wheeler. While Specter was careful and meticulous and Wheeler tried to appear calm and reasonable, Nomura was more like what Joe Pinto had called him—"a fucking Japanese Zero," one with his machine guns pointed at Wayne Soucie. Nomura's cross-examination was rapid-fire and unrelenting, the questions coming in staccato bursts. Where Specter had allowed Rakowicz and Darold *some* freedom to give lengthy answers, Nomura demanded largely yes or no responses. He phrased some very lengthy questions and permitted Soucie only brief responses. Sometimes he didn't even bother letting Soucie answer, cutting him off when he pondered too long. Nomura was using this testimony, in part, not to try to debunk Soucie but to reiterate some of the plaintiffs' highlights in the case, to put things into a nutshell of sorts. His caustic style—plus a new voice echoing in the courtroom—had the members of the jury sitting up in their chairs.

Nomura started by noting that Ford had paid for Soucie's trip to Reno and that Soucie had spent time earlier with Wheeler and his associates going over his testimony. Nomura, in a typical exchange, asked about the 1,149 rollaways eventually reported.

> Q: He [Wheeler] didn't ask you: "God, how are we going to explain
> that away?"
> A: No.
> Q: How are you going to explain that away, sir? I'll ask you. Can
> you?
> A: Basically, the . . .
> A: I need, sir, just a yes or a no, and then I'll ask another question.
> Can you?

But Nomura didn't really want an answer. He was making a speech. He pressed on, mentioning that trucks that had had the wedge installed did not have the same incidence of rollaways. He tried to get Soucie to admit that this meant the original brake system had caused the problem. Soucie wouldn't do it but that didn't stop Nomura from pushing.

> Q: You're starting to lean in this direction, aren't you?
> A: No.
> Q: Just a little bit?
> A: No.
> Q: Just a *little* bit?

Soucie wouldn't budge. His tests had not proven the brake system caused the rollaways.

> Q: And as you see it right now, then Ford should tell the public
> about these rollaways, correct? Something is wrong with the
> brake.

A: Yeah, I believe they've been working on it.

Q: Well, have they told the public?

A: They did it. They did recall . . .

Q: Sir, have they told the public about rollaway?

A: Not that I know of.

Q: Okay. Should they?

A: It's basically a statistic. It's based upon the overall population and I'm not sure what that would mean.

Regardless of whether spontaneous disengagement had been proven, Ford had approved a temporary and, later, a permanent fix for the brake system. But it hadn't made sure to get it into all of its trucks by October 9, 1994, the day Walter White lost his life.

Q: Certainly the existence of spontaneous disengagement as a theory and the fact of a rollaway on a number of vehicles were known to Ford well prior to his death. Correct?

A: Yeah, those are data points.

Q: Certainly the wedge fix was available over a year before his death, correct?

A: Yeah, parts were available.

Q: The cam-in was available prior to his death by, looks like nine, ten months. Correct?

A: Correct.

Q: None of that information was disseminated by Ford to the public, was it?

A: Not to my knowledge. I don't know.

Q: It's Ford's responsibility, right? Correct?

A: Correct.

Q: But they didn't do it, did they?

A: Yeah, they're . . . I'm not sure why that would be.

Q: And afterwards, when you have 1,100 vehicles roll away plus fifty-four injuries, the vast majority of which are on non-fixed vehicles, non-cam-in and non-wedge . . . They haven't sent out anything. Have they?

A: Not that I know of.

Now Nomura walked along the edge, launching into what amounted to a speech, a speech about the previous jury's verdict and the fact that its decision "must be accepted as true: Ford knew the parking brakes were prone to failure prior to this accident but continued to sell [the trucks] without recalling [them] and without warning consumers of the danger. The jury was also asked if it found by clear and convincing evidence that Ford acted with oppression or malice in the conduct upon which it based its finding of liability for the death of Walter White . . . Now you know what happened in 1998 when the jury came back with that finding in that verdict. Correct?"

There was little Soucie could say. His response, though, wasn't bad, considering.

"I know that they came back with a verdict," he said. "I'm not sure that I understand all the particulars."

On re-cross, Wheeler kept it brief, having Soucie repeat for the jury that no engineering evidence showed that spontaneous disengagement actually occurred. Hearing this, Nomura bounded from his chair.

Q: The fact of the case is that this brake is prone to failure. Ford knew about it, didn't warn, and didn't recall. Those are the facts of this case, are they not?

A: I don't believe that the mechanism is prone to failure. I've demonstrated that it's not.

Q: Are those the facts in this case, sir? The judge says they're facts. Are they facts?

A: If the judge says they're facts, I guess they're facts.

NOMURA: And then they are. Thank you.

That concluded testimony in the case of *White v. Ford II.*

The plaintiffs' team looked approvingly at Nomura. He had boxed Soucie in, given him little room to equivocate. Nomura had kept Soucie's answers brief and on point, preventing him from making speeches while getting in a few of his own. Nomura seemed to have been a smashing success.

Except, it would turn out, to the jury. Virtually every member of the panel, including those who may have been leaning toward the plaintiffs, had a visceral reaction to the cross-examination of Wayne Soucie. The jurors genuinely liked and believed the affable, soft-spoken engineer from Mobley, Missouri. They hadn't liked Nomura's examination.

CHAPTER 26

Closings

SPECTER ROSE FOR HIS closing speech. Much of it would be similar to that of the first trial, with Specter rehashing the facts of the case as he saw them. This would bore the jury, but it was necessary. One way to alleviate the tedium was for Specter to be quick about it. He singled out the exhibits he wanted to stick out in the jury's collective mind. His case was about facts and these were the highlights. He had them ready to go, with Caputo working the TV monitor and poster exhibits as he called for them one after another. Bang, bang, bang. It made a statement: My case is about the facts. There will be opinions and emotions, but my case has a solid foundation in the facts.

After laying down the cinder blocks, Specter stated the plaintiffs' view of the case. He would give the plaintiffs' opinion of what had occurred, of what Ford had intentionally done wrong. Also, although Judge Hagen would tell the jury that "a verdict may never be influenced by sympathy," Specter would remind the jurors, in a somewhat novel way, that this was about a little boy, the death of a little boy, which had caused great pain and suffering. To this very day.

Ford could have done something, he told the jury. It had known about the brake problem early on. "Every rollaway and every skip-out that occurred from the very beginning was preventable, was known about. Should never have occurred," said Specter. The problem, he said, "was discovered, opened, discussed and closed, but it was never solved." Early on Tim Rakowicz had recommended a recall—and Ford's insistence now that his white paper did no such thing was folly. "How can that be seriously maintained?" Specter asked. "The cover of the document says 'F-Series Parking Brake Control Self-Releasing Field Campaign and Owner Notification Paper.' That is synonymous with a recall."

> And they knew they had vehicles rolling away all across America, they knew that there was property damage being sustained,

they knew that people were being injured, they knew that people were at risk for being killed, and they swept the issue under the rug. Period.

Ford denied and delayed. Even when the government agency NHTSA requested information, Ford didn't reply within the required forty-five days. NHTSA made its request on September 14, 1993. Ford complied on February 9, 1994—"five days short of five months." Specter told the jury that Ford's claim that it had voluntarily recalled its vehicles after a request to do so by NHTSA was also absurd. "They say (they were) urged to do so, but let's face it, it's forced to do so by NHTSA because the next thing for NHTSA is to force a recall by bringing a legal action. And Ford cannot withstand the publicity of having an enforcement action brought by NHTSA." He cited Darold's testimony that such an action had never been filed by NHTSA.

Ford had not fully reported the number of known injuries to NHTSA, including one of which Ford—and Specter—had intimate knowledge. That was the case of Derick Bobb, an infant whose skull had been crushed by a Ford F-150. Withholding such an injury from NHTSA, said Specter, "is reprehensible."

Maybe, just maybe, if Ford had not delayed, had decided to issue a timely recall, and had told the truth about the cause of the rollaways, Walter White would still be alive. Specter reminded the jury that he had deposed Rakowicz for the Bobb case—asking him about such a recall— before the tragic incident in Elko.

Have you considered the unbelievable irony of that, that Mr. Rakowicz, in September of 1994, came to my office in Philadelphia, and we talked about what Ford was doing, and they had a chance to save Walter White's life because it wasn't for another three weeks that he was killed.

And Mr. Rakowicz told me that he and his colleagues had been discussing since July whether to include rollaway, spontaneous disengagement, in the recall information going to people. And I said to him, "Well, don't you think you have to? People aren't going to bring their trucks in if they just think it's skip-through." We knew from that transcript, you can see that these two men sitting in a conference room in Philadelphia, we could see into the future. We knew what was going to happen!

Specter said this last sentence with his hands to the heavens. Jimmie White flushed, his face twisted with remorse, his jaw clenched tight with anger. Rakowicz sat, the impassive look still on his face, staring straight ahead, but his face turned crimson now as Specter looked in his direction. The lawyer looked back to the jury and softened his tone.

> And if he knew . . . then his superiors knew. They knew what they were buying. They were buying deaths and injuries all across the country.

Indeed, Ford knew there was a problem. The proof: It fixed it. First with the wedge and, in later models, with the cam-in design. There were just a few problems. The company took too long to do so and it failed to warn people of the true and hazardous nature of the problem. Not even when they finally issued a recall. That notice had mentioned only skip-through on apply, a minor inconvenience.

> Walter White is not in a grave in Elko, Nevada, because of skip-through on apply. He is dead because of spontaneous disengagement. So this is an effort to take your eye off the ball. Don't let them do it.

Worse, Ford had still not issued a proper warning. Not even after paying off at least one multimillion-dollar settlement and losing the first case before a jury in this same courtroom. Not even after documenting 1,149 rollaways and fifty-four injuries as of January 1999—and those were just the cases that drivers reported. How many more had there really been? "And how many have been injured since January 1999?" Specter asked. People were still, to this day, riding around in F-Series trucks with bum parking brakes. Without knowing it. Didn't that prove that Ford didn't give a damn?

Perhaps the worst thing Ford had done, still was doing, was insisting in the face of the evidence, even a jury verdict against it, that it had done nothing wrong. Ford showed no remorse.

> And from the evidence at the last trial, a lawyer for the Whites could well have assumed that Ford would come in and say, "We know that we made a mistake, we know we did wrong, we're

sorry, we're sorry about these vehicles rolling away, we're sorry about spontaneous disengagement, we know it happens. We know that you've been told as a matter of fact and a matter of law by His Honor that you must accept, must accept as true that these vehicles are prone to failure and that we at Ford acted maliciously, but we're sorry and we won't do it again."

They didn't say that to you. I mean, of all of the outrageous, outrageous—what is more outrageous than saying, oh, no, no, no, no, no, no, spontaneous disengagement doesn't occur? We know that you've been told by the judge that you must accept as true that these brakes are prone to failure, but we're going to tell you it doesn't happen. We're going to try to get you to nullify the court's charge to you. What a manifest outrage. How offensive!

Specter believed Ford was lying, concocting a new story for this trial, a story about how spontaneous disengagement never existed. Despite the facts of the case—the pin test, the fixes made to solve the problem, the recall, the injuries, and one death. And the fact that a jury had already found Ford was responsible for that death and should be punished. Ford was spitting into the wind.

This new story necessitated that Tim Rakowicz change his story as well. Suddenly he knew that the pin test was invalid and realized that his white paper had been wrong. He didn't remember being involved in the recall at the first trial, but now he did. Specter compared Rakowicz to Sergeant Schultz of the TV show *Hogan's Heroes*, who was noted for saying, "I see naawwwwthing." But now, more than a decade after dealing with the brake problem, he recalled all sorts of things. He had twisted and turned, Specter said, to suit Ford's new trial defense. Ford made Rakowicz a victim of sorts.

"They should not have done this to him, turning him into a pretzel," Specter said. "And that's being kind about it. And now he knows everything about everything, when he used to know nothing about nothing."

Now Specter reached into his pocket to make sure his props were in place. He was about to talk about net worth and what the jury should consider in assessing punitive damages. This would be a repeat performance, one Ford had tried to block but one that Judge Hagen had approved before trial. Ford was worth $11,651,000,000. Specter wrote the number out for the jury.

Since Ford was "entitled to be treated just like a person," Specter asked the jury to imagine that the mammoth company did not have $11 billion but was a person with just $10. He placed a $10 bill on the wooden railing of the jury box. Then he showed them a penny, which would be equal to one-tenth of 1 percent of $10, or roughly equivalent to 0.1 percent of Ford's net worth.

> Now if you think taking one penny from that guy is going to deter him and it's going to vindicate Nevada's legitimate interests in punishment and deterrence, then you go ahead and you award one-tenth of 1 percent, which is $11 million. But you know, I think, as well as I do, that a person that has $10 in their pocket who has taken from them one penny as punishment will thumb their nose at the person punishing them. That is not effective punishment. Just like Ford has thumbed their nose at everyone and everybody, including you, and will apparently continue to do so into the future unless they are punished.
>
> Now, I've got a dime here somewhere. Ten cents. That is 1 percent of $10. Now you take 10¢ away from a guy that's got $10, and he may start to think about it.

Finally Specter took a $1 bill from his pocket. He didn't really expect the jury to award the equivalent—more than $1 billion—but he wanted to conclude with the jurors having a large number, a very large number, in mind. With that kind of penalty, he said, waving the dollar bill in the air, "a person is going to start to shape up."

He urged the jury to punish Ford, not only for Walter White but also to protect the interest of fellow Nevadans who might have been hurt, who still might be hurt, by Ford's pickup. "These people, by the way," he said, pointing at Jimmie and Ginny seated in the first row of the courtroom, "these are citizens of Nevada and they've had the courage to see this through. They had the courage to stick this out for nine and a half years since their boy was killed." Specter sniffled. For the first time his voice turned raspy.

Now Specter did something he had never done before in a trial. He walked to the plaintiffs' table and picked up a book, a paperback he had bought over the weekend in San Francisco. He stood before the jury and leafed through the pages, stopping at a poem titled "Dirge Without Music" by Edna St. Vincent Millay, the Pulitzer Prize–winning poet. This poem, at least to Specter, embodied what the court case meant to the Whites. It was about survivors determined to avenge an unjust death. His voice cracked as he read parts of the poem.

I am not resigned to the shutting away of loving hearts in the
    hard ground.
So it is, and so it will be, for so it has been, time out of mind:
Into the darkness they go, the wise and the lovely.
Crowned with lilies and with laurel they go; but I am not
    resigned. . . .

The answers quick and keen, the honest look, the laughter,
    the love,
They are gone. . . .

Down, down, down into the darkness of the grave
Gently they go, the beautiful, the tender, the kind;.
Quietly they go, the intelligent, the witty, the brave.
I know. But I do not approve. And I am not resigned.

Several jurors reached for tissues. Specter had had cases before that had caused his eyes to well up, but he had always managed to control them from spilling over. Now they ran like rivulets, tears dripping down his checks. Yet he steadied his gaze and his voice for the last words of this closing speech.

And it's up to you to not be resigned. It's up to you to say that the death of this boy will not produce in you resignation. It's produced in Ford resignation. They have been resigned from this problem since 1994, but this problem does not go away. This problem continues. Your fellow citizens are still at risk. This company must be deterred. They must be punished. They will not do it on their own. It must come from you. The government will not do it. You are all that is left. You are all that is left to vindicate the truth that is this case.

    Thank you.

MALCOLM WHEELER WAS ready for his shot at the jury, more than ready. He had so much he wanted to say, needed to say. He had laid out a plan early in the trial, a plan to make major points in his opening and then at the end show the jury that he had proven those points. But Specter had gotten in the way. Now he not only had to make his case but also rebut Specter on every point possible. Or at least try to.

    Wheeler rose from the defense table, rolling a wadded tissue in his palms as he walked past Specter and the plaintiffs' table, then tossing it in a wastebasket. Was this act symbolic, meant to convey a message to the jury? *Yes, I'm sympathetic to the Whites too, but now it's time to get down to the hard facts, to the legal issues.* Wheeler leaned his forearms on the podium in front of the jury box and held his wire-frame glasses between two fingers, dangling the spectacles from one thin temple.

He began his speech in a soft, almost singsong fashion, telling the jury that he was not asking them to go against the judge or the jury in the first trial. He was not asking this panel to diverge from its duties. It was within their discretion to award nothing, zero, if they so decided. "You *may* . . . award these additional damages," he said, noting the judge's instructions to the jury given before Specter's closing argument. Punitive damages—"*if any*"—could be awarded to punish and deter Ford. He noted Hagen had mentioned that the Whites "have already been fully and fairly compensated."

> We are asking you, ladies and gentlemen, to comply with these instructions. We're asking you to exercise your discretion in determining whether to award punitive damages, if any, to decide not to award any punitive damages.

Now, Wheeler urged, "go with me down a trip of common sense." He told the jury they could even choose to believe that the folks at Ford were "nameless, faceless people . . . who are evil, all they care about is money, their blood in their veins is green, all they care about is profits, they don't care about people." It still defied common sense that they would delay fixing the brakes and delay a recall. Even if Ford didn't care about the people who bought its cars, as Specter had suggested, such a delay would only cost the company more in the long run. Delaying a fix would result in more cars being recalled.

> What is that going to do to the Ford Motor Co.? Well, for starters, it's going to ruin the company's reputation because if, as he's suggesting, there can be thousands of these things happening over a twenty-year period, on every one of those vehicles, there's a great big blue oval, and in the middle of the blue oval it says "Ford." It's on the front of the car and it's on the back of the car and it's inside the car and it's in the owner's manual. There's no hiding that.
>
> The longer they delay, the more of these vehicles they're manufacturing and selling. The more they manufacture and sell before recalling, the more extensive the recall is. . . . Mr. Specter and Mr.

Nomura have not identified for you one single reason, not one, why anybody at Ford could possibly have thought if they believed that this was a defective design and it was actually causing injuries and deaths, that they could possibly have thought that it was a good idea to delay the recall into some distant future time. Not one reason has been given to you, and it defies common sense.

He mocked what he termed Specter's "conspiracy theory." It was inconceivable, Wheeler insisted, that everyone from Tim Rakowicz to Ford's top executives to "Missouri farm boy" Wayne Soucie to the federal government (NHTSA) could be involved in a conspiracy to hide a dangerous defect. "It defies common sense," he said.

It also defied common sense that if Ford were trying to hide the fact that spontaneous disengagement occurred in its brakes that it would have tried so hard (and asked Orscheln to try hard) to prove the phenomenon existed. "Does that make any sense?"

Wheeler ended many of these statements with a sharp, short chuckle. A belittling huff. "Teh!" He did it often.

And what about all that stuff about Rakowicz's boss, Ken Gutowski, "purging" comments about his writing a recall paper. Specter had made that sound so insidious. "He just wanted the document to reflect correctly the name of the committee or the group." To make that sound so devious—Teh!—was ludicrous.

Wheeler knew, had to have known, that Rakowicz hadn't come off well on the witness stand, that he had contradicted statements he had made in the past. But, he asked the jury, how many people could withstand several days of grilling as Rakowicz had without making a mistake or two? "I mean, it's a common joke, men can't even remember their anniversaries."

He likened Specter to Cardinal Richelieu, a figure from the 1700s, who had executed hundreds of innocent people. Richelieu was quoted as saying, "Give me six lines written by the most honest of men and I will find an excuse in them to hang him." Rakowicz had contradicted some past statements because he had been better prepared for this trial, taking the time to study more than a thousand documents "to come here and let you know what the real truth was." For instance, said Wheeler, Rakowicz didn't remember in 1994 that he had attended the CPPRG recall meeting but now, a decade later, he did recall being there because he saw an attendance sheet with his name on it. Simple.

What about Rakowicz's white paper recommending a recall? "Tim didn't understand the nature of the tests and he thought, on February 19, which was Friday, which was the date he completed his report . . . all he thought that had been done was they slammed one of the doors ten times, that somebody sat on the bumper." Once he found out (the following Monday) that a man had jumped on the bumper and had kicked at the brake pedal, Rakowicz understood that his theory of spontaneous disengagement had not been proven.

"And lo and behold," said Wheeler, "that very week he gets the written report from Orscheln and he looks at it and says, 'I had the test all wrong.'"

As far as Rakowicz's stark admission that the nation should have been warned about rollaway in Ford's recall notice, Wheeler chalked that up again to the witness not having the proper documents at his disposal at the time.

> Mr. Specter got Mr. Rakowicz to say, yes, America should be told about rollaway, [but] what document didn't Mr. Specter give Mr. Rakowicz before he started asking that series of questions? He didn't give him the recall notice. He didn't give it to him. Mr. Rakowicz was up there bare, trying to remember, what does the recall notice actually say? And you now know that it does talk specifically about rollaway. It talks about unintended vehicle movement. That's rollaway. It's pretty tough to sit up there on that stand for three days and have lawyers do that to you.

Rakowicz wasn't an evil person. And neither was Ford some "nameless, faceless, green-blooded"—Wheeler would repeat the phrase ten times in his closing speech—corporate entity. In fact, he said, the decision as to whether to issue a recall was "a tough call. It was a really tough call." Wheeler held his thumb and index finger barely an inch apart to demonstrate the point. On one hand, Ford, despite its best efforts, could not prove that its brakes spontaneously disengaged. Yet it was getting reports of rollaways and property damage due to rollaways.

> What do you do? . . . Here's the choice. The choice is, do you recall 884,000 vehicles that have this beneficial feature, beneficial both safety-wise and customer convenience-wise, and disable on an unproven theory because it's possible that some of those rollaways

might be being caused by something having to do with this design? Or do you not?

You've done everything that you can possibly do to try to show that it's actually happening and you can't do it. Do you go on a theory and disable a safety and convenience feature in 884,000 vehicles?

And Ford made a tough decision. It recalled all those vehicles. "They could have gone the other way," noted Wheeler. Now, asked Wheeler, despite the ruling by the first jury: "Is it a reprehensible decision?"

WHEELER REFUTED CLAIMS by Specter that Ford had been reluctant to acknowledge a problem with the brakes because they saved the company warranty costs in the long run and Ford did not want to disable the self-adjust feature or change the brakes. But Wheeler said the brakes themselves, even after deducting warranty savings, cost Ford more than $2 extra apiece. Wheeler had been talking for almost two hours now. There were still so many things he wanted to say, pieces of evidence he wanted to remind the jury about. "During the closing I just felt it getting away from me," Wheeler would acknowledge after the trial. He was tired and a bit befuddled, occasionally searching for a misplaced chart or interrupting himself when he tried to inject a missed point. ("I'm going to try to answer, to the extent that time permits, every accusation that Mr. Specter made," he had promised earlier. And he meant to keep the promise.) Wheeler apologized repeatedly to the jury about how long he was taking, then pressed on anyway. Afterward he would say, "There's a saying: 'There's the argument you plan to give, the argument you give, and the argument you wish you had given.'" Wheeler knew it was not going as well as he had hoped. What he didn't know was that he was actually convincing a number of jurors.

Despite some rambling, his main argument was getting through with resonance. Ford tried hard to find the problem, it made various fixes—shortening the control rods, installing the plastic wedge, switching to a cam-in design. It had sent a bulletin to dealers. Finally, and even though it couldn't prove the brakes caused rollaways, Ford issued a recall for all 884,400 vehicles. And NHTSA had had no quarrel with the wording of the recall, despite the fact that Specter and Nomura had characterized it as "almost fraudulent. I'm not sure what words they used." (At this, Specter smiled, looked at David Caputo, and mouthed the correct word—"phony.") Ford, said Wheeler, had done nothing wrong.

So should there be punitive damages? . . . Here's my question for you: If you award $1,165,000,000 to Mr. and Mrs. White and take it away from Ford, will that help Tim Rakowicz make a better engineering judgment tomorrow? Next week? Next month? Next year? . . . Will it help any other Ford engineer?

Now Wheeler sought to hedge his bet. He had to blunt Specter's demonstration, the one with the penny and the dime and the dollar. That had been powerful stuff at the first trial. But Wheeler took a few other approaches instead.

First he told the jurors that should they decide to award damages, they must reduce the award to reflect the harm caused only to people in Nevada. He noted that there were 1,387 Ford truck owners in Nevada who received recall notices, or 1 for every 600 owners nationally. That meant the jury should divide whatever award it might decide by 600.

In addition, any monetary judgment against Ford would hurt, submitted Wheeler. If employees at Ford hid the brake problem and that resulted in a judgment against the company, well, said Wheeler, "that's just like stealing from Ford Motor Co." Imagine, he said, if, say, Tim Rakowicz stole $10 million out of Ford's bank.

. . . and his boss found out. And his boss would say, ahhh, $10 million. It's nothing. Doesn't matter to me unless it's $100 million. It doesn't matter to me unless it's at least a billion. Do you think that's what his boss would say? . . . That's what Mr. Specter would have you believe.

If the jury was determined to punish Ford, to send it a message, Wheeler was telling them that $10 million—an amount roughly equal to the penny in Specter's demonstration—would be enough to do it. But he really wanted to leave this courtroom without Ford having to pay even one penny, not the symbolic kind worth $10 million in Specter's demonstration but the kind worth 1¢.

Wheeler concluded by telling the jury that Tim Rakowicz and Ford had already endured enough. They had heard and taken to heart the first jury's verdict years ago, had heard the verdict that Ford's brake was defective and that it had acted with "malice and oppression." Wasn't that enough? Tim Rakowicz did not have green in his veins; the young engineer was not "heartless or uncaring." Neither was Ford.

Does he need another message? Does his boss need another message? And does the message have to be some astronomical number? That's not what this case is about.

So I'm finished, I'm going to—I'm going to finish where I started. The plaintiffs' lawyers have to have one of two theories. Either there's a giant conspiracy of really, really bad people at Ford and Orscheln and the government, which makes no sense. Or there is no conspiracy and those folks genuinely believed the rightness of the decision they made. Now, that's not what the first jury thought, and I'm not asking you to quarrel with the first jury. I am asking you, asking you to look at the evidence and asking you to think about the testimony of Mr. Rakowicz, Mr. Soucie, Mr. Darold, how they were questioned, what the style was. And I am asking you to conclude that the conduct was not reprehensible and that you should not award punitive damages.

Thank you very much for your patience, and I'm sorry to have taxed it.

LUNCH. SPECTER WAS GLAD for the break. A chance to regroup, wolf down his daily ration of half a tuna sandwich, and gather his thoughts for his rebuttal. He already knew what he wanted to say and that he wanted to keep it short. He had timed Wheeler's speech: 2:20. Too long.

Jimmie White was steaming as he walked back to Durney's office across the street. He had tried to remain calm throughout the trial and even for Wheeler's closing. But likening an award against Ford to someone stealing money from the company—Wheeler had used the example of a Ford employee—was too much.

"He's saying I want to steal money from Ford Motor Co., after they stole my son's life?" said Jimmie, his voice shaking. "When he said that I wanted to come out of my chair and smack him."

Specter was glad that Jimmie hadn't.

Specter had several subjects to hit in his rebuttal. He galloped through his final points.

An award of punitive damages, Specter told the jury, was not only called for but also necessary. It was ridiculous to think the first jury's verdict, without severe monetary consequences, was punishment enough for Ford. That would be like absolving criminal convicts of any real punishment. "We could open up the jails, let everybody out because the mere fact that they were convicted is enough," he said, looking at the jurors. "Do you believe that?"

Ford had claimed it would only have lost more money by delaying a recall since the faulty brake system would have been installed in more new cars. But Specter noted the company had stopped putting the bad brakes into its trucks by February 1994, instead opting for the cam-in design. "It had been capped at 884,000, so they had no worry about an expanding number of vehicles," he said.

Wheeler had said that Ford also did not stand to gain anything by delaying because the ratchet-and-pawl system actually cost more, about $2 more per vehicle. But, said Specter, "he doesn't mention to you the biggest cost involved in having a recall. That's the recall itself. That recall cost $22 million. That's *$25* a vehicle."

Specter said he didn't unfairly question Rakowicz. The witness spent several days on the stand because it took that long to wring some shreds of truth out of him and to demonstrate how the engineer had changed his story. In 1994, when Pete Durney had interviewed Rakowicz in his deposition, he had denied knowledge on several fronts, including whether rollaway was more dangerous than brakes skipping through when they were applied.

> And the idea that he doesn't remember now what he said to Durney isn't the point at all. It's the fact that he said those things to Durney and tried to hide his role because what they do at Ford is they make you dig and dig and dig and dig and dig. They don't produce documents. They don't keep documents. They give you a witness whom you ask to produce them who tells you, I don't know anything, and then you try a case, what, eight years later, and the man becomes an expert on everything.
>
> The same thing on this issue about, oh, in the first trial Mr. Rakowicz wasn't shown an attendance roster of who was present at that recall committee meeting. That wasn't the point at all. The point was I asked him in my office in September 1994 if he had any involvement with the recall, and that happened to have been one month earlier when he was at the meeting. Now, how could he have forgotten that in good faith?

Ford delayed responding to NHTSA and, said Specter, pointing to Jimmie and Ginny, "all that . . . was more time off the clock that mattered a lot to those people because their son wasn't killed until October 9, 1994."

Specter disputed Wheeler's assertion that the recall notice really did warn about the danger of rollaways, even though the term was not used.

First, Specter read Rakowicz's testimony, testimony in which he acknowledged that Ford only recalled the trucks because the government was concerned about rollaways and had called for the recall.

> Q: And rollaway is a safety issue, correct?
> A: Yes, sir, absolutely.
> Q: And skip-through on apply is not a safety issue, correct?
> A: Yes, sir.

Specter walked across the courtroom to the exhibit bearing the recall notice sent to Stewart Brothers Drilling, Jimmie's employer.

> During rapid pedal application of the parking brake, the pedal may go to the floor with little or no effort. Should this occur, the parking brake system may not achieve full tension, potentially resulting in parking brake ineffectiveness or diminished effectiveness.
>
> Ladies and gentlemen, that is skip-through on apply, just as Tim Rakowicz said. That is not spontaneous disengagement. That is not rollaway. Rollaway was never warned of.
>
> This argument in this closing speech is atrocious, that this was done for reasons of rollaway. It is atrocious. Down here at the bottom, note: "Never leave your vehicle unattended while it is running." Not when you have already parked it and you go away and then it disengages. That's different, right?
>
> And it says: "If you do not take these precautions, your vehicle may move unexpectedly and injure someone." Is that notice to people that if you put the vehicle in first or in neutral and you turn the ignition off, you put the parking brake on, and you get out of the vehicle, and you leave and you go away and you go into the house, that sometime later the parking brake may disengage spontaneously? Of course it is not.

Specter told the eight men and women looking at him now that Wheeler was trying "to sell you this idea that this language warns against rollaway." If Ford really wanted to warn people of an impending danger, why didn't it say something that was clear and direct? Specter suggested this:

> The National Highway Traffic Safety Administration is concerned that your parking brake may disengage spontaneously. If this happens, you or someone else may be injured or killed.

The finish line was near. Specter raced for it.

[Six] of your fellow citizens sat in these seats and made these decisions six years ago, and it was all upheld. And nothing has changed
at Ford, and they're proud of that. They're proud to tell you, oh,
yeah, everybody's got the same jobs and they're just happy and
we're just moving along.

So we know that a verdict isn't sufficient, just saying it isn't sufficient. They tell you, we have every motivation to want to recall as
soon as we can. But look at the truth of this case. They didn't—they
wouldn't have recalled on their own, despite what they say were
their own pure motivations. It took NHTSA to tell them to do it.
And then when they did it, they were untruthful about the reason
because they wanted to keep people from knowing because they
didn't want to have claims against them, like this claim.

He [Wheeler] argues that everybody will figure it out. Bull! Do
you know how you figure out what happened there at Ford? You've
got to go out and hire a whole bunch of lawyers who have to spend
ten years unearthing every darn thing imaginable . . . [and] we still
haven't figured it all out.

What they decided to do was they decided to do everything possible to avoid telling people the truth. And they're still doing that
because they don't want to be sued. They know there are not less
than fifty-four people as of January of '99 who were injured from a
rollaway. They know that Walter White was killed from that. God
knows how many others there are.

And you know what? You know how many people there are in
this country who know the truth about this? It's the people that
are in this room right now in Nevada. And it's the [six] people who
had your jobs six years ago. And people have to know about this.
Because it's a matter of saving lives. Thank you.

JUDGE HAGEN GAVE his final instructions to the jury and sent them on
their way. A verdict was unlikely that same day. It was already late afternoon. The courtroom emptied out. There was nothing to do now except
wait. Specter spoke to the Whites briefly, then adjourned with Durney,
Nomura, and Caputo to the lawyer's lounge, a stark room with bare
walls located several floors below the courtroom.

"Well, now you've seen two defenses by Ford that were completely
opposite," Specter said.

"This was a ballsy defense," said Nomura.

Ballsy and dishonest, Specter felt. How could Ford at the first trial have basically acknowledged it was wrong and beg for mercy before the jury set punitive damages, yet claim at the same stage at this trial that the company had done nothing wrong? Yet maybe the jury would buy it.

Specter felt he had put on a solid case, but he also doubted the jury would come back with a huge verdict, at least not as big as the last jury's. Getting $150 million again probably wasn't in the cards. Things had changed since 1998. For one, Ford's net worth was now $11 billion, not $30 billion. And the judge, fixing an error the appeals court had cited from the first trial, pointedly instructed the jury to consider only Nevada's interest in this case, a factor that also was likely to reduce an award.

"I'm also worried that there won't be the same emotional involvement as in the first trial," Specter told Durney. This case had been about the amount of punitive damages, not whether the Whites deserved compensation. It was not about their pain. Jimmie and Ginny had not testified. Neither had said a word in open court.

But all the plaintiffs' lawyers felt there would be some award. The evidence, they felt, was too strong. The first jury's verdict was a fact; the judge had instructed so. Ford had acted with malice and oppression. Fact.

Specter called for a pool. The lawyers wrote their predictions on slips of paper. Each kicked in $5. Jimmie had already put in his money, guessing $50 million. Compared with the first trial, in which he and others had testified, this one seemed flat to him, devoid of emotion. How could this jury be as upset at Ford's actions as the first? Still Jimmie felt certain he had won the case, and a $50 million verdict would satisfy him just fine. He wanted to sting Ford and that would do it.

Just as six years earlier, Nomura was the most optimistic, predicting $75 million. Durney speculated $60 million and Caputo, $55 million, or one-half of 1 percent, calculating the jury might adopt Specter's penny-dime-dollar analogy but pick something in between, a nickel. Specter wasn't quite as optimistic, or maybe he was afraid to be. He wrote $35 million on his slip.

"If we get zero dollars it will be the biggest surprise I've ever had," Specter said, "and I've had some where I thought I won and didn't."

You could never tell what a jury would do. He'd come out on the losing end when he hadn't suspected it. But this case was different, wasn't it?

It was inconceivable to Specter that the jury could have bought Wheeler's argument that Ford did nothing wrong, inconceivable that even a single juror could vote to award nothing—zero!—in punitive damages. Never mind several of them.

Inconceivable.

CHAPTER 27

A Jury Divided

THE JURY HAD BEEN pent up emotionally and intellectually. For nine long days of testimony and arguments, its members had sat shoulder to shoulder in a wooden box, albeit one containing comfortable high-back leather chairs. The jurors had not been allowed, as the judge had constantly admonished, to discuss the case with each other or any other person. Now they were free to speak about the case. And speak they did.

The second they entered the jury room, a spartan space containing a long table and adorned only with two forlorn plants and a solitary, lopsided picture (a framed landscape), the ladies and gentlemen of the jury unleashed a torrent of free expression. Some discussed issues while sifting through documents and exhibits from the case. Some talked about the witnesses. Some talked about the lawyers. All at once.

"You ever seen so many lawyers in one room?"

"How'd you like that Wheeler guy? He wouldn't make eye contact."

"Specter made too much eye contact. He was, like, staring at us."

"I didn't like that little one. What's his name, Nomura?"

"Was Rakowicz lying through his teeth, or what?"

"That Al Darold was smooth, wasn't he?"

"Yeah, a little too smooth. He was full of baloney."

"If I never see another ratchet and pawl . . . I think I could assemble one blindfolded."

"Hey, you know what?" said Connie Martin, Juror No. 1, a single woman in her thirties. "Maybe this is a reality TV show. Maybe they're all in on it except for us. Where's the hidden camera?"

Connie would prove to be the most outspoken and light-hearted of the bunch. A large woman with bright brown eyes tinged with green, she had a ready laugh that softened the take-charge personality reflected in her gait, a stiff, shoulders-back way of walking evident each time she had led the procession of jurors into the courtroom. For Connie, this group of jurors was fairly tame compared with the people she was used to dealing with at her place of employment—Lakes Crossing Center, a wonderfully euphemistic name for a maximum security facility for the criminally insane. Connie was a security supervisor.

"Let's pick the foreman," someone said.

Cynthia Lavan volunteered but she was ignored. A few of her peers felt she craved too much attention to be put in charge. How tacky that she kept taking calls on her cell phone during breaks in the trial! There was silence for a few minutes. Then Steve Maximov, a Reno croupier with a glib sense of humor that belied deadpan eyes, spoke up.

"Well, anytime I've ever seen a movie about a trial, the foreman's always the one who sits where I'm sitting," he said, noting his position at the very left end of the first row.

"Good, you're the foreman," someone said to a chorus of relieved agreement, which was followed by disagreement as the cacophony erupted once again.

"Ford's done something very wrong here," said Bonnie Coe, a grand-mother who ran her own at-home day care center.

"I don't agree," countered Allen Humphreys, the mechanic.

"Neither do I," said Catherine Armour, an elementary school secre-tary who was friends with Pete Durney's wife.

"I'm with Bonnie," said Connie. "Ford definitely did some wrong things."

IT WAS APPARENT from the outset. Reaching a verdict wasn't going to be easy.

Finally things settled down. It was time for some serious exchange. The jurors had been friendly throughout the trial. Many had lunched together, talked about their families and the beautiful weather for this time of year, how the Truckee River that coursed through downtown Reno had swollen, flowers blooming along its banks.

Catherine Armour and Cynthia Lavan, who called each other Cathy and Cindy, had become fast friends, chatting and going to lunch together, though not discussing the case and never having any idea how far apart their opinions would be or ever dreaming that they would become fierce opponents when the deliberations began. In fact, none of the jurors or the attorneys in the courtroom could have imagined that they would be so evenly—and widely—split.

Allen kept talking about how Ford had done all it could reasonably have been expected to do. "They had the wedge made. They developed the cam-in. They issued a recall."

Cathy, a mother of two grown sons, both in the Air Force, couldn't let go of the notion that Walter White had been left alone to play in that truck. "I never left my kids unattended," she said.

Cindy broke in, loudly.

"Helllooo?! That's not the point! We're not here to decide who's right and wrong. That's already been established by the first jury. We're not starting from scratch. The point is . . . Ford could have done something faster. So what if the kid was in the truck? That's not what we're here to decide. Those brakes should have held and Ford knew it! They should have sent the recall sooner. It should have said, 'Warning! Your truck could roll away.' Even that there was the *possibility* that it could roll away. If they did, more people would have come in to have them fixed."

Cindy was burning inside. She looked over at Allen, who was handling the ratchet and pawl. Allen had told his fellow jurors more than once that he was a car mechanic and that he understood how these things worked.

"So what?" Cindy blurted out. "I don't even know why that thing's in here. We're not deciding if Ford's guilty or not. We already know they are. There's already been a verdict by the first jury. We're just here to decide the amount of punitive damages."

"I guess you're right," Allen said as he put the brake parts down. But he was clearly steamed. Allen was already upset with Specter, specifically a remark he had made about mechanics. The lawyer had referred to J. E. Davidson, the Pittsburgh mechanic who had first pinpointed the brake problem, as "just a mechanic" or "only a mechanic." Allen felt that was a put-down. (Specter, who liked Davidson and respected his opinion, had actually been making a different point: How could the experts at Ford not have recognized the brake problem when it was so clearly evident to someone not as highly trained? Specter's answer was, of course, that they could. Just that they didn't want to.)

Specter thought he had an ally in Allen Humphreys. If anyone, he would see through Ford's flak and understand the brake problem. "I don't know if we're going to win or not," he had told Caputo when the jury went out to deliberate, "but I'm glad we kept that mechanic on the jury." How wrong he had been. Specter was unaware when the jury was chosen that Ford was the mechanic's employer. Allen told his fellow jurors now that he was a car mechanic who for twelve years had worked at a Ford dealership, mostly on Suzukis but occasionally on Fords, and always side-by-side with Ford mechanics.

Steve broke in now, doing his job as foreman. "Look, it's almost five o'clock," he said. "The judge is going to call a recess soon. We all ought to try to think about a dollar amount. We need to think about it overnight. Let's do that and come back tomorrow and discuss a dollar amount."

The jurors had only had a little more than an hour since the closing arguments and the judge's instructions. That was barely enough time to vent some emotion and pull out a few key documents from the piles in the jury room. Humphreys had been most interested in the exhibits, just as the lawyers had guessed. The plaintiff's attorneys had given Humphreys a nickname—"Bowling Ball Guy," because of his lawsuit against the bowling alley. The plaintiffs felt that someone with such a litigious nature, combined with Humphreys' knowledge as a mechanic, would be terrific for their case. They considered him one of their linchpins on the jury. They couldn't have been more wrong.

The jurors left for the day, laughing loudly as they got on the elevator to leave the federal courthouse. They seemed relieved and friendly. They obviously got along well. It was a good sign, thought Specter. Wrong again.

THE NEXT DAY, a balmy and beautiful Friday, started quite differently from the way day one of deliberations had ended. It was time for serious talks now, time for everyone to reveal how, and if, they wanted to punish Ford. To almost everyone's surprise, Bonnie Coe, a demure and diminutive grandmother of seven with short and straight, pageboy-style white hair, insisted that she wanted to speak first. She'd been thinking about the case all night, and she had to say her piece right away or she was going to burst.

"I'm going to throw this out and I know it may seem farfetched to some people, but I just feel like we need to prove a point," she started. "In the ten years since Walter White died, Ford has done nothing that I can see. There's still trucks out there with that problem and it could happen again. What will it take to send a message to Ford? And I don't care if it's only one in a thousand that could roll away, but we saw nothing that showed that they really cared at all. Ford was saying, 'Well if something happens, no big deal. We'll just sweep it under the rug.'"

Then Bonnie threw the first pitch: $100 million.

The response was immediate.

Allen: "Well, I say zero."

Cathy: "So do I. Zero."

Steve: "Same here. I say zero also."

Bonnie shrank back in her chair. *Maybe I'm all wrong about this,* she thought.

Until Connie spoke up.

"I'm with Bonnie," she said. "I say $100 million."

The oldest of the jurors, a woman who gave her name as Eileen in an interview after the trial, had sat in the back row of the jury box (occasionally nodding off, her muffled snores audible to her fellow jurors). She chimed in with $1 million, stating that to her, "That's a lot of money." Specter had been concerned about this juror, knowing that older folks remembered all too well when a Milky Way cost a nickel and a movie was a quarter. They remembered the days when $1 million was truly "a lot of money."

But not Bonnie. "One million?" she said incredulously. "You might as well say zero. If it's $1 million, Ford will be cheering—Yahoo!"

Glenn Ostrander, a tall young man with a goatee, had been fairly quiet so far. He had mixed feelings. He was "floating," as he would put it. On one hand, he thought Ford had made an effort to fix the problem and had not acted with bad intent. On the other, he was convinced that Ford knew there were problems with the brake system before it put it into its F-Series trucks—and put it in anyway. Maybe more than anything he was bothered by the way things had transpired in the courtroom, bothered by the case Ford had put on and the behavior of its witnesses and its lead lawyer, who, like Ford, he felt, was "trying to pull the wool over our eyes." It was eating at him.

"I'm still not convinced that Ford did anything wrong," he said. "But it's like Ford was trying to hide a lot from us, Mr. Wheeler and Tim Rakowicz. Mr. Specter was trying to get everything he could from Rakowicz and he kept saying he didn't recall."

Still, no one had proved, really *proved*, that Ford intentionally did anything wrong and Glenn would say later that he was ready to give the Whites nothing, not a penny, "if most people felt that way on the jury."

Nevertheless, he threw out a number, just to keep the ball rolling. It wasn't zero, but it wasn't very high. "How about $10 million?"

The battle lines were drawn, with the majority tipping in Ford's favor—three jurors at zero, one at $1 million, one at perhaps $10 million. Bonnie and Connie, at $100 million, were outnumbered.

But one juror still had not mentioned a number. Cindy had sat in the back row and had seemed especially attentive throughout the trial, often leaning forward to read exhibits on the large TV monitor or to get a better look at a document. She also seemed, at least to Specter, to be with the plaintiffs. He thought he had seen tears in her eyes after his closing argument. Indeed the poem he read had moved her. Cindy had had to reapply her makeup after returning to the jury room. Bonnie had also cried. But not all the jurors were so moved by Specter, a usually unemotional man who himself had shed tears. A few thought he'd been faking it, his tears part of a well-rehearsed acting job. A few speculated with a chuckle that he had planted some substance in the pages of the book, smelling salts perhaps, to make his eyes overflow.

Cindy certainly appeared to be sympathetic to the Whites. But jurors were hard to read. Hell, impossible. Specter had had jurors smile at him, even wink at him during a trial, then vote against his client. Cindy was a middle-aged woman with dark brown hair and glasses. She was a wife and mother of two grown children, daughters, a bartender and a biologist. Cindy worked as an employee trainer. The lawyers knew all this. What they didn't know, hadn't asked, was the name of her employer. If they had, Cindy Lavan might have been excused by the plaintiffs' attorneys. She worked for General Motors. A car company.

Now her opinion would be critical. She could leave Bonnie and Connie standing alone in calling for a big award. Or she could move the jury toward a 50–50 split, with three jurors at zero and three seeking a nine-figure punitive award. Everyone looked at Cindy, waiting for her vote.

"I say $116 million."

Cindy had been swayed by Specter's demonstration with the dollar bill, the dime, and the penny. To truly punish Ford, to even start to punish Ford, you had to at least take a dime—or 1 percent—from its corporate pocket.

Wheeler's gambit—to insist, despite the upheld verdict of the first trial's jury, that Ford had done nothing wrong—had worked for three of the jurors. But, as Specter had predicted, it had backfired for those who weren't swayed, making them angry with Ford over its refusal to accept any responsibility. And now they—Connie, Bonnie, and Cindy—wanted to punish the car company. Severely.

"They lied to us," Cindy said. "They said there was nothing wrong. That really makes me mad."

"And how about the way they sugarcoated the recall letter? And that delay in responding to NHTSA, five days short of five months," said Connie. "I can't get over that point. Ford wants to be treated like a person? Well, you try not paying your rent for five months and see what happens. Not only should the Whites have been warned, but also everyone driving one of those trucks." Had Ford acted more quickly, none of the jurors might be here right now, said Connie, "because Walter White might still be alive."

"I'm not sure they did it as fast as they could," argued Cathy, "but they were within the law, within what NHTSA was requiring."

Connie: "Yeah, but remember, NHTSA didn't require more because Ford told them that only one person was injured, when they knew about eight. And look at how many more ended up hurt."

Steve: "I think they did the recall notice as fast as they could because they thought it was a nuisance issue, not a safety issue."

Cindy: "Oh, c'mon."

Steve: "Really. Everybody has cars roll away."

Then Steve told a story about his own experience with a rollaway. It had happened a few years earlier. He and his wife, Dawn, were in the garage sitting in their Toyota RAV4 when they spotted their neighbors across the street. Steve hopped out of the passenger seat and walked over to say hello. His wife got out after him. As he was talking to his neighbors, he spotted Dawn walking leisurely down the driveway to join them. Not far behind was the RAV4, rolling down the driveway, picking up speed as it headed directly toward his wife. She had her back to the SUV and didn't see it coming.

"Look out! LOOK OUT!" Steve and his neighbors screamed at her, pointing at the RAV4. Steve's wife turned, saw the truck, and jumped out of the way just in time. It rolled to the end of driveway, across the street, and into a lot where a new house was being built.

"It almost killed her," said Steve, a former Navy jet pilot. Then he delivered the punch line, the reason this was an example of why he had a hard time blaming Ford for the death of Walter White. "You know why that vehicle rolled away? Because she didn't set the brake. She forgot."

Steve said that a rollaway doesn't mean a brake malfunctioned. "It means someone screwed up," he said, adding, "Nobody ever proved spontaneous disengagement. Not NHTSA or Ford or Orscheln. They tested and never proved it, not even banging that brake system with 5-pound weights."

"Rollaway is a result, not a problem," Allen chimed in.

But several other jurors disagreed with his assessment. These brakes *were* defective and there were many, many reported cases of rollaways, they pointed out. Ford's brake was clearly defective—after all, there was a recall—and the company had fudged on admitting the problem. And Ford was still refusing to admit the real problem.

THEN THINGS TURNED nasty in the jury room. Jurors who had voted for zero protested the thought of giving more money to the Whites, who had already received compensatory damages from the first trial, though they didn't know how much.

"I don't want to see the Whites get another dime," said Cathy.

"Zero!" said Allen.

Cathy added, "And I don't care if we sit here 'til doomsday."

A few jurors suggested sending a note to the judge asking how much the Whites received in compensatory damages from the first trial. But Bonnie put an end to such talk. "Forget it! It doesn't matter who gets the money. It's about punishing Ford."

And how about the lawyers? No one wanted to give a big award that would line the lawyers' pockets. No one.

Even Connie said, "It bothers me that the attorneys make out like rats." But she felt that Ford had done wrong and had to pay the price, no matter the recipient.

Bonnie: "Big business needs to be slapped down once in a while."

Cathy: "You sound like you're just against big business, that big business is always wrong."

Bonnie: "In this case they are."

Allen chimed in with a political statement of sorts. "Large punitive damages are a problem in this country. That's why doctors' medical malpractice insurance is so high. Large punitive damages just raise the price of everything."

Steve Maximov would recall when the jurors were interviewed later, "We were very, very close to a hung jury at that point. We couldn't have been more separated and none of us wanted to budge."

But as the hours wore on toward lunchtime and the panel continued to debate the issues, both sides seemed to soften.

Cathy had to admit that if Ford had sent its recall notice sooner, Walter White's life might have been spared. Allen persisted that Ford made a "reasonable attempt" to warn people and only could have prevented the tragedy "if it had a time machine" to go back before Walter's death. Yet some of the conviction had left Allen's voice.

Cathy also had to admit that she didn't like the way Ford had put on its legal defense. Cathy and the other jurors felt that Wheeler had addressed them as though they were dumb. "Like cowpokes," said Cindy. "Like we were a bunch of farmers and casino workers and prostitutes in Nevada," offered Bonnie. And they felt that Rakowicz had made up one lie after another.

"He changed his story so much," Cathy said, adding that the trial's chief witness had been evasive and reluctant in answering the plaintiffs' questions. "It got to the point that when Mr. Specter asked him a question, we could answer it before he did."

A few things were bothering Steve as well. He was particularly troubled by the fact that Ford had insisted the brake problem was merely one of customer satisfaction and not safety. If that was the case, why had it recalled only trucks with manual transmissions—those trucks susceptible to rollaways? "That didn't go unnoticed," he would say later. "That was one of the trickier points. That was why most of the jury felt that Ford had pulled a tricky one."

Yet Allen had also made a good argument for keeping any award low, that the jury was to limit the punishment—and thus the deterrence factor—to protect only Nevada's interest, not that of the entire nation. (He didn't know it, of course, but the judge's failure to stress this fact in his charge to the jury in the first trial was primarily the reason for this second trial.) While no one believed Wheeler's argument that this meant any award had to be divided by 600, it nevertheless mandated some limit on the verdict.

Eileen appeared more convinced now that Ford had acted badly and realized that $1 million was not, in the current scheme of things, "a lot of money." She announced that she now could see her way to awarding $20 million.

Glenn, too, was on his way up from $10 million. He agreed that what Ford did—the delay in recalling the cars, the nebulous language of its recall notice—showed bad faith. Why did it take almost five months to respond to NHTSA? Why so long to send the recall notice? Why—and this still bothered him—did Ford's witnesses sound like they were not telling the truth in court? He had a feeling that Ford's lawyer had not been truthful. Glenn was bothered most by the piece of paper Wheeler held before the jury in his closing argument that purported to show Nevadans had bought just 1,387 Ford trucks with the brake problem. Out of 884,400? How could that be? Glenn did the math. If Nevada had even 1 percent of the nation's population—and Specter had said it was more—that would be at least 8,800 trucks. And folks out here drove more American-built trucks than in other parts of the country. "You go to any ranch in Nevada and you'll see a Ford pickup there," said Glenn.

The more Glenn heard from the others, from Bonnie and Connie and Cindy, the more upset he began to get with Ford.

"When people finally knew about the brake problem, it was two and a half years later, after Tim wrote his white paper. That bothers me," he said. "Ford could have mailed something to people instead of just sending a Technical Service Bulletin to dealers. For me, credibility counts. If Ford would have said, 'We experienced a problem with the parking brake. . . . Get to a dealer and we're working on it.' Or if they told people to take precautions, chock your wheels or park where your truck won't roll. That's my problem. They didn't tell the public anything. They still haven't! And with a million vehicles on the road? That's amazing."

Maybe Ford had not broken the letter of the law. But had it acted differently, had been more forthcoming, perhaps Walter White would not have died. And that hit Glenn especially close to home.

"My world changed when I had my little man," he told his fellow jurors, referring to Gavin, his seven-month-old son. "One night I was giving him a bath and I was thinking about the Whites and how horrible it would be."

"You can't ever replace him. This little guy's my life now. . . . All I could think of was, 'What if it was him? What if Ford hadn't sent me a notice?'"

Glenn reconsidered his initial vote for $10 million in punitive damages. "That's a drop in the bucket for Ford," he said. He could indeed see raising the award to at least $20 million, even $50 million.

Now Steve said he could also see his way clear to an award. Cathy said she might vote for $20 million, maybe $25 million, but no more. Allen was still sticking to zero, but he had a strategy in mind that would allow him to agree to an award. Even one as high as $50 million, an amount he guessed correctly was low compared with the first jury's award. ("I didn't know the result of the last jury," he would say later. "But I knew that if our near-socialist Ninth Circuit threw it out, it was damned high. And I figured that the next jury, if we hung and there was a next jury, would be high also. So I just tried to keep it as low as I could.")

Several jurors also now expressed the notion that whatever they decided would be appealed by one side or the other, so why not come up with a number? Why end all this with a hung jury?

Maybe a compromise was possible.

Finally Connie took charge. She had been writing the numbers on a paper flip chart, drawing a line with zero at one end and $116 million on the other. Now she suggested adding the votes and dividing by eight. She borrowed Cindy's calculator, punched in the numbers—roughly estimating what Glenn, Eileen, and Steve were willing to give based on their comments—then announced a number: $58.75 million. Then she did the same for the numbers the jury believed Wheeler and Specter had suggested, even if somewhat subliminally—$1 million by Wheeler, $116 million by Specter. That averaged out to $58.5 million. Almost the same number.

"We must be on the right track," beamed Connie.

Not everyone agreed.

"Forget it. I'm not going for fifty-eight," said Allen. "Not a penny over fifty."

"Then we're going to be here for a long time," Cindy shot back. She hinted she would come down from $116 million.

"C'mon guys. We've got to compromise," said Connie. "It's all about compromise."

Cathy didn't want to go beyond $20 million, if she voted to award anything. "I don't think Ford is at fault nearly that much," she said. "I'm sorry, but I don't see anything Ford did wrong. They did everything on time."

"You're kidding me!" said Cindy.

"And besides, they should have been watching that child."

"Cathy, it happens," said Cindy. "I kept an eye on my children too, but there were times I turned my back. My daughter once got away from me in the supermarket and I couldn't find her right away. It happens."

"Well, I never let mine out of my sight. With my kids . . ."

"We're not talking about your kids!" said Cindy.

"And if Ford was wrong, why didn't the government fine them?" asked Cathy.

Connie now: "NHTSA didn't know. They told them there was only one injury when they knew of eight. They delayed responding about the recall notice five days short of five months. Five months!"

Allen: "You can't get off that, can you? 'Five days short of five months, five days short of five months . . .'"

Connie: "That's right, I can't. That's one helluva long delay."

Allen: "Ford didn't do anything wrong."

Connie: "How can you say they didn't do anything wrong?"

Bonnie: "Just look at that recall letter! Look at how they downplayed the danger . . ."

Connie: "If I would have gotten a recall letter like that, I probably would have put it off. I probably would have said, 'Oh, I'll get to it.' And never gotten around to it. I would have blown it off. But if it had said the brakes are dangerous and I had a three-year-old kid, well, that's different. And I do think the reason Ford said it the way they did was because this was their best-selling product . . ."

Cathy: "I drive a Ford and I've never had any problems . . ."

Cindy: "Jeez! What does that have to do with the price of tea in China?"

Connie: ". . . And they still don't own up to it!"

Bonnie: "Even knowing this child was killed."

Cathy felt her colleagues' eyes focused on her. They were angry that she was so stubborn. She started edging away from zero. Maybe if Ford had sent the notice sooner, that cute little blond boy's life could have been saved. Maybe she could find a way to award the Whites some money, even though she hated the idea. Hadn't they already gotten millions from Ford in compensatory damages?

By this time Steve, resigned to give some punitive award, said he might be able to live with $50 million. It was a beautiful day outside, sunny and 70 degrees, unusually warm for March 19. It had been gorgeous all week, a week Steve was supposed to have been on vacation. Several of the jurors expressed a desire to leave the courtroom and enjoy what was left of this glorious Friday.

"Okay, $50 million," said Connie, seizing what appeared an opportune moment. "Can we all agree on $50 million? That's a fair compromise."

She went around the room. There were seven votes for $50 million.

There was just one holdout. The General Motors employee wouldn't budge. Cindy had started at $116 million. Any less would be a pittance for Ford, no great punishment at all. Taking $50 million from Ford was like taking a nickel from Specter's fictitious man, the man with $10 in his pocket. It just wouldn't do. "Maybe I'll go to $75 million," she said. "No lower."

"I repeat, not a penny over fifty," said Allen, his arms crossed against his chest.

"No way, "said Cindy. Maybe she'd go down to $60 million, but that was it.

Steve stood up and walked over to the flip chart, the one on which Connie had drawn a line with zero at one end and $116 million at the other. She had written in several other numbers along the continuum, including $50 million and $100 million. Steve took the black marker and beneath $50 million he wrote the number "7." Beneath $100 million he wrote a "1." It was 7–1.

Cindy jumped from her chair.

"I don't need this crap! You're all backing me into a corner. Did you hear His Honor say, 'Don't let anybody influence your decision, change your mind, or convince you to do other than what you think is right?' I don't need an ultimatum."

"We all came to $50 million. Why can't you?" A voice from among the seven.

"I don't care what you did. It's not fair. And now you're going to gang up on me?"

"Don't take it that way."

"How else am I supposed to take it?"

"Oh, come on."

"No. I'll stay here all week if I have to. I'm in no hurry. I'm not working next week," said Cindy, who had recently had back surgery and was on leave from her job.

Connie tried to bring peace and a resolution.

"All right. What about $54 million?" she asked hopefully. "Can we agree on $54 million?"

"No," barked Allen.

"No way," said Cindy.

"Okay," offered Connie. "Let's split the difference. What do you say about $52 million? That's a compromise. That's fair."

"No," said Cindy, her face stern. "I won't go below $60 million."

By now Allen had had enough. He'd gone way beyond what he felt was a fair compromise. Cathy was angry as well, at herself as much as anyone else. She had let the group pressure her into moving to $50 million and now she was starting to regret it.

"Listen," said Allen, "if we don't agree on $52 million right now, and I mean right now, I'm going straight back to zero. I don't care if I hang this jury." His peers could see he meant it.

"Same for me," said Cathy. And she meant it, too.

The room fell silent for the first time in many hours.

CHAPTER 28

A Nickel

SPECTER USED THE waiting time to work on his father's campaign.

"Book the radio ads as late as possible," he instructed over his cell phone as he walked along Reno's Virginia Street.

"How much are they spending in the Lehigh Valley? How much of that is the Club for Growth?" he asked of the conservative Republican group opposing his father.

In the coming weeks the younger Specter would watch the Club's preferred candidate, Pat Toomey, inch closer and closer in the polls until he was just a few percentage points away. Nerves were starting to fray among some in the Specter campaign, but both father and son remained calm. The candidate wore a confident face for the media, whose members covered the race more closely as Election Day drew near and as the prospect of an upset seemed more possible. His son and campaign manager kept a close eye on internal polling data as well as campaign expenditures, making sure his father's ads had a steady presence on television while monitoring campaign cash to ensure there was enough for the critical final days, including "street money" to help get voters to the polls. April 27 was only weeks away.

Durney and Nomura walked nearby. They tried not to interrupt Specter while he was on the phone or to talk about the case. On this second day of deliberations, there was nothing they could do, so why keep talking about it? But they did, almost to themselves. Durney was trying to figure out what the jury might be talking about while Nomura was hoping for a sign, any sign. Their chatter was nervous.

"Wheeler had to convince all of them, or almost all of them," said Durney. "No way he did that."

"It would be a good sign for us if they asked the judge for a calculator," Nomura said, smiling at the notion.

"No way. I can't see it."

"Or, remember the movie *The Verdict*?" Nomura went on, "Where the jury comes out during deliberations and asks, 'Are we limited to the amount requested by the plaintiff?'"

Nomura laughed. As the lawyers and the Whites sat down for lunch at an outdoor café on the banks of the Truckee River, Durney guessed at what was going on in the jury room. "You know," he said, "if you swear at a dog in a nice voice, he'll wag his tail. And that's all Wheeler did. I think some of the jurors may have fallen for it. I think the stronger wills will prevail but it will take some time."

If Durney was nervous, he didn't show it when his food arrived. He scarfed down a steak topped with shrimp. Then he gulped down a cup of seafood chowder that someone else at the table had left. He ate his sweet potato fries, then scooped a handful off Nomura's plate. His dessert arrived but he never got to eat it. At 12:58 p.m., the *William Tell Overture* crackled in the air. It was Durney's cell phone. Everyone grew quiet. Durney put the phone to his ear and listened intently, nodding his head.

"Uh-huh. Uh-huh. Uh-huh," he said, then hung up. "Let's go! The jury's back."

JIMMIE AND GINNY took their seats in the courtroom, holding hands, stern expressions on their faces. The lawyers took their places impassively. The judge called for the jurors, who filed into their seats slowly, solemnly. The clock on the courtroom wall ticked toward 2:00 p.m. as juror Steve Maximov rose and handed a large manila envelope containing the verdict to a clerk, who carried it to Judge Hagen. Hagen tore open the sealed envelope, pulled out a white sheet of paper, and read it to himself. Then he had the clerk read the verdict aloud.

> SPECIAL VERDICT. We, the jury in the above-entitled action, find as follows:
>
> What amount of punitive damages, if any, do you award to plaintiffs Ginny and Jimmie White against defendant Ford Motor Co.?
> ANSWER: $52 million.

There was no outburst in the courtroom. No handshakes, no high-fives. For such a significant moment there was little outward reaction. The lawyers knew not to openly celebrate or lament. Still Specter felt vindication, both for his case and for himself as a lawyer. He had stood by the Whites, encouraged them to turn down Ford's settlement offers after the first trial.

Jimmie and Ginny looked at each other after the verdict was read and exhaled, releasing years of frustration and the last two weeks of intense emotion and uncertainty. Jimmie allowed a small smile to creep from his heart to his face. But what he felt was relief. Not joy.

Afterward, the Whites and their lawyers walked back to the parking lot of Pete Durney's office. Jimmie was satisfied. The verdict was enough to embarrass Ford, to punish those he believed had been responsible for his son's death and had tried to cover up the true cause. He and Ginny had won; Ford had lost.

"This was never about the money," said Jimmie. Then he added something Specter had heard many times from clients who'd lost loved ones. "You'd give every penny back for one thing, but you know you can never have it."

The Whites and their lawyers walked across the street to Durney's office after the trial and said their goodbyes. Specter didn't talk much with the Whites. There was little left to say. He looked at Jimmie and the two men shook hands. He hugged Ginny softly. Specter turned and walked to his already packed rental car, and then he and Caputo headed for the highway, the Lincoln Aviator cutting through the Sierra Nevada en route to San Francisco and a red-eye home to Philadelphia.

JIMMIE AND GINNY drove back to Elko that night. On the drive they talked again about moving to the Northwest. They wanted to be near the sea, so different from the remote desert town where they lived now, where Walter was buried. The next day they would go together to visit his grave in the small cemetery next to Elko High School, a school where Walter would have been enrolled the following year had he lived.

CHAPTER 29

Deal

ONCE AGAIN THE CASE had Specter's desired effect. There were head-lines the morning after the trial from Reno and Elko to Kansas City and Miami. Specter and the marvels of modern technology had made sure of that. Working his cell phone while coursing through the Sierra Nevada, Specter had called the Associated Press to report the verdict. The story hit the wires before Specter reached San Francisco. By the time he and Caputo had been seated in the rear of a small San Francisco restaurant and popped the cork on a bottle of champagne, the AP story had already been posted on websites by several major newspapers, including *The Miami Herald*. The AP had summed up the case in fewer than 300 words.

NEVADA JURY AWARDS BEREAVED PARENTS $52 MILLION
IN SUIT OVER FORD TRUCK BRAKES

By SCOTT SONNER
Associated Press Writer

RENO, Nev.—A federal jury awarded $52 million in damages Friday to the parents of a three-year-old killed when a Ford pickup truck rolled over him because of a defective parking brake. Jimmie and Ginny White of Elko said in their civil lawsuit that Ford Motor Co. knew about the parking brake defect but didn't warn consumers. Ford said it plans to appeal.

"I think it is a reasonable and relatively modest number under the circumstances," said Shanin Specter, lawyer for the Whites, whose son, Walter, was killed in October 1994. "Ford has been having these parking brake problems for 10 years with these trucks, these F-Series vehicles," he told The Associated Press. A month after the boy died, Ford recalled 884,000 1992–94 F-Series pickup trucks and Broncos, 1993–94 Ranger pickups, Explorers and Mazda Navajo SUVs to repair the parking brake mechanisms. But Specter said the recall notice told consumers only that the problem with the brakes was that they sometimes would fail to engage initially. "Ford did not say that after the brake had been engaged it later could disengage spontaneously for no reason," said Specter. He said there have been more than 1,100 incidents in which Ford trucks' parking brakes have disengaged spontaneously, resulting in 54 injuries and the one death. The Whites received a recall notice in March 1995, after their son Walter had climbed into their 1993 Ford F-350 pickup truck and fell or jumped out. He went under the wheels as it rolled down their driveway.

Ford spokeswoman Kathleen Vokes in Dearborn, Mich., confirmed the company plans to appeal Friday's ruling. She said she was not aware of plans for an additional recall.

While a number of newspapers ran the story, many more did not. Most major papers, including *The New York Times* and even Specter's hometown *Philadelphia Inquirer*, didn't print a word. Nor did TV stations carry the story. Specter had just wanted to spread the word about Ford and its faulty brakes and even more faulty recall. The media reaction had been good, not great.

Specter had also known that the case was not yet over, though it was nearing a final solution. When Specter read the newspaper articles on his BlackBerry the night of the verdict he noted that the AP reporter had managed to reach Malcolm Wheeler and that Ford's lawyer promised to appeal the case again. Which Ford dutifully did.

Ford asked that the verdict be tossed out entirely. The grounds for appeal had, of course, been minimized since the first trial. Specter and Judge Hagen had corrected those things the appeals court had cited as errors. Hagen, for one, carefully instructed the jury this time that it was to consider only Nevada's interests in assessing punitive damages.

Nevertheless Wheeler believed he saw numerous grounds for the verdict being tossed out. Ford's appeal rested in large part on a Supreme Court ruling handed down after the first Ford trial in 1998. The high court, in a 6–3 decision, ruled in *State Farm v. Campbell* that a punitive damages award of $145 million was excessive in a case in which $2.6 million was awarded in compensatory damages. In that case a jury found for plaintiffs who alleged the insurance company had acted in bad faith in failing to settle an auto coverage claim and that the carrier had engaged in a long-standing pattern of dishonest practices. The court ruled that except in extreme cases punitive damages should generally not exceed compensatory damages by a double-digit ratio, or by more than nine to one. At the most.

Wheeler cited one case that came after *State Farm* in which a California jury awarded $290 million against Ford over the roof design of its 1978 Bronco. The California Court of Appeals had upheld the $290 million award, but on remand from the Supreme Court for further consideration in light of the *State Farm* case, the same California appeals court reduced the punitive damages to a 3:1 multiple of the compensatory damages in the case.

In its appeal—which would first go to Judge Hagen—Ford sought first to have the punitive damages thrown out entirely, stating a number of reasons. Failing that, it asked for a fire sale of sorts. The company argued that if a punitive award was upheld it should be set at no more than a 4:1 ratio to the $2.3 million compensatory damages already paid to the Whites, even if the court agreed that Ford's actions were highly reprehensible. Then, Ford figured, the amount should be discounted by 40 percent, the percentage of negligence the first jury attributed to the Whites. Ford noted in its appeal "that the accident would not have occurred but for the contributory effect of plaintiffs' carelessness."

When the numbers were crunched, Ford figured the proper punitive award should be somewhere between zero and $5,553,042.80. At the most. Ford made a slew of arguments for zero.

Also it claimed that the Whites had failed to prove that the compensatory damages were insufficient to punish and deter Ford. How could they? It was the plaintiffs who had argued to leave the amount of compensatory damages out of the trial and the judge had agreed. That, as Ford put it, had left the jury "in the dark" and had created an "evidentiary vacuum." Had it known the amount, perhaps the jury would have felt that was enough to satisfy Nevada's interests and to punish Ford.

If any award was to be upheld, Ford argued that the correct amount would be $1,383.260.70—a 1:1 ratio minus 40 percent. Also, Ford argued, as it did at the trial, that it had not acted in a reprehensible manner, that it had in fact acted quite responsibly. The company made every attempt to find the problem and to fix the brake problem. "The record does not support a conclusion that Ford was indifferent to safety. To be sure, Ford made some mistakes . . . but that is, at most, negligence."

Ford had gone so far as to issue a recall, and before the fatal mishap had occurred. And even if that recall notice was lacking, as the first jury had found, it didn't matter. The wording of that recall notice didn't matter at all. Why not? Because Jimmie White had received it *after* the death of his son.

The automaker cited the *State Farm* case: "A defendant should be punished for the conduct that harmed the plaintiff, not for being an unsavory individual or business." And in that case, said Ford, the recall notice found faulty by the jury had no bearing on the case of Walter White. According to Ford, "The evidence in the case supports, at most, a finding that Ford's conduct falls on the low end of the reprehensibility spectrum."

Caputo spent weeks working on the Whites' response, which, after editing by Specter, was a blistering mix of legal argument laced with layman's words that showed the attorneys' disdain for Ford. The rebuttal began by noting that two juries separated by six years had come to virtually the same conclusion—punitive damages equal to roughly one-half of 1 percent of Ford's net worth at the time.

Ford's actions were even more reprehensible than known at the first trial, Specter charged. "The retrial also exposed the depths of dishonesty to which Ford is willing to sink in an attempt to limit its liability for Walter White's death."

The response to Ford's appeal also argued that compensatory damages were irrelevant, that no court in the land requires that a second jury be told the amount awarded by a first. (To Specter, Ford's argument that the jury might have awarded no punitive damages if it had known the amount of the compensatory award was ludicrous. If the jury had known the Whites had gotten $2.3 million, would it have scrapped its award of $52 million and instead voted for no punitive damages at all?)

Specter termed Ford's reasoning and calculations for a sharply reduced award "mental gymnastics." His rebuttal also cited *State Farm* but argued that the court's 9:1 ratio was only a guideline and that it had noted some cases could be exceptions. (He cited several post–*State Farm* cases in which courts approved punitive awards of more than nine times compensatory damages, including an Arizona case in which a $60 million award represented a 153:1 ratio.)

The White case, Specter wrote, was one of those cases that warranted an exception. In allowing exceptions to its "ratio" the Supreme Court had cited the degree of harm done to a plaintiff, especially if that harm was physical as opposed to economical. In this case, wrote Specter: "The harm—the violent death of a three-year-old child—is the worst kind of physical harm imaginable."

It also noted that a defendant's actions could be considered. Specter argued that Ford's actions were worse than even the first jury had known. For instance the second jury had learned the following: (1) Ford informed the government of just one injury before Walter White's death when it knew of at least eight; (2) some 170,000 vehicles with the defective brake system never made it in for the recall "and may still be on the road;" and (3) "By June 1999, Ford had 1,149 reports of rollaways, including fifty-four injuries and one fatality, yet it continued to deny—and continues to deny today—that spontaneous disengagement happens."

"Finally," Specter's response noted, "the court knows one more thing it did not know in 1998: Having to pay the compensatory damage award (plus interest) and living with the possibility, for more than four years, of having to pay more than $69 million in punitive damages, have not appeared to change Ford's behavior with respect to this parking brake one bit. Ford has not fired anyone, nor has it sent a new recall notice to owners of unrepaired vehicles still on the road and there is no evidence that it has plans to do either of these things—or anything else—in response to the juries' verdicts in this case."

If Hagen upheld the verdict—and he had ruled for $69 million the last time—the case would go once again to the Ninth Circuit. It was anyone's guess how long the Ninth Circuit might take to issue a ruling. Specter hoped it would be less than four and half years this time. Wheeler in this appeal was not asking for a new trial, and Ford probably didn't want one. Its legal bill for the case so far probably reached into the millions. A number of the attorneys involved predicted that the court might simply keep the second verdict intact, except that it might lower the amount. Perhaps by about half to, say, $25 million. If it did so, Ford might just pay that amount—or try to negotiate a somewhat lower sum—and then pay it, happy to see the case finally go away. Specter would not settle the case on the cheap and Ford knew it. Neither would Jimmie White.

Nobody expected there to be a third trial. Nobody wanted that, though everyone knew by now that Specter was willing to try the case a dozen times if that was what it would take to get justice for the Whites.

SPECTER RETURNED to Philadelphia after the Ford trial to a full caseload. As usual.

In the month following the verdict against Ford, Specter found himself in a Philadelphia courtroom delivering an opening speech for a child hurt in a fall from an apartment window. The child had smashed his head on a concrete pavement and suffered brain damage. Oddly, the incident had occurred on the same date as another tragedy—September 11, 2001.

On investigating the case, Specter had discovered not only that there had been a long-standing problem with screens popping out of windows at the apartment complex but also that the management knew about it. Other tenants had complained, and five months earlier another two-year-old had fallen through an improperly secured screen.

The trial opened with Specter holding a large color photo of Nicholas Woolfolk in front of a jury and describing the incident and the injuries suffered by the little boy, including blindness in one eye and brain damage that was likely to cause learning difficulties. "He will never see again from that eye," Specter said, as the child's mother lowered her head onto the counsel table and wept, her shoulders bouncing lightly.

The trial lasted two weeks and ended in a $7 million verdict. However, Specter had negotiated a prior agreement stipulating a set amount that the defendant would pay if it lost, generally a way for a defendant to limit an award and insure against a "runaway verdict." In this case the amount was $12.25 million. The landlord would have to pay that amount. As part of the deal, it also agreed to provide window guards in its upper-floor apartments for families with children.

SPECTER WAS STILL working on his father's election, frantically poking messages into his BlackBerry and his cell phone during courtroom recesses and at the end of each day of testimony.

Election Night would prove to be a long night for Arlen Specter. As the returns trickled in, the Republican primary election was going exactly the way his son had predicted. It was incredibly close.

Specter should have been an easy winner. He was in his twenty-fourth year in the Senate and had spent nearly $15 million on the race, far outspending Pat Toomey. But Toomey was being backed by the GOP's farthest right wing, which had targeted Specter from among all the Republican incumbents nationwide.

Specter was ahead as the early tabulations came in from Pennsylvania's sixty-seven counties. But his lead was withering with every passing flash return. More than a million votes would be cast, but Specter was clinging to a slim lead of only a few percentage points. As the hours passed, his lead grew ever thinner. Conventional wisdom had Specter going down to defeat. Toomey, it appeared, would surge ahead as the last of the votes were tabulated from the state's farthest reaches, the most rural—and most conservative—counties, some of which still used paper ballots, which took longer to tabulate.

But politics would once again turn conventional wisdom on its head. Those remote counties instead went for the moderate Specter, not necessarily because they liked his politics but because they liked him. Specter had always made a habit of visiting even the tiniest town and most rural outposts of his large state. He kept a book in which he logged every constituent visit. Over nearly twenty-four years, that meant a lot of visits. And the people of those areas didn't forget it. Specter won the small and rural counties over his right-wing rival. And he won the election, his closest since his first Senate race in 1980. Specter finished with just 17,146 more votes than his rival, or 50.8 percent.

JOE PINTO DIED on August 19, 2007. Shanin Specter attended the funeral and spoke with Pinto's wife, Lillian. One newspaper ran an obituary about the long-time lawyer, which read in part:

> Joseph V. Pinto Sr., a giant in the products liability defense bar who was often called on by the Ford Motor Co. to handle some of its toughest cases, died Saturday due to complications from colon cancer. Mr. Pinto, who was a longtime partner at White & Williams before retiring three years ago, was 71.
>
> Mr. Pinto took summer associate William Conroy under his wing 25 years ago and the two maintained a close relationship even after Conroy left the firm nearly five years ago as a partner with a substantial amount of Ford business in his pocket. He said Mr. Pinto had a unique talent for taking the complex mechanical issues that often dominate products liability cases and distilling them into simple themes for juries to digest.
>
> "When it comes to products liability defense, he was the best I've ever seen do it, and I've seen a lot of people over the past 25 years," said Conroy, now a partner at Campbell Campbell Edwards & Conroy. "He was an understated guy with tremendous courtroom skills and sense, and juries loved him for it."

Eleven days later, Specter was on trial in Pittsburgh. But this afternoon, instead of at the bar of the court he was seated at a sports bar called Hi-Tops. His medical malpractice trial had recessed early for the day and Specter relaxed with co-counsel Andy Youman, sipping a club soda while watching his beloved Phillies play the first-place New York Mets. It was a critical game. A win would give the Phillies a four-game sweep of the Mets and put them two games out of first place in the National League East Division. Winning the division would mean their first playoff berth since 1993. The Phils had started off the game with a 5–0 lead but squandered it and fell behind. Specter watched intently as the game went to the bottom of the ninth inning, his team trailing 10–9. Jayson Werth started the inning with a single, then stole second and third bases on consecutive pitches. Tadahito Iguchi followed with a single to bring Werth home and tie the game. Iguchi stole second, Jimmy Rollins walked, and Chase Utley came to the plate. The All-Star second baseman had missed a month of games after breaking his hand and had only been back in the lineup for a few days. It was uncertain if he had regained top form. The pitch count went to 3–2. The fans at a packed Citizens Bank Park rose from their seats. On the next pitch, Utley lined a single to right field to score Iguchi and win the game. Specter smiled broadly and high-fived Youman. While he was watching the game, Specter's BlackBerry had vibrated. It was important news.

The Ninth Circuit Court of Appeals had handed down a decision in *White v. Ford*. Nearly three and a half years after the $52 million verdict, which had been upheld by Judge Hagen, a three-judge panel of the appellate court had again made a ruling in the case. And again it threw out the punitive damages award. Although naturally disappointed, Specter took some solace in the narrow scope of the decision and the fact that the appellate judges had upheld much of the case—including the punitive verdict, just not the amount. It ruled in Ford's favor on only a few issues. If it came to a third trial on punitive damages—and Specter was ready and willing—he felt the court's concerns could be addressed and that he could again convince a jury to hand down a large award.

The appellate panel that decided the latest case pointed out Ford's reprehensible behavior in the case on a number of things. It noted Tim Rakowicz's white paper that stated the parking brake "will intermittently self-release." It noted that "Ford management worried about a recall and its potential cost" of $22 million. It noted that Ford had reported to the government (NHTSA) 44 cases of rollaways with resulting property damage but that the Whites proved at retrial that Ford knew of at least eight injuries and that it had received reports of more than 100 rollaways at the time it submitted its letter to NHTSA. It noted that "it was clear to Ford that there was a potential rollaway problem" at the time it sold the F-350 to Jimmie White's employer.

The appeals court noted further that it had upheld most of the plaintiffs' claims, including the allegation that when Ford engineers discovered the brake problem the company "covered it up with a euphemistic notice to dealers" rather than an immediate customer recall. The court agreed that Ford knew about the brake problem "and failed to warn people . . . in conscious disregard of their safety."

But the judges found fault with several aspects of the $52 million verdict. One was the fact that the judge in the case had failed to instruct the jury *not* to consider other people who were hurt as a result of Ford truck rollaways. While the jury could hear evidence about those other injuries, it was only to punish Ford for the harm to the Whites, not other victims. Ford had requested that Judge Hagen include such a "limiting instruction" in charging the jury but he had refused.

The court also determined that Hagen omitted three pertinent facts: (1) the Whites had received $2.3 million in compensatory damages; (2) the first jury had found that it was not the defective brake that had caused Walter White's death but that it was Ford's failure to warn; and (3) the Whites had been 40 percent responsible for the accident. Had the latest jury known those things, the court said, it could have issued a lesser punishment.

The court did not address the broader issue of whether the $52 million verdict was excessive based on recent precedent but instead ordered a new trial for a new jury—armed with the additional instruction and information—to again decide punitive damages.

Specter's disappointment was not personal. He had enjoyed trying this case. But he felt that the appellate court had abrogated its responsibility, that it had handed the case back to be tried a third time instead of deciding whether the award was fair. If it had affirmed the $52 million verdict or set a lower number, the case would likely have been concluded. After all these years the court could have sent everyone home once and for all, both the Whites and Ford. Instead it had punted. The court had ordered a do-over based on narrow issues of Judge's Hagen's instructions to the jury, instructions that veteran court observers knew most jurors only half-listened to. Specter felt the jury had understood the case and that it had also comprehended that the intent of the verdict was to punish Ford, that it had nothing to do with compensatory damages the Whites had received or the facts of Walter's death.

But the appellate panel's decision was not entirely bad for the Whites. While reversing the amount of the award, it upheld a number of things that Specter had fought for, such as the plaintiffs' ability to introduce as evidence Ford's full financial statement and annual report for the jury to decide a punitive award.

Nevertheless another trial would be needed to punish Ford. This latest court decision would perhaps tamp down an award by another jury. And there was no way to tell whether even after a third large verdict, if that were to occur, such an award would not run afoul of what the appellate court might find "constitutionally excessive" in a broader sense.

Still, while this reversal was a defeat, it removed some of the defense arguments, reducing its grounds for further appeals. And, even with the added instructions the jury would receive a third time around, who was to say that Specter could not once again convince a jury to slam Ford with a big punitive verdict. He was certainly willing to try.

IN JANUARY 2008 Ford made an offer in the White case. It was much higher than the amount it had put on the table before the $52 million verdict but one that Specter and his client felt was not high enough. He doubted Ford would up the ante much more. A third trial appeared imminent.

The Whites had by this time sold their place in Elko to Jimmie's sister and moved to a town in Washington State about 45 miles east of Portland, Oregon. They had liked Nevada, but, noted Jimmie, "It got to the point there you couldn't go around the corner without everybody knowing who you were." He and Ginny did not welcome the celebrity.

When he got word of Ford's latest offer, Jimmie gritted his teeth for yet another round in court.

"Me and Ginny had talked about it, that we had wanted to settle the case, and we set a number in our heads that if Ford made or exceeded the amount, we would settle. We were not in it for the financial gain, and once we made it to a certain point, it wasn't worth the continued stress to stretch this thing out for another two or four years," Jimmie said. He mentioned a settlement sum that he said he and his wife "could live with."

Ford's latest offer, though eight figures, had fallen short of that number. And from comments made during the negotiations, Ford intimated it would never get there. But then in the spring of 2008 Ford made another offer. This one was above what Jimmie and Ginny had set their minds on.

Specter still wanted to fight on, to take it to a third trial, but his was only one vote. His chief co-counsel in the case, Pete Durney, was wavering. In his sixties, older than Specter, Durney had joked during the second trial that he hoped to get some of the money from the case before he passed away.

The Whites were split. In a way Jimmie also wanted to fight on, to join Specter in another battle. He wanted the public punishment of another verdict against Ford. His "whole goal," he said, was a verdict against the automaker. But the linchpin now would be the person who had been the quietest throughout, who had silently endured the long and hard legal battle. Ginny White did not want to go through it again. She had had enough. She was suffering from lupus and didn't think she could go through another trial. "Let it end," she told her husband.

"This was the point that it had to stop," said Jimmie thirteen and a half years after the tragedy that killed his son. "You begin to get a feeling that it's never going to end. Ginny was getting to the point where she felt that it never was going to end. One step forward and two steps back. Walter would have been seventeen now."

"I was ready for it to be over," echoed Ginny. "No more of that stress about what is going to happen next."

So on May 8, 2008, the Whites and Ford signed a settlement agreement. It stipulated that the amount would remain confidential. A check was sent overnight.

Was the settlement enough in Jimmie White's mind to punish Ford? "No, but I don't think we would ever be given enough to punish Ford . . . because with the size of Ford and their net worth and everything, I don't think the Supreme Court would have ever upheld an amount high enough to punish them."

And although Ford never acknowledged liability, the fact that it was willing to pay such a large settlement translated into such an admission for Ginny White.

"I'm pretty satisfied. . . . As long as they acknowledged they were in the wrong, that's enough for me," she said.

Jimmie said he was relieved that the case had finally come to a conclusion, but he still had odd emotions about it all. "It's kind of hard to explain," he said, "It's hard to accept the fact that it is over because it was a part of our lives for so long."

When the parties finally cashed the check from Ford, Jimmie and Ginny got relatively little from the settlement, though enough for them to live modestly well for the rest of their lives. But they would not be rich. One reason was that much of the money, roughly half, would be paid in taxes to the federal government. It was a little-known fact that while plaintiffs do not pay taxes on compensatory damages, punitive damages—and settlements—were subject to federal levies. Not only that, but Uncle Sam double-dipped when it came to such payments. A plaintiff had to pay taxes on the full amount of the settlement, including the portion that was paid to the attorneys. Then the attorneys had to pay taxes on the amount they received. (For example, on a $10 million settlement, a plaintiff had to pay taxes on the full amount—at the top rate of 35 percent, that would be $3.5 million. If the attorneys, for example, had a 40 percent share in a case, they would also then have to pay 35 percent on their $4 million fee, or another $1.4 million. The government's total take would be $4.9 million.)

THE WHITES SETTLED into life in the Northwest. Far from their trailer in the desert of Nevada, they bought a wooden, six-bedroom rancher on 20 acres of wooded property in Washington State overlooking the Columbia River, which formed the border with Oregon to the south. It was a beautiful, shaded spot with a view of the river gorge. Neither worked, but Ginny volunteered at the local library, helping to run book and bake sales. Jimmie spent much of his time felling dead trees and clearing brush from his property, landscaping around the house, and chopping wood for the small stove in the basement. "We try to keep busy," he said, noting that they owned a small boat they used for fishing and traveling on the Columbia.

Jimmie and Ginny never did adopt another child. "We talked about it but, ah . . ." said Jimmie, his sentence and thoughts trailing off. "You kind of get the feeling that you're trying to replace somebody, and that's the wrong reason to do it."

As the years passed the Whites managed to part with some of Walter's possessions, giving his old toys to charity. They did not keep a bedroom for him. But they still kept his clothes safely tucked away in a cedar chest and memories of him in their hearts. They tried to visit his grave site in Elko once a year, on his birthday.

"It can still be very rough, very rough, especially around his birthday and all, it's still pretty rough around here," Jimmie said in 2010. He paused for a few seconds, swallowed hard, and continued. "You sit around and you think as the years go by, *he'd be seventeen and a senior in high school now . . . he would have graduated now*. Things like that. He'd be going on twenty now. And you wonder what kind of man he'd be."

PART III
Blumer v. Ford

CHAPTER 30

Joe

Jennette blumer sat in the back of the snug Pittsburgh courtroom and fumbled with the gold wedding band that hung from her necklace. Nerves made her right leg bounce a rapid beat. Her vapid, ash-blue eyes bobbed in puddles of tears.

Her lawyer had warned her that he was about to display photos of the accident. He advised her not to look up.

"I saw his shoes," testified the first plaintiffs' witness, Jim Walendzie-wicz, a large video screen to his right showing a photo of a red tow truck with a pair of sneakers several feet away on the asphalt driveway, "and then I saw him lying underneath it."

The screen flipped to the next photo, which showed a man pinned beneath the tow truck, the rear axle pressing on his chest. Jennette looked down, trying to stare at the design in the courtroom's dark blue carpeting. Now her whole body shook, her shoulders trembling as she hugged her sister Sharon tightly, as if she were holding on for her life. Several seconds later, Jennette allowed her gaze to move upward slightly, still avoiding the large screen. But she caught sight of another screen, a laptop computer being used by a technician a few feet away from her, and her eyes held to the screen, locked momentarily against her will, unable to move away.

And she saw him. Joe. Lying beneath his truck, suffocated, lifeless, his entire face the color of his widow's sad eyes.

Jennette began to sob. Shanin Specter walked to the back of the court-room and placed a hand on his client's shoulder as members of the jury watched, several also visibly upset by the sight of Joe Blumer's corpse. Specter's attempt to console Jennette proved futile. She suddenly jumped up and ran, bursting through the courtroom doors as if fleeing a demon, sobbing uncontrollably.

"Oh my God!" she blurted. Her words and her anguish reverberated in the marble hallway, plosive sounds crashing like shrapnel through the doorway and back into the courtroom. "Oh my God! Oh my God!"

A FEW DAYS EARLIER, on a Sunday evening in March 2009, Specter had boarded a twin-engine King Air en route from Philadelphia to Pittsburgh. He and a young associate, Kila Baldwin, worked on his opening speech for the trial as the small plane jounced lightly in the clouds, traversing the 300-mile breadth of Pennsylvania at 12,000 feet. Specter worked a pen with one hand, an Amstel Light with the other. He liked chartering a plane on such occasions because it saved what to him was life's most precious commodity—time. He dreaded getting to major airports early and then standing around for hours, hours he could have been spending at work or at home with his four daughters.

Baldwin prepped her boss on the specifics of the case, on the technical aspects of the parking brake system of the Ford F-350 that had killed Joe Blumer. They pored over information and changes since Specter's last case against Ford. Some things had changed, but not that much. The brake manufacturer Orscheln had been taken over in a merger with a Michigan company named Dura Mechanical Components Inc. (becoming Dura Automotive Systems), but the brakes were still made in the same factory and, despite some changes, had remained problematic until Ford took over and redesigned the brake system itself for model 2005 vehicles.

Specter needed to know some things before he walked into the courtroom and cross-examined Ford's expert witnesses. But he was a quick study. And even if he didn't yet know every detail that Baldwin had down pat, in some ways he knew this case better than any lawyer in the country. Specter knew about this tragedy, knew it before it happened. He had seen it all before, had watched the terrible sorrow play out before his eyes in Central Pennsylvania and in Nevada years earlier. He could close his eyes and see the grim faces of Jimmie and Ginny White and Tammy and Dave Bobb before them. This time the unsuspecting victim had been a grown man, a husband and father.

On a brisk autumn day four and a half years ago, Joe Blumer had driven his tow truck to rescue a broken-down pickup truck. He parked his vehicle, pressed down on the parking brake, and got out of the wrecker. He was behind it when the Ford F-350's parking brake disengaged and the large vehicle jolted backward, rolling over Blumer and crushing his chest. The cause of death was suffocation. Blumer's life ended at 43.

The incident also ended the life that Jennette Blumer and her family had known. Things would never be the same. She and her daughters were left without the happy-go-lucky, doting man who had cooked them dinner and cheerily washed the dishes, who had taken them out and helped with their homework. Both daughters had become distraught in the days and weeks and months after their father's death. They were now seeing a therapist.

Years ago, Specter had never imagined that he'd be spending such a large chunk of his career fighting Ford. But here he was again, in an airplane on his way to another trial against the nation's number two carmaker and its still number one–selling vehicle. Especially in light of his courtroom record, he had thought that Ford might settle this latest case involving an allegedly faulty parking brake. And Ford had made an offer but it was not a serious one, at least not so far as Specter was concerned. Ford had tried the same tactic that General Motors had used on his client John Smith years earlier, dangling an offer of $1 million before Jennette Blumer. It was a lot of money for Jennette, whose husband had made maybe $20,000 a year before his death. But Specter advised her against considering it and Jennette vowed to follow her attorney's lead. She would refuse to surrender.

He estimated the "value of the case" if a jury delivered a verdict against Ford at between $5 million and $7 million. But there was also a chance he could lose and get nothing. So he decided that he would settle the case—or, technically, recommend that the Blumers accept a settlement—if Ford went up to $3 million. Of course Jennette could order him to take a lesser amount, but she had followed Specter's suggestions up until now and he felt certain she would continue to heed his advice. Still if Ford offered $2.5 million or even $2 million, it would be awfully tempting to the client. It wasn't near what he had negotiated in his previous cases against Ford, but Joe Blumer earned a low income and was much older than Walter White and Derick Bobb, who would need care for the rest of his life. And the Blumer family, Specter knew, needed the money. Perhaps even more, the family needed the peace that closure might bring.

He started the negotiation with Ford on the high side. He would settle the case, he initially told Ford, for $12 million. Specter had several things going for him, not the least of which was his history of jousting with the company. Did Ford have any reason to believe he was anxious about going to trial? Just the opposite—he relished the opportunity. It had taken the better part of a decade for Specter to accept a large settlement for Jimmie and Ginny White, and even then he had been ready to stay on the battlefield had the Whites been able to stand with him. In the Blumer case, Specter's original offer was soft and, after Ford offered $1 million, he would soon lower his demand. For $10 million, he told

Ford, he would drop the suit. The two sides were far apart and would remain so.

So Specter would once more face a company that fate had made his nemesis, the Ford Motor Co. And its damned parking brake. In the Blumer case, the parking brake was the successor to the device that Ford had put into the F-350 and that had injured Derick Bobb and killed Walter White. Another bad brake. It had spontaneously disengaged—or so Specter's experts had determined—and caused a rollaway. Another rollaway. This one killing Joe Blumer and shattering his family.

Specter's partner had, in the meantime, had his own run-in with Ford. In 2007 Tom Kline went before a Philadelphia jury on behalf of Dina Anthony, who at the age of twenty-seven had been rendered a quadriplegic after an off-road accident in which a Ford Bronco had flipped over onto its roof, a removable fiberglass roof that had failed to withstand the impact of the crash. Anthony had been in the rear passenger seat, was crushed by the roof, and suffered severe spinal injuries. The mother of two children would never walk again. Kline claimed in the lawsuit that the roof was defective, that the flimsy fiberglass it was made from was not crashworthy. He demonstrated as much for the jury, holding a piece of the material in his hands and breaking it, an audible snap resonating through the courtroom. The roof of the 1985 Bronco, an SUV-type vehicle based on the F-150 pickup truck, was to blame for Anthony's injuries, Kline told the jury. In his closing speech, in a remark he would repeat years later in his one-man show, "Trial as Theatre," staged at Philadelphia's Wilma Theater, Kline told the jury, "If there was a museum of defective products, this roof would be in the lobby." Ford settled the case before the jury reached a verdict.

Specter undoubtedly would have put the F-Series parking brakes in the same museum lobby. Those brakes now brought him to the eve of his third major trial against Ford. On checking into his hotel in downtown Pittsburgh, the Omni William Penn, Specter ordered dinner for what he dubbed the "war room," a first-floor conference room where he and his team would hunker down for the duration. The windowless room was stocked with twenty-nine boxes of transcripts and documents that had been compiled during discovery, several laptops, a printer, a projector for viewing exhibits, pens and notepads, plates of mini-Milky Ways, and a small refrigerator whose contents included only one item—beer. This room was for reviewing and deciphering, for planning and plotting, with some sessions that would last late into the night. Baldwin had worked up much of the case, particularly the expert witness testimony. The young lawyer knew the mechanics of the brake—and its problems. A Pennsylvania State University graduate, Baldwin possessed the small features and blue eyes of an Irish face framed by strawberry blonde hair that she wore alternately curly and ruler-straight. Though young, Baldwin had a lengthy resume, having worked for both plaintiffs and defense firms and also as a government attorney for the Securities and Exchange Commission. She spoke Italian and Spanish fluently.

Baldwin wasn't sleeping much these days, fretting over the case and negotiating unsuccessfully with an unfamiliar hotel bed. But she appeared sharp and alert when the moments demanded it, and there were many such moments. Brought in late to help in the case was Dominic Guerrini, who at the University of Pennsylvania Law School had scored an A+ in what would turn out to be the most important class he took—Specter's. Throughout the trial, Specter would bounce questions and ideas off Guerrini, who answered the way Specter liked. Decisively. Guerrini's opinions were never wishy-washy. He was a yes-or-no man.

"I need to get through this twice before I can have a beer," Specter said of his opening speech for the start of trial. He had written and rewritten portions of the speech with Baldwin, now rehearsing and trying to synchronize his words with the exhibits flashed onto the big screen by a technician, Evan Wolfe.

"Evan, you can't see the pinion in this one. . . . Can't you get a better picture than this?" Specter barked about a photo of the parking brake's components. He decided instead to show the jury the actual brake mechanism. "I'll hold it up instead. . . . I'll need that handed to me immediately when I mention it in my opening."

After several hours, Specter, now ready, twisted open a beer bottle and walked over to Baldwin. He patted her on the back.

"This is good, Kila. Good job."

"Will you say that to me at least once tomorrow?"

"Only if you deserve it," deadpanned Specter.

THE NEXT MORNING brought a slight chill. Specter, working his Black-Berry, briskly walked the few blocks from the hotel, his rapid pace leaving Baldwin and Guerrini lagging 50 yards behind by the time he reached the Allegheny County Courthouse. When they walked into the courtroom, they saw Bill Conroy, the one-time protégé to Joe Pinto and now a partner in the Philadelphia firm of Campbell, Campbell, Edwards & Conroy.

The proceedings began with Specter and his team, and Conroy, flanked by two associates, discussing various matters with the presiding judge, Michael A. Della Vecchia, before the jury, a panel of twelve Allegheny County residents plus two alternates, was ushered into cushioned seats. Opening speeches ensued in short order. Both Specter and Conroy were brief, each finishing in under an hour. They had, naturally, differing views on what had happened on September 29, 2004, the day Joe Blumer died. Specter would claim—and promised the jury he would prove it during trial—that Ford's brake broke. A hardworking man with a loving family believed that his Ford F-350 and all its parts had been "built Ford tough," as advertised. And he'd been let down. Joe Blumer trusted that the parking brake would hold, trusted it with his life, and the brake had spontaneously disengaged. It was not strong enough to hold the large, heavy tow truck equipped with heavy equipment and a top-mounted hoisting engine. Photos of the brake system showed chipped and broken teeth in the gear-like pinion and sector wheels that were supposed to have held all that weight but couldn't because the parts were made deficiently. Specter had the testimony of two experts to support his position. And he had records of prior incidents involving Ford truck parking brakes, evidence that showed a pattern of problematic and dangerous brakes. Specter also had the conviction from his own personal knowledge that the auto company was not above selling dangerous products, knowing about them and keeping those products out on the street. He had—though he could bring up none of this at the Blumer trial—knowledge of tragedies that had befallen two little boys.

Conroy argued something totally different: Nothing was wrong with Ford's brake. The problem was that it had been improperly installed and maintained by Ed Butler, who owned and operated the towing company and who did most of the repairs. Butler was a mechanic but only part-time—he mostly drove and towed trucks—and he had had no formal training. And Joe Blumer was at fault. Desperate for that particular tow job—he had wanted to get back in the saddle following a hospital stay and was paid on commission, with no salary—Blumer had risked using a truck he knew had a bum parking brake. He took a chance that, even when the truck was parked on a hill, the 4-inch wooden chocks he placed behind the left wheels would hold the truck long enough for him to set up his tow and get out of there, with no parking brake applied. Conroy had his experts too. And he would pose a simple question to the jury:

Who do you trust more, a multinational corporation that over a century had sold millions of automobiles, or two guys in Pittsburgh hustling to make a living?

Specter spoke first. He started by walking to the front of the courtroom, picking up the parking brake that had been in Joe Blumer's truck, and explaining that this was the system used in Ford's model year 1999–2004 trucks. He pointed out the logo stamped on the brake, the famous Ford oval first put on Ford vehicles in 1912. He held the brake aloft in front of the jury box.

"These were bad brakes. Ford had lots of problems with these brakes. And this brake right here, the one in my hand," Specter said, turning and pointing to Jennette Blumer, "killed her husband."

The brake, he said, was not strong enough to withstand normal use. He showed the broken teeth on the pinion and sector portions of the brake, the gear-like wheels that were supposed to mesh and hold tight. Not only were the teeth broken, Specter said and later photos would depict, but there was also lateral play between the two pieces. That misalignment, coupled with the broken teeth, caused the pieces on occasion to become unmeshed suddenly, to "skip out." The brake would disengage and a vehicle, if parked on an incline, would roll away.

Specter showed photographs of Joe Blumer—"a father . . . a husband . . . a working man . . . a citizen of this community"—when he was alive and with his children.

> And if they look to you like a happy family, it's because they were a happy family. They weren't fancy people. Joe didn't have a fancy job. He didn't have a fancy education. Jennette didn't have a fancy job. She didn't have a fancy education. But there was a lot of love in that house, and that was a very fine family.

Specter took the jury through the incident that occurred on that early autumn day when Blumer drove his truck to the Ace Bindery at 5000 Centre Avenue, where Jim Walendziewicz's Ford Ranger had broken down. Blumer had hoisted the Ranger and begun towing it up the hill from the bindery but then realized he couldn't make the sharp turn to the top of the hill and had to back the Ranger off his wrecker. In the process, with Walendziewicz back in his vehicle, looking over his shoulder, the tow truck suddenly rolled back and smashed into the Ranger. Walendziewicz jumped out of his truck and saw Joe Blumer lying beneath it.

Then Specter splashed a photo on the large TV screen that had been set up for the jury and on a larger screen against a wall at the side of the courtroom.

> This is the final resting position of those vehicles. Joe Blumer died underneath that truck. He was struck by the truck when the parking brake disengaged. He was trapped underneath the truck. The undercarriage crushed his chest and suffocated him. This photograph shows you his sneakers. As he was struck, he was propelled out of his sneakers. Now, what happened here was that when Jim backed off the L-arms, the pinion and sector teeth in this brake that I showed you, those broken and chipped teeth, which would normally be in contact with each other fully—they should be fully mated—they separated. They skipped out, disengaging the parking brake. Unknown to Joe Blumer, the brake teeth were barely engaged when he got out of his truck and therefore they were ready to separate at any moment. So just the slightest vibration, which could be from the truck engine or the power take-off or the backing over the L-arms or some combination of those things, caused the brake to give way.

Bill Conroy rose for the defense. At 6-foot-6, he was easily the biggest person in the room, 3 inches taller than Specter and certainly more solidly built. But his demeanor was that of a Gentle Ben. Soft-spoken and bespectacled, Conroy had longish, wavy black hair flecked with gray, and a thick moustache, a look that made him appear relaxed and confident. He rarely raised his voice or appeared agitated or emotional. He was steady. He seemed sincere. A class act. He started his opening by acknowledging the Blumer family and its loss.

> This is indeed a very tragic, tragic case. Mr. Blumer, by all accounts, was a very decent guy, a loving father, a loving husband. And you'll hear about this from his family. But despite our sympathy for what happened to Mr. Blumer and his family, on behalf of Ford Motor Co. and McCrackin Ford, we do not believe this accident is Ford's fault or McCrackin Ford's fault.

The latter reference was to the local Ford dealership that was Ford's co-defendant, from whom Ed Butler had leased the truck. McCrackin had since closed, but it still had insurance to cover claims against it.

Conroy would base his case on the "physical evidence"—he used that phrase repeatedly in his opening argument—not sentiment or sympathy but cold, hard facts. And, he asserted, those facts were on Ford's side.

It was Ford's contention—the crux of its case, really—that Joe Blumer's boss, Ed Butler, had installed the brake improperly. Conroy flashed up enlarged photos that showed marks and nicks on the brake parts that he said demonstrated the brake had been mishandled. Another photo showed two marks where the take-up spring (which pulled the pedal back up) rested, proof, said Conroy, that it had been moved and incorrectly repositioned. "That is the reason," he told the jury, "why the parking brake, after he installed it, began to have issues, issues that became progressively worse and worse with time."

Further, marks on the pinion and sector gears showed, he asserted, that the brake had been depressed all the way to the floor on some occasions, proving it had been out of whack. And, he said, scratches on the bottom of the pedal were evidence that it had been kicked or pulled up from beneath. It was this kicking, submitted Conroy, that also broke the metal teeth inside the parking brake system, not normal usage.

A second main contention of the defense was that Joe Blumer had known the brake wasn't working and so he never bothered to set it at all on that fateful day. The evidence suggested, said Conroy, that Blumer parked the truck in gear, turned the engine off, got out, set 4-inch wooden chocks behind the tow truck's left rear wheel, then climbed back inside the vehicle, restarted the engine, put the truck in neutral, and then got out to work the towing equipment, relying—hoping—that the chocks would hold his truck in place. The proof, said Conroy, was that after the accident, emergency personnel had found the parking brake pedal in the upright position, meaning the parking brake had never been set. If the brake had spontaneously disengaged because of a defective or malfunctioning brake system, the pedal would likely have remained pressed in a down position. (Specter had espoused the opposite, saying that a brake pedal could have popped back into the upright position, that in fact one of the system's springs was designed to do just that.)

This argument seemed dubious. Who would have intentionally parked on such a steep hill (the grade was measured at 25 degrees at some points) without a parking brake? According to Conroy, Joe Blumer would have. He had recently been released from the hospital and badly wanted to get back to his regular life and paycheck. So he took a chance with a truck with no parking brake. It all seemed oddly implausible, but Ford had a slew of photos and exhibits and experts to back up its theory.

SPECTER AND HIS TEAM left the courtroom after Conroy's opening speech with a list of questions. Not necessarily concerns, but questions. Did Conroy's photos and exhibits prove Ford's theories of the accident? Or, more pointedly, could the exhibits convince the jury? Specter wasn't willing to take the chance. He set out to examine each claim and every photo Ford presented. He wanted to try to explain—and then debunk—each one. "We need to knock down everything they said, from top to bottom," said Specter as he convened a meeting that evening with Baldwin, Guerrini, and his main expert witnesses, who were on hand to help out. And they were beauts.

The first to take the stand for the plaintiffs would be Bob Nocivelli. With a white goatee and a wispy mane of gray hair, sort of a Wyatt Earp look, Nocivelli was a hybrid of sorts. He was a certified master technician but he was also a mechanic, and a bit of a bumpkin at that. He hailed from a smaller town outside Apollo, Pennsylvania. Nocivelli wore a dark suit and a crisp shirt and tie to court, but there was no hiding his rough, large hands that had dirt embedded beneath their nails. His deep voice had a slow cadence. Nocivelli was self-assured, with a disarming, grandfatherly friendliness.

Specter's second expert was as refined as Nocivelli was rough-hewn. Campbell Laird, a small, bespectacled man with a ring of white hair circling an otherwise bald pate, was the expert Specter had used before in the *White v. Ford* case. The professor was more polished than Nocivelli but no less charming. He looked a jury in the eye and sprinkled scientific terminology with everyday words like "stuff" and "things." Laird used his hands a lot when he spoke, often with heartfelt excitement over some esoteric scientific finding or principle, his every word accented by his native Scotland.

As was his practice, Specter had his experts come to trial days before either would testify. Most lawyers didn't do this, often timing their experts' arrivals to the day they were to testify, then shipping them out immediately afterward. Since most charged by the day, Specter's way was expensive. But he wanted his experts to have some experience with the trial before they actually took the stand, to get a feel for the case, the judge, the defense lawyers, the jurors. It also gave them the opportunity to hear testimony and learn about the defense case. Nocivelli and Laird got along great, not only examining exhibits together but also chitchatting about their families and personal interests. They often met for lunch, when Specter and his lawyers largely shunned them, not wishing to be seen in public (particularly by a member of the jury) fraternizing with experts who, despite being paid for their work on the case, were supposed to maintain their objectivity.

"It goes out of adjustment." Nocivelli said as he turned the parking brake over in his hands, a plate of meat loaf and mashed potatoes awaiting his attention. "It goes out of adjustment because it can and will. It's not one thing but the whole system that's bad."

"I'd agree with that," said Laird, who had taken a seat beside Nocivelli at the large conference table, a covered dish of chicken pot pie nearby.

Specter interrupted. "Let's go over each picture the defense showed in their opening and figure out who's going to say what. Kila, you do the examination. First we will tell the jury what happened. We tell our story first. Then we debunk their story." If that was possible.

The case would turn on a few key elements. One was whether the jury believed Ed Butler, who installed the brakes and who said they had been working fine before the mishap, or if they believed the defense claim that he was essentially a liar. Another was whether the jury believed that Joe Blumer would have parked his tow truck on a hill when he knew there was a problem with the parking brake. And it would turn on the experts, on whom the jury believed more—the professionals and exhibits presented by the Ford Motor Co. or the mechanic with the grease-stained hands from Apollo, Pennsylvania, and the diminutive, professorial Scotsman.

Ed Butler, Specter felt, would hold his own before a jury. He was unkempt and uneducated but he had experience in the towing business and enough know-how with parking brakes to install one correctly. And he was smart enough to do something if one wasn't working properly. In fact Butler had come to the same conclusion about the brakes that formed the core of the Blumers' case.

"I need to talk to you," Butler had whispered to Baldwin in court during pretrial motions. He seemed excited. Baldwin walked to the back of the courtroom.

"I know exactly what's wrong with this brake," he continued, his voice rising. "Let me tell you what the problem is."

Baldwin shushed Butler and ushered him outside the courtroom and around a corner of the marble hallway, where, highly animated and using his hands as he spoke, he explained how he felt there was too much play between the pinion and sector gears. Baldwin listened patiently as the mechanic with no formal training detailed the plaintiffs' experts' own theory about the case.

"That's just what we're going to try to prove in court," said Baldwin.

In addition to possessing a good understanding of the brake, Butler seemed like a sincere fellow, someone Specter and Baldwin felt the jury would believe. Yet Butler did have a reason to lie. If the brake had not been installed correctly and indeed wasn't working on the day of the mishap, then it wasn't Ford who was responsible for the death of his employee and friend. Joe Blumer's demise would then be on the hands of Ed Butler.

Specter had dismissed the second defense theory that Joe Blumer knew his brakes were shot and parked on the slope anyway. He dismissed it—and felt the jury would, too—the second he saw the defense photo of the hill where the accident had occurred, a photo presented in Conroy's opening speech. While his own experts had photographed the slope from the bottom of the hill facing upward, Ford's had shot it from the top down, an angle that made the hill look far steeper.

"To park on that hill without a parking brake on, you'd have to be suicidal!" yelped Specter when the photo was flashed on the war room screen. "I'm going to use that in my closing."

But again, crazy as it seemed, he had to admit to himself that perhaps the jury could see even this Ford's way, that maybe Joe Blumer would have taken such a foolhardy chance. He was desperate to work again for both his state of mind and the paycheck.

And despite Specter's confidence in his paid experts' own theories, only time would tell if Bob Nocivelli, whom he'd never actually seen on a witness stand, and Campbell Laird would stack up against Ford's hired guns.

As they examined the defense photos now, Nocivelli and Laird offered explanations for a number of exhibits Ford had presented. They had reasonable responses to most. Except one. Conroy had shown the jury a close-up of the brake system in which one of the gear-like plates bore a dark mark, almost a scratch but ruler-straight. It also had a little nick, a sort of notch, along the top edge. This, Ford claimed, was evidence of damage caused by Ed Butler as he installed the brake. Nocivelli and Laird looked at the photo and then at the actual brake system from Joe Blumer's truck. Nocivelli used his own flashlight—a peculiar-looking device that he had rigged with little arms and legs so it could stand and point on its own—and a magnifier to make sure the photo and the brake were the same object. They were. But how had those marks gotten there? Nocivelli and Laird looked at the photo and the device again and again and from every possible angle but remained confounded as to what might have caused the marks. Then, out of nowhere, Specter had an idea.

"Take a look at the exemplar," he said, referring to the new and unused brake the firm had purchased as part of its investigation. "Where do we have that?"

A search of the room began but Baldwin interrupted. "Actually, it's up in my room," she said, adding with a grin, "I've been sleeping with it." A few minutes later the brake arrived from her hotel room on the seventh floor.

"And it's never been installed in a truck?" Specter asked.

"No, that's brand new, just out of the box," said Nocivelli. "I bought this one myself. Ordered it direct from Ford." He had operated it maybe fifty times, gently, just using his hands.

Out came the flashlight again as he and Laird peered into the guts of the contraption. It took only a few seconds for them to make the same discovery and, simultaneously, to reach the same conclusion.

"The mark is on it!" exulted Nocivelli.

"And the notch!" said Laird.

They looked up at Specter, both men smiling broadly. Identical marks—particularly the straight line, which was exactly the same in thickness and length—were on both the original brake from Joe Blumer's truck and the new, never-used brake. It could mean only one thing. Nocivelli started the next sentence and Laird completed it.

"It's in the manufacturing."

"A machine made that mark."

It meant that Ed Butler hadn't made the mark; Ford's own manufacturing process had.

"That's really funny," said Specter.

"Almost hard to believe," said Nocivelli.

Specter was chuckling now. "We're here looking at that photo and wondering how those marks were made and they're on the exemplar. That's really funny."

Had Ford not bothered to check the marks against a new brake? Had its experts missed that entirely? Or had they known the mark was on the exemplar and decided to use it as "evidence" anyway?

No matter. It didn't prove anything any longer and certainly did not fault Ed Butler's competence. If anything, it said something about Ford's.

CHAPTER 31

Ed Butler

SPECTER HAD ED BUTLER take the witness stand on the first day of testimony. He was an important witness, perhaps the most important. The case hung in large part on this little man's stooped shoulders.

Butler had hardly gotten gussied up for court. He had on a plaid flannel shirt in hues of maroon, green, and beige that he wore untucked over old jeans. On his slightly pigeon-toed feet Butler wore running shoes that had long ago turned from white to gray. His face bore stubble and his hands were large and calloused, the ends of his fingernails indelibly black. Butler was short but because of his posture he appeared even shorter, his head pushed forward and down into his shoulders, like a cartoon turtle. Butler was frazzled as he took the stand so Specter started with something simple to ease him into his testimony. It didn't help.

"How old are you, sir?"

"I am fifty-four," he replied, then looked up at his wife, Linda, a younger, rotund woman with a pretty face, signaling him from the back of the courtroom.

"Fifty-five," Butler corrected himself. "Fifty-five. I am not very good at these things."

"Are you nervous?"

"Very nervous."

"Are you very, very nervous?"

"Yes."

Specter stopped and poured his witness a glass of water. After he took a few sips Butler was asked about the name of his towing business, Edlin Automotive Services. He explained that the name was a combination of his name and his wife's, Ed and Lin.

"Why Edlin instead of LinEd?" Specter smiled as he asked the question and a few people in the courtroom chuckled. Butler took a few seconds, then smiled as well. "I couldn't tell you that," he responded.

Butler was getting over his jitters. Until Specter asked him to recall the day he hired Joe Blumer. Butler began to answer, then stopped, put his head down, and started to weep. A few seconds went by before he raised his head, cleared his throat, and continued telling the jury about Joe Blumer.

"He was one of those people who you knew right away . . . he was a very likable person," said Butler, wiping his eyes with his hands. Specter handed him a box of tissues.

Butler acknowledged that he was the one who likely had installed the new parking brake since he did most of the mechanics at the tow service. He had gotten this particular truck, a red Ford F-350 Super Duty, new from a local Ford dealership. He denied that he had ever tinkered with the part of the brake called the take-up spring in an attempt to fix the brake, as the defense had suggested. He wouldn't have bothered, said Butler, because the brake was so cheap, just $56. He would have simply returned it for a new one.

Nor did he ever kick at the brake pedal, as the defense had also alleged. Butler said he never used his foot at all to move the pedal back to the upright position. And he couldn't recall Joe Blumer ever doing such a thing either.

Nor did the brake ever feel "weak," a condition that he said would occur when a parking brake was nearing the end of its life, not in the months before he had replaced it in the truck nor on the morning of September 29.

The new brake had worked fine, never any sign of trouble, he testified. With the truck's work log projected onto the courtroom screen, he noted how he'd taken the same vehicle out on 189 calls since installing the brake in May and thirty-one times the week before the incident that killed his employee. Butler had even gone on two calls earlier that same day.

He remembered that day with clarity. He remembered being surprised to see Joe walk into the shop since he had only recently been released from the hospital with some sort of heart scare.

"And I even asked him, I says, 'Joe, does your wife know you're here?' And he had said no, she did not. I really didn't want Joe working."

He even told his office assistant, Candy, not to take any calls for tows because he didn't want Joe to go out on a job. It was his strategy to just keep Joe hanging around the garage with nothing to do. "I was just going to get Joe bored enough so he would say, 'Okay, I'm going back home.'"

And they didn't take any calls. Until AAA called. Butler was under contract to AAA, and while he could push off some calls to other companies,

he couldn't turn down calls from AAA. Ed Butler told the jury what happened next.

> At that time Candy had come out and told me, "You have a triple-A
> call." And I think I told her—I said, "Joe is still here. I got to try and
> get rid of him." Joe had overheard us. And he said, "I'll go do the
> call." And I said, "No, Joe. I'll go do the call." He said, "Come on.
> Let me go do the call."
>
> So Candy and I discussed it. And Candy even said, "Hey, he
> looks good. Let him go do the call. He needs this maybe for him—
> something to do, get him something to do." So we decided to let
> Joe do the call. And I told Joe when he left that if he had any prob-
> lem, if he was getting out of breath, if he was tired, if the drive over
> there was too much, anything, to give me a call, and I would jump
> in the Ranger, one of the smaller trucks, and come over and give
> him a hand. I said, "I'll even go with you."
>
> Well, he didn't want a babysitter. He did not want me to go
> with him. And so, of course, naturally, I didn't, knowing that Joe
> knows what he's doing out there. He was well capable of towing
> that Ranger.
>
> And then the next thing I know, Candy is hollering in the office
> because we got the phone call and said that Joe was in an accident.
> And at that time I didn't believe it was anything because Joe was in
> an accident before and that's what we had insurance for.
>
> I didn't think twice about it. And then when I asked Candy, I
> said, "How bad could it be?"
>
> She said, "You better take the phone."
>
> And that's when whoever was on the other side told me I better
> come over to the scene. And then that's when it dawned on me that
> it was bad. And it still really didn't hit me until I got there how bad
> it was.

Butler paused and swallowed hard. His eyes welled up and he looked
downward, his face cast in crimson. He began to sob as he blurted out
loudly his next words.

"That should have been me in that truck. It should have been me! It
should have been me!"

Linda, in her seat in the courtroom, was also crying. She said, softly
and to no one in particular, "It shouldn't have been either of them."

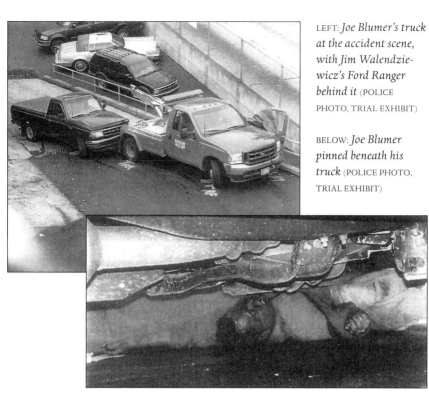

LEFT: *Joe Blumer's truck at the accident scene, with Jim Walendzie-wicz's Ford Ranger behind it* (POLICE PHOTO, TRIAL EXHIBIT)

BELOW: *Joe Blumer pinned beneath his truck* (POLICE PHOTO, TRIAL EXHIBIT)

Joe Blumer with his stepchildren Paul and Kayla (Jennette's children from her first marriage) and Shirley (back row, right) and Joanne (in front) (COURTESY OF THE BLUMERS, TRIAL EXHIBIT)

ABOVE: *Plaintiff experts Bob Nocivelli and Campbell Laird inspecting a parking brake while Kila Baldwin looks on* (AUTHOR'S PHOTO)

LEFT: *Ed Butler, Joe's former boss* (AUTHOR'S PHOTO)

BELOW: *Mel Blumer, Joe's brother, with Jennette* (AUTHOR'S PHOTO)

A close-up of the brake system with marks Ford claimed were made by Ed Butler during installation. The same marks were found on a new, unused brake.
(PHOTO BY CAMPBELL LAIRD)

Trial exhibit showing the brake system's gear-like teeth (PHOTO BY CAMPBELL LAIRD)

Derick Bobb at 17 at Fenwick Island State Park in Delaware (COURTESY OF THE BOBBS)

ON CROSS-EXAMINATION, Bill Conroy's strategy seemed straight-forward. He was out to attack Ed Butler's abilities as a mechanic and his credibility as a witness. Butler had come across as sympathetic. He seemed concerned and sincere, and his testimony—as the person who serviced the truck that killed Joe Blumer—was critical. Conroy sought to make Butler out to be an incompetent and a liar.

Butler, Conroy ascertained, was licensed to do state inspections of vehicles but he had never taken any formalized mechanical education courses. He serviced his own fleet of twelve trucks as best he could but Butler was no trained master mechanic. If a brake was shot, he'd throw it out, buy a new one, and pop it in. Maybe he had screwed one up.

Conroy quizzed Butler on the proper installation of the parking brake system, spending much of the time on a part of the brake known as the take-up spring, a coiled length of metal. Conroy flashed on the screen a photo that seemed to show that the spring had been somehow moved from its original set position, pointing to a mark showing where the spring had started out. It had moved from the factory "design position." Conroy asked if that could possibly have an effect on the brake tension and how the parking brake pedal felt when the brake was applied.

"Oh, most definitely," answered Butler.

"It would affect how far the parking brake would actually travel, right?"

"It could possibly."

"It would also have an effect, once the parking brake is depressed to whatever location it's in with the spring in this less than properly adjusted condition, when the parking brake is released, it can have an effect on how far back the parking brake returns when it's released. Right?"

"I didn't know that."

Clearly, Butler was not as well versed on the braking system as, say, a Ford-certified mechanic. Yet he possessed practical knowledge. Did one need to know why a lightbulb had burned out to replace it? When Conroy asked about the brake's inner workings and whether Butler knew what had gone wrong with previous parking brakes he had replaced, his answer seemed to satisfy the jury.

"They were broke," he said.

Part of Conroy's strategy was to create suspicion that something insidious had occurred in the case, that the testimony of this simple man who ran a simple business had been manipulated by the plaintiffs' experts and attorneys. The defense lawyer briefly mentioned that Nocivelli had contacted Butler "within days of the accident"—actually nine days—to join him for an inspection of the tow truck and said "that you knew that Mr. Nocivelli was an investigator on behalf of the plaintiffs."

Butler's response was straightforward but it did make him sound awfully chummy with the plaintiffs' expert. "I know when Bob called," he said, using Nocivelli's first name, "and introduced himself, he said he was going to be working with Edgar Snyder on this case." Snyder was the local attorney who first took the case on the Blumers' behalf.

Then Conroy abruptly switched to another target, to a man whose name the jury had not heard before—David Caputo. He was the attorney who had developed the case but had since left Kline & Specter for a position with the U.S. Attorney's Office in Philadelphia. He had met with Butler when the case was being explored and before Butler's seventeen hours of deposition testimony.

"Do you recall Mr. Caputo meeting with you the night before your very first deposition?" Conroy wanted to know.

"It's possible," said Butler, seemingly confused and curious about the question. "I don't remember. But go ahead."

The attorney pulled out a copy of Butler's deposition and showed him the page and line in which he had acknowledged having met with Caputo that night for "approximately an hour, maybe an hour and a half."

> Q: And your testimony is that during this time period that you did not review any photographs with Mr. Caputo?
> A: Correct.
> Q: That you didn't review any documents with Mr. Caputo?
> A: Correct.
> Q: That you did not talk about the accident at all?
> A: No.
> Q: That you didn't talk about this particular truck at all. Right?
> A: Not to my knowledge. I can't—you know.
> Q: What you talked about, according to your testimony, was . . . the weather. Right?
> A: Yes.
> Q: You talked about family?
> A: Yes.
> Q: This was the first time you had met Mr. Caputo. Correct?
> A: Uh-huh.
> Q: And you talked about, I think, Mr. Caputo's trip up to visit you for this meeting, right?
> A: Yes.

Q: And all this took place over an hour and a half?

A: Approximately.

Q: And you never discussed this particular case in terms of the truck or the records or the accident or photographs or anything?

A: Basically what we talked about was the deposition that was coming up and that I was to tell the truth, to the best of my knowledge. And I understand this happened in 2004. And four years later a lot of things I don't remember without being prompted. I need things to prompt me. That's when other things happen that I remember things.

Q: Mr. Butler, it's fair to say you didn't need Mr. Caputo to remind you that you should tell the truth?

Specter rose to object, but was overruled.

A: Oh, no.

Q: I'm sorry.

A: No. I didn't need him to tell me that.

Q: So for this hour to hour and a half, there was discussion about weather and family?

A: Basically, the hour and a half—there again, my times—if you asked me right now how long I've been sitting on the stand I couldn't tell you. Basically what I would call it is a meet-and-greet. You know, "Hey, how you doing? I'm so-and-so. How you doing? How is the family? How is your family? Where are you from? Such-and-such. You know, you have a deposition tomorrow. I just want to remind you just tell the truth, to the best of your knowledge." That's basically was what the meeting was about.

Q: I'm just curious, Mr. Butler, because everything you just said to us took place in less than a minute. I just want to better understand everything that was discussed during this hour and a half.

A: I can't remember what was discussed in that hour and a half. I don't even know if it was an hour and a half.

Conroy also pressed Butler about an affidavit the plaintiffs had asked him to sign, and he noted with raised eyebrow that some changes had been made and some things were crossed out. There were, Conroy noted with Butler's assent, "some things in there that you did not agree with." The defense attorney also asked Butler if he had met with plaintiffs' counsel before his testimony here at trial. Yes, acknowledged Butler, for about a half-hour.

On redirect, Specter almost immediately went to the questions surrounding his former colleague, David Caputo, a lawyer whom he trusted not to coach or manipulate a witness, a lawyer who had left a lucrative practice to work for the government putting crooks in jail.

As Conroy had done, Specter carried a section of Butler's deposition up to the witness stand. Butler had also been questioned in that earlier testimony about his meeting with Caputo.

"Let's look at page ten of your deposition," Specter began, pointing to several lines in which Butler had told defense counsel Nancy Winschel that besides the "weather and family" he had spoken with Caputo about the questions that might be asked of him at the next day's deposition. And also generally what to expect at the deposition. And the relevant documents Butler would bring with him to the deposition.

> Q: So you didn't spend an hour and half talking about the weather. Correct?
> A: Oh, no.
> Q: And you didn't tell Ford's lawyers that you did either. You told them that you did a lot of other things as well. Correct?
> A: Correct.

So who was being devious? Was it Ed Butler trying to cover up being coached in his testimony by Caputo, or was it Ford for making an innocuous, routine meeting seem like a nefarious deed? A few minutes later, Specter tried to sum up this little chapter of the trial with one question to Butler.

> Q: Have you cooperated with everybody's questions of you at all times?
> A: 150 percent.

Specter finished with Butler by asking about a previous incident with the tow truck, when Joe Blumer had found a problem with the parking brake and Butler had told him to bring the vehicle right back to the shop. Joe had done just that.

> Q: So Joe's practice if he felt the parking brake wasn't working was to call you and tell you. Correct?

A: I would . . .

Q: Sir, on the twenty-ninth of September, the day that Joe Blumer died, did he call you and tell you the parking brake wasn't working on the truck?

A: No, he did not.

Q: Was the parking brake working on the truck that day, as far as you knew?

A: Oh, it was. I was using the truck that day.

Q: I think you told Mr. Conroy, in answer to his questions, that when the parking brake was broken, it would feel limp?

A: Yes.

Q: Do you recollect that?

A: Yes.

Q: Did this parking brake, the one involved in this accident, ever feel limp?

A: No.

Q: Now, Mr. Conroy asked you about occasions . . . when you would purchase replacement parking brakes from Ford dealerships?

A: Yes.

Q: Do you recollect that?

A: Yes.

Q: And I think the questioning was to the effect of you didn't tell them what was broken on the brake itself. Is that correct?

A: Correct.

Q: Now, are you even expert on the innards of the brake itself?

A: No. I'm not an engineer.

Judge Della Vecchia excused the witness, telling him, "If you wish, you may go home or back to work." Butler stepped down from the witness box, looking like the most relieved man on Earth. But he wouldn't go home or to work. He stayed for the rest of the trial.

CHAPTER 32

The Mechanic and the Professor

WITH BUTLER'S CRITICAL TESTIMONY over, the trial now moved to a phase that could have been dubbed "the Battle of the Experts." Both sides paid their experts to render scientific opinions on what had caused Joe Blumer's demise. They had arrived at completely opposite conclusions. At least one side had to be wrong. And it would be up to a jury of Allegheny County citizens to listen to these experts and view a variety of exhibits and measurements and calculations and decide which theory was correct. The jurors would have to decide which experts were the most credible—the most qualified, the most knowledgeable, the most capable, the most honest—and which of their theories made the most sense.

Baldwin would examine Bob Nocivelli. She started with the usual rundown of the witness's resume, education, and experience, so the judge would admit him as an expert. Nocivelli did not have the formal credentials of the other experts at trial. He didn't have a master's degree or a Ph.D. Nocivelli had been schooled largely at the University of Hands-on Experience. He was a mechanic by trade, having worked on his first auto, for pay, when he was fifteen years old. Before that he'd worked on clunkers, go-carts, anything with wheels. He had gone directly from high school to working at an Esso station, where he worked as a mechanic and towed cars. He was the only expert, so far as Specter knew, who had actually operated a tow truck. Nocivelli hadn't made grander plans after graduation because he figured he was about to be drafted to go to Vietnam. And he had been right. (Nocivelli had told Baldwin before his testimony that he didn't want to be asked about the war and she abided.) From the witness stand Nocivelli joked that the Army must have had made a mistake when it assigned him to operate a tow truck to remove disabled vehicles from the field of battle.

"Usually they make a mechanic a cook in the Army or something like that," he said, "but that wasn't the case. I went in doing exactly what I was doing outside."

And he came out doing it. Nocivelli never attended college but he went to a handful of vocational schools, starting with the Forbes Trail Area Technical School, which was part of his high school program. He later attended the Kinman School in Indianapolis, which he described for the jury as "wrecker school," and the Consolidated Industrial School/ Heavy Truck Division, where he took classes on brake repair among other things. He also earned certification as a master technician and later attended classes and seminars, including those offered by several brake manufacturers. In 1983, after working for years as a mechanic, Nocivelli started the RAN Group (his initials) in which he offered his professional services to help determine whether equipment failures had caused accidents. He often worked with police and lawyers, both defendants and plaintiffs. He had inspected plenty of accidents and had testified in eleven states, in some cases for the authorities, including the state attorneys general in Pennsylvania and West Virginia. In the Blumer case Nocivelli had gone to inspect the tow truck on October 8, nine days after the accident.

Q: After reviewing all these materials, did you make a determination about what caused this accident on September 29, 2004?

A: Yes, I have.

Q: Can you tell us what that determination is?

A: The determination, in as few words as possible, is the parking brake system on that 2002 F-350 truck is defective.

Q: Can you just briefly tell us why you believe it's defective?

A: The system is defective because in the manner in which it's constructed they actually self-destruct upon application. As you apply the parking brake pedal, it develops lateral play as you place your foot upon the pedal in the manner that is very conventional, very normal. It shoves the pedal arm to the side and forces it into a disengagement position.

Nocivelli had prepared an elaborate exhibit that provided an open view into the front corner of a 2002 Ford F-350, similar to Joe Blumer's vehicle. It was even painted red like his actual truck. Nocivelli and Baldwin then explored the exhibit, followed by a technician operating a video camera that projected parts of the contraption onto a TV screen for the jury. Nocivelli's rather long-winded explanation—"That was probably the longest answer in history," he said at one point, laughing at himself—combined with the swinging, bouncing hand-held camera projection, produced an unintended effect. It was dizzying, literally.

After his first day of testimony, Judge Della Vecchia commented to Specter that Nocivelli had seemed like a "mad professor," expressing that he hadn't been impressed by the examination so far of the plaintiffs' first expert witness. The comment worried Specter, who was leery of beginning his case behind in the score. He knew he had ground to make up.

BUT WHEN NOCIVELLI returned to the stand, he managed—reined in somewhat by Baldwin—to keep his answers shorter and on point. And his prior demonstration did seem to have at least one beneficial effect on the jury, particularly when Nocivelli pulled the brake release, which snapped the pedal up hard, almost violently. The jury could easily imagine how normal use over time could damage the system, how, as Nocivelli explained, "the teeth were worn severely, chewed out, chunked out." He had also wiggled the brake pedal from side to side when explaining the lateral movement of the brake gears, which he said could also have contributed to disengagement, or "skip-out."

Questioned further, Nocivelli next disputed the defense assertion that the brake pedal had traveled all the way to the truck's floor. It had gone, his inspection showed, perhaps as far as 1 inch from the floor, which he described as "the end of the allowable by-design travel on the sector." The brake obviously needed adjustment, but it wasn't broken before Joe Blumer had taken his last run.

"It's quite obvious," Nocivelli testified, "that the parking brake had to work and hold the vehicle or Mr. Blumer would have never been able to get out of that truck to do the activity that he needed to do to disengage Mr. Walendziewicz's truck."

He concluded, "The parking brake skipped out. The sector and pinion became disengaged and the truck rolled."

Q: Mr. Nocivelli, should a properly designed parking brake system ever spontaneously disengage?
A: No.
Q: Did this brake malfunction?
A: It did.
Q: How do you know it malfunctioned?
A: It disengaged. It skipped out.
Q: Was this parking brake used in a normal fashion by Mr. Blumer and Mr. Butler prior to this accident?
A: Yes.

Q: Are there any reasonable secondary causes for this accident?
A: None that I can think of.

Lastly Baldwin asked Nocivelli to explain the mysterious marks Conroy had shown on one of the brake gears during his opening speech. The implication was that the marks had been made by Ed Butler's shoddy workmanship. But as Nocivelli and Campbell Laird had discovered, the same marks had been present on a brand-new brake. The marks were not evidence, as Conroy had suggested, of mishandling of the brake.

Q: Was this parking brake controller ever installed in a truck?
A: Never.
Q: Do you know what causes this mark?
A: I don't, with certainty.
Q: Was this mark caused by anything in the installation process?
A: It's never been installed in anything.

Conroy would score some points on cross-examination, though he would not rattle the mechanic from rural Pennsylvania, who now seemed steady and relaxed in the witness stand.

"How you doing, all right?" Conroy asked Nocivelli.

"Yep."

The defense attorney flashed up a photo of the inside of the brakes from Joe Blumer's truck. He asked if the photo showed the two gears, the pinion and the sector, meshed together. But Nocivelli refused to see what Conroy saw in the photo.

Q: When we look at this photograph, we can see, can't we, that the pinion gear and the sector gear are in alignment, aren't they?
A: They are not.
Q: They're not in alignment?
A: Not in my opinion, no.
Q: I'm sorry?
A: Not in my opinion, they are not.
Q: Is there any contact between the pinion gear and the sector in that photograph?
A: There is contact, but they are not aligned.
Q: You think they are out of alignment?
A: They are out of alignment.

The difference in what the two saw could be explained by point of view. Yes, the sector and pinion gears were meshed together, the teeth of one set in the "valleys" of the other. But looked at straight on, one part was a little to the left and the other a little to the right. To Conroy, a layman, the gears were in alignment. To Nocivelli, a mechanic, they were "right on the cusp, right on the edge of holding."

Then Conroy showed the "dimple" part of the brake, a depression in the metal casing or frame intended to hold the gears in place. The dimple, or depression, was what prevented the gears from moving much within the brake system. If they moved laterally too much, they would bump up against the dimple, preventing the teeth from disengaging.

Yes, Nocivelli had to admit, he recognized the dimple and its purpose. But he said that didn't prevent the parts from being pushed and forced and worked to a point over time where the gears, especially those with broken teeth, would move enough during a hard application—despite the dimple—to disengage.

Conroy again tried to undercut the plaintiffs' case with intimations of skullduggery. About those marks that had appeared on both the exemplar brake gear and the same part in Joe Blumer's truck, had anyone besides Nocivelli ever had possession of the exemplar brake?

"Attorney Baldwin," said Nocivelli, a puzzled look on his face.

And, Conroy wanted to know, apparently implying some sort of impropriety, wasn't it true that Nocivelli had socialized with Ed Butler?

"On one occasion," said Nocivelli, and left it at that.

CAMPBELL LAIRD, the second expert witness, deeply tanned from a recent trip to Hawaii to visit his son who lived there, bounced to the stand. He was in his seventies but possessed a youthful exuberance and a devilish smile. He seemed always upbeat and up-tempo. He was clearly a man who enjoyed what he did. His resume was a thing to behold, twenty-seven pages single-spaced.

On questioning by Specter, Laird told the jury he hailed from Scotland, though his accent made that hardly necessary to mention. He had earned his bachelor's degree, master's, and Ph.D. at the University of Cambridge in England.

Laird was smart but not stuffy. To chuckles from the jury he said his current post at the University of Pennsylvania was "professor emeritus, which means that they're willing to accept my work if they don't have to pay me." Laird had kept current in his profession, only in the last year having been made a fellow of the Metallurgical Society, a 150-year-old organization that limited membership to 100. For years he had studied what makes metals hard and soft, what makes them deform and break and, said Laird, who moved breezily between technical and common language, "this sort of stuff."

Laird was comfortable on the witness stand. He looked directly at jurors when he spoke, using frequent gestures. He testified, he told Specter, for both defendants and plaintiffs, depending on the facts of a case.

Conroy deferred questioning on Laird's C.V. He also didn't ask the routine question about how much Laird—or Nocivelli, for that matter— was being paid for his report and trial testimony. That number tended to produce looks of astonishment among jurors, middle-income folks who included a nurse, a county elections worker, a manager of a research lab, a Veterans Administration employee, a manager with a vacuum manufacturer, and a student who had worked odd jobs at fast food restaurants, including Subway and Popeye's. Conroy doubtlessly didn't ask because he didn't want Specter asking the same question of the defense experts.

After hearing Laird's resume, Judge Della Vecchia smiled and ruled that the puckish professor was indeed qualified as an expert on the matter at hand.

Laird told the jury that he had reviewed "a great mass of material" on the Blumer case, including eight boxes of documents and a number of brake systems, and he had also visited the scene of the accident. He had reached this conclusion on what had caused the accident that led to Joe Blumer's death:

> The causes are, one, that this controller, as designed and manufactured, was defective in a number of respects. It is insufficiently robust. The parts don't hang together well and don't work. There are inconsistencies within it. For example, there are two sectors of importance and two pinions of importance, each of which mate with one another. It is defective in my view to design a system wherein the interaction of a sector and a pinion can destroy each other where you mate those gears, the stops that allow them to bring each other abruptly to an end of things, because in the process of doing that, they destroy each other.
>
> And, as a result of that and other aspects . . . it undergoes distortions and movements throughout the life of the controller that ultimately result in its ineffective operation. And a parking brake is an essential safety tool. And if the thing doesn't work, a skip-out can occur and the brake doesn't operate properly, doesn't hold properly.

And it can and did unpredictably break free and release a rollaway with tragic consequences.

Laird was asked by Specter if he had photographs that backed up his theory. He did, replied the scientist, and he pulled a pile of pictures from his jacket pocket. That was not the normal way exhibits were introduced in court. Specter passed the photos to Bill Conroy to inspect.

"Would you ask him to keep them in order, please," Laird instructed regarding Conroy.

As he flipped through the photos, projecting them on the larger screens for the jury to see, Laird explained the significance of each. Occasionally he used a laser pointer to note specific areas of interest. Laird wasn't so much testifying as conducting a lecture, a show-and-tell.

Laird suggested that the metal dimple Conroy had shown that was intended to keep the brake gears from moving laterally was insufficient to do that job. For one, Laird pointed out the slight gap—"displaced by half a tooth width"—between the dimple and the gears. He termed that gap "slop," which allowed for some play. He demonstrated how the gear moved against the dimple with only a gentle push. "That is bad," he tsk-tsked.

Specter started to ask another question but Laird would not be deterred. "I wish to make one further point," said the professor. Laird went on to explain how this "play" would worsen when the brake parts were subjected to force, such as the parking brake pedal being depressed and the tow truck holding on a hill with another truck as its load. He explained that the brake mechanism held the rear wheels by a steel cable that "stretches like toffee" under the weight of the large vehicle.

He pointed again to the photo and said, "This picture is not taken under load. I have just tickled the pedal. And when things are out of alignment, the application of a load is going to distort it further, and that distortion is what we call 'elastic.'"

Even though Conroy had shown that the dimple was situated so that the gears could only move so much, Laird explained that looks were deceiving. "All materials are elastic to some degree," even steel, he said. Using a mix of highly technical terminology and layman's language, he went on to explain how elasticity and reversible deformations and stress and gears not mating properly work in tandem.

Laird said, "And it is these complexities in the overall interaction of the controller that ultimately produce the misfortune that we have seen today."

At this point in the trial the jury was ushered from the courtroom and the lawyers debated before the judge a matter that would prove critical to the case. It concerned whether to introduce evidence that similar problems had occurred across the country with the Ford F-Series brakes. Specter wanted forty-one reports—made by Ford owners to the company—allowed as evidence, evidence he felt would help convince the jury that Ford's trucks were defective and that Ford had known and done nothing about it. Conroy and the defense team badly wanted this information excluded, kept from the jury.

"There are some situations where they say parking brakes did not hold and the vehicle rolled. That to me, Judge, is not enough," said Conroy. "It doesn't tell us why it's happening. There could be any number of reasons why it's happening. The reasons could relate to issues that are totally unrelated to what the specific defect issues are in this case in terms of design and in terms of why this accident happened here. And what is really happening, Judge, if we just let this in—because there is a claim that the parking brake didn't hold and the vehicle rolled—[it] is basically indicting the entire design of the parking brake, regardless of the reason why it's happening. When I believe . . . the focus of the Court needs to be much more specific, because this kind of evidence can be explosive. It can be highly prejudicial. It can be very confusing to a jury."

But Judge Della Vecchia disagreed. Although he removed some of the incidents, he allowed Specter to present twenty-eight of them to the jury. "In its naked sense, those claims in those documents are identical to the claim here. We're on an incline. It stopped. We get out. It rolls backwards. That's what we have here. Ford opted not to investigate any of those claims . . . Generally speaking, their tack in all those claims is, 'This is an insurance matter. You should see your liability insurance carrier.'"

Conroy was unrelenting, raising his voice. "Just the idea that Ford is getting reports that a parking brake has failed and vehicles rolled on a hill, that in and of itself should not be enough to allow these events to come in when it's unexplained as to what happened."

But the judge had heard enough. He turned to Specter. "Do you want to say anything?"

"Not really," replied Specter.

The judge turned to Conroy. "To me they [the twenty-eight incidents] meet the bare necessity of the substantial similarity. Had they done some testing or done some investigation here, maybe we would know that this wasn't a defective product. This was driver error. This was whatever. We don't. They opted not to look into this further."

WHEN THE TRIAL resumed, so did Campbell Laird. Specter supplied some questions and the professor took flight, lecturing the jury. With a microphone pinned to the lapel of his dark suit, Laird seemed quite at home in the courtroom. "I'd like to speak next on . . ." he would say as he embarked on another technical explanation. "May I have some water?" he'd asked the tipstaff. "Take a look," he instructed the jurors at another point as he stepped down from the witness stand to show them a matter of interest in an exhibit, professor to his students. The judge and the defense gave Laird great latitude, not that either had much choice.

Asked at one point if Ford could have made a better brake for its heavy trucks, Laird volunteered, "They could not only have made it better but for a lower cost."

Asked what he thought happened in the case of Joe Blumer's death, he leaned over closer to the jurors. Several tilted toward the professor.

> The scenario, as I see it, was Mr. Blumer went up the hill with the Ranger in tow, raised on the stinger and strapped on the L-arms. He had plenty of power to get around that corner, but it was geometrically too difficult. So he had to stop. He was stuck. He put the vehicle parking brake on. It was sufficient to hold both vehicles under those conditions. And it was sufficient to allow him to put an auxiliary help in the way of a four-by-four chock under the driver's wheels. Then Mr. Walendziewicz arrived and they lowered the stinger. The stinger went onto the floor—before he arrived, I think he had undone the straps.
>
> So all he had to do in the presence of Mr. Walendziewicz was to lower the stinger. He lowered it to the ground. He may have taken a little bit of weight off the rear wheels. He may not have. The Ranger at this point was . . . held sufficiently by the L-arms so Mr. Walendziewicz could get into it, start it up, and begin backing it off. The L-arms at the back end where it's at the rear of the front wheel, when the Ranger is lifted, is sort of triangular in shape. And so as it goes over that, the weight of the wheel would press down on the stinger, add additional weight to the stinger, and add, actually, an additional frictional force retaining the pair of them on the hill. As it goes over the L-arm, it probably gave it a nudge upwards,

and that could well have been one of the—a possible initiator to triggering the escape of the parking brake.

And then he backed off, and then that or some other event of vibration and release occurred, causing the truck to then start down the hill in pursuit of the Ranger as it backed down, and striking it. And then you know the rest. Mr. Walendziewicz put on his brakes, held it, and Mr. Blumer was entrapped under his tow truck.

Like a one-two punch, now Specter introduced the twenty-eight reported similar instances in which Ford truck brakes disengaged. He went over a number of them with Laird, one by one, cases in which a truck owner claimed the parking brake disengaged on its own and a truck rolled away. And how Ford never investigated the incidents.

"Should a parking brake ever disengage once applied if it is properly designed?" Specter asked his witness.

"It should not," replied Laird.

ON CROSS-EXAMINATION Conroy began by discussing the marks, including the straight line, on the brake gears. He had shown these marks in his opening arguments, claiming they showed that there had been damage, proof that the brake had been installed improperly by Ed Butler. But Nocivelli and Laird had already noted the identical marks on the exemplar brake, meaning they had been on the original as it came from the factory. Meaning Conroy's theory was wrong.

Conroy questioned how the plaintiffs' experts had discovered the marks must have been made at the factory. He doubted it could have been discovered so suddenly and so fortuitously for the plaintiffs. He tried to make Laird sound disingenuous.

> Q: Now you issued a number of reports in this case and the latest one you wrote about a month ago. What you said about this was that "If the tool mark had been imposed by a person manipulating the tool in that confined space, I find it hard to believe that the mark would be as straight as it is. There must be many other explanations for that mark." Now back at that time period you weren't of the opinion that it was a manufacturing issue. Right?
>
> A: No. But I have seen some very important evidence since.
>
> Q: So I think what you're telling us is that this important evidence is that the controller that Mr. Nocivelli had . . .

A: Well, the one that he had and which he sent to Ms. Baldwin, and I hadn't seen this before in its assembled condition, and you can see that mark on this controller in this part.

Q: And that's the other controller Mr. Nocivelli obtained?

A: Correct.

Q: So the source of those two controllers from wherever he got them from, right?

A: That's correct.

Q: And you didn't know about these marks that are on these controllers until this week?

A: That's correct.

Q: Now, you're telling us that Mr. Nocivelli . . . you were here yesterday when he told us that he had had this one part for close to a year?

A: Yes.

Q: What I want to find out, Dr. Laird, is this: You're telling us that Mr. Nocivelli never picked up the phone and said to you, "Hey, I've got this controller, and there is a mark on there"? He never said that to you?

A: He did not, no. He did not call me to say he got this mark on there.

Q: And . . .

A: I don't know that he knew that he had that mark on there.

Q: And, counsel, I take it, never told you "There is a controller that Mr. Nocivelli has that has this mark on there"? Until you came back . . .

A: I was the one that saw this mark out here, and it came as a surprise to the assembled people.

Q: So you had this controller in your hands as well?

A: This week I had it in my hands and there it was.

Q: So you found it?

A: I found it.

Q: You alerted counsel to it?

A: I did.

More technical testimony followed, with Laird pointing his laser and largely commandeering the dialogue. And that's what the cross-examination had become, a dialogue. Not so much a lawyer attacking the testimony of a witness but a chat between two professionals about a parking brake system. And with Laird leading the dance. The defense attorney seemed to be losing his authority in the courtroom with this witness, as when Conroy asked one question and the professor replied that his premise was wrong and offered, like a schoolteacher helping a pupil, "Let's look at the previous picture and see if we can figure this out."

It got to the point where the judge had to step in.

"Doctor," he said, "we have this problem with experts. This is how the system works. The lawyers ask the questions and the witness answers. Okay?"

"Okay."

Conroy kept at it, patiently attempting to pick apart Laird's testimony but hitting a wall at every turn. Laird stuck to his theories, immovable. Finally Conroy, exasperated, called it quits.

"Dr. Laird, that's all I have," he said. "Thank you."

"Thank *you*, sir," said the witness.

CHAPTER 33

A Man's Wallet

IT WAS TIME. Members of the Blumer family would have to do what they had dreaded all along. One by one the people who had been closest to Joe would take the witness stand. This had little to do with proving the case but everything to do with demonstrating for the jury that there had been real pain and real suffering for all those Joe had left behind. It wasn't a phase of the trial that anyone, including Specter, enjoyed. But such testimony was necessary for the plaintiffs' case. If the jury was going to be asked to hand down an award to Jennette and her children, they had to know what the family had gone through, were still going through, would go through for the rest of their lives. The jury not only had to be told about their horrible loss. They needed, in some measure, to feel it. And there was only one way for that to happen.

"OH, HE WAS GREAT," said Joanne Aubrey about her deceased son-in-law. She had a sad, worn face that looked older than her years, her down-turned mouth sunken. But she managed a smile as she recalled a tidbit from Joe's life.

"He'd put the lights on the tow truck," she said, moving her finger in the air in a circular motion, a reference to the vehicle's flashing amber lights. "He'd take them to school in the tow truck. They liked that."

Specter asked her how Jennette was doing, her daughter watching from the front row of the courtroom with the rest of her family, more of whom had come to court this day, including MaryAnn and Betty, two of Jennette's four sisters.

"Not good. Not good," said Aubrey. "I don't want to say 'nervous breakdown,' but not good. Not good. She shakes all the time."

The jurors looked between Aubrey and Jennette. Two female jurors were crying. A man in the front row of the jury box tilted his head back and focused his eyes on the ceiling, though it was difficult to discern his feelings. Was he rolling his eyes in disdain for this display of emotion or was he looking upward to stem a flow of tears?

"You need anything?" the judge asked the sobbing jurors. "Tissues?"

One took a handful and blew her nose.

Specter kept Aubrey on the stand only a few minutes. While he knew this testimony was necessary, he didn't want to overwhelm the jury. Emotional testimony, he knew, had limits. Jurors could begin to feel a plaintiff's attorney was playing on *their* emotions and then things could turn quickly from sympathy to resentment. Specter was determined not to reach that point.

He had the judge excuse Aubrey from the witness stand and called his next witness.

Mel Blumer, at fifty-seven, was quite a bit older than his brother, Joe. After Joe died, Mel moved Jennette and Joe's kids into his house and they were still all living together. One thing Mel brought to the witness stand was a knowledge of his brother's skills as a tow truck operator. Mel, who once owned his own towing business with three trucks, had started Joe off and had taught him to drive a wrecker.

"Joe drove for twenty years . . . he observed all the rules," said Mel. "Joe started driving in the ninth grade. He loved the towing business. I think he drove a tow truck before he drove a car."

Like many of the jurors Mel was unmistakably a Western Pennsylvania native. Heavyset, with a moustache, Mel came to court most days proudly wearing cowboy boots and a black Pittsburgh Steelers jacket with yellow leather sleeves. A few months earlier the Steelers had won a record sixth Super Bowl, and it was clear that Mel was no Johnny-come-lately fan. The arms of his coat were worn and slightly blackened.

Mel concluded his testimony by talking about Jennette, who was trying to "stay strong for the kids." He told the jury that the nervousness she displayed was not merely a symptom of the moment, not something that only overtook her in the courtroom.

"Jennette should probably go get herself some help," Mel said, almost off-handedly. "She shakes."

If Mel sounded matter-of-fact, Shirley, Jennette and Joe's fifteen-year-old daughter, sounded almost robotic, her words coming in a clipped cadence. Although she sounded rehearsed, Shirley was simply anxious. And, possibly, a little shell-shocked. Since her father's death she had undergone severe difficulties. Her behavior had become odd at times. She had trouble with other kids.

"Me and my dad were very close. We did homework together and watched football together," said Shirley, also telling the jury about riding to school in her father's tow truck. "Now I have to ride the bus and get beat up and stuff."

Asked how she was doing now, she told Specter in a monotone voice, "I'm not doing good at all. I miss my dad."

She added that her mother wasn't doing well either and added, "I'm afraid I'm going to lose my mom next."

Joanne, more than a year younger but bigger than her sister, burst into tears on the witness stand the second she saw a photo of her father. One of the jurors handed her a tissue box. Joanne spoke in a small, scratchy voice barely more than a whisper.

"I'll be fourteen tomorrow," she told the jury, then launched into all the things she missed about her father, in no particular order, scattered remembrances. "He always took us everywhere he went. He taught us how to swim."

Joanne said she and her mother and sister moved in with Mel partly to get out of a house that held too many memories of her father. "The house smelled like him," she said.

"I miss him coming home," she said, her voice cracking. "He used to take us to school and give us a kiss and say, 'Have a good day.' I miss everything about him."

Joanne began to sob. She was excused as a witness and she rushed to the back of the courtroom and threw her arms around her mother. Both were still crying loudly when a recess was called and the jurors filed past them and out of the courtroom.

JENNETTE WALKED UP to the witness stand visibly shaken, and shaking.

"Relax, just relax," the judge's tipstaff, an older gentleman named Ray Bender, told her. Jennette's mannerisms were peculiar and so was her testimony, as though she were bewildered, quiet and shy on one hand, but relieved to finally be able to address the jury. Almost gleeful. She rambled from one memory to another. Specter let her go, only occasionally using a question to focus her.

She told the jury about the day Joe had proposed marriage. So proud was he to ask for Jennette's hand—and certain of her answer—that he had taken to one knee in front of everyone, strangers, at the food court of the North Hills Village Mall.

"Out of the clear blue Joe got down and he said, 'I want you to marry me. And I'm not going to take no for an answer.' He had the ring and everything. When I said 'yes,' people stood up and applauded. It was hard to say no to Joe. He was so passionate."

Jennette showed the jurors her wedding ring, now worn on a chain around her neck with gold charms her husband had given her in the years after their marriage. "When I wear it around my neck, it's like he's there with me," she told them.

Specter asked Jennette about Joe's wallet. She had kept it in a box since his death, never touching it in the years since. Specter asked her for it and she handed him the large lump of brown leather, starting to cry as she did so.

"Do you mind if I open it up?" he asked.

Jennette shook her head no, blinking away tears. She looked away as Specter opened the wallet, as though he were pulling a pin from a grenade. Choking back tears himself, Specter moved toward Jennette, finally standing beside her as he began to remove the wallet's contents. She grew more comfortable, even smiling as she saw Joe's wallet stuffed with memories, the photos of her children and happy times. First Specter withdrew a photo of Paul, Jennette's son from a previous marriage.

"That's Shirley," she said as Specter gingerly removed the second photo.

"Paul."

"Joanne."

"Joanne."

"Joanne as a baby."

"Shirley."

"Shirley."

"Shirley."

"He never took the old ones out of his wallet, just put the new ones in front."

There were eighteen family photos in all. The wallet contained one credit card, issued by Target stores, and a small pile of lottery tickets, a working man's dream of wealth. Some of the tickets—with numbers using his mother's home address, her phone number, Joe's birth date, his radio number in the tow truck—were dated September 29, 2004. They were tickets Joe never had the chance to check. (None was a winner.)

Specter asked Jennette about the good times and she told him, occasionally speaking of Joe in the present tense. "Joe gets bored, like really quick," she said, relating how he liked to do things with the children. "Just watching the kids' faces. I got a lot of pleasure watching Joe with the kids."

"Do you worry about them now?" asked Specter, jarring Jennette back to the present.

"My kids . . . they have their good and bad days. It seems there's so many bad days," she said, her smile vanishing.

She talked about Joe's scare with heart problems and how the man whom friends used to call "Smokin' Joe" had given up cigarettes, cold turkey, and had changed his diet, switching from fast foods and soda to soups and salads. She talked about how he had cooked and cleaned for the family.

"He was funny. And he cooked. He made *pasghetti*. I don't say it right, but he really made *pasghetti*."

She talked about the dreams that still haunted her about the day he died. And about how much she missed him. "When Joe was there, you could talk to him. He never felt like arguing. He said life was too short. Unfortunately, it was."

CHAPTER 34

No Deal

Jennette's testimony concluded the first week of the trial. Specter had his bags packed and the plane on notice to be ready to leave. He was tired and eager to get home after five days on the road.

But Judge Della Vecchia put a halt to his hasty retreat. He ordered both sides to stay until 2:00 p.m. He wanted them to talk, to try to settle the case. He knew that Specter had last demanded $10 million and that Ford had offered $1 million. Any negotiation had stopped there. Surely, the judge figured, there had to be some agreeable middle ground.

"Your Honor," said Specter back in the judge's chambers, "I'm willing to make a substantial move if they do."

But Specter wasn't willing to go too far too soon. He had just had a big day in court, with moving testimony. After one week there had been a cumulative effect from the physical evidence, the photos, the experts, the family. He knew the defense went next, but he felt good about the trial so far, very good.

Jennette had placed her financial fate in Specter's hands and turning down $1 million demonstrated her faith in him. Even after Specter had taken his share of such a settlement plus his firm's expenses, Jennette still would have roughly $600,000 tax-free. That was a lot of money for a woman whose husband had made $20,000 a year and who now had no visible means of support for herself and her two children.

But Specter didn't want her to simply exchange a husband's income with a Ford (or insurance company) paycheck. There was no way to compensate for the loss of love and companionship. To exact a measure of punishment against Ford would be to obtain a measure of justice. The case was about money and yet it wasn't just about money.

And Specter had been an attorney long enough to have learned from his mistakes and his clients'. He harkened back to John Smith, the young man who had been found dead within a year of cashing an inadequate settlement check from a car company. Never again, Specter had vowed. Not if he could help it.

Specter and his team sat in the courtroom, waiting for Ford to meet with the judge, then talking with Della Vecchia themselves. Then waiting while Ford's lawyer in Michigan, Kristin Pil, who was in charge of negotiating a settlement, was called. Then waiting some more.

"I feel better about the case than I did a week ago," Specter told Baldwin as they sat in the empty courtroom.

Previous attempts to settle the case had gone poorly. In an e-mail on February 24, only ten days before the scheduled start of the trial, Specter had written Conroy, urging, threatening really, a settlement before it was too late. He noted Conroy's previous comments about Ford's financial problems and indicated he was willing to take that into account, but only so much. Money woes wouldn't get Ford off the hook for what had befallen Joe Blumer. Specter's e-mail used a velvet hammer approach, trying to be civil while reminding Ford that he wasn't one to back down from a fight. He reminded Conroy of the settlement in the Bobb case and the two large verdicts in the White case. His e-mail read in part:

> Bill—I wanted to give Ford a little more to think about on their approach to this case, so please consider passing on this e-mail to Ms. Pil.
>
> I know Ford has no reason to question my resolve to try this case, ability to obtain a huge verdict, or willingness to wait to be paid. I've dealt with the parking brake problems in the F-Series trucks for 16 years. Ford paid [amount confidential, but known by Ford] to settle Bobb in 1995. White was a fourteen-year odyssey, with a $151 million verdict in 1998, a $52 million verdict in 2004, and an [amount confidential] settlement in 2008. . . . Liability is far clearer in Blumer. While I try to avoid trash talk, I'm obliged to tell Ford that I don't think the judge or jury will be happy with Ford's explanation for what occurred in this incident. I know I'm not.
>
> In Blumer, Ford at least seems to acknowledge through their relatively early approach to settlement and their initial offer of $1 million the difficulty of defending on the merits. Bobb was settled early and fairly. White was grossly misadjusted by Ford, with a silly offer of $250,000 before and during trial and a too-little-too-late offer of $2.5 million during jury deliberations. The negative publicity alone from those two big verdicts [in the White trials] of the unreliability of the brakes on the best-selling line of motor vehicles in the world was worth more than those offers. That could happen here, too.

The post-1998 legal battle in White proved only that both sides had a lot of money and patience. The case should have been settled fairly before trial, which is what I'm urging here.

What I know to be missing from Ford's analysis in Blumer is a realistic understanding of the damages picture. This is the principal reason for this e-mail. . . . It's easy to look at Joe Blumer's background and say, "Hey, look at this guy—ninth grade education, lifetime behind the wheel of a tow truck"—and conclude he couldn't have been much of a husband or dad. How wrong that would be. He came to the marriage with Jennette's two children as a point of pride, not an obstacle. Their two natural daughters together, Joanne and Shirley, are horribly affected. They had a phenomenal relationship with their dad.

Ford does have some measure of Jennette so I needn't dwell on her except to say that she is heroic and sympathetic.

This family deserves a lot of money. As much as anyone can predict an outcome in the civil justice system, I believe the jury will see it this way. Joe Blumer's life was taken in a ghastly and painful way due to what obviously was a malfunction of this brake. But to get the case settled the Blumers have to compromise. So must Ford. I will work with you or Ms. Pil . . . to get this matter resolved, but if we are to do so we must recognize the realities here, on both sides, and work to achieve true fairness. I'm willing to do my part.

Shanin

Ford had presented a counteroffer: $1,150,000. A joke, and a bad one at that, thought Specter. To inch up a mere $150,000 amounted to no new offer at all. Ford was playing hardball.

Now after a week of trial in Pittsburgh the judge wanted the two sides to try again. Specter again was willing. He sat in the courtroom until 2:00 p.m. this Friday afternoon with no word from Ford. The judge finally adjourned but in the belief that Specter and Ford would try to hash things out over the weekend.

Within an hour Specter was headed for the airport. At 3:36 p.m., just as he was about to board a leased twin-engine King Air, his BlackBerry buzzed with an e-mail from Kristin Pil.

"I understand the court expects us to talk," messaged Pil, who invited Specter to call her in Dearborn.

Specter responded icily, "Kristin—the court told me that you wanted to talk. The court does not expect us to talk. Please let me know if you want to talk."

Almost an hour passed before Pil e-mailed back.

"Shanin—In response to a request by the court, Ford is willing to continue settlement discussions in this matter. However, if we are to continue negotiations, Ford needs a response to its last offer of $1,150,000. Thank you."

Pil wasn't willing to make the first move. She wanted Specter to go first, to offer a large reduction in a settlement price. Specter's terse answer came within eight minutes and it set a deadline. Two could play hardball.

He wrote: "$9,850,000 payable in three days (as in White)."

Specter would budge only as much as Ford.

Ford would not respond with another offer.

CHAPTER 35

In Ford's Defense

THE SECOND WEEK of the trial gave the defense a chance to play offense. Conroy would counter with Ford's expert witnesses. He only needed to blunt the effect of the plaintiffs' professionals. If, at the end of the trial, the jury didn't know which side to believe, that was fine for Ford. A tie went to the defense, as the judge would instruct the jury before deliberations.

Ford's first expert was Aaron Jones, who, in his mid-forties, was much younger than either Nocivelli or Laird. Jones, thin, with receding brown hair, had a handsome face and a just-the-facts-ma'am manner. Even though he had testified plenty of times in the past, he appeared physically uncomfortable on the stand, particularly following Campbell Laird, who had seemed as if he were sitting in his living room. Jones shifted his body often and crossed his legs back and forth.

Jones was a metallurgical engineer who had a master's degree and was working on his Ph.D. He had attended the Illinois Institute of Technology and much of his education had focused on failure analysis of materials, an expertise much like Laird's. His title was senior director of materials and transportation engineering at an Illinois firm called Packer Engineering, where he'd been involved, as he put it in his heavy Midwestern accent, "in investigations of numerous products from tower cranes to elevators, escalators, trains, planes, automobiles."

He told Conroy and the jury that he worked for plaintiffs as well as defendants. But on cross-examination about his resume, Jones acknowledged to Specter that in reviewing more than 100 cases involving the Ford Motor Co., not once had he testified against the company. He had also testified in cases involving Chrysler, Specter ascertained, and again always for the car company. He had also testified for American International Group Inc., or AIG, the insurance giant that had been bailed out by Uncle Sam.

Specter asked Jones how much he was being paid by Ford to work on this case. Jones at first said he didn't know, then guessed the sum to be about $80,000. So, calculated Specter, if this was a typical case and Jones had done more than 100 for Ford over the past eleven years with Packer Engineering, that would amount to at least $8 million Ford had paid to Packer. At least.

"Is my math correct?" asked Specter.

"I believe your math is correct."

On the question of Jones' resume, Specter mentioned that Dr. Laird—he stressed the "doctor"—had authored 300 articles, and he asked Jones how many he had had published.

"Not that many," said Jones. The number, Specter would coax from Jones later, was three.

The brunt of Jones' testimony was that there was no demonstrable defect in the Ford parking brake system and that there had been no spontaneous disengagement of the brake. Of these things Jones was certain. As certain as Laird was that a problem with the brake had made it spontaneously disengage. Jones pointed to the dimple, the bump in the casing that held the gears and prevented them from moving laterally far enough to disengage. "There is physically not enough room for that to happen," he told the jurors, the defense photo showing little space for the gears to shift. (Conroy did not ask his expert to comment on Laird's theories of force and elasticity). The witness also said that in examining the brake from the tow truck he did not see evidence of lateral movement on the gear teeth, no marks to indicate such a skip-out had occurred.

> The way I understand the theory proposed by plaintiffs' expert is that because there is a little bit of misalignment, there is a possibility for a little bit of misalignment between the sector and the pinion, that you can get a situation where you have the sector gear hanging on by a very, very small amount onto the pinion gear such that any small movement would trip that off. However, there is just physically not enough space for that to happen. Secondly, there is no evidence that that actually happened.

Jones also pointed to marks the dimple had made on the gears that, he said, indicated significant wear and proof that the brake had been pressed down as far as it could go, and many times. And that, he said, was further evidence that there was a problem with the brake adjustment.

Jones disputed Laird's assertion that "you could have skip-out of one tooth." He explained, "If we had a skip of one tooth at any given time with that pinion gear being engaged, you would actually have two and a half teeth engaged in the sector gear at any given time. So if we lost one tooth, the tooth behind it would pick up the slack."

Jones also pointed to the mark on the take-up spring part of the brake system that, he said, showed it had not been in its proper design location at the time of the accident, which would have caused slack in the cables leading to the rear brakes and resulted in the brake pedal moving closer to the floor of the truck when applied. This misplacement of the spring would have been Ed Butler's fault in installing the brake system.

Markings beneath the rubber brake pedal—and the fact that it had come off and had to be glued back on—indicated that it had been kicked, said Jones, and provided proof of mistreatment by Butler and Joe Blumer.

Jones' theory of the mishap was that Joe Blumer must have known the parking brake was not functioning but was able to park his truck on the steep incline without it rolling downhill. Jones testified that a number of factors made that possible. Blumer had initially parked the truck in gear, there was a small hump in the road that helped to hold the truck in place, the truck had been turned to the side against the slope, and the disabled Ranger pickup had put weight behind the tow truck and helped hold it still.

But, said Jones, when Blumer got back into the truck and took it out of gear to start the engine and operate the hoist and then the Ranger was unhooked, the wooden chocks were not enough to prevent the wrecker from rolling backward. That explained, he said, why the tow truck began to roll almost immediately after Walendziewicz moved his Ranger from the tow truck.

NO SOONER HAD Conroy finished his examination than Specter jumped up to cross-examine the witness. In his hand was a batch of bills that Jones' company had submitted to Ford for work on the Blumer case. He started to add them up with the witness: $21,000 for work done through August 2007, the next bill for $11,000, then $4,000, then $15,000, $9,000, $12,000, $6,000, $17,000, $11,000, and finally $35,000. The total was $141,000 and, since Jones was still working, Specter noted, the meter was still running.

"So we're somewhere approaching twice what you told the jury you had billed in this case so far. Would that be fair?"

"Yes, sir," said Jones.

Next Specter asked about the mark on the brake gear that showed it had been depressed all the way to the bottom teeth. He was willing to concede the point that the system had on some occasions been fully depressed. But then he asked, "If the parking brake is engaged and is holding the vehicle on an incline, it shouldn't later disengage. Correct?"

"No, sir," acknowledged Jones.

Specter asked about the other marks on the brake gear that Conroy had introduced as evidence of damage but, to the surprise of both sides, were found to be on the brand-new exemplar brake. When Jones started to take the brake from Specter to inspect the marks, the attorney held it from his grasp. "I would prefer to handle the equipment," he said tersely. "It's my examination." Specter wasn't going to let the witness control any aspect of his cross-examination the way Laird had done with Bill Conroy. At this point the questioning became tense. Jones sat stiffly, his body turned awkwardly toward the jury and away from Specter, as if he were trying to ignore the lawyer's presence.

"You didn't know before this trial started that there was such a line on the exemplar parking brake, did you?"

"That's the only exemplar parking brake I have ever seen with that line on it, sir."

"Sir," Specter shot back, "that's not responsive to my question. Please answer my question. You didn't know until this trial started that this line was on the exemplar parking brake?"

"I did not know that line was on the exemplar parking brake, sir."

And about his testimony that if there had been a broken tooth on the brake gear, the next tooth would still hold the brake, Specter had a simple question.

Q: How many teeth were damaged?
A: There was one that was missing a portion of it . . . then there were also three others that had some damage on them.
Q: There were four damaged teeth?
A: There were four damaged teeth, not one, that's correct, sir.

Specter pounded Jones about his theory that Joe Blumer knew the parking brake was broken. He mentioned the 25 percent grade of the hill and asked Jones, "And your testimony to the jury is that you believe that Mr. Blumer intentionally stopped his vehicle on a tremendous grade without applying the parking brake. Correct?"

"Correct." Jones was sticking to his guns.

And Jones, who had said the brake had been installed improperly, told Specter that he believed it had never worked, that it had been nonfunctional since Ed Butler had put it in the truck.

Even earlier on the day of the accident, when Ed Butler drove the truck?

"Yes," Jones told Specter.

> Q: And the same for the month of September, correct?
> A: Yes, I believe so.
> Q: And August?
> A: Yes, I believe so.
> Q: And July?
> A: Yes, I believe so.
> Q: And June?
> A: Yes, sir.
> Q: And May? That's your testimony, correct?
> A: I believe that the parking brake was never working properly from the time it was installed, that's correct.
> Q: And your testimony is it flat wasn't working on the twenty-ninth in the afternoon, on the twenty-ninth in the morning, on the twenty-eighth, on the rest of September, in August, in July, in June, in May. Correct?
> A: Yes, it was not installed properly.

Specter found this implausible, that two men would have operated such a heavy truck without a parking brake. So he asked again, "Flat wasn't working, right?" And again, Jones answered, "Yes."

The lawyer noted that the truck had been used on 189 recorded jobs since Butler had installed the brake in May. And then, feeling confident that Ed Butler had done well on the witness stand days earlier, that the jury had believed the little man who ran a local tow truck operation, maybe even liked him, Specter put it all on the line. He took the intimations Conroy had made since the beginning of the trial and asked the tantamount question of credibility before the twelve members of the jury. It was a gamble, but one he felt he had to take. Specter took a step toward Jones and locked eyes with the witness.

> Q: Do you know that Ed Butler testified that the brake worked just fine on the morning of the twenty-ninth? Do you know that?
> A: Yes. I believe I read that in his testimony.
> Q: So in order for you to be right, he has to be either mistaken or lying. Correct?
> A: That's correct.

JAMES VARIN WAS Ford's answer to Campbell Laird. A Michigan resident, he was an engineer who had earned a master's of science in metallurgy from Rensselaer Polytechnic Institute and had 40 years of experience in automotive design. Wearing a dark suit and neatly coifed white hair, Varin had the look of a distinguished professional. He had been in a courtroom before on a number of such occasions. He had faced Specter in *White v. Ford*. Varin had worked much of his career, from 1969 through 1991, for Ford and now worked as a consulting engineer.

When questioning him about his resume, Specter wanted Varin to tell the jury a little more about his work at Ford. "Is it correct that in the last ten years that you worked for Ford your job was to provide support to the office of general counsel in the defense of product liability lawsuits and to provide expert testimony in the fields of brake design, brake system analysis . . . and failure analysis?"

"Yes."

"In fact, I've read right from your resume. Right?"

"Apparently so, yes."

Varin had been working on his own since 1991, he told Specter, as an independent consultant.

"But in reality," Specter pressed, "you spent the last eighteen years, since 1991, largely defending the Ford Motor Co. in product liability lawsuits. Correct?"

"No, I would not agree with that," Varin shot back, sitting straight, peering at Specter through wire-rim glasses. "I have certainly participated in that activity, but I have a much wider range of activities than just that."

Varin acknowledged that he had been called on to evaluate allegations against Ford 100 or more times from 1991, when he left the company, to 1997, a fact Specter had dug up from an earlier deposition. And between 1997 and now? Varin agreed with Specter's estimate that it could have been 200 more.

> Q: How many times have you testified that a Ford product was defective?
>
> A: I don't ever testify that a product is or is not defective. I just give my opinions.
>
> Q: How many times have you testified that Ford acted unreasonably?
>
> A: I don't remember ever giving that testimony.

Q: Would it be correct, sir, to say that for the last twenty-eight years a large percentage of your professional time has been spent defending the Ford Motor Co.?

A: It has been spent in giving testimony in which allegations have been leveled against Ford . . . again, I don't defend Ford.

The interchange was close to a replay from Specter's examination of Varin from the first trial. Varin was paid $240 an hour for his consulting services and, Specter reminded the witness from earlier depositions, did most of his work for Ford, perhaps as much as two-thirds. And while he didn't "defend" Ford, Varin acknowledged that he had never testified against Ford, not once. He never testified that Ford had made a defective product or that the company had acted unreasonably.

Conroy finally returned to question Varin about the Blumer case and the witness espoused his theory of the tragedy. First, he said, evidence suggested that the brake pedal had been forced to the return position "repeatedly very violently." He noted damage to the rubber bumper and the fact that it had been glued back on. He also pointed to marks on the underside of the pedal, though they appeared relatively faint, even on the blow-ups. This proved, Varin suggested, that the drivers of the vehicle had been improperly banging the pedal to the return position, which showed that the brake had not been functioning the way it should have been.

Next Varin pointed to the photo that showed two distinct marks where the take-up spring rested. That meant the spring had been moved from its original position, also potentially affecting its function. And that, he said, proved that the spring had come loose somehow and had been reinstalled. Varin didn't say the words but this could only lay blame on the man who had installed and worked on the brake system—Ed Butler. Asked about Laird's theory that the spring had simply "migrated" to another position, Varin disputed such a notion.

"There are no marks between the two," he told the jury. "If there were a migration, it would be a progression, a progressive movement from one to another."

"What caused this second mark here?" Conroy asked minutes later.

"The spring is removed and then reinserted. It cannot be wound up to the same degree of tightness as it is at manufacture."

Conroy asked his expert witness if Ford's brake system was a "safe design" and Varin responded that it was. He looked directly at the jury as he explained, "It satisfies all the requirements for a safe automotive design. It meets all federal, it exceeds all federal requirements and all Ford internal requirements, which are more restrictive than the federal requirements. It functions properly as it is intended to function."

"And," Conroy wanted to make the point one more time, "if a parking brake system is not properly installed in a vehicle by someone, can that affect its functionality?"

"Yes."

Conroy didn't identify that "someone." But his point was clear. Butler did it.

IT WAS DIFFICULT to say, even at this point in the trial, which way the jury was leaning. Some jurors had wiped away tears at several points but they only felt bad for Jennette Blumer and her family, not necessarily believing that Ford was responsible for the death of a husband and father. Their emotion was no proof that they believed Campbell Laird over James Varin, or Ed Butler over Ford Motor. Juries were almost impossible to read. It would come out only after the trial, for instance, that at this point Conroy and his experts had convinced at least one juror that Butler must have installed that brake improperly. Barb Keller, a young woman, was convinced and would remain so for the duration of the trial, that Butler had screwed up when he installed Ford's replacement brake. She felt sorry for the Blumers, but Conroy's questions and Butler's answers had left her feeling doubtful of Butler's competence. If this case boiled down to Ford workmanship versus Ed Butler's mechanical ability—and it would—if one had made a tragic mistake, Keller, for one, felt certain that it was the tow truck operator with the grimy clothes from downtown Pittsburgh, not the corporate giant from Dearborn. "I felt he installed the brake wrong," she would say flatly in an interview after the trial.

Specter would try to chip away at Varin's credibility and his theory of the fatal incident. He asked if the expert had investigated any of the other twenty-eight rollaway reports the plaintiffs had entered as evidence. Varin had not. Over the last eighteen years in which he had worked as a consultant on Ford cases, had he investigated a report of a brake failure in a Ford truck resulting in a rollaway? Again, Varin had not.

"So when you told the jury a few minutes ago that this was a safe design, that testimony was not made with the benefit of personally investigating these rollaways or these alleged rollaways or being asked by Ford to do the same sort of thing with respect to this parking brake system. Correct?"

"Yes."

Specter went back to Varin's testimony about those mysterious marks on one of the brake gears, the identical marks his own experts had discovered on the exemplar. Had Varin ever made the effort to learn whether the marks could have been made as part of the manufacturing process before he concluded they were evidence of damage made to the brakes after they had left the factory? Had he called the manufacturer? No, Varin acknowledged, he had not.

Specter decided to wisecrack a bit with the witness.

"Do you know their phone number?"

"No, I don't."

"Do you think you could find it, if you wanted to?"

"Yeah, I'm sure I could. Yes."

Varin's expert report had concluded that the broken gear teeth were caused by someone kicking at the brake pedal. So, Specter wanted to know, had Varin read or heard any testimony during the trial in which anyone ever said they had kicked the parking brake? No, Varin had not.

And since Varin had concluded that Joe Blumer had never applied the parking brake on that fateful day because he knew that it wasn't working, Specter had a simple question, so simple it seemed to catch Varin by surprise.

"You never met Mr. Blumer. Correct?"

"I'm sorry?"

"You never met Mr. Blumer. Correct?"

"That's correct, yes."

"But you're able to say what he knew because you say you're sure the parking brake wasn't working on that tremendous grade for him at all, and that's why he never applied it?"

"Yes."

Was Varin saying the brake wasn't working on September 29, "flat wasn't working?" Varin said, "Yes." And, he said to Specter's questioning, that he believed it wasn't working—"flat wasn't working"—on September 28 as well. Or for the 31 towing jobs Ed Butler had gone on the week before the tragedy. Or the 189 jobs since the brake had been installed.

Next, and finally, Specter produced deposition testimony in which Varin had said that although he never investigated those 28 similar rollaways, he had looked into more than 100 claims of "unintended vehicle movement" in various vehicles, including many with automatic transmissions. This was not a parking brake problem, he told Specter now.

But the lawyer's question was not about the brake system. It was about Varin's credibility.

"You had investigated more than 100 claims of unattended vehicle movement and you had decided that in each of those cases it was the driver's fault because the driver had failed to apply the brake. Right?"

"Probably right in both cases, yes."

"No further questions," Specter told the judge.

THE DEFENSE WOULD close its case with Jeffrey J. Croteau, a forty-one-year-old mechanical engineer from Massachusetts who had blond hair and cherubic good looks. Croteau worked for a scientific consulting firm called Exponent Failure Analysis Associates. The company had 800 employees located in twenty-three offices throughout the world. Croteau was a principal in the firm. He had published eleven articles.

Specter tried to chip away at the witness's objectivity before he addressed the Blumer case directly. In response to questioning, Croteau acknowledged that most of the work he did was for the Ford Motor Co., probably 75 percent, and that his company relied heavily on Ford's business. Croteau, who so far had billed $157,000 for this case, estimated that he had worked on about 150 cases for Ford. And that over the past five years he had testified nine times in court and ten other times in depositions in cases involving Ford, and all on Ford's behalf. He agreed with Specter that his occupational performance—and thus his compensation—was based in large part on the work he did for Ford.

"Have you ever concluded that a vehicle is defective?" Specter asked him.

"No."

"How many vehicles have you looked at in your career? Hundreds? Thousands?"

"Definitely hundreds."

"Have you ever testified on behalf of a plaintiff bringing a lawsuit against any car company?"

"No."

"How much has Ford paid Exponent, say, over the last ten years?"

"I've been presented with information that Ford has essentially paid Exponent about $90 million in the last ten years, which on average is about $9 million a year."

Conroy took over the direct examination, though Croteau essentially launched into a lengthy lecture, complete with slides and a video, about his inspection of the accident scene and how events had likely unfolded that sad day. He had run tests at the Arizona Proving Ground that approximated the accident scene to prove his theories. Croteau concluded that the defense argument was on sound ground, that it would have been possible for Joe Blumer to have stepped out of his truck without having a parking brake and put chocks behind the wrecker's left rear wheel. "It would be risky, but you could do that," Croteau testified.

Again Specter rose to cast doubt. Smiling, he asked Croteau, who hailed from Massachusetts, if he was a New England Patriots fan.

"Hard not to be." Croteau returned Specter's smile.

Specter, who of course had read the expert's report, noted that his testing had been on a 20 percent grade—not 25 percent, as was the slope at the actual scene—and that he had not used the actual vehicles that had been involved. Specter wanted to know why he had not. Why hadn't Croteau tried to recreate the scene exactly, or as closely as possible? The witness said that doing so would have been "pretty dangerous," but he still would have tried—except that "they" chose not to.

"Who is 'they'?" Specter asked.

"Counsel."

"Who?"

"That would be collective counsel. So Mr. Conroy, Tiffany Alexander, and Nancy Winschel." Alexander was an associate at Conroy's firm, while Winschel was a partner with the local firm that had conducted discovery in the case. Both were seated with Conroy at the defense table.

"Did you discuss with them what might happen if you went and did that?"

"No. I mean, if it was up to me, I wouldn't mind trying to prove that theory."

"So you wanted to do it? Is that what you're saying?"

"Yes."

"You told them, 'I want to go do this.' Correct?"

"I didn't tell them I wanted to go do it. I told them it could be done."

"But you were overruled by them?"

"In essence, yes."

And, Specter continued, wouldn't the best way to try to support his theory have been to run his tests on the actual hill where the incident occurred? "Yes," Croteau agreed.

"So," Specter said, starting to wrap up, "you know from all your experience in this field that one of the things that you want to try to avoid doing, as somebody who is going to have to come into court and defend your position, is doing a test that turns out badly. Correct?"

"Well, you certainly don't want to do a test that doesn't support your opinions. And if that is what you mean by the definition of 'badly,' yes, I agree."

"But I guess what I'm trying to get at here, isn't for you, isn't the courtroom supposed to be a search for truth and not something that doesn't support your opinions?"

"Are you telling me that the courtroom is the search for truth?" asked Croteau. "Yes, I believe that's true."

CHAPTER 36

Common Sense
and Credibility

CONROY BEGAN HIS closing speech with an acknowledgment of the tragedy that had befallen the Blumer family and the emotion, the sadness that had hung over the trial like black crepe.

"There have been tears through this trial, there have been tears," he said. And although he didn't offer an apology to the Blumers, Conroy seemed genuinely sorry for their loss. He wasn't a phony and he didn't come across as one.

But, he said—a "but" anticipated by everyone in the courtroom—the jury should look at the facts, the cold, hard evidence, and "make your decision in this case not based on emotion, not based on sympathy, and not based on your heart. We can't do that."

And what were those facts? First, and quite simply, was the testimony, uncontroverted testimony, that the parking brake on Ford's truck exceeded the standards of the federal government. The government specified the performance of parking brakes and Ford not only met those standards but also set its own, higher criterion. What more could one be humanly expected to do?

Second, and this was disputed, Ford contended that its federally approved brake system had been improperly installed in Joe Blumer's truck. There were marks on the brake's inner workings that Ford's experts said proved that was the case.

And third, Joe Blumer never set the brake on that tragic day. This was disputed as well. How could anyone know what Joe Blumer had done before the disaster, what his intent had been? But there was proof for that theory as well, Conroy told the jury. For one thing, when the truck was inspected after the accident the brake was found in the released position, not set with the pedal depressed.

Those were the straight, unadorned, stripped-of-emotion facts.

The slides went back up on the large screen and Conroy showed his proof. He spent much of his allotted one-hour closing speech on the spring inside the brake system. He showed the two marks left by the spring—one where it had rested when originally purchased, the second where it wound up after Ed Butler allegedly reinstalled it—even though Butler denied ever touching the spring. But reinstallation of the spring was the only explanation for the two different marks, Conroy told the jury.

He pointed to the other marks on the brake gears that he said were proof of someone mishandling the system. The plaintiffs' experts had shown that the same marks existed on a new exemplar, or "controller" brake, but Conroy questioned how those marks got on a brake that had been in the possession of the plaintiffs' experts and attorneys.

"And what is significant is the history of that controller and how it . . . was just through this trial that this observation was first made about this mark and where this controller was and where it came from and how all this just unfolded in the past two weeks."

He pointed to other marks on the brake gears that suggested the brake had been pressed to the end of the sector, meaning it had been depressed to the floor of the truck or close to the floor, and that the brake had been in need of an adjustment.

Conroy noted that Ed Butler had said he had no problems with the brake before the accident and that he had signed an affidavit to that effect. But on cross-examination during trial, stated Conroy, "he told us something quite different." Conroy pulled out the testimony and began to read it back for the jurors.

When asked if the brake pedal was traveling to the floor, Butler had answered, "Not all the time, no."

> Q: But sometimes it did. Correct?
> A: When you gave it that extra [Butler indicated a little extra force]. Correct.
> Q: It would go to the floor.
> A: You could make it go to the floor. Correct.
> Q: I think you told us that when the pedal went to the floor, there was a problem with it?
> A: Correct.
> Q: And you knew that before this accident?
> A: Correct.

Conroy also said the evidence was clear that the brake, after installation, had been abused. The rubber stop had been damaged—the defense concluded from kicking—and had to be glued back on, and scratches were found on the bottom of the pedal.

"So when you tie this all together from beginning to end," Conroy told the jury, his long arms outstretched, "it all points to before the accident the parking brake isn't working right. The parking brake is going to the floor. It wasn't a parking brake that one could or should rely upon."

And knowing that, according to the defense theory, Joe Blumer didn't bother to set the brake. Because he knew it didn't work in the first place. He instead relied on several other factors, Conroy said, to hold the truck on that steep hill—the turn of the wheels, the angle of his tow truck, the weight of the pickup truck on the lift, having it in low gear initially and later placing the large wooden chocks behind the left rear wheel. These maneuvers had all been enough to stabilize the truck. Until the pickup truck was released from the wrecker. Shifting the truck out of gear to run the hoist had come first, then removing the weight of the pickup and the large stinger moving toward the ground and allowing some lift to the truck's rear. Those actions all created an avalanche of sorts. The tow truck could no longer hold without a parking brake, and it had moved backward suddenly, violently, crushing Joe Blumer in its path.

Conroy next debated the plaintiffs' claims that an inadequate parking brake had skipped out and caused the tragedy. Despite the broken teeth on the brake gears, he said, there was no evidence that the gears moved laterally and separated, causing a skip-out. The dimple on the adjacent metal housing would have prevented that. And finally, the proof that this did not occur was the fact that after the accident the gears were found still enmeshed, the pinion and sector gears were not apart but in their original design alignment.

"I submit to you," Conroy told the jurors about the plaintiffs' contention of a failed parking brake, "that these theories do not work. The physical evidence doesn't support a skip-out."

Conroy urged the jury to consider the facts, and only the facts.

> I know for some of you what I'm asking you to do here is a very hard thing. There is a very fine family here. And I know for some of you it will be a very difficult thing to say to them that Ford is correct about what happened here and that you shouldn't recover. I know how hard that can be. But I submit to you that in this case

with the facts that you've heard that the evidence justifies this result. Thank you.

Specter walked slowly to the jury box. Before greeting the jury and pressing his case, he uttered, without introduction or attribution, a few words from the W. H. Auden poem "Funeral Blues," words that spoke powerfully to the Blumer family's loss.

> He was my north, my south, my east and west, my working week and my Sunday rest, my moon, my midnight, my talk, my song. I thought that love would last forever. I was wrong.

Specter let the words hang in the quiet of the courtroom before going on.

"I want to start with talking about credibility," he said, then launched into how "our side" had presented "people who have lives and professional existences outside of sticking up for one entity for their entire livelihood." He mentioned specifically Campbell Laird, a Ph.D. in metallurgy, who had forged a lengthy academic career and won the praise and respect of his peers in the profession.

He mocked Ford's experts as a "traveling road show" out to protect and defend Ford. Many of them derived much or even most of their income from the automaker. "Who did they bring you?" he asked, pointing toward the defense table, then answering his own question. "They bring you people whose entire lives are spent on airplanes traveling around from courthouse to courthouse in this country."

He singled out James Varin, who, said Specter, had retired from Ford—where he worked his last ten years in the company's product liability defense department—and had looked at 100 claims of vehicle rollaways.

"And," said Specter, his voice soaked with sarcasm, "every single time he's concluded that, 'Oh, the driver didn't set his parking brake.' Isn't that amazing? Isn't that remarkable? We apparently have a lot of really stupid people in America who don't set their parking brakes. It could never be the brake, could it, Mr. Varin?"

Next Specter posed a direct question to the jury that got to the heart of the matter. "Now, what is this case about? The case is about—did Joe Blumer engage this parking brake on that hill on that day? Yes or no?"

He peered at the jury, then glanced at Jennette Blumer, then back at the jury. "If you decide in your deliberations that Joe Blumer did not engage the parking brake on the hill that day, throw her out of court. Throw her right out of court.

"But, of course, Joe Blumer engaged his parking brake on that—as it was correctly described by Mr. Aaron Jones—'tremendous' grade."

Specter backtracked to his argument and urged the jury to use common sense and not to rely on, as he put it, again mocking the defense's case, "a bunch of shadows and squiggly lines." Wasn't it more sensible to assume something other than the defense theory that Joe Blumer intentionally got behind a truck that weighed almost five tons and was on a hill and had no working parking brake? Didn't it make more sense that he believed the brake was working and that he would be safe?

"If he doesn't apply his parking brake, he is suicidal!" Specter shrieked the words. "It's suicidal not to apply your parking brake on that tremendous grade. Is there any doubt about that?"

If, Specter continued, Joe Blumer knew he had no parking brake, why hadn't he simply put his truck in reverse and lowered it, along with the Ranger in tow, down the hill to a more level spot and unhitch it there?

Specter concluded, "Of course, he had what he thought was a fully functioning parking brake."

Specter scoffed at the defense's strategy of blaming Ed Butler, saying, "Without a scintilla of a shred of evidence, they called the man a liar." The defense was asking the jury to believe that not only did Butler install the brake wrongly, but he also knew it didn't work and drove the truck anyway. And he let Joe Blumer drive the truck.

"That," Specter suggested, "defies common sense. That parking brake and that truck was in service for those four and a half months between mid-May and late September. It had done two tows on the morning of the twenty-ninth of September. It had done thirty-one the previous week, all done by Ed Butler. How could he go without a functioning parking brake? You must be joking!"

And, Specter said, it was ludicrous for the defense to try to cast suspicion on his team's discovery during trial that marks found on the brake gears from Joe's truck were the same as those found on a spanking new brake, disproving the defense claim that the marks proved the brake was mishandled.

"Now what do they want you to believe? Do they want you to believe that Ms. Baldwin here got some sort of a screwdriver or something and made the line on the exemplar brake? And Mr. Nocivelli . . . he did the same thing? That they would engage in tampering with evidence and obstruction of justice and a fraud on His Honor and the court system?"

He said Ford tried to explain away the broken teeth on the brake gears by blaming the drivers for kicking at the brake pedal. "Ladies and gentlemen, in a fight between my shoes and this brake, this brake is going to win," suggested Specter, pointing toward his soft Italian loafers, incredulity building in his voice as he went on.

"You're not going to break these metal teeth with leather shoes or a pair of sneakers kicking a pedal, even if there was any evidence whatsoever that anybody ever did that—which there isn't."

As evidence of skip-out, Specter pointed to misalignment between the brake gears and the fact—allowed into evidence by the judge over Ford's objections—that the company had changed the brake system in later years.

He also pointed to the twenty-eight other rollaways that were put into evidence and reminded the jury that "all involve this parking brake." And that Ford did nothing about those incidents. It didn't investigate them, merely told the victims to settle with their insurance companies.

About the pedal being found in the upright position after the accident, Specter said that was only natural. "Well, of course it was. . . . It was no longer engaged and the brake pedal came up," he said, explaining that four "return springs" connected by a cable leading to the rear of the truck would return the pedal to its upright position. It wasn't proof that the brake never worked, Specter said. It wasn't proof of anything.

"It's meant to try to confuse, to make you throw up your hands and say, 'Oh, this is too complicated for me. I'm not a mechanical engineer. The burden can't be met by the plaintiff because I just don't understand.' Don't let them do it. This case is pretty darn simple."

SPECTER BEGAN his windup where Bill Conroy had begun his closing speech, by recognizing the emotion of the trial.

> There have been a lot of tears in this courtroom. But nobody here should apologize for the fact that tears have been shed. There is nothing to be ashamed of in that regard. The fact is that this was an enormous and is an enormous wrong that was committed and a terrible thing to happen to this fine man and this fine family. And whether we cry about it or whether we don't cry about it isn't going to change the fact that the harm here is unimaginably great.

Specter's job now was difficult. He had to remind the jury, graphically expose the loss that the Blumers had experienced. Much of the verdict, should the jury hold Ford responsible, was not for Joe Blumer's pain and suffering, but for those who survived him. But Specter had to be careful not to insult the jurors by seeming to play on their sympathies.

He started with Joe Blumer's wallet, showing them again its contents, contents that epitomized his closeness with his family and at the same time demonstrated to the jurors that he was not unlike themselves.

"A man's wallet, like a woman's purse, tells no lies. It speaks the truth. Joe Blumer had eighteen photographs of his family in that wallet, eighteen photographs," said Specter. "He didn't have a fancy credit card. He had a Target card. He didn't have a gold American Express card."

Specter mentioned that Joanne, Joe's youngest daughter, was nine years old when she lost her father. Jennette would care for Joanne, he said, "But she's lost a lot, Joanne Blumer has, as all of these people have. Her sister and her mother. And, let's be honest about it, a part of each of them died on that hill that day."

The older Blumer daughter, Shirley, was "having a very, very rough time," said Specter. Both children were getting professional help, he said, "but help is not a father." Help wasn't riding to school with your father or doing your homework with him or having "those conversations that only a father can have with his girls."

Or that a wife can have with a husband.

"I want to talk to you about Jennette," continued Specter. "She had a beautiful marriage. What a beautiful marriage. How many of us could say that if we were to pass away today that our spouses would take our wedding rings and have them on their person forever?"

Specter's voice had been growing softer as he spoke about the children, then Jennette. He moved now to the wooden lectern that stood near the jury box and began to read a poem, one he adapted from "We Remember Them" by Rabbi Sylvan Kamens. Specter did not explain or introduce the passage. He simply read the words:

> At the rising of the sun and its going down, I recall him.
> At the blowing of the wind and the chill of winter, I recall him.
> At the opening of the buds and in the rebirth of spring, at the shining of the sun and in the warmth of summer. At the rustling of the leaves and in the beauty of autumn, I recall him.
> At the beginning of the year and at its end, I recall him.
> For as long as I live he, too, will live. For he is now a part of me, as I recall him.
> When I am weary and in need of strength, I recall him.

When I am lost and sick at heart, I recall him.

When I have joy I crave to share, when I have decisions that are difficult to make, when I have achievements that are based on his, I recall him.

When I fulfill his dreams and my own, I recall him. As long as I live, he, too, will live, for he is now a part of me, as I recall him.

"Ladies and gentlemen, I ask you to render a verdict for the Blumer family and against the Ford Motor Co.," concluded Specter. "I ask you to award the full measure of damages for each and every element of those damages, and I ask you to do justice. Thank you very much."

The judge read his instructions to the jury, explaining the lengthy list of questions on the verdict slip and the rules for deciding the case. To find Ford's parking brake was defective, the jury must, he said, find that it "malfunctioned under normal use." When it came to witnesses, he told the jury to consider their qualifications and whether they appeared to be "biased or unbiased, whether they are interested or disinterested persons . . . which witness or witnesses and which evidence you consider most worthy of belief."

He noted that unlike a criminal case, in which the prosecution had to prove its case beyond a reasonable doubt, a civil case was decided on a preponderance of the evidence. If the jurors felt the scale tipped, however slightly, to the plaintiffs, then they should hand down a verdict for the Blumer family. If the scales tipped toward the defense or were perfectly even, then they must hand down a verdict for Ford. And then Della Vecchia sent the jurors home for the night.

CHAPTER 37

The Jury Is Back

THE TWELVE JURORS came to court at 9:00 a.m. the next day and were ushered behind closed doors to begin their deliberations. Jennette and Mel Blumer sat at a concrete table outside the courthouse. Jennette's sister, Sharon, worked a pile of scratch-off lottery tickets. No winners. Specter and his co-counsel, Baldwin and Dominic Guerrini, remained in the courtroom, reading and talking. Baldwin sat in one of the jury chairs, her feet up propped up on the wooden railing. Conroy and his defense team had left the building, reachable by cell phone.

At 10:20 a.m., the jury asked to see certain exhibits—four of the photos, the exemplar brake, a photo of the accident scene. What did it mean? Was it a good sign for the plaintiffs or for the defense? Nobody knew.

By 11:00 a.m., Jennette and Mel and other members of the family had moved indoors. Jennette fiddled with Joe's gold wedding band. She was shaking slightly, as she had been throughout most of the trial. She looked at Mel and confided, "My stomach's all in knots."

Around noon, the jury was brought lunch. Specter ate in the courtroom, spooning down a cup of soup from a cardboard container. There was some discussion of what the jury might be considering. Was the fact they were beginning a fourth hour of deliberations good or bad? Was it ominous for the plaintiffs if this went on much longer? Was it a sign of disagreement or perhaps had the jurors settled the question of Ford's negligence and now were taking time to crunch the numbers, to add up the millions? Nobody knew.

At 1:50 p.m., Judge Della Vecchia wandered into the courtroom, his sparse gray hair tussled, his judge's robes off, his thumbs tucked behind suspenders. He looked at Baldwin. "I think you'll do fine," he said. But then the judge chuckled and added, "Now that I said that, I probably jinxed you." Baldwin eked out a small smile.

AS CHURCH BELLS rang outdoors, the jurors, faces somber, filed back into the courtroom at 2:00 p.m. on March 19, 2009. It was the exact date—and even the same hour—that the verdict had been read in the second *White v. Ford* trial five years earlier.

"Do we have a verdict?" Della Vecchia asked.

The jury signaled that it did. Specter rose from his seat and walked to Jennette, taking a seat beside her and holding her hand. It was something he rarely did, especially since he was not supposed to speak in court from behind the bar. Technically, a lawyer became a spectator when he left to join the gallery. But in this case, Specter felt that his client needed him by her side.

The verdict slip was handed to the judge, who looked it over and then began to read aloud.

Do you find that the Defendant Ford Motor Co. was negligent?
Yes.

QUESTION 2: Do you find that the Defendant Ford Motor Co.'s negligence was a substantial factor in causing Joseph Blumer's death?
Yes.

QUESTION 3: Do you find that the parking brake system on the subject vehicle malfunctioned on September 29, 2004?
Yes.

QUESTION 4: Do you find that this malfunction was a substantial factor in causing Joe Blumer's death?
Yes.

QUESTION 5: Do you find that the parking brake system was defectively designed?
Yes.

QUESTION 6: Do you find that a design defect or defects in the parking brake system was a substantial factor in causing Joseph Blumer's death?
Yes.

QUESTION 7: Do you find that the defendants failed to properly warn of a defect in the parking brake system before the subject vehicle was sold?
No.

Answering "no" to No. 7, you don't have to answer No. 8.

QUESTION 9: Do you find that the defendants failed to properly warn of defects in the parking brake system after the subject vehicle was sold, but before September 29, 2004?
Yes.

QUESTION 10: Do you find that the defendants' failure to properly warn of a defect in the parking brake system after the subject vehicle was sold, but before September 29, 2004, was a substantial factor in causing Joseph Blumer's death?

The answer is "Yes."

The issue was settled. The only thing that remained was the monetary award. In some cases, Specter knew, juries could find for the plaintiffs but then be stingy about money. In a deep recession and in a region like Pittsburgh, which had been hard hit with job losses, perhaps this jury would feel disinclined to award a large sum. Perhaps for a family like the Blumers, whose breadwinner had only made $20,000 a year, jurors might feel that a large award was not necessary. Della Vecchia continued:

QUESTION 11: State the amount of damages that you award for Jennette Blumer's loss of her husband's services, society, and comfort— $2,300,000.

QUESTION 12: State the amount of damages that you award for Joanne Blumer's loss of her father's guidance, tutelage, and moral upbringing—$2,250,000.

QUESTION 13: State the amount of damages that you award for Shirley Blumer's loss of her father's guidance, tutelage, and moral upbringing—$2,250,000.

QUESTION 14: State the amount of damage that you award for Joseph Blumer's pain and suffering—$1,500,000.

QUESTION 15: State the amount of damages that you award for the economic loss caused by Joseph Blumer's death—$450,000.

The judge totaled the numbers. "I get $8,750,000," he announced. "Okay. Ladies and gentlemen, is this your verdict?"

The jurors indicated agreement. Bill Conroy nevertheless asked that the jury be polled. All but one, Juror No. 6, Barb Keller, answered that they agreed with the verdict. But the vote had been closer than that at one point only hours earlier. When the twelve members of the jury initially walked from the courtroom after the judge's charge—they had been prohibited from talking about the case among themselves before that moment—they sat at a table and took a poll. Six were for the plaintiffs, while six said they were undecided. At the end, all but one decided for the Blumers, and Barb Keller was alone in her views, particularly on the veracity of Ed Butler.

"Bottom line, I honestly didn't believe that Ed Butler put that brake in wrong," said another juror, Jennifer Cusick, the jury foreperson, manager of a pulmonary research laboratory in Pittsburgh. "He did it for many years. My heart went out to him. He seemed like a decent, honest guy and you can't fake that." Other jurors said they, too, had believed Butler.

It was Ford's witnesses, particularly its experts, that many of the jurors felt had not been completely honest. "Kind of sleazy," was the way Dan O'Malley put it. "The way it was brought out that they basically made a career of working for Ford . . . it seemed like they got paid to state Ford's opinion, whether it was right or not. They were not very credible witnesses. The family's witnesses seemed much more believable. They were honest types of people. They were night and day as far as credibility."

O'Malley, forty, the father of two small boys and manager of planning and procurement for a small Pittsburgh company, admitted that he went into the case somewhat "biased" in Ford's favor after hearing an outline of the basic facts during jury selection.

"I was probably more in favor of Ford because you hear so many people suing big companies. So I kind of thought, 'Here we go, somebody suing a big company.' But the facts, and the way they were presented, changed my mind."

That and his own personal experiences. A self-described "technical type" of person, O'Malley, who would be among the leaders on the jury, said the parking brake seemed flimsy. He did not believe that the alleged kicking by Ed Butler or Joe Blumer had damaged the brake. "No, that's impossible. It damaged itself."

Why had it been necessary for Butler to replace the brakes so many times? O'Malley asked himself. He himself had owned a much older pickup—fifteen years old with more than 200,000 miles on it—and he had never had to replace the parking brake.

He also doubted that Joe Blumer would have parked on that steep hill, knowing he didn't have a functioning parking brake. O'Malley recounted an incident that occurred years earlier when he was working on a job with a friend who was using his 1979 truck to tow a piece of heavy machinery. The friend knew his parking brake wasn't working when he stopped on a hill. He parked the truck in gear and placed a 6-inch chock—2 inches larger than the one Joe Blumer had used—behind the wheels. But when he removed the equipment from behind the truck, it broke loose and rolled away, smashing some concrete and finally coming to a stop about 100 feet away when it crashed into a car. O'Malley thought about that incident and Joe Blumer, whose truck could not even be parked in gear to operate the hoist.

"No! I don't think a tow truck driver would take that chance," he said.

"On that incline? No way he didn't use the brake," agreed Dan Yeskey, who was unconvinced early on that the plaintiffs had a case and even had some doubts upon starting deliberations.

But for him and many of the other jurors, the case hinged on the experts and the jury believed those the plaintiffs put on the witness stand. "I'm a working man and it impressed me that they had grease under their fingernails," said Yeskey, who once had been employed as an auto mechanic for Allegheny County and now worked on its voting machines.

He said those experts had disproved Ford's theory that marks on the brake gears were evidence of damage since the same marks were on a new brake. "To make an identical tool mark like that would be insane," he said.

And Yeskey, who himself once owned a Ford truck, said he didn't believe that kicking the brake pedal had damaged the system. "I experienced kicking the brake up. You can't do it. You can't put that much force kicking upwards. I drove five trucks and I tried to impress that on the jury."

When it came to setting a monetary award, many of the jurors initially wanted to hand down a large verdict, a very large verdict. But they were concerned that too much might make the verdict susceptible to appeal.

"Give them something that's just, and make Ford pay" was the general sentiment, said Yeskey, "but if you give them too much, say $25 million, we know Ford is going to appeal. . . . If it's too much, this lady [Jennette] will never see this money, or she'll see it too far down the road." Another juror, Rhodora Woodson, said she wanted to award more but she, too, was wary of future litigation. "Maybe this will stick," she said.

AS JENNETTE AND MEL walked slowly out of the courtroom arm in arm, crying, they noticed the jurors sitting on a wooden bench in the corridor. Once strictly instructed to avoid even saying hello to jurors outside of court, now they could no longer resist. Jennette rushed over and hugged Jennifer Cusick, who stood and hugged her back, tears in her eyes as well. Then Jennette went down the line, one by one, hugging and shaking hands with each and every juror, even Barb Keller, who had voted against her case but now gave Jennette her best wishes.

"Thank you," said Jennette. "Thank you. Thank you. Thank you."

She had also hugged and thanked Specter earlier in the courtroom. He wished Jennette luck but noted Ford might have new legal maneuvers. Don't worry, he assured her, he would take care of it all.

As he drove home alone after trial, Specter relaxed with his thoughts and the sounds of Van Morrison and Bonnie Raitt and Louis Armstrong's "What a Wonderful World." His mind kept rerunning the trial and the verdict. He knew that the award plus delay damages—interest the plaintiffs could charge starting one year after suit was served—would bring the total award to about $10 million, basically the amount he had demanded from Ford to begin with. He also knew that this latest battle with Ford wasn't over, that within a few days the company would file motions for post-trial relief, protesting various aspects of the proceedings and of course its outcome. Likely failing on those motions, it would appeal. But for now he had beaten Ford one more time and there was reason to be happy.

Without a stop, Specter managed to traverse the Commonwealth of Pennsylvania in just more than five hours. His eight-cylinder Audi hummed along the turnpike, his iPod blaring an eclectic mix, Gordon Lightfoot and the Goo Goo Dolls, Sinatra and Springsteen, while his mind raced over the case of Joe Blumer, then back to the Whites, to Jimmie and Ginny and Walter, then further back in time to Derick Bobb, the "lucky" one among the trio of victims. Derick had had his head run over as an infant yet had lived to talk about it. Specter thought about that, about luck, how Ford's parking brakes had failed all across the country, and how some people, the vast majority of people, had escaped tragedy. Many, maybe most, probably hadn't even realized that there had been a problem with their brakes. A lot of trucks had rolled away on their owners, Specter knew, but most were lucky not to have been in the way when it happened, or had been nimble enough to have moved out of the way in time. This whole idea of fortune, of chance and destiny, consumed him for a long part of his drive.

What if Walter White hadn't jumped out of Jimmie's truck when it began to roll? Or if he had jumped out the other side, or if the tire had narrowly missed him? Couldn't Joe Blumer have been standing alongside his truck when the brake released instead of behind it? And what about all the other people who had jumped out of the way in time to avoid injury or death? How did fate pick and choose its victims and its survivors?

When he arrived home, Specter told his wife and daughters about the verdict. He told them about Jennette and her kids and how happy the verdict had made them. He told them about his closing speech and the fine man who had died with eighteen photos of his family in his wallet. And he asked Tracey to gather photos of their children and have them laminated. If, God forbid, something happened to him, he wanted to be found the same way they had found Joe Blumer. With a full wallet.

CHAPTER 38

Derick

DERICK BOBB STEPS OFF the school bus and walks to the mailbox, extracting a small pile of letters. He takes his time walking down the driveway to the brick and aluminum siding rancher where his mother and father, Tammy and Dave, sit on the front porch on a hot and muggy May day.

Derick, by now seventeen and a student at Big Spring High School in Newville, Pennsylvania, looks like any typical adolescent. He wears jeans low on his waist and his black baseball cap backward on his head. A necklace of black beads peeks out from under his T-shirt and a tiny diamond adorns one earlobe. Derick wears a fuzzy blond goatee that partially conceals a slight case of acne.

"What's up, D.?" his father shouts out. Dave, a burly man, sits with his shirt off in a plastic chair sipping water from a plastic bottle. He casts a jolly smile at his son.

When Derick reaches the porch, he greets a visitor with a grin and a firm handshake. At his father's request, he pulls up a chair and sits back, relaxed. Derick is a "miracle." That was the word doctors used to describe his recovery from having his skull crushed a month before his first birthday. A miracle. After the incident with the Ford truck, doctors had told the Bobbs their son might die. Even if he lived, he would probably be in a vegetative state forever.

"Well," says Dave, pride and defiance in his voice, "you see him standing here. He ain't in a vegetative state."

After his initial recovery Derick flourished physically. He grew bigger and stronger. After five eye surgeries he could see well enough with glasses, though he was legally blind in his right eye, which also was missing a chunk of peripheral vision. He could run around and throw a football and ride a bike and swim as well as most kids. But that was where the similarity to most kids ended. Derick, even in middle school, could not recite the ABCs, could not tie his own shoes.

Now, at seventeen, Derick is quiet, very quiet, rarely speaking unless spoken to and, when he does, his few words come in muffled bursts. It is when he speaks that Derick's shortcomings become most evident.

"How was school today?"

"Fine."

"What do you like about school?"

No answer. There is only a pause as Derick, his pale blue eyes staring off, magnified by his wire-rim glasses, wrestles internally for a response. His father, seeing that there will be none, breaks the silence, speaking, as the family often does, about Derick in the third person. Derick doesn't seem to mind. "He remembers some things a long way back, but not simple things," explains Dave.

Derick has progressed considerably over the years. So have Dave and Tammy. Their marriage, once on the rocks, has survived twenty years, and the couple seems happy. Tammy works full-time as a teacher's aide at the local middle school supervising in-school suspensions. Dave still drives a truck full-time, but is home more often with his children now that he has a dedicated run and works the night shift. The couple had another child after Derick's injury. Rebekah is fourteen.

The Bobbs still live in the same house—"I'll probably die here," says Tammy—that they bought outright with the money from the Ford settlement. Most of the modest sum of money Tammy and Dave received directly from the settlement is gone, used to pay off the house, to buy a recreational vehicle, and for other expenses. The bulk of the settlement money is tucked away in a trust for Derick, plenty to last his lifetime. The Bobbs still own their cabin in the woods, though Tammy rarely goes there anymore. Too many bad memories, one in particular. The kids visit the cabin in the nice weather, particularly the oldest, Scott, who is now married with two children of his own.

Dave sits back on the porch on this particular day and talks about the future. When he mentions his plan to buy the house next door for Derick, his son rejoices loudly, "They have a pool!" It is the most he has said in a half-hour. But when the conversation shifts to food and Derick is asked his favorite thing to eat, he can only smile, then grimace, struggling momentarily for an answer, finally putting his head down and giving up.

"What if I said, 'Let's order out. What do you want?'" prompts Dave. Still no answer.

But when his sister, Rebekah, mentions pizza, Derick pipes up. "No one's asking you, so shut up!" Then he laughs, showing Rebekah that he didn't intend to be mean. But when he stops laughing he still isn't able to mention a single food.

Derick has an appetite but the family has to be careful to make sure he eats and eats right. If food isn't set before him he'll sometimes forget altogether. Or he'll rummage through the cabinets and consume whatever is handy, maybe a large bag of chips or an entire box of granola bars. Which is better than it had been.

When he was younger Derick had been very fussy about food. At one time he refused to eat any two foods combined, such as cheese on a hamburger. During another period he would eat only round foods, things like Cheerios, doughnuts, hamburgers. On one trip in the car Tammy had to fight with him when he wanted to drink what he thought was Kool-Aid from a gallon jug stored behind the backseat. The blue liquid was windshield washer fluid.

Derick is very conscious of the texture of foods, refusing those that don't feel pleasant in his mouth, such as gooey condiments of any kind. He will not eat ketchup, mustard, or mayonnaise. It's also a daily fight to get him to use toothpaste. Derick is thin but not because of a poor diet. It is because of a side effect of a drug he takes to help with his short-term memory. Aricept, normally used to treat dementia in patients with Alzheimer's disease, can cause a loss of appetite.

"I want him to be out on his own," says Dave, continuing to talk about the house next door, which his divorced neighbor has promised to sell whenever Derick is ready to move in. "But he can't cook. He'd burn the house down. He can't handle money. He'll never be able to drive." Derick, hearing this, smiles and nods slightly in agreement. He rolls his eyes when Dave mentions having Derick's grandmother make the move next door with him someday.

Despite years of practice Derick still has trouble telling time on a standard clock, often unable to calculate minutes by the large hand. He has learned to tie his shoes but ties them too loosely, and the bows come apart. He can count but has difficulty with money. He knows the difference between a $1 bill and a $100 bill, explains his brother Andy, but the difference holds no meaning for him. He doesn't understand the values—that $100 can buy so much more than $1. Although officially now in high school, Derick still cannot consistently recite the ABCs, getting through about the first eighteen or nineteen letters and then losing his way. He cannot read and he uses a preschool primer with his teachers. He takes speech lessons every Tuesday. At Big Spring, where Derick can remain enrolled until he is twenty-one, he takes special education classes and does light job training, learning to stock shelves and other basic tasks. He learns things such as cleaning, doing laundry, and making himself lunch at a Life Skills House used by his high school. Special instructors also take him and other students shopping at the local supermarket or Target store. Sometimes his group goes to eat at a restaurant. "I only do cooking on Monday," Derick volunteers.

The Bobbs are determined not to coddle Derick. They treat him like their other children, praising his good efforts and pointing out his weak ones. Derick gets teased just as much as his siblings. Despite warnings against it Dave and Tammy let Derick ride a bicycle and occasionally the tractor they use to mow the lawn.

"I know he has issues but you can't shelter him. You gotta let him be a boy," says Dave. On one occasion Dave, a long-time volunteer fireman and now a deputy chief, put an air pack on Derick's back and took him with him on a training course—inside a burning building. "I heard from ten or fifteen people later on, criticizing me, saying, 'Why did you take him there?' Because he wanted to go inside, that's why."

Derick, he says, wasn't scared. He loved the experience. Derick continues to go on occasional calls with the fire squad, though he knows to stay where he is told and to keep his hands off much of the equipment. "He knows his limitations," says Dave.

Dave and Tammy don't worry too much about Derick's limitations. "I look at it this way," says Dave. "The good Lord gave him to us for seventeen years. Anything he does is a blessing to us."

Tammy nods in agreement. She also cringes as she listens to Dave's firehouse exploits with Derick but she doesn't interfere. She knows Derick has to be given some slack, has to be allowed to live as normal a life as possible. Although she prefers the high school swim team, of which Derick is a member, to firefighting. Swimming is his favorite activity. "He's our little frog. But he hates wearing his prescription goggles and he usually wears them upside-down," laughs Tammy, always maintaining a positive, happy tone.

She says that Derick needs to be pushed to do activities; otherwise he'll sit on the couch all day and play video games. Not unlike other kids his age. He's been swimming on the high school team for a few years, and Tammy says the other boys are kind to him. They stand at the end of the pool and cheer as he finishes every race, usually a little behind the competition. When asked if he likes swimming, Derick nods happily. And he seems generally happy except when he struggles to do tasks or remember simple things, such as his best stroke in swimming, or his favorite movie, or his friends' names.

"Do you have friends at school?"

"Yeah."

"A lot?"

"Too many to count!"

"Who's your best friend?"

No answer.

"Can you think of one?" Dave pushes him.

Derick pauses. It's obvious that he wants to answer, just that he can't. Finally, he surrenders and says, "Not inside my head."

Derrick knows what happened to him all those years ago at the cabin, or at least what he's been told. He understands that he is different from other kids. And why.

"I was eleven months old and somehow the parking brake lost . . ." Derrick stops mid-sentence and scratches his face, looking off into the distance. His mother prompts him. "How the truck rolled over your head . . . ?" There is another long pause, but Derrick doesn't answer. Instead, he lifts his face to the warm sunshine and closes his eyes, allowing his thoughts to drift somewhere else.

Acknowledgments

THANKS TO THE FAMILIES who agreed to be interviewed, often many times. Also to the defense attorneys who graciously spoke with me, including Bill Conroy, Malcolm Wheeler, and Joe Pinto before his death.

Thanks to Avery Rome, my wonderful editor (even though she uses a faint pencil and still doesn't believe that *adamance* is a word) and a continual source of encouragement. And special thanks to Josh Goldstein, the *Inquirer* reporter who got me started on all of this, calling me years ago asking if I'd be interested in writing a book about the work of a couple of Philadelphia lawyers.

Glossary of Names

Todd Albert—Philadelphia orthopedic surgeon and friend of Shanin Specter whose wife, Lauren, was killed in an auto accident while the two families vacationed in Morocco

Tiffany Alexander—Defense co-counsel at the Blumer trial

Catherine Armour—Juror in the second *White v. Ford* trial

Joanne Aubrey—Joe Blumer's mother-in-law, who testified at trial

Michelle Bailey and Michelle Thornall—Witnesses who provided deposition testimony, later barred at trial, that found "comparative negligence" on the part of the Whites

Kila Baldwin—Specter associate who prepared the Blumer case and was co-counsel at trial

Manuel Barbosa and Harry L. Worosz—Ford employees who wrote a 1984 article about the new parking brake system developed for the Ford Aerostar

James E. Beasley—Legendary Philadelphia trial lawyer for whom Shanin Specter worked before starting his own firm

Stephen Blewett—Consulting engineer who testified for Ford at the first trial

Jennette Blumer—Joe Blumer's widow who was represented by Specter along with her children Shirley and Joanne

Joe Blumer—Tow truck operator who was killed when his employer's Ford vehicle's parking brake failed and rolled over him

Mel Blumer—Joe's brother who testified at trial

Derick Bobb—Infant who was hurt by a rollaway Ford F-Series truck

Tammy and Dave Bobb—Derick's parents; other children are Scott, Andrew, and Rebekah

Dr. Louis T. Broad—Defendant in the first case Specter took to trial

Stuart Brown—MIT-educated mechanical engineer and executive of Failure Analysis Associates who testified for Orscheln Company, Inc.

Ed Butler—Joe Blumer's boss and owner of Edlin Automotive Services in Pittsburgh

Linda Butler—Ed Butler's wife

Candy—Ed Butler's employee at his tow truck operation

David Caputo—Attorney at Kline & Specter who worked on both the White and Blumer cases with Specter

David Caruso—Plaintiff in a medical malpractice case tried by Specter that resulted in a $49.6 million verdict

Jeffrey J. Croteau—Mechanical engineer who testified for Ford at the Blumer trial

Jennifer Cusick—Juror at the Blumer trial

Alfred Darold—Former chairman of Ford's Critical Product Problem Review Group

Joe Davidson—Pittsburgh mechanic and consultant in forensic automotive mechanics who wrote an early letter to the National Highway Traffic Safety Administration about bad Ford truck brakes

Judge Michael A. Della Vecchia—Allegheny County Common Pleas judge who presided at the Blumer trial

Pete Durney—Reno attorney and partner in Durney & Brennan who initially investigated the White case, co-counsel with Shanin Specter

Dr. Diana Eberstine—a California clinical psychologist who reviewed the Whites' case for the plaintiffs

Sergeant John Aubrey Fosmo—Elko County Sheriff's Department official who investigated the White tragedy

Grant Gerber—Elko attorney who worked for Durney & Brennan and the first attorney contacted by the Whites

Jeffrey Germane—Professor and accident reconstructionist who testified for Ford

Dominic Guerrini—Specter co-counsel at the Blumer trial

Ken Gutowski—Tim Rakowicz's boss at Ford

U.S. District Judge David Hagen—Federal judge who presided over the first *White v. Ford* trial

Johnson Halldor Gunnar Hooks—Ginny White's brother who lived with the Whites at the time of the tragedy

Judge Louis G. Hill—Philadelphia Common Pleas judge who presided at Specter's first trial

Allen Humphreys—Juror in the second *White v. Ford* trial

Aaron Jones—Metallurgical engineer who testified for Ford at the Blumer trial

Robert W. Kearns—Inventor of the intermittent windshield wiper who sued several auto companies for patent infringement

Barb Keller—Juror at the Blumer trial

Judge Andrew J. Kleinfeld—Judge of the U.S. Court of Appeals for the Ninth District in San Francisco

Tom Kline—Founding partner, with Shanin Specter, of the Philadelphia law firm Kline & Specter

Campbell Laird—Scottish-born professor and metallurgist, a key plaintiffs' expert witness

Clarice LaRose—juror in the first *White v. Ford* trial

Ray LeBon—Ford attorney who served as co-counsel with Joe Pinto in the first *White v. Ford* trial

Adelaide Lusky—Plaintiff in Shanin Specter's first trial, which he lost

Connie Martin—Juror No. 1 in the second *White v. Ford* trial

Steve Maximov—Juror in the second *White v. Ford* trial

Irene Mendelsohn—Rehabilitation counselor who provided expert opinion on the future education and employment of Derick Bobb

U.S. District Judge Malcolm Muir—Federal judge assigned to the Derick Bobb case

Bob Nocivelli—Mechanic and expert witness for the plaintiffs at the Blumer trial

Don Nomura—Co-counsel, with Shanin Specter and Pete Durney, in the second *White v. Ford* trial

Dan O'Malley—Juror at the Blumer trial

Don Orscheln—Patriarch of the brake company in Moberly, Missouri

John Osgood—Attorney who managed the Ford Product Litigation Group

Glenn Ostrander—Juror in the second *White v. Ford* trial

Kristin Pil—Top-level Ford attorney at the Michigan headquarters

Joe Pinto—Outside Ford counsel and lead attorney in the first *White v. Ford* trial

Lillian Pinto—Joe Pinto's wife

Ragna—Daughter of Ginny White

Tim Rakowicz—Ford product design engineer and a main witness for the Ford brake trials

Diane Robinson—Jimmie White's sister who testified at the first *White v. Ford* trial

John Smith—Pseudonym used for a Specter client injured in a lap belt case against General Motors

Wayne Soucie—Orscheln manager of design development when the self-adjusting brake was invented

U.S. Senator Arlen Specter—Veteran senator from Pennsylvania and Shanin Specter's father

Shanin Specter—Lead plaintiffs' attorney in the Ford cases

Tracey Specter—formerly Tracey Pearl, wife of Shanin Specter and mother of Silvi, Perri, Lilli, and Hatti

Max Steinheimer—Attorney for Orscheln

Bill Tyson—Executive at Orscheln

James Varin—Former "principal reliability engineer" for Ford's light truck division

Destine Weightman—Philadelphia drowning victim represented by Specter in a case that produced a $24 million verdict

Malcolm Wheeler—Denver-based attorney who was lead counsel for Ford in the second *White v. Ford* trial

Jimmie and Ginny White—Plaintiffs in *White v. Ford* on behalf of their deceased son, Jon Walter Douglas Wayne White

Chris Wicker—Ford co-counsel in the second *White v. Ford* trial

Nancy Winschel—Defense co-counsel at the Blumer trial

Nicholas Woolfolk—Child hurt in a fall from a faulty window at an apartment complex and represented by Specter in a case that won a verdict

Dan Yeskey—Juror at the Blumer trial

Andy Youman—Attorney at Kline & Specter